Moments of Discovery

UNIVERSITY PRESS OF FLORIDA

Florida A&M University, Tallahassee
Florida Atlantic University, Boca Raton
Florida Gulf Coast University, Ft. Myers
Florida International University, Miami
Florida State University, Tallahassee
New College of Florida, Sarasota
University of Central Florida, Orlando
University of Florida, Gainesville
University of North Florida, Jacksonville
University of South Florida, Tampa
University of West Florida, Pensacola

Dwain Warner with southernmost bobcat (*Felis rufus*) specimen, above Cuernavaca, 1953. Photo courtesy D. W. Warner.

Moments of Discovery

Natural History Narratives from Mexico
and Central America

EDITED BY
KEVIN WINKER

University Press of Florida
Gainesville/Tallahassee/Tampa/Boca Raton
Pensacola/Orlando/Miami/Jacksonville/Ft. Myers/Sarasota

Copyright 2010 by Kevin Winker
All rights reserved
Printed in the United States of America. This book is printed on
Glatfelter Natures Book, a paper certified under the standards of
the Forestry Stewardship Council (FSC). It is a recycled stock that
contains 30 percent post-consumer waste and is acid-free.

First cloth printing, 2010
First paperback printing, 2012

Library of Congress Cataloging-in-Publication Data
Moments of discovery: natural history narratives from Mexico and
Central America/edited by Kevin Winker.
p. cm.
Includes bibliographical references and index.
ISBN 978-0-8130-3417-1 (cloth: alk. paper)
ISBN 978-0-8130-4439-2 (pbk.)
1. Natural history—Research—Mexico—Anecdotes. 2. Natural
history—Research—Central America—Anecdotes. 3. Mexico—
Description and travel. 4. Central America—Description and travel.
I. Winker, Kevin.
QH107.M66 2010
508.729–dc22   2009030437

The University Press of Florida is the scholarly publishing agency
for the State University System of Florida, comprising Florida A&M
University, Florida Atlantic University, Florida Gulf Coast Uni-
versity, Florida International University, Florida State University,
New College of Florida, University of Central Florida, University of
Florida, University of North Florida, University of South Florida, and
University of West Florida.

University Press of Florida
15 Northwest 15th Street
Gainesville, FL 32611-2079
http://www.upf.com

This work is dedicated to the contributing authors,
who took the time to preserve an extract of their explorations.

Books are not absolutely dead things, but do contain a potency of life in them to be as active as that soul was whose progeny they are; nay they do preserve as in a vial the purest efficacy and extraction of that living intellect that bred them.

John Milton, *Areopagitica*

Contents

Preface and Acknowledgments xi

1. In Search of the Horned Guan 1
   Miguel Álvarez del Toro
2. From Rain Forest to Cloud Forest in Mexico, Guatemala, and Costa Rica 19
   Robert F. Andrle
3. Studying Birds in the Sonoran Desert 49
   John M. Bates
4. Back Roads with Ben 58
   Lula C. Coffey
5. A Collecting Expedition to the Isthmus of Tehuantepec 71
   Walter W. Dalquest
6. Some Mexican Experiences 83
   Robert W. Dickerman
7. Sabbatical Trip to Panama, 1970 92
   Stephen W. Eaton
8. My Early Mexican Travels 121
   Ernest P. Edwards
9. Adventure Is Where You Find It 142
   John T. Emlen, Jr.
10. An Ornithological Expedition to the Lowland Tropical Rain Forest of the Sierra de Los Tuxtlas, Southern Veracruz, Mexico 158
    Paul D. Haemig
11. The Rancho del Cielo 181
    Joyce Heck
12. Bird Specimens Collected at Lake Olomega, El Salvador 194
    Joe T. Marshall, Jr.

13. Green Mansions of Tamaulipas   197
    Paul S. Martin
14. A Kekchi Odyssey   238
    Don Owen-Lewis
15. Civil War and Rain Forests in the Chimalapas   250
    A. Townsend Peterson
16. Lost in the Tuxtlas   260
    John H. Rappole
17. Six Trips to Mexico, 1939–1950   268
    Charles G. Sibley
18. Fifteen Years of Studying Birds in El Salvador, 1966–1980   297
    Walter A. Thurber
19. Recollections of Mexico: People and Places   327
    Dwain W. Warner
20. Studying the Birds of Los Tuxtlas   335
    Kevin Winker

Afterword   371
Literature Cited   377
Index   385

Preface and Acknowledgments

The purpose of this book is to capture some of the wonderment and history of biological exploration in Mexico and Central America (Middle America) through autobiographical accounts by those who were there. The authors constitute a group of seasoned Neotropical hands, and most saw and did things in the course of their work that make for the tales of a lifetime.

These entertaining and illuminating events are rarely if ever told in written reports or scientific papers. Thus some of the most exciting aspects of biological exploration are not recorded but rather live, for a time, in the oral history of the profession. Humorous and incongruous situations, captivating people, places, and wildlife, moments of discovery, and the inevitable trials provide the essence of this rich history.

I began assembling the book to see some of this history recorded so that a wider audience could appreciate the people, places, and events that make up the human side of the natural sciences. This history complements the science that was the authors' primary focus, and it serves as an autobiographical view of this important period of biological field exploration. The geographic region selected is mostly northern Middle America, which has undergone rapid change in the past decades. The authors' experiences in the region extend from the 1930s to the 1990s—more than sixty years of firsthand accounts from Mexico south to Panama. (See the accompanying map, p. xiv.) I asked the authors to have fun writing their chapters, to revel in the memorable highlights of their Middle American adventures, and to tell some good stories.

The resulting accounts represent many human-years of excitement and toil in times gone and places irrevocably changed. From the biological perspective, the stories provide firsthand observations of ecosystems in many cases gone forever. From the historical perspective we see snapshots of times and places past that enable us to grasp the often phenomenal changes that have since occurred, not only among the countries, environments, and peoples concerned but also in the natural sciences. And from the human perspective, we share a connection with explorers going into unfamiliar environments to push forward the frontiers of personal and scientific knowledge. Through it all we find the curiosity, humor, and wonder of the field biologist.

Biological exploration often occurs at the rough edges of humanity's homogenizing influences. This is where discoveries are made and lasting impressions formed. These explorations and the myriad experiences that accompany them stimulated our careers and continue to push us forward. The natural world and its human surroundings are endlessly fascinating, the more so as the natural component shrinks. When I began writing to potential authors, I felt it was important not only to find good stories but also to obtain autobiographical accounts of the history of this scientific endeavor and geographic area. It turned out that the stories were important to the authors as well. Sadly, for several these words were among the last they wrote.

In these chapters we get insights into the souls of the authors as they adapt to new customs, learn to communicate in a new language, and often give searching retrospectives of times and events past. For example, the glimpse we have into the mind of a young Maya Indian agent fresh from England, who gives up pipe smoking after participating in the local habit of pipe sharing, speaks eloquently to the various adaptations that occur to get on with life in a new and different environment. And the juxtaposition of the behaviors of humans and animals provides the reader a rare opportunity to turn the lens around to study the observers, a remarkable and varied group.

Birds form an important part of this work. I sought authors whom I knew either in person or by reputation, and since I am an ornithologist, the group was biased toward people who had studied birds for all or a portion of their careers. The diversity among the authors is striking, however, and signs of change can be found in the natural sciences, such as increasing specialization and diminishing use of guns in field study. The use of specimens in ornithology remains important, although specimen-based research represented a larger proportion of ornithological investigation in the past than it does now (see Winker 2004, 2005). Readers can be assured that scientific collecting represents an almost insignificant factor in annual avian mortality, and yet it yields information critically important for the management and conservation of biodiversity. More on this topic can be found in Remsen (1995) and Winker (1996).

Another change that has occurred is the rapid growth of appreciation for the natural sciences in Latin America; today a scientist exploring a country's biological diversity is as likely to be a national as a foreigner. The professional role of women, too, has blossomed. Insofar as biological research is an egalitarian pursuit and the planet's biodiversity is integrally linked (especially through migratory birds), this increasing integration of all stakeholders is very positive. I know that the educational efforts and enthusiasm of at least some of these authors helped in part to stimulate these developments.

Biological explorations necessarily include names for many of the species (or higher groups, such as genera) of the flora and fauna encountered. At the first use of an English common name in each account I have tried to include in parentheses the scientific name when it can be determined. This is done to provide a common language and biological reference point for all readers interested in the biology of these narratives. Latin scientific names are the lingua franca of these studies and are generally the medium through which English-speaking biologists communicate with Spanish-speaking colleagues about our mutual biological research. English common names for bird species in North America have been formalized as proper nouns by the American Ornithologists' Union and other professional societies. These names are thus capitalized, just as one would capitalize Mexico, Tlacotalpan, and Poughkeepsie. Such standardization has not occurred with other vertebrates, nor with plants, so these English names are not capitalized. Scientific names for all organisms are rigorously standardized and thus provide the common language for reference.

Each chapter is given mostly as the author wrote it. My editorial hand has generally been light. For most of the authors, Spanish is a second language, and I have not imposed homogeneity on their use of it. I did not wish to make an author appear to be more at home in a foreign language than was the case, and I wished to retain the use of local names, dialects, and slang. This can cause terms to be present that may be understood only in that country (or in that time). Spanish terms that have been adopted into English are spelled in their anglicized form (for example, Mexico or Panama rather than México or Panamá), but because this is an ongoing process there is some heterogeneity (for example, Rio Grande versus Río Bravo).

A short biographical sketch about the author precedes each account and includes citations of works given in the literature cited for those who wish to learn more of the authors and their scientific contributions (the latter usually associated with the fieldwork related in the accounts). An afterword provides more background about how this book came to be.

I sincerely thank Shirley Barnett, Karen Klitz, John Byram, Harry Greene, Frances James, Floyd Hayes, Robert Norton, Leonard Kamerling, Sally Antrobus, Rose Meier, and the staff at the University Press of Florida for their expert advice, comments, and assistance in the development of this book. The authors themselves deserve special thanks. I am far richer for having had the opportunity to communicate and work with this remarkable group of people, and I am pleased to dedicate this work to those who answered my letters with the autobiographical accounts presented here. Thanks to all for allowing us a glimpse of your explorations.

Figure 0.2. Middle America, comprising the countries between the United States of America and South America, from Mexico to Panama.

I

In Search of the Horned Guan

MIGUEL ÁLVAREZ DEL TORO

Miguel Álvarez del Toro (1917—1996) was a renowned Mexican biologist, naturalist, and conservationist. His experience and success in biological exploration, popularization, and conservation in Chiapas, Mexico, were without peer. He was founder and director of the Instituto de Historia Natural in Chiapas; author of important books on the region's birds and natural history, including *Las Aves de Chiapas* (1971, 1980); and recipient of numerous awards, including the Paul Getty Award (World Wildlife Fund) and the Roll of Honour for Environmental Achievement (United Nations). This essay is his last writing. For more details, see Cuarón (1997) and Navarro and Morales-Pérez (1999).

The imposing sierra arose before our eyes and far away, so distant that it seemed beyond our reach. Through the mist and behind the hills we made out the goal of our trip: El Triunfo. Beforehand, about an hour from Mapastepec, we had stopped at the town of Guadalupe Victoria, where our guide Don Rodrigo had his house. There we remained for the obligatory lunch, which we calmly ate as if our goal were merely over the next rise. After the meal we proceeded, having also rearranged the cargo that the mules carried on their miserable backs; we men mounted horses, the appearance of which inspired my serious doubts that they could climb this rocky sierra, besides traveling up and down the innumerable gorges within.

As we neared the foot of the sierra we passed through several towns; some, like Nosillero, El Tesoro, and El Paval, are well known as places where the feared onchocercosis is an endemic disease. Everywhere we noticed the peculiar look of the inhabitants with their reddened eyes and numerous scars on the head that testified to the operations they had suffered to avoid the inevitable blindness. If the *filarias* (worms) responsible for this disease are not removed immediately, they invade the eyes and cause total blindness. All of this had as a result our frequently swatting whatever flying insect might try to suck our blood, because a biting fly is the transmitter of this parasite.

El Paval was the last little town. It was already night when we arrived there, and our beasts could not take another step. In fact, some threw themselves and their loads down, which would oblige the muleteers to untie everything to make readadjustments. This brought forth a torrent of curses on the ancestry of the poor animals and increased our impatience on account of the delay. As we were approaching the sierra the trail was becoming more and more difficult and really dangerous in not just a few places. Furthermore, we had to cross the Novillero River an infinite number of times. It seemed to me that whoever had made this path undoubtedly liked to take a bath every few kilometers. We all agreed that the trail was indeed bad. How far we were from imagining what was waiting for us the next day! We spent the night in El Paval, sleeping in the hallway of the *casa principal* and practically besieged by dozens of skinny, barking dogs that at the least movement of any of the sleepers let loose an infernal din, unnoticed by the owners of the house, whose peaceful snores were heard even in the corridor.

Given the bunch of dogs, self-appointed guardians to prevent anyone from going out on the patio, even to urinate, and also given the fear that we could be the target chosen by some insect to satisfy its hunger and in exchange leave us a share of the feared *filarias*, we all slept poorly. My two helpers were truly terrified by the prospect of the disease, and I had to explain to them several times that the apparent transmittor does not bite at night. But the question concerned me until dawn, because we had actually been in infected territory all day, and faced with the impossibility of escaping bites, our only remaining hope was that those insects did not carry in their saliva any young *filarias* to transmit. To make matters worse, in the hours before dawn a tremendous rainstorm broke out, and in spite of our not being directly exposed to its fury, we still thought about how the trail would be at daybreak.

This time we were indeed prepared to leave when there was scarcely sufficient light to distinguish the road. We set out, leaving behind the level lands and beginning to climb the first foothills. There was a dense fog hiding the landscape, and although we were still in the tropical zone, it was somewhat cold, and the chilly water that fell on our backs when we involuntarily brushed a rain-soaked branch gave us a disagreeable sensation. Day broke when we were already going up the steep sides, and from time to time as we passed through tree-filled woodlands our eyes captured a view of the splendid coastal plain. We breathed the pleasant scent of the wet earth, and of pines and cypresses that begin to dominate the vegetation at these heights. But a sad atmosphere was noted in this zone: it was the hour when the fields should have been ringing with bird songs, but here only an occasional cry indicated the presence of a bird.

The explanation was that over the smell of pine and rain-washed earth, there dominated the aroma of field and forest demolished by fire. How many lives cut short, how much injured land! All the previous day we had crossed uninterruptedly the devastated land, the scorched forest, and with astonishment we understood that the fire must have been terrible and was stopped only when it arrived at the rain forest, a woodland entirely saturated with water. A fire that extended from the rail line to the highest peak of the sierra! Did anyone worry about trying to stop it? No one, not one authority indicated any knowledge of this. And even less the eternal destroyer of forests: the Forest Authority.

We climbed, we climbed, and we climbed almost vertically and on a trail good for goats but not for horsemen, let alone for beasts of burden; in some places, we noted uneasily, this precarious path had been supported with the help of poles hammered into the earth to prevent it washing away. At times a mule's hoof would split off a piece of the path that would roll down the steep slope, while the animal desperately fought with its other three feet to regain its balance and not follow the destiny of the loosened pebbles falling away until lost from sight in the cloud-covered abyss. My respect for these unfortunate animals increased: malnourished, carrying voluminous loads, panting on account of the altitude, and at each step fighting to keep from slipping to a frightful death. Although we carried no loads, our hearts threatened to burst from our chests, and we opened our mouths wide to suck in the air our lungs demanded; our legs ached with the effort, sweat drenched us in spite of the cold, and the mountain continued upward seemingly to heaven. We had mounts, but most of the time it was necessary to go on foot because the trail was so treacherous. In some places we were forced to wait until each animal proceeded far enough forward from the next one for safety, because the pebbles and occasionally huge rocks that were loosened would fall directly on those coming up behind. Thus were these slopes—almost vertical. And the path turned and turned again like a spiral staircase. The caravan looked like a line of ants climbing a cliff.

All morning the clouds surrounded us, moistening our faces with cold dew, but around noon the sky cleared, and as if a curtain were being raised, we viewed an astonishing panorama that unfolded before our eyes and stretched out to the sea. This mountain range rises sharply from the coastal plain, but it is not a single massif; one must descend and ascend mountain after mountain, crossing ravine after ravine to arrive finally at that very high peak that always seemed almost within arm's reach and yet was always hidden by the clouds, like a timid maiden hiding among the swathes of heavy veils, occasionally removing them partly to encourage the traveler who painfully climbs and climbs.

The day went on, and the cold intensified; the mists frequently enveloped us and scarcely allowed us to see the little path, which was now passing through more level areas, apparently covered with dense woods, although because of the thick mist, only fantastic shadows could be seen. For some minutes it seemed to me that we were floating suspended in the air—perhaps we had already reached the sky; we were traveling among cotton clouds, seeing only a few meters ahead, nothing on the left, nothing on the right. At one point, in all that misty uncertainty, the dense cloud cleared a little and—horrors! We saw that the land provided only just enough space for the narrow trail; it was but a tiny strip of land, a narrow ridge situated between two very deep abysses hidden by the clouds. One simple misstep could send one directly to eternity. I could not believe how we had been able to get through this place; and on horseback! The merest stumble of a horse would have sent us to compete with the regal buzzards at soaring through the mist, to collide after several minutes with the treetops a thousand meters below.

As the mist thinned, I realized we were traveling through vegetation that was not scorched. Yet we did not smell the odor of pines and cypresses; we smelled eternal wetness—moss impregnated with water and rotten tree trunks about to disintegrate. The very fine mist droplets invaded us everywhere, entering our bodies and giving us the sensation of being inside a refrigerator. It was so dark that it seemed the beginning of night, but the clock said five in the afternoon; and we were still far from the opening where we would camp: El Triunfo. It would indeed be a triumph to get there. A well-chosen name.

We continued onward; we had to get to our stopping place. I felt as if I were traveling through a fantastic country, inhabited by phantasmal forms caused by the dense vegetation and the thick mist, which permitted us to see, with difficulty, only a few steps ahead. Suddenly the guide, who was leading, brought me back to reality. He was saying something about a snake, and as everything is usually interesting in these regions, I dismounted with such agility as my frozen and weary body allowed and went forward, threading my way between the animals and the thick, water-soaked undergrowth. It was a small but adult *nauyaca*, a species native to high places, called *nauyaca del frio* (*Bothrops goldmani*). As we were still en route to our camp, we had no implements readily to hand that might facilitate the capture of poisonous snakes and, at this juncture, not even anywhere to keep it securely. But it was a good specimen, and probably we would not run across another. Finally, taking advantage of the fact that the snake, too, was sluggish on account of the cold, I succeeded in putting it in a rifle case. This unplanned halt provided us a more important discovery, which we would otherwise surely have overlooked. A little beyond the *nauyaca*, at the edge of a small muddy pool, we distinguished some excrement and a track that, considering the fauna of the zone, could only be the desired Horned Guan (*Oreophasis derbianus*). Finally, a tangible sign of the species that constituted the principal objective of this difficult trip! The discovery granted us good hope that we should not fail. As though to dispel any remaining doubt, a few meters ahead was a feather; an insignificant little feather, but it was white with a tiny black line in the center. Undoubtedly it came from the breast of a Horned Guan, and so, with renewed optimism, we resumed the difficult journey.

Darkness was coming on, but the twilight was imprecise on account of the mist. It was an unchanging light, so that it could as well have been noon or six in the evening, but at least we had sufficient light to see where we were going. There had not been a sign of the sun all day except while we were still climbing the initial steep slopes far below. When it was almost nightfall, we arrived at the little valley known as El Triunfo—a level area of about three hectares, crossed in the center by a stream with icy, crystalline water and banks hidden by enormous and thick stands of watercress, among the lush leaves of which large numbers of frogs were singing without the cold bothering them at all. Toward the far side of the clearing was a little shingled house, and close to where we stood were the remains of a corrugated metal roof. This was the stopping place where the few travelers who went by spent the night. In times past the place had seen the arrival of frequent mule trains loaded with coffee on their way to the coast. But when I visited El Triunfo, the products of the plantations had for a long time been transported from Tuxtla on government-built highways.

This small clearing must surely have been deforested for many years, because there was not the slightest sign of any scorched trunk; the ground was covered with thick, short turf except for those portions invaded by chaparral. Formerly, as I was informed by the efficient Don Rodrigo, the mules had grazed at night in this little valley while the muleteers rested beside bonfires or beneath the corrugated roof, which had been built cooperatively by various plantation owners for the mule trains that transported coffee.

At the time of my first visit to the zone, the clearing served as an open space for the mating flights of Resplendent Quetzals (*Pharomachrus mocinno*). During the sunny hours (very few indeed), it was quite a spectacle to watch the males chasing each other and crossing the diaphanous sky in all directions, flying repeatedly downward from the nearby ridges or from the edges of a dark forest of tall trees that surrounded the clearing. Near where we camped on the shore of the stream was a lone dead tree of medium height where the quetzals paused to show off their splendid metallic plumage while they watched for the arrival of a rival male; the newcomer was warned by the cries they hurled as soon as he emerged into the light of the clearing. I never saw, nor shall I see, so many quetzals as those that frequented this small opening and astonished me with so much beauty, showing off all their splendor in their aerial maneuvers.

In spite of the cold, it was a pleasant camp site. The canvas tents placed in the center of the clearing captured the intense heat of the morning sun when the sky was clear, effectively relieving the dampness that invaded everything. Situated on moderately high ground, the camp also allowed a view of the whole valley and the surrounding ridges. I remember the amazing spectacle the clouds presented almost every day at around one o'clock in the afternoon: they accumulated at the tops of the mountains and then, like whipped cream ladled over a dessert, they dripped downward over the slopes toward us, covering the forest until they reached our valley, turning the whole universe white. It took the fog about two hours to get to the camp; we watched it advance like something thick and milky that hid everything, until it enveloped us, and then we could not see anything beyond a distance of three meters. The area remained thus shrouded all night and part of the morning, until at about nine o'clock, the clouds began to tear apart and send puffs upward into the sky or downward into the deep gorges. Then, very slowly, the sunlight increased, dominating in the illuminated areas for longer and longer periods until finally the day cleared up; but this pleasure lasted only three or four hours, because then the white darkness invaded once more—what a paradox! We were living in limbo, enveloped in cotton or swimming in milk, depending on individual imaginations. When the fog rolled in the only things we could do were sleep and leave the tent once in a while to eat. Even on clear days, by afternoon one could not do anything besides climb into a sleeping bag; partly clear afternoons that allowed us to hunt a few birds near the camp were uncommon—but the resulting soup was very tasty.

Once we were well settled in our camp, Don Rodrigo came out with the unexpected news that he had to leave with the animals and would come back on the day fixed for our return. I did not like that much; I had already noticed that this man was well acquainted with the region. He left us his oldest son to take his place, which I feared was not the same, because no one else knew the forest as Don Rodrigo did. We would either have to mark trails so as not to get lost or find a local guide, improbable because only one family lived in this area. We said good-bye to Don Rodrigo, missing his witty conversation, but in the long run it turned out that his son, named Jorge, was an excellent young man. On the way up he had helped with the animals but had been somewhat withdrawn, and I had had little communication with him. I was not confident of his abilities, but later I had to modify my opinion, and finally he pleased me so much that I offered him a job at our institute, where he served me for several years with excellent and efficient performance as a field helper until a stupid rich drunk hit him with an automobile, causing his death. It was a lamentable loss for his family and the institute.

The weather was clear on the morning I initiated the preliminary exploration, accompanied by Jorge and Jesús, one of the helpers from Tuxtla. But the thick night fog, after condensing on the vegetation, had left it dripping in an endless drizzle. We traveled by way of an ancient trace, almost invisible, having been abandoned for years, but at least the vegetation allowed us to pass. The fog obliged us to travel slowly; the altitude made breathing difficult, and double effort was needed because of the slippery ground. For every few steps forward we slid halfway back, and we advanced with great difficulty, receiving continuous baths of freezing water from the branches that we moved with each step. It was intensely cold, but effort kept our bodies warm; to cap it off the ground was extremely uneven, either rising or falling, and only once in a while did we encounter short level stretches that were a real respite.

Finally the fog dissipated, allowing us to see the marvelous forest where we were: a jungle in perpetual half light, where beautiful tree ferns vied for space with innumerable varieties of palms and unknown shrubs beneath the gigantic trees. Ancient trees; the trunks could be encircled with difficulty by several men with extended arms. Their tops were lost in the heights, and their trunks and branches were covered by veritable gardens of epiphytes, plants that constantly oozed water. Other trees were festooned with a kind of hanging loose moss like an immense green veil that oscillated with the soft breeze, giving the trees a strange and venerable appearance. The thick vines and the slender lianas fastened everything with countless knots covered with brilliant, dewy moss. The big trees here steal light from the small ones and in turn are invaded by vines that cover the trees with their tentacles; it is an eternal battle for light, but not necessarily a cruel one. Whether the strong dominate the weak or the weak dominate the strong, it is only a juncture of balanced natural forces that we consider brutal, judging them with our simplistic anthropomorphism. In these forests the ground is never dry; the thick carpet of leaves is impregnated with water, keeping fresh the large patches of terrestrial moss and the innumerable little umbrellas of a great variety of mushrooms of capricious forms and colors.

A rain forest, or forest of mist, is one of the most interesting regions for a naturalist. There were birds everywhere: Emerald Toucanets (*Aulacorhynchus prasinus*) projected their ridiculous bills from the foliage, spying on us, later to fly away with the noisy beating of damp wings. Trogons, dressed in their metallic plumage, chased each other in the perennial game of "hide and seek" so typical of many birds during mating season. An iridescent purple hummingbird, resplendent, unexpectedly flew toward my face and fluttered there for some seconds until, its curiosity satisfied, it flew off toward some nearby flowers to suck its daily ration of nectar combined with tiny little insects. Melodiously above everything came the song of a goldfinch, and a little farther away two splendid quetzals challenged each other with their strange squawks. A few steps farther on a large butterfly lost the last shreds of its chrysalis and, helped by the heat of the sun beginning to penetrate the fog, would soon extend its wings to begin flight, adorning with its colors for a few days the eternal half light of these marvelous forests.

It is painful to think that one day, perhaps soon, some peasant family will arrive at this place and, without any regard for it, will cut down the trees and annihilate the little animals. In place of the huge, ancient, oxygen-producing trees, the fragrant orchids, and the brilliantly colored birds, there will be men, dogs, pigs, chickens, and plantings of corn or coffee. These men, gathering before their huts, will probably talk about their miserable harvests and will spend whatever money they ephemerally extract from the place but will never consider that the primitive forest and the flight of the quetzal were much more attractive than chickens or cornfields; or how infinitely sweeter are the voices of the tinamous or the song of the goldfinch than the hysterical barking of starving dogs or the satisfied grunts of the pigs that devour everything. These men, and their leaders, will never come to believe that one may coexist with nature; that it is not necessary to destroy everything, to burn everything; that one can extract sustenance without taking from us oxygen and water, indispensable elements for the very lives of the destroyers. Thinking along such lines about the destiny of these forests in the hands of human ambition and ignorance reduces me to weeping.

Ten days went by in our zoological exploration of the region. From daybreak, if the weather permitted, or more frequently from nine in the morning—the hour when the fog lifts on clear days—until the thick afternoon fog rolled in, we walked through these woods collecting interesting examples of birds, reptiles, and insects. But the Horned Guan, the principal objective of our trip, continued to elude us; we had only one brief view of this desired species. As we were traveling along the edge of a deep gorge, we heard a furtive noise among the foliage of an immense tree. On looking upward we could make out a dark form that ran along a branch. Doubt continued until a tiny shaft of sunlight illuminated the bird's head and we glimpsed a little red horn, which left me immobilized with emotion and with the word *pavón* stuck in my throat. Disappointment followed hope when the bird glided away before our astonished gaze and, leaving me mute before the marvel of the spectacle, was lost in the mist of the gorge without our being able to see in which direction it went—although it would have been impossible to chase it anyway because evening was coming on, and the mist was beginning to cloak everything with its damp coverlet.

As if in a compensation for the let-down, on our return to camp I distinguished among some bushes at the edge of the clearing a small dove. Although the mist prevented seeing it clearly, I found something strange about it that awakened my scientific interest, now dormant because of the tiring day and the frustration of a few hours before. I pursued the dove until, helped by the mist, I got it within range. What a surprise! The specimen turned out to be nothing less than a Maroon-chested Ground–Dove (*Claravis mondetoura*), a species of which there existed only four examples in the museums of the world. This was a positive find—the fifth known specimen!

The twelfth day in camp dawned, and in spite of the fact that it was apparently going to be an exceptionally clear day, considering that the morning fog was not very thick, we set forth again rather reluctantly; we were all discouraged about the possibility of locating a guan, undoubtedly a scarce bird. We searched without resting, with the futile hope that overpowers the subconscious of the collector or hunter, impelling repeated visits to the place where one has seen the coveted prize. With the idea of finding the bird where we had seen it before, we again walked the edge of that same deep gorge, perhaps for the fifteenth time. Silently, favored by the constant moisture that kept the leafy ground soft, we advanced like ghosts of the forest through the last shreds of mist, which at times obscured the surrounding area and at other times let us see the forest clearly, as if someone were playing with an immense curtain. Unexpectedly, a strange sound left us frozen into immobile shadows. It was an unusual clicking, something none of the three of us had heard before; we heard the sound two or three times before realizing that it came from above our heads, at the top of an immense tree. Whispering, we argued about what it might be, and then we heard a croak that sounded like the word *a-g-uuaa*. Imagining that the call could be that of the guan, since no bird we knew had been heard to utter such a noise, I found my heart pounding rapidly. We remained motionless, almost without breathing, moving only our eyes. We saw nothing in that dense foliage, and nothing sounded again in the area except a multitude of little birds and the occasional song of the mandolin frog. Suddenly there was a noisy beating of wings—and then nothing.

With the feeling of a new defeat, perhaps the last opportunity to find a guan specimen, we slowly continued along the now well-known trail; it was very steep and hugged the edge of the fog-filled ravine, but at the altitude where we walked the light of the sun still illuminated the opposite side. I was some meters behind the others when I realized that Jorge had stopped abruptly up ahead and was pointing out something while summoning me with his hand.

From his side, through a small window in the vegetation, I saw some branches moving on the far side of the ravine. Jorge told me he thought he had seen a large bird, black in color, among the foliage. Quickly I took out the binoculars, and just as I was focusing them the bird emerged into the clear sunlight that bathed the outer branches. I was so surprised upon viewing those white eyes on the black velvet head and the very conspicuous little scarlet horn that I almost dropped the glasses. The Horned Guan was in full view, and it was a magnificent specimen!

Finally we had found the most sought after bird of that trip. But alas, it seemed so far away that it would be nearly impossible to reach it with a shot. Going down to the bottom of the ravine and climbing the side where it was would take too much time—perhaps several hours to climb those steep, slippery, wooded slopes. I decided to lay it all on the line. With very little hope, calculating that the guan was probably 150 meters away, perhaps more, I tried to conquer the throbbing of my heart and steadied the muzzle of my .410—.22 on a branch. Taking careful aim—because the success or failure of the trip could depend on that difficult shot—I softly squeezed the trigger. At the shot the guan flew—what luck!—*toward* us, and it tried to land on a tree rooted in the slope on our side, with branches at our level. Not being able to light, it took off again, making an undulating curve before us. Already warned by the direction it was taking, and with the extra seconds in which all this transpired, I had the chance to shoot at it with the .410, having previously used the .22 on account of the distance. At the shot, instead of falling flat as I expected, the bird glided downward until it was lost from sight in the misty abyss. We could not even see the approximate direction in which it fell—it simply entered the thick fog.

Desperately, without acknowledging the futility of the action or measuring the danger, we hurled ourselves in pursuit, alternately rolling and slipping down the slope. We were somewhat separated, each going where he could among those entwined lianas, when unexpectedly I felt the earth give way beneath my feet. Several square meters of small trees, plants, and I were sliding toward the abyss in a tangled heap, until an enormous tree trunk blocked the trajectory, stopping the uncontrollable plunge. To the great relief of my frightened companions, I emerged from the pile of earth and branches, brushing off my clothes and looking for my gun, but I discovered I had twisted my leg and could walk only with difficulty. There was nothing to do but curb my desire to hunt for the specimen, and I entrusted the task to my two helpers while I stayed behind to wait for them.

Jorge and Jesús went on down toward the bottom while I, limping and falling, slowly climbed toward the trail and sat down on a log. My hopes for finding the bird were minimal—practically nil, since the only thing we knew was the general direction it had been going when it entered the mist. But we were not even completely sure of this; the bird might have recovered sufficiently to change its course and then fallen who knew how far away in that ravine. Disappointment invaded me as I waited. To find that specimen would be like the proverbial hunt for the needle in the haystack.

After three full hours of waiting, by which time I was convinced that besides not finding the guan Jorge and Jesús had lost their way in the fog, with relief I saw my helpers materialize in the clearing like someone appearing from behind a white curtain. With great joy I realized that Jesús was carefully carrying the fantastic specimen! Extended in death like a fan, the bird's tail showed the characteristic white band. When they arrived breathless at my side, emotion overtook me at having in my hands that magnificent rare bird, so beautiful and so spectacular. I examined it with wonder, and my tension finally eased because this assured the success of the expedition. From here on I could pay more attention to the other animal life that surrounded us, always interesting and abundant in little-known species. This was the first guan I saw up close and held in my hands.

Later the two men told me that after an unsuccessful search in the thick vegetation and rocks at the bottom, everything hidden by the fog, and as it was already getting late and they lacked even an approximate idea of where the bird had fallen, they had decided to return defeated. But fate ordained that right on top of a rock they had passed earlier, Jorge glimpsed a little red leg, and on examination he discovered that it belonged to the prize they had sought so diligently. The irony was that they had passed under this same rock at the beginning of the search; only upon returning did they have an angle of view that made the bird partially visible.

Those who have not had this kind of experience may have difficulty understanding that one step forward or backward can change the viewing angle enough to find something we have given up for lost. This has happened to me many times in my specimen collecting, especially in regard to hummingbirds, those tiny but incomparably beautiful birds. And so it happened this time, because it is not easy to see any object within the dark tangle of lianas, with everything brilliantly covered with dew and the fog only allowing one to see once in a while. You have to experience it to understand it. The guan was among the lianas, its wings extended and its head hanging down; being black made it even harder to see. In the case of the guan, frequently the first thing that identifies it is the little scarlet horn that stands out against the black background of the shadows and the green of the foliage. On the other hand, when the bird is found among the multitude of epiphytes covering the branches, the abundant red flowers make the little horn inconspicuous. The important thing was that we had our first guan specimen and returned satisfied to the camp, although I had a hard time walking with my injured leg.

The next day, very carefully and meticulously, I prepared the specimen; I had all the time I might need, because for three days I was simply limping too badly even to leave the camp. To make the best of the time when the sun was out and its welcome warmth offset the chronic coldness of the place, I had my field table for preparation of specimens set up outside, near my tent; from there I could admire the comings and goings of the quetzals crossing the sky. Nearby on the trunk of a dead tree I saw something green, very green, slowly climbing up the rotten trunk. Immediately I became alert; it was a little lizard that I did not recognize, and because I could not move well, I called for my two helpers. Quickly I gave them instructions to capture the interesting reptile, which they managed to do using a long pole with a loop on the end when the lizard was about five meters above the ground. It was a beautiful example of the *Abronia* group, peculiar lizards that have little horns beside their ears, giving them the appearance of little dragons. Later, carefully observing the tree trunks, we were able to capture three more specimens for a total of two males and two females, the latter being a dull yellow in color. Afterwards in Tuxtla I identified the reptiles as *Abronia ochoterenai*.

The woman who lived in the little farm house mentioned earlier, who was the mother of several children and who daily sold us tortillas, eggs, and a few vegetables, arrived with her delivery just as we were completing our capture of the first reptile. She made a huge to-do, and there was no human power or protestation that could convince her it was an inoffensive lizard. For her and her family, the *Abronia* was an extremely dangerous animal, the bite of which would cause the loss of hands or feet, not to mention eventual death. Every day that she came to our camp she asked about my health, confused, because my fingers, which I had allowed the lizard to bite as a proof of its not being dangerous, had not turned black. When we left she still did not understand why I had not died. Because her husband was almost never around, several times we asked this woman about the neighboring woodlands, as I did not want our collecting to be limited to the areas we already knew. One day she offered to send me a good guide to lead us to various places in the mountains.

On the agreed day we got ready early, had breakfast, and waited for the arrival of the guide. As soon as the mist cleared, at about nine o'clock, we saw approaching a short, chubby kid. I don't think he was a meter in height. We supposed the most logical thing—that he had been sent to tell us the guide would not be coming. None of us could have imagined what happened a few minutes later. The boy showed none of the usual timidity found in country people from areas where strangers are infrequent. On the contrary, with great self-confidence he planted himself before me; he took off his hat, an enormous hat for someone his size, and bowed deeply, saying at the same time: "Patrocinio Hernández, at your service." I have never forgotten how comical the scene was, nor his words. I asked him what he wanted, and he left us astounded by informing us that he would be the guide. Incredulous, we did not know whether to laugh or take him seriously. We were expecting a man, or at least a youth, not a child less than a meter tall with an enormous hat that gave him the appearance of a thumbtack, armed with a machete over one shoulder, so long that it dragged on the ground, and on the opposite shoulder a knapsack likewise too large for him.

The boy was chubby and very charming in his manner. Not quite so charming, his head showed several of the little tumors associated with onchocercosis, and he also had inflamed and reddened eyes. He was a candidate for blindness, which caused us much sorrow. In later conversation we found out that he had formerly lived in El Tesoro, a zone where onchocercosis is found, which explained his condition; in El Triunfo the fearful disease does not exist. Although the insect that transmits it, a sorrel-colored *simúlido*, was bothersome and abundant on sunny days and this never ceased worrying us, fortunately no one on either this trip or later ones came down with the dangerous disease.

We worried that the boy would go blind sooner or later, and we could not know whether treatment might cure him. His mother did not show the slightest mortification about the parasite, as is frequent among country people, and I doubt she would have taken him to Huixtla, which at that time was the best center to care for those afflicted with this suffering. I explained many times to the woman what caused the sickness and the great danger the boy Patrocinio was in, and she always answered me that when she had time she was going to take him. I never found out the fate of this child because the family had moved away before my next visit; in their place we found a family named Gálvez, who live there to this day.

Patrocinio informed us that he was going to take us to the mountain, but I doubted his capacity to such an extent that I sent Jorge to ask the mother if it was true that this little boy, eight or ten years old at most, knew the trails within the forest. The woman sent back the message that I should have confidence, that Patrocinio knew the area very well, and that he was in the habit of moving around on his own all through the area, looking for fruit, robbing nests, and trying to catch some animal. Astonishing! And indeed the boy left us dumbfounded at his expertise about everything—trees, animals, and trails—and also for his absolute lack of precaution. He stuck his hand into every hole in the ground or in the trees. How did he stay alive? We could not comprehend it; among other things because the poisonous *nauyaca del frio* was abundant in the area. It might not be as dangerous as other snake species in warmer climates, but it was still a risk, especially for a child. But when Patrocinio encountered one coiled on the trail, he simply jumped over it.

It cost us a lot of effort to convince him, at least when in our presence, to leave in peace the little birds in their nests; with the skill of a thief he stuck his hand into every nest without bothering to ascertain whether instead of chicks, it contained a coiled serpent; he pulled out the victim by a leg and before we could say "no," with a twist he had already wrung its neck. He put his hand into hollow trunks as far as his arm would go and brought out baby rats or even an adult one—stuck to his finger on more than one occasion. He was a true-born pillager, only thinking about getting something to eat. It was not that he was he dying of hunger, because his family always had tortillas, eggs, and fruit. Rather, the uncontrollable depredation typical of peasants is a product of ignorance that makes people see nature with indifference and so with total coldness; they cut down, they burn, and they destroy everything animal or vegetable.

We had another little adventure during our stay at El Triunfo. As noted, it had previously been a stopover for mule trains—a resting place for the drivers. At the time of my first visit, travelers passed through only occasionally. On this particular day, I went out walking nearby accompanied only by Jorge, while the other helpers stayed in camp preparing some specimens. My intention was to look around with the hope of finding some rare species, perhaps a little-known bird or even a new species, the dream of every scientific collector. I armed myself with a .22 loaded with cartridges shooting tiny grains of birdshot suitable only for very small birds. We walked southward along the only trail crossing the area, following a level stretch, then rising, arriving at a ridge, and then going down the side of the mountain toward the ocean. As usual, it was fairly cold. Wisps of fog were still floating around, covering and uncovering the landscape and at times enveloping us in moisture that penetrated our bones. Upon topping the ridge and seeing inviting sunshine beyond, we began descending the slope, enviously viewing the faraway cars traveling along the coastal highway, looking like speedy little ants. In the distance was the sea, with its warm waters, while we were wrapped in heavy clothes and still feeling the cold.

Going around a bend in the path we saw bathing in the loose dirt three *gallinitas del monte* (*Dendrortyx leucophrys*), a rare and extremely shy quail that almost no one has seen in its natural habitat. I profoundly regretted not having brought the shotgun to acquire what would have been a valuable specimen. Nevertheless, begging for a miracle, I began trying to put myself into range for the .22 birdshot, something practically impossible given the shyness of this animal. As I expected from previous experience, at my slightest movement the birds slipped into the grass. Precaution no longer mattered, and we ran over the sandy ground to where the birds had been. They were still at the edge of the thicket, but on seeing us they ran in deeper, still shaking the dirt from their plumage. Even though it was almost useless to try to get close enough because of the short range of .22 birdshot, I tried to catch them, followed closely by Jorge.

Once in a while we caught a glimpse of these timid birds, which encouraged us to follow them despite the fact that the ferns were growing thicker and the darkness of the forest was enfolding us. The ground was steep—so steep that several times as we climbed, we slid downward as if on a toboggan. After a period of futile pursuit, we lost track of where the birds had gone and finally considered the attempt lost. Then we realized we also didn't know where *we* were. We had committed a beginner's error: pursuing something beyond the path into deep forest. We went down some gullies and climbed some slopes, and this disoriented us further. The situation was not too alarming, in that by walking downward we were bound to encounter the trail, which wound around and around the steep mountainside. It cost us no little effort, however, because on the way down we were leaving behind the high forest and entering dense thickets with huge cypress trees here and there. Finally, when we least expected it, we came out on the trail on a narrow section along a crest dividing two deep ravines. We had not intended to go down that far, and now we would have a long climb back up to reach the cloud forest. It was already about noon, and the fog would soon lower, covering the whole area with its milky blanket.

Before beginning the ascent, we looked farther down the trail to where it formed a bend protected by a small rock outcrop. This was the widest part of the path, about two meters across. But what caught our attention were some pale objects and something that looked like a hat. We were about forty meters away, and we did not want to go a step farther down the slope, but curiosity overcame our weariness and we approached to discover a macabre spectacle. Up against the outcrop was a small, burnt-out fire, and nearby lay the clothing of a man and woman, all torn up and bloody. Nearby lay a machete, an emptied knapsack, and a hat. A little farther away there was a piece of fabric like those used by the indigenous women of Chiapas to cover the head. And all around us were jaguar (*Panthera onca*) tracks—many tracks, and signs of rolling. It was perfectly clear that a jaguar, or perhaps a pair of them, had come across these people and attacked them. Obviously the people had had no chance to defend themselves; the machete was still in its sheath.

We were still looking over the scene and wondering about it when Jorge said he thought he heard a whirring like that of a Great Curassow (*Crax rubra*). Joking that the cat was probably still around, he took a big rock and hurled it into a little wooded area on the side of the gully. Exploding from the thicket came loud, threatening roars, and we ran into each other trying to flee. It is unwise to bother a jaguar protecting its prize, and it is pure foolishness to molest a man-eating jaguar. The gun I had with me would scarcely even tickle a jaguar. Concluding that discretion was definitely the better part of valor, we took off running, hardly conscious of the steepness of the ascent, fearing every second that we would have the cat on our backs. In our rush back up the slope we frightened an innocent little deer out of a thicket, and this noise caused us such an additional fright and adrenaline discharge that our hearts almost leaped out of our breasts.

Nothing followed us, but we both saw the jaguar in every stump and in every running squirrel, and we reduced our pace only when we fell down from exhaustion. I have never gone up a steep slope so fast; my chest was bursting, and Jorge was in the same condition. I think we broke a speed record. The whole trail was surrounded by thick forest, with the only clear spot being the one where we had camped—if we stepped on a *Bothrops*, we never knew it. Arriving at the camp, we collapsed on the ground like stones, forgetting the folding chairs. And scarcely a moment too soon, because within minutes a fog began to descend, so thick that one could not see two meters. Naturally those who had stayed at the camp, noting our elegant entrance, badgered us with questions and asked if we had seen the devil. We answered them only with gestures, too out of breath even to speak.

For several more days we continued walking the slopes, gullies, and trails. Besides admiring the landscape I acquired a good collection of birds and reptiles. Everything was novel, from the smallest insect up to the birds and larger mammals. On two occasions we saw solitary tapirs (*Tapirus bairdii*), which surprised me because they typically inhabit warmer places. One day we were making a trail along the edge of a ridge to the west of the little valley of El Triunfo—climbing up and down through rocky hills covered with thick vegetation, so thick that in some places darkness reigned—when we saw something shining among the vines in a spot illuminated by the sun. We pushed apart the bushes to get a clear look, and found ourselves gazing upon something that seemed quite unreal—perhaps we had discovered a traditional fairy castle, perhaps some crystal ruins? We had to cross a rocky gully to alleviate the doubt. It was a large outcropping, probably of quartz, and almost bare of vegetation. No large trees grew there, and only a few bushes were rooted in the crevices. We saw almost transparent blocks, and I lamented that they were too heavy for us to carry away. I took a large lump of joined prisms that I used for many years as a paperweight in my study, and it was greatly admired by visitors. It seemed to be pure crystal.

What we had found was not a fairy castle or the crystal ruins of some fabulous kingdom, as imagination suggested. It was simply a strange quartz hill that must still be there. We continued our journey, opening a path because one did not exist along this way. Not very far from the quartz hill we unexpectedly came upon a clearing formed by a large landslide, something relatively frequent in this range. From the edge of slide we could clearly see the sea, far away beyond the coastal plain. But what drew our attention more immediately was a disturbance below us at the opposite edge of the slide, where it formed a sharp dropoff. A young *temazate* or red brocket deer (*Mazama americana*) was desperately fighting to secure a foothold on the edge with its front hoofs, while its rear legs were thrashing in the void. A beautiful Harpy Eagle (*Harpia harpyja*) besieged the deer with extended claws and delivered tremendous blows with its huge wings. The little deer was fairly young, though it no longer had white spots on its pelage. What we did not know was how all this had started—whether the eagle had taken advantage of an accident or had simply attacked the deer as it moved along the edge. We were the witnesses of a drama worthy of being filmed. The powerful raptor circled in the air and then hurled itself on its victim, striking the deer with its talons so hard that the noise of the blows reached us where we stood. It seemed that occasionally the claws dug in, while the great wings caused a huge commotion in the foliage. The drama concluded fatally when the eagle grasped the deer strongly by the neck with its talons, the little deer let go of its precarious support, and with a final howl fell downward over the loose and sandy soil of the landslide. The enormous raptor immediately fell upon its victim, grasping the animal in its claws when the pair came to a tangled mass of earth and vegetation farther down the slope. Apparently the eagle lifted its prey; we last saw it flying with difficulty among the huge trees.

This scene gave me an idea of the Harpy Eagle's immense strength. Formerly I had only seen it pursuing monkeys and attacking *pavas cojolitas*. We were astounded by the spectacle we had observed, and some of my companions encouraged me to intervene. But there was no reason to kill this magnificent example of an uncommon bird going about its natural business. As we lost sight of the eagle and turned to follow our path, at our backs a racket broke out from several lesser birds, also witnesses to what had happened, the most noticeable being chachalacas and some *pajuiles*, which with their cries and whistles were alerting all the forest inhabitants to the presence of a predator.

Some days later, on the agreed date, Don Rodrigo returned with the mounts and pack animals for the trip back to Mapastepec, where our ancient jeep was waiting to take us home. So many interesting things to collect, or simply to observe, had kept me occupied during the periods of clear weather. We had spent twenty days in the camp, and we were tired of the fog and cold; even on the sunniest days it was too cold to bathe without heating water. We struck the camp, bade farewell to the resident family, and went off down the mountain.

At around noon, in a cypress grove on a little tree charred by the forest fire, I suddenly saw a tiny bird I had never seen before, brilliant bluish green on top with a blue back and whitish blue beneath. I engraved it in my memory and made some notes. Later when I looked for it in my books, it turned out to be one of the rarest of birds: the *alinegra* tanager, or Azure-rumped Tanager (*Tangara cabanisi*).

We returned to Tuxtla with the Horned Guan and a good collection of lesser birds and reptiles. From then on I remained enamored of El Triunfo, and after a few days I began to consider how the area could be protected; there should be no invaders, colonizers, or small farmers who might destroy that habitat. As always happens in such cases, it took many years of effort and negotiations for the politicians to understand the affair and offer the necessary support. By one means or another we succeeded in stopping several attempts to colonize the place. As usual, the bureaucracy seemed to care about nothing. Some surveyors supported establishment of an *ejido* (collective farm) in that beautiful valley, but through an appeal to officials, that attack on nature was avoided. Later Dr. Manuel Velasco Suárez, while governor of Chiapas (1970–76), promulgated a state law declaring El Triunfo a biological preserve. Engineer César Domínguez Flores, my right hand at the institute, and I spent many hours of work and worry to safeguard El Triunfo, protecting it with every means available to us. I believe it unjust that today certain factions wish to take control of that region. If it were not for the work of the Natural History Institute of Chiapas, the Horned Guan would have ceased to exist some time ago, and El Triunfo would have been converted into just another bleak plateau with an ejido planted in the center.

Considering the state of the world, perhaps in the end El Triunfo will become a sterile wasteland; human agglomeration can never find enough space, and having done away with everything, people fight among themselves for the last crumbs. I do not wish to be a prophet of doom, and for the well-being of my descendants I hope I am wrong about this, but seeing the symptoms certainly makes one pessimistic.

2

From Rain Forest to Cloud Forest in Mexico, Guatemala, and Costa Rica

ROBERT F. ANDRLE

Robert F. Andrle conducted pioneering biological work in southern Veracruz and Guatemala, much in association with his Ph.D., which he obtained from Louisiana State University in 1964. The studies related here continue to be recognized as landmark contributions in northern Neotropical ornithology (Andrle 1964, 1967a, 1967b). He went on to a long career at the Buffalo Museum of Science in Buffalo, New York. He has secured natural history specimens for the museum since 1948 and continues to do so. Since the 1980s, he has professionally consulted on various projects involving the museum and its nature preserve and has led natural history tours in the United States, Canada, Latin America, and Africa. He is currently a Fellow of the Buffalo Society of Natural Sciences (founder of the Buffalo Museum of Science) and a Research Fellow of the museum. His most prominent research there is the *Atlas of Breeding Birds in New York State* (Andrle and Carroll 1988).

On March 2 in the year 1793 the inhabitants of San Andrés Tuxtla, a small Mexican town near the Gulf of Mexico in southern Veracruz, heard a sound like violent thunder. At about 6 p.m. a fiery glow appeared to the north over nearby Volcán San Martín Tuxtla. During the night the thundering occurred again and became so loud that people in the vicinity of Orizaba, about 150 miles away, believed they heard cannon fire. San Martín continued erupting at intervals over a period of several months. On May 22 there was a severe disturbance, and the sky grew so dark from ash emissions that lamps in San Andrés had to be lit at midday. This great ashfall reached eastward from the volcano for about eight miles and in places attained a depth of ten feet. It drifted in the air as far away as the states of Tabasco and Oaxaca, and westward in Veracruz to the towns of Orizaba and Córdoba. At times, lapilli, cinders, and other ejecta showered down on the mountain. Some of the forests on the more than mile-high volcano were destroyed by the ashfall and by the streams of basalt lava that flowed over the lip of the huge crater and in places reached the Gulf waters about twelve miles away.

Figure 2.1. Robert Andrle at 5,400 feet (1,646 m) on the crater edge of Volcán San Martín Tuxtla, August 25, 1962. In the background clouds are beginning to move in from the Gulf of Mexico and will soon envelop the mountain. Photo by R. F. Andrle.

It was in this way that Don José Mariano Moziño Suárez de Figueroa, botanist to the Royal Expedition of New Spain in the summer and autumn of 1793, described this tremendous event in a small and isolated tropical mountain range. This is just one recorded occurrence in a history of volcanism that, since the Tertiary, has profoundly sculpted the Tuxtla Mountains. Today San Martín, its subsidiary cones, and its neighboring volcanoes in the adjacent Volcán Santa Marta massif are quiescent; a mantle of luxuriant vegetation clothes the loftier peaks, crater walls, ridges, deep gorges, and lava flows. The town of San Andrés Tuxtla is now a thriving community nestled in the hills and surrounded by fertile fields where cattle graze and crops of maize, beans, and tobacco flourish. About ten miles to the west rises the beautiful, isolated cone of Cerro Tuxtla, formerly a holy place of the local people, from whose olivine-rich basalt lavas were said to have been carved the curious stone toad and rabbits seen by early visitors to Los Tuxtlas. Tourists occasionally stop to view the massive, strangely helmeted basalt head near the plaza in Santiago Tuxtla, a type of work believed to date from the ancient Olmec civilization of more than three thousand years ago. Many other interesting artifacts have been unearthed in this coastal region from archaeological sites such as Tres Zapotes, below Cerro Tuxtla, and others in the lowlands to the south of the mountains.

Some visitors also come to enjoy beautiful Lago Catemaco, a broad blue expanse of water lying near the center of the range in a great depression bordered by foothills and volcanic cones. Several large springs of highly mineralized water gush forth on its northern shore, from which the liquid is bottled and shipped to Sierra towns and various parts of the country. Many glistening white Snowy Egrets (*Egretta thula*) and contrastingly somber-hued Neotropic Cormorants (*Phalacrocorax brasilianus*) fly over the lake and roost on or forage from its islands, rocky points, and shores. The surface of the large island, Agaltepec, shows evidence of possibly having been shaped by people of a bygone age. Indeed, since some of this land has been inhabited by humans for centuries, there is no doubt that archaeological treasures are yet to be discovered from the mounds seen in various places and also in the lower elevations along the Gulf slopes of the mountains.

In the Tuxtla Mountains

To one interested in the natural world, the Los Tuxtlas region offers such a wealth of living things that a person could easily spend "days without time," as Arthur Loveridge once put it, studying and enjoying them. My interest in the Sierra was first stimulated by Alexander Wetmore's (1943) excellent paper on the birds in part of the range, and by Frans Blom and Oliver La Farge's (1926–27) fascinating book *Tribes and Temples*, in which they described the region, its people, and some of its archaeological objects and sites. Later, translating Immanuel Friedlaender's (1923) intriguing paper concerning his exploration and geological investigations in Los Tuxtlas in 1922 served to increase my attraction to the area. It was in May 1951 that I first stood near the small village of Tapalapan on the southwestern slope of the range, watching the yellowish white glow of the rising sun etch the rounded outlines of Volcán San Martín Tuxtla and its subsidiary peaks and listening to the swelling dawn bird song chorus issuing from the nearby forest and thickets. Here was a place where the natural attractions were clear and compelling to me. I knew then that I wanted to return someday to explore the region more thoroughly and learn more about its birds, other animals, and plant life.

Since then I have made several short trips to the Sierra, and in 1962 I was fortunate to conduct doctoral program field studies there for about a year, with a research grant from the National Academy of Sciences. This was truly a memorable and often exciting period. I followed intimately the progression of the seasons with all their attendant interaction of weather and the varied elements of the region and its people. On foot, by horse and mule, by jeep, power boat, dugout canoe, and aircraft I traveled through and above the Sierra, into its magnificent humid tropical forests, through elfin cloud forest in the high peaks, the montane sweetgum forests and pine woodlands in the southeast, semideciduous forests at lower elevations, and savannahs and fields on the inland slopes. I slept in thatch-roofed villages and solitary mountain huts, in *rancho* buildings, in a hammock slung between trees, and in a sleeping bag on the ground. I boated on Lago Catemaco, on mangrove-fringed Bahía Sontecomapan, in coastal lowland rivers, and off Gulf shores. Thus I experienced fully this wonderful display of tropical nature in all its variety and beauty. It was a year in my life of rich satisfactions and unforgettable experiences.

One moonlit night we lay in our sleeping bags just after dusk at the small level place called La Cocina on a ridge high on the flank of Volcán San Martín Tuxtla. We savored the moods of this fine climax forest that covers much of the mountain and listened to the deep roaring of the *saraguatos* (howler monkeys, *Alouatta palliata*) as they chorused in the distance. And as it darkened we heard the subdued rustlings and chitterings of the kinkajous (*Potos flavus*) as they began to feed on ripe fruits in the leafy lower parts of the canopy. At about 3 a.m. we were awakened by a distant sound, at first a faint murmuring, then a louder cacophony of voices, horns blowing, and finally flickering torches visible on the trail below between the great tree boles. Soon more than a hundred men, women, and children of all ages filed into and past our small camp with much calling, laughing, and excited conversation. They were from San Andrés, a vocal and happy throng on their annual Semana Santa or Easter Week pilgrimage to the volcano crater to gather bundles of fragrant branches from the *camedor* shrub for use in the holiday religious ceremonies. It was bedlam for a time. I recall how some of our visitors commenced to play cards, and two began to skin an opossum they had secured en route, throwing its entrails on the ground beside our sleeping bags. With the main volcano peak trail running through our camp, we got no more sleep that night.

Dawn in the montane forest on that April morning was heralded by the clear, flutelike notes of those fine singers the Slate-colored Solitaires (*Myadestes unicolor*). Whistled songs of the diminutive White-breasted Wood-Wrens (*Henicorhina leucosticta*) mingled with the hooting of Blue-crowned Motmots (*Momotus momota*), the loud barks of the Barred Forest-Falcons (*Micrastur ruficollis*), and the low calls of Emerald Toucanets (*Aulacorhynchus prasinus*). Early one morning, while walking on the peak trail above camp, I stopped abruptly as two large, lithe weasels stalked purposefully across the path less than twenty feet away. They were the epitome of agility and grace, these tayras (*Eira barbara*), obviously on the hunt as they ran along the trunk of a fallen tree looking alertly to and fro. The whitish fur on their heads is a reminder of one of their apt Spanish names, *cabeza de viejo*, or head of an old man.

Figure 2.2. Aerial view of the almost unbroken forest on the Gulf slope of the Tuxtla Mountains, March 27, 1962. The village of Montepío is in the foreground near the river mouth, and Volcán San Martín Tuxtla is at the upper right, covered by clouds. Photo by R. F. Andrle.

Another time at La Cocina we were sleeping peacefully in our jungle hammocks, suspended between the tree trunks, when I was rudely awakened in the middle of the night by the shock of my back and head hitting the forest floor. I shouted and reached for my flashlight and trusty gun, thinking someone had cut the rope with a knife or machete. Zipping open the hammock insect netting and emerging rapidly, I found that the rope had suddenly parted entirely of its own accord, apparently having aged enough since its manufacture during World War II to have become weakened. My startled companions found all this most amusing.

One late afternoon, my local assistant Andrés Baxin was leading along the trail down the volcano when he suddenly yelled and began running rapidly. Traveling barefoot, as he often did on the trail, he had stepped into an army ant column, and the aggressive little creatures had reacted immediately. We found it difficult to stop laughing at Andrés's antics. I once got into a similar predicament myself in the great climax rain forest near the Cumbres de Bastonal, southeast of Volcán Santa Marta, when I encountered a column of these ants being followed by various woodpeckers, woodcreepers, tanagers, and brush-finches. I had just secured a specimen of Golden-olive Woodpecker (*Colaptes rubiginosus*), which fell into the ant column and was immediately set upon. Jumping into the middle of the column, I snatched up the ant-covered woodpecker and tossed it aside, following as fast as I could. But I was not swift enough. Amid the laughter of my companions, I was forced to shed almost all my clothing to rid myself of the biting ants.

High in the rugged Volcán Santa Marta massif, near the great semicircular crater wall of Cerro Campanario, the Río Coxcoapan begins its rushing course through montane forests down to its wide, slow-flowing debouchment in Bahía Sontecomapan near the Gulf of Mexico. One day on a forest trail far up this stream, I came upon several young Mexicans from a nearby rancho frolicking in a deep pool. As I paused to watch them, I noticed a medium-sized fer-de-lance (*Bothrops atrox*) moving slowly along the opposite bank near the water's edge and thought it best to call the boys' attention to its proximity. Their response was instantaneous. Never was a pool vacated so rapidly! With a surprisingly swift and accurate fusillade, they hurled stones at the unfortunate pit viper, killing it. They then took it back to show their people at the rancho, and I was not able to persuade them to sell it to me for preservation as a specimen. These highly venomous reptiles are fairly numerous in the region. Although mainly nocturnal and not usually aggressive, *Bothrops atrox* is an ever-present danger, and carrying antivenin during fieldwork is a wise precaution.

One morning Harold Axtell and I were walking on a well-worn trail in lowland foothill forest west of Sontecomapan just after two barefoot local women had passed. Suddenly a five-and-one-half-foot (1.67 m) fer-de-lance crossed the trail, which at this point was bordered by rather dense ground vegetation. I wonder how many of the local people here become victims of this viper. We used the shotgun barrel to move the snake into position for some close-up (telephoto) photography, and it struck once or twice but otherwise remained quite docile. We admired its beautiful colors and striking pattern. Gary Ross from Louisiana State University encountered a big one while studying butterflies throughout the mountain range. Pursuing a butterfly through the forest, he paused to retrieve it from his net and felt something strike his boot. It was a large fer-de-lance, which his local assistant killed with a machete. Luckily, Gary was wearing knee boots at the time. The people living near my house on Lago Catemaco, knowing I was interested in bird and other animal specimens, draped a dead fer-de-lance over my gate. It measured over six feet in length. This viper has a large elevational range. I once encountered a smaller one crossing the trail to El Triunfo at about 8,000 feet (2,439 m) elevation in the Sierra Madre de Chiapas when I was studying the Horned Guan (*Oreophasis derbianus*).

During my investigations in the Volcán Santa Marta massif I stayed for a time on the south slope in Ocotal Chico with John Lind and his family, who were working as missionaries in the region. The Popoluca people there were surprised to see how I traveled alone in the forest reaching up toward the volcanoes. I was told some of them believed that little men lived in the forest above, and that it was dangerous to go there alone. The Popolucas occasionally watched me prepare bird study skins, not having seen this done before. They were impressed, I was told, that I could secure the birds undamaged, particularly hummingbirds, about which they seemed to possess some superstition. I very much enjoyed this stay with the Linds, who were gracious hosts.

One day Epigmenio Tegoma and his friend and I were ascending toward Volcán San Martín Tuxtla through the forest above Tapalapan when an armadillo (*Dasypus novemcinctus*) sprang from cover and bolted away. Both my friends immediately fired at it with their shotguns, but, though possibly wounded, it made the supposed safety of its burrow, hotly pursued. Their dog yapped and jumped frantically about the burrow entrance as Epigmenio quickly dropped to his knees and with great energy began to dig into the earth with his machete, occasionally pausing to reach down into the burrow to try to grasp the animal by its tail. In a very few minutes he had dug a trench about two feet deep and five feet long, finally pulling out the struggling armadillo by the tail and dispatching it with a machete blow. The armadillo's flesh is highly prized by the local people. Epigmenio later posed proudly for a photograph with the animal on his lap.

His dog had been running through the forest in all directions, nosing into various holes and crevices. Later it came back to us whimpering, with its muzzle starting to swell greatly. Epigmenio thought the dog had probably had been bitten by a fer-de-lance. He then produced a dirty old pop bottle from his bag and proceeded to force the dog to drink some of the liquid it contained. I did not find out what this was, but when I returned some weeks later he told me that the dog had recovered completely, only to be killed soon afterward by a car. He and his family in Tapalapan told me how some years earlier they had assisted A. Starker Leopold during his zoological investigations in the Tuxtla Mountains while he was gathering information for his book on Mexican wildlife. They proudly showed me photographs of his expedition on the walls in their home. I hope that those I sent them of our times together are similarly displayed. The fine cooperation and friendliness of these people were an example of the same attitude that I encountered almost everywhere I traveled in the region.

Laguna Tisatal at that time was a beautiful, forest-bordered body of water lying in a small crater in the foothills on the southwestern side of Volcán San Martín Tuxtla. Early one morning, with Epigmenio and a friend, I reached its shore to find it thronged with at least three hundred Least Grebes (*Tachybaptus dominicus*). My companions immediately began to stalk the nearest grebes, and after shooting and killing or wounding about a dozen from the shore, they stripped off their clothes, plunged in, and began to retrieve the birds, clamping the legs in their teeth. Ashore, they tied a cord around the grebes' legs and carried them back to the village dangling, a few of the birds wounded and still struggling. On this trip they also shot two Keel-billed Toucans (*Ramphastos sulfuratus*), which they said were good to eat.

Throughout the Sierra I selectively collected plant specimens, especially of trees and shrubs that appeared to be major components of habitat types. To identify them more easily, it was best to collect flowers and/or fruits in addition to leaves, if possible. Unfortunately, I could not always secure such specimens from the larger forest trees, because their lower branches were so high above the ground. Hence I was obliged to use a shotgun or rifle to bring some specimens down. One giant tree from which I collected specimens in this unconventional way was in the undisturbed climax forest on the Gulf side of the Sierra. This specimen was later identified as *Engelhardtia guatemalensis*, a Central American species of the walnut family, otherwise unknown in Mexico

Figure 2.3. Epigmenio Tegoma digging with a machete in pursuit of an armadillo in its burrow in the humid forest above Tapalapan in the Tuxtla Mountains, May 31, 1962. Photo by R. F. Andrle.

at that time. The botanists at the U.S. National Museum complained good-naturedly about the pellet holes in some of the specimens that I sent them. Another specimen sent to the same museum was a bamboolike vine that I secured in the understory of the magnificent cloud forest in the Sierra Madre de Chiapas southeast of El Triunfo; at the time it was not identifiable and was possibly an unknown species.

Another collecting situation involved butterflies. Gary Ross was unable to collect a large white species called *Morpho polephemus* that flew through the forest usually out of reach, just below the canopy. I was able to secure several specimens for him relatively undamaged by using very small shot in light loads. In another instance, one afternoon in the lowland forest north of Tres Zapotes, I fired at a Black Hawk-Eagle (*Spizaetus tyrannus*) perched some distance away in the top of a tall tree. It glided down into heavy vegetation, and I could not find it despite diligent searching. Thinking it might still be there, I returned the next morning and indeed found it, but it was by then covered with maggots. Nevertheless, I was able to preserve the specimen as a study skin, the first of this species to be secured for the expanding zoological collections at the Louisiana State University Museum of Zoology.

Volcán San Martín Tuxtla

It was a calm, cool evening in late April with a waning sliver of moon giving almost no illumination under the closed forest canopy. Leopoldo Castillo and I had set up camp in the great forest on the Gulf slope of Volcán San Martín Tuxtla as dusk fell and the gloom thickened, eventually obscuring the closest of the lofty, buttressed trees. A short distance away to the southeast we listened to the impressive roars of the howlers, a sound that to me embodies the real essence of this tropical wilderness. The kinkajous were active in the trees overhead, and a loud chorus of frogs commenced, some sounding very much like the barking of small dogs. As the light faded, the insect chorus began until it formed a continuous background to the other forest sounds. Shortly before first light a Mottled Owl (*Ciccaba virgata*) uttered its low hoots, and we could hear the penetrating, resonant booming of a Great Curassow (*Crax rubra*). Later, in the depths of this virgin forest, I encountered two of these great birds high in the trees; they were feeding on fruits about 50 feet (15 m) above the forest floor, and they peered down at me as I moved around to obtain better views.

The early morning avian chorus in this climax forest is remarkable for its magnitude and diversity. The still, humid air is filled with the tremulous whistles of Great and Slaty-breasted tinamous (*Tinamus major* and *Crypturellus boucardi*), the calls of Barred and Collared forest-falcons (*Micrastur ruficollis* and *M. semitorquatus*), the loud, chanting notes of Spotted Wood-Quails (*Odontophorus guttatus*), the resonant calls of Scaled Pigeons (*Patagioenas speciosa*), and the cooing of Tuxtla Quail-Doves (*Geotrygon carrikeri*). Chestnut-capped Brush-Finches (*Arremon brunneinucha apertus*) utter their high, thin songs. Rustlings and heavy wing flapping of feeding Crested Guans (*Penelope purpurascens*) can be heard from fruit-laden trees. Black-headed Nightingale-Thrushes (*Catharus mexicanus*) sing their high-pitched, musical songs, contrasting with the *caows* of Collared Trogons (*Trogon collaris*) and the peculiar, froglike calls of Keel-billed Toucans. Giant, iridescent blue *Morpho* butterflies beat erratically through sunlit openings, and large red-bellied squirrels (*Sciurus aureogaster*) forage in the trees. Tall, long-fronded tree ferns, some exceeding 20 feet (6 m) in height, grow in the ravines and are sometimes scattered in the understory among the spiny-trunked palms. Mosses of varied green hues, long vines looped and twisted, and large-leaved climbers and air plants with orange-red, spiked inflorescences festoon tree limbs and trunks. Each canopy tree is a vibrant world in itself. Once I counted more than seventy brilliant Red-legged Honeycreepers (*Cyanerpes cyaneus*) feeding on the nectar in the orange flowers of a giant *Bernoullia flammea* tree at least 150 feet (45 m) tall.

In the damp silt of a small stream I came upon tracks of the little red brocket deer (*Mazama americana*), and farther along were the pug marks of a small cat, perhaps an ocelot (*Felis pardalis*). Near a forest opening a fluttering caught my eye in a wet and muddy place where soil had washed into a stream pool. Two hummingbirds, a Violet and a Long-tailed sabrewing (*Campylopterus hemileucurus* and *C. excellens*), had become bogged down in the mud. I carefully extricated them, rinsed them in the pool, and held them in a patch of sunlight until they began to dry. It was a real thrill to study these exquisite creatures at such close range, and I admired their glittering, iridescent feathering as they preened in my hand before flying away.

Later, when we left the forest, moisture-laden air began to move in from the Gulf, and then dense clouds enveloped the mountains, saturating the vegetation. These two massifs form an orographic barrier to the air masses brought to the coast by trade winds, northers, and occasional easterly waves, the air absorbing moisture as it moves across the water. The luxuriant growth of vegetation in these mountains is a response to the abundant precipitation that results from this uplift and condensation, often coming in the form of heavy downpours. The weather station above Coyame, on the northeast side of Lago Catemaco, has recorded over 160 inches (4,064 mm) of rain in a year.

On my aerial survey over the region in 1962 I was able to obtain a good impression of the existing vegetation community types as well as the overall extent of forest. I was impressed with the largely unbroken tropical forest on the massifs and its extension to lower elevations, particularly on the Gulf-facing slopes. I also noted the extensive agricultural and pasture lands on the inland side of the range and the clearings for new *milpas* and *colonias* at the edges of and within the forest on both northern and southern slopes. This was a new and revealing perspective, and I enjoyed swooping low in the aircraft over my home on Lago Catemaco and waving to my family before returning to the airport.

One beautiful June evening as dusk fell on the Gulf shore below Volcán San Martín Tuxtla, we prepared to retire to our hammocks in a thatch-roofed, earthen-floored hut in the little village of Montepío. Howler monkeys chorused in the forest, which commenced near the village and stretched inland, almost unbroken, from the confluence of the Ríos Col and Máquina up to the volcano crater. We spent a wakeful night as rodents scurried about the loose earth floor below our hammocks, leaving a maze of tracks visible at first light. According to an old map and an account in a German publication (Kerber

1882), "seven hours from San Andrés Tuxtla" there is a large archaeological site composed of at least nineteen mounds or structures of various sizes, some of them attaining a height of 12 meters and a length of 120 meters. From the map the site appears to be in the vicinity of the present town of Montepío. This is just one of the many sites found in the Gulf coast region in and around these mountains, some of which have been shown to have been inhabited as early as 1500 B.C.

While exploring the great crater of Volcán San Martín Tuxtla, which is at least 800 feet (243 m) deep and about half a mile (800 m) in diameter, we found the tracks of a Baird's tapir (*Tapirus bairdii*) in a muddy place on a small volcanic cone within it. These all-terrain mammals (the Brazilian and Baird's species) are known to ascend to heights of over 6,000 feet (1,829 m) in Latin America. Later, while moving at night at lower elevations in the primary forest southeast of the volcano, I noticed a large bat hanging on the limb of an understory tree about ten feet above ground. This proved to be a woolly false vampire bat (*Chrotopterus auritus*), one of two widespread but uncommon to rare species in the Neotropics, with very large ears and a sword-shaped nose leaf. These bats feed on small mammals, birds, lizards, and large insects. As a group, false vampire bats are the top predators of their order, and some have wing spreads of up to 36 inches (91 cm); this species attains wingspans of up to 28 inches (71 cm). Occasionally, when we camped in open areas at the edges of the forest and put our horses out to graze, there were streaks of blood on their necks in the morning, indicating that vampire bats (*Desmodus*) had fed. We always had to take care not to leave any bare skin exposed when we used our sleeping bags on the ground. Sometimes, while mist netting for birds, I left the nets up until dark, only to find that bats had become entangled in them. In some cases they had cut holes in the nets with their teeth and escaped before I could release them.

Occasionally I rode horses or mules during my investigations in the Tuxtla Mountains. One year Harold Axtell and I planned to ascend Volcán San Martín Tuxtla. Harold had never ridden a horse before and was reluctant to do so. But since this was the best way to carry us and our equipment from San Andrés, I persuaded him to ride. Andrés Baxin selected a docile horse for him, and I had a mule. My mule was small, so I looked rather odd on it with my feet not far from the ground. We watched with some trepidation as Harold slowly crossed the one or two paved roads on the north side of town. Luckily, in the early morning there was little traffic. Harold managed quite well in the cultivated land en route and also as we ascended through the montane forest to La Cocina. The trail was narrow and winding, and we had to be careful to keep the horses and mule clear of the tree trunks, otherwise we could be brushed off or could injure a leg between the mount and the trunk. Mules were usually more surefooted on the trails than horses, but they were generally quite independent and stubborn; one had to be careful to keep a tight hold on the reins when dismounting, or the mule might take off rapidly on its own.

Wooden saddles were quite common in the Sierra, and sometimes I would have to use one, which was rather uncomfortable. Once I rode on a horse with such a saddle in a descent from the mountains above Cuetzalapan. The route was steep at times, and I kept sliding forward; later I discovered that I had acquired several slivers in my posterior. At another time it was a pleasure to borrow John Lind's fine, large horse with its comfortable leather saddle and ride it down from Ocotal Chico. I had to cross several streams, in one of which the rushing water was up to my knees. The horse was sturdy and surefooted, though, and it was a pleasant ride on which I was able to see many birds and view the natural surroundings at leisure.

Hunting was quite common in the Tuxtla region, and I met several lone hunters and hunting parties in various places. One group of four whom I encountered in the forest near the crater of Volcán San Martín Tuxtla had shot a Crested Guan and a paca (*Agouti paca*). A party of six hunters armed with shotguns whom I met in the heavy montane forest on the Gulf slope of this volcano were as piratical looking a group as I have ever seen. A number of times when I observed guans and curassows I was impressed with how easy it would be to secure them, as they were often quite unwary, peering down at me from fruit-laden trees and drawing my attention with various low calls and wing flapping. In my conversations with hunters and with my assistants, I heard of tapirs, peccaries (*Tayassu tajacu*), jaguars (*Panthera onca*), red brocket deer, agoutis (*Dasyprocta mexicana*), pacas, and other animals being taken, and some meat, especially from the last two, was for sale in the local markets. In one market I saw a fresh puma (*Puma concolor*) skin for sale. Frequently I saw farmers tilling their fields with a shotgun slung over one shoulder, particularly in new *colonias* or *milpas* near the forest edge. Young people were often seen hunting with slingshots. Sometimes visitors to the hotel at Playa Azul on Lago Catemaco shot the Snowy Egrets (*Egretta thula*), Green Herons (*Butorides virescens*), Least Grebes, and other birds that frequented the trees and nearby lakeshore areas. I also learned that guns were highly prized. More than one person offered to buy my rifle and shotgun.

A number of friends came to visit us while we were residing on the shore of Lago Catemaco, and it was always a pleasure to see them and enjoy their company. Two such visitors were Allan Phillips and Bob Dickerman. Among other research tasks, Bob was securing vertebrate blood samples for encephalitis testing. My wife, Patricia, recalls particularly the odor of the vulture that Bob's assistant skinned beneath the kitchen window! Allan carried a smoothbore .22 caliber rifle for collecting small birds. In the forest on the Bastonal one day I was walking slightly ahead of him when he called out that there was a Golden-browed Warbler (*Basileuterus belli*) ahead. I glanced back to see him raising the rifle in my direction. Having had the unpleasant experience some years before of being wounded by gunfire, I quickly ducked low before he fired. He secured the warbler.

Another time, Allan was not as lucky. He thought he had collected a Long-tailed Sabrewing, but when shot, the hummingbird fell into a large, flat-topped pile of branches about five or so feet high alongside the dirt road through the forest. We were amused to see an irritated Allan hopping around on top of the branches looking for the hummingbird, uttering various expletives. I don't believe he ever found it.

Howler monkeys and spider monkeys (*Ateles geoffroyi*) were fairly common when I was working in the Sierra. I heard and observed small groups of them in various places, usually in the larger areas of contiguous forest or at the edges in more remote sections. Two howlers had favorite trees on the slopes above Dos Amates, and I frequently paused to watch them. They would sometimes commence roaring when the daily commercial aircraft passed southeast overhead. On one occasion a howler came down fairly close in the lower branches of a tree, and I was able to obtain some fairly good photographs of it. I have a picture of it stretched lazily lengthwise on a limb gazing down at me. This individual demonstrated the propensity of monkeys to defecate and urinate, apparently deliberately, on a person below them, so I carefully kept out of the way. Once when I was close to a band of spider monkeys they became quite excited and, calling loudly, hurled twigs and small branches at me. Apparently there was some trade in spider monkeys in the Sierra, and I heard of females being killed to secure their young.

While at our home on the lake we acquired a young spider monkey that became rather tame, although, as expected, he never became housebroken. The arm of a chair was no different from a tree limb in this regard. Chango had the run of the house. He delighted in scampering outside to sit on an upper porch railing and eat a banana. He particularly liked to sneak up on the two sleeping dogs belonging the house's caretakers, Miguel and Elena, and tickle and tease the dogs until they made off. Green Herons, Snowy Egrets, Ringed Kingfishers (*Megaceryle torquata*), large iguanas, and occasionally a basilisk (*Basiliscus*) frequented large trees and the lakeshore in front of our house. Once I found a Central American wooly opossum (*Caluromys derbianus*) eating oranges in the trees on the grounds. It bit through my heavy gloves when I tried to move it into better light for a photograph.

A variety of resident and migratory birds also occurred at our home there. Nesting in the trees in and near our yard were Green Herons, Brown-crested Flycatchers (*Myiarchus tyrannulus*), Yellow-throated Euphonias (*Euphonia hirundinacea*), and Clay-colored Thrushes (*Turdus grayi*). Blue-crowned Motmots hooted nearby, Green-breasted Mangos (*Anthracothorax prevostii*) and Rufous-tailed Hummingbirds (*Amazilia tzacatl*) flitted about, and there were Melodious Blackbirds (*Dives dives*), Scrub Euphonias (*Euphonia affinis*), Band-backed Wrens (*Campylorhynchus zonatus*), and Piratic Flycatchers (*Legatus leucophaius*) in evidence. Least and Pied-billed grebes (*Tachybaptus dominicus, Podilymbus podiceps*), Ruddy Ducks (*Oxyura jamaicensis*), and Neotropic Cormorants were frequently offshore. At night we listened to the Common Pauraques (*Nyctidromus albicollis*), Mottled Owls, and Vermiculated Screech-Owls (*Megascops guatemalae*). It was a pleasant place for the family and a good, centrally located base of operations for my studies.

When I first moved into the house on Lago Catemaco, local people told me that there was an armed murderer living in a house near the bridge in Catemaco, and they warned me to avoid the area. Later I met an American living near the lake who showed me his guns, including automatic weapons, and said he would use them if necessary to protect himself from a perceived threat to his land. He seemed somewhat stressed, but not being familiar with the local political situation at the time I was not sure what provoked this attitude. There was an apparently authentic report of an attack by local farmers on a police station near Acayucan, resulting in some casualties. Otherwise, it was a peaceful time during our stay in the region.

One day I visited the malaria control office in San Andrés and noted with interest their large wall map upon which dots showed numerous cases of the disease in the region, especially at lower elevations near the base of the mountains. At intervals the control personnel would arrive at my house and spray its interior walls with DDT, marking the spray date on the garage wall. I particularly remember the day I had arranged with a resident of Sontecomapan for him to take me out in the bay in his boat. But when I arrived early in the morning on the appointed day, he was in a hammock in his home, sweating and shaking with malaria and unable to accompany me.

Those richly satisfying days in this wild land I will always remember with satisfaction, and the desire to return will always remain with me. But eventually there may be few or no such wild places in the Tuxtla Mountains to experience again. This region is blessed with a mild climate, high rainfall, and volcanic-derived soils, factors which, when combined with its comparatively low relief and considerable extent of gently sloping terrain, make much of the area accessible to settlement and suitable for agriculture. Consequently, the high human population increase in Mexico and immigration from other parts of the country have exerted pressure on the natural environment in the region that has been increasing, and in some areas this has produced deleterious effects. New *colonias* and *ejidos* have been established, some being carved out of the virgin forest in a way reminiscent of pioneer days in the eastern United States. Individuals have moved in with farming and cattle ranching.

These developments were brought home to me vividly one evening as I paddled a canoe slowly along the edge of Bahía Sontecomapan, watching basilisks skitter across the shallows and listening to the night sounds commence. As darkness came I could see at least fifteen fires burning high on the forested mountain slopes as farmers burned the felled forest trees, branches, and grass to expose the soil for their maize, beans, and other crops. An example of this was a large area I traversed on the Gulf slope that had been cleared of forest a few years earlier and was then covered largely with grass or bare earth. Tall, isolated forest trees were scattered about, some still festooned with lianas, climbers, and epiphytes. Some of them were showing the adverse effects to foliage and attached plants that often occur to such single trees when they are deprived of the protection of the forest and exposed to sun and wind.

The increasing population in this region and people's need for more land has not allowed forest regeneration to occur as it once could when populations were sparser and shifting cultivation was prevalent. In one way it is fortunate that some of the soils in this region are more fertile than in many places in the tropics. Growth of plants is comparatively rapid, and many slopes have low gradients. Consequently, there is less erosion and plots can be used longer for agriculture than in some other tropical regions. I think, however, about the real loss to Mexico and its people of this great forest and its rich array of living things.

A few years ago I enjoyed visiting the biological station on the Montepío road and hearing of the studies that were being conducted there. During this trip I had the pleasure of meeting and going into the field with Bill Schaldach, who had long experience in research on Mexico's bird life. It is good to read of the increasing number of Mexican and American biologists working in the Tuxtla Mountains and elsewhere in Mexico during the last decade or so. I recently obtained a copy of *Historia Natural de Los Tuxtlas* (Soriano et al. 1997), a large volume containing a wealth of valuable information on the biology of the region. From a practical standpoint, however, I doubt that stronger efforts for conservation and preservation of the Tuxtla forests thirty or forty years ago by Mexican scientists and environmentalists would have been effective, considering the economic, demographic, and other factors during that time. I hope that such efforts, coupled with knowledge among local people of the regional importance of this mountain watershed, will succeed in preserving higher-elevation forests in the region, though they are only a small portion of the magnificent expanse that once existed.

My Mexican friends in Los Tuxtlas expressed an awareness of the environmental changes taking place in parts of the region and voiced concerns to me about possible long-term adverse consequences, not only to the land and its flora and fauna but to the people living there. Dr. Rodolfo Hernández Corzo, former director of the Mexican Department of Wildlife, once emphasized that the country is still learning and trying to adapt scientific techniques of resource management to the mounting pressures of a rapidly growing population. At a conference some time ago he made some observations about his country that I think are important: he said that at that time Mexico was still coming out of the first phase, of total harvesting or exploitation, and into the second phase, of conservation and preservation of resources. Rural populations still represent a large percentage of the country's total population, with a rather low standard of living, and it is clear that any conservation movement will have to confront apparently insurmountable problems. For a good account of the history of conservation in Mexico I recommend Lane Simonian's *Defending the Land of the Jaguar* (1995). Corzo also said:

> I am very sure that if we go to our people and tell them that they are supposed to preserve wildlife because of the aesthetic value they will understand, they will even shout "Ole," but will not find themselves able to act accordingly.... We must emphasize the practical aspects in preference to aesthetic aspects in dealing with the wildlife resources. In Mexico now, according to the actual trends of our economic and social progress, whether we like it or not we have to concentrate on the economic values of these four entities (land, water, forests, wildlife) constituting our natural physical background.

My good friend Professor Carlos Ramírez of San Andrés Tuxtla presented my wife with a book as a parting gift when we left the Sierra in 1962. It is entitled *Estampas de Mi Tierra* (Sketches of My Land) and contains poetry and prose about life in Los Tuxtlas by Eduardo Turrent Rozas. Among the many delightful drawings in this small volume is one depicting a large hourglass with a supporting frame of moss-draped tropical trees above a little house. To me this simple sketch has significance that is probably not what the author intended. It could mean that time is running out for what remains of the natural world in the Sierra. The *campesino* toiling in his maize field above lovely Bahía Sontecomapan probably neither knows nor cares of such things, because his chief concern is survival. The crude wooden sign he had erected among the maize plants read: *"Aqui, mi vida"* (In this place, my life). Let us hope that somehow among the people living in these beautiful mountains there will come to be a sufficient understanding and appreciation of the aesthetic and physical benefits that a properly protected, wisely used, and cherished natural environment can provide.

Travel and Research in Veracruz, Oaxaca, and Chiapas

In the early 1950s, about two-thirds of the approximately 125-mile (200 km) road across Mexico's Isthmus of Tehuantepec was under construction or being improved, and it was in rather poor condition. In April 1952, while traveling from Chiapas to the Tuxtla Mountains, we set out from Tehuantepec northward across the Isthmus. It had begun to rain—possibly an early start to the rainy season. No bridges had yet been built across the streams, and we had to go off the newly constructed raised portions of the road five times to drive across the waterways. We did not have a four-wheel-drive vehicle, so we often had to stay in lower gears to keep moving as the rain turned the road to mud. Part of the way across we came upon a bus that had gotten stuck, canted to one side and partially blocking the road. Several cars and trucks were held up by this vehicle. After consulting, we all agreed to band together to help one another, thus managing to get past the bus, which was irretrievable, and continue. Eventually we reached the better stretch of road toward Acayucan without further serious problems. What stands out in my mind about the area at that time is the great extent of tall tropical forest present on both sides of the road. Crossing the Isthmus about ten years later it was a shock to see how most of this forest had disappeared. There was none near the road, and on both sides it was hard to see any forest at all for great distances. Instead, houses and villages now occupied the area, illustrating precisely how opening and improving a road through a veritable wilderness can drastically change the landscape.

During our 1950s investigations in Chiapas there was an acute shortage of gasoline. Most stations had none. Miguel Álvarez del Toro knew that there were Resplendent Quetzals (*Pharomachrus mocinno*) in cloud forest remnants near Pueblo Nuevo, about fifty miles north of Tuxtla Gutiérrez, so he gave us specific directions. We contacted the state highway chief and explained our purpose. He graciously gave us a half tank of gas and we set out, though not at all certain that we had enough to reach our destination and return over the steep and winding roads. Unfortunately, we had to turn back before reaching the cloud forest. It was especially disappointing as my companion, Bert Wright, had never seen this beautiful species. Along this road we reached a small mountain village and, as it was quite warm, decided to stop at a local store for a cool drink. There was much noise and gaiety, and we realized that a celebration of some sort was in progress. Many people, most of them apparently inebriated, were sprawled over the road and near the houses. I had to be careful not to run over anyone. As I zigzagged slowly along, an obviously drunken man with a machete came running across the street toward our vehicle, shouting and gesticulating. His attitude seemed menacing, so I tensed to be prepared for whatever might be coming. As it turned out he was friendly, had apparently spotted my binoculars, and merely wanted to look through them. We decided it would be wiser not to stop for a cool one in that particular town.

Also during these studies in the Chiapas highlands, one evening I spotted a small trailer parked off of the road in a pine forest. It proved to belong to Byron Harrell, who was carrying out fieldwork in Chiapas. I could not find him but left a note, which I don't think he found. Bert and I slung our jungle hammocks for the night between pine trees. Occasionally I had seen people walking nearby through the forest, sometimes with a dog. They did not stop at my greeting and, as I found with some local people in remote areas of Chiapas, were somewhat shy or aloof. Sometime during the dark, moonless night I was startled by Bert's loud yell that someone was there. I immediately bailed out of the hammock, reaching for flashlight and pistol. Not accustomed to camping in the wild, Bert had been uneasy about it, but now he sounded really alarmed. I quickly determined that there was no one about. Bert said something had struck the bottom of his hammock, hard. I could only surmise that a local dog or perhaps some other animal had blundered into it, possibly running. Bert got little sleep during the remainder of that night.

He and I also stayed at the Mocambo, a large resort hotel along the Gulf coast south of Veracruz city. We had been in the field for some time, and it was refreshing to rest at this pleasant place along a beautiful wide beach. We wondered how such a large hotel could persist; all the tables were set and a large staff was present, but there were hardly any guests evident. Bert had been experiencing some mild dysentery, and we had been bitten by many ticks and chiggers. I counted about seventy-five bites on my body. It was a poor use of whiskey, but dabbing it on the bites provided some relief from itching. When Bert's dysentery grew worse and did not seem to be alleviated by the usual medicine, I went down to the bar and asked the bartender if he had anything that might relieve the malady. *"Sí, señor,"* he declared, and promptly began mixing liquids from various bottles, finally giving me a large glass of weird-looking orange-red liquid. I delivered it to Bert, who downed it. What the stuff was I never learned, but it must have been powerful and effective as it helped the already weakened Bert sleep for several hours. He awakened completely cured, and we were soon able to continue on our way.

During my investigations of the Horned Guan in Mexico and Guatemala I initiated a trip to the Sierra Madre de Chiapas with my good friend the late Miguel Álvarez del Toro. On March 9, 1965, Miguel and I, four of his assistants, the noted artist Albert Gilbert, and Ron Andrews from western New York traveled together in a truck and the Land Rover of the Instituto de Historia Natural. We went to Finca Prusia, a coffee plantation on the south slope of the range at about 3,300 feet (1,006 m). Proprietors Herman Kahle and his wife were fine hosts to our party. Besides providing a place to leave our vehicles, they generously supplied us with overnight accommodations as well as horses and men to transport us and our equipment up to our camp at El Triunfo in the cloud forest near the crest of the range. They informed us that the finca was operated largely on water power from the mountain streams. At dinner that night there was a cuckoo clock on the wall and, if I remember correctly, a picture of the kaiser. Some of these plantations had originally been established in the eighteenth century by German settlers. Herman told me the finca employed many local Indians, who were dependent on it for their livelihood. Finca Prusia was remote enough from populated areas for the manager to become, in effect, the local law. He oversaw the finca's employees and was sometimes called upon to settle problems and incarcerate offenders. Herman said one day there was a fight among the workers and one came asking to see the manager. This individual came in with his arms behind his back. When asked what he wanted, the Indian brought his arms forward, one holding a severed hand from the other, and asked whether it could be reattached. Apparently it had been cut off by a machete blow during the fight.

One of the highlights of our stay at El Triunfo was that each morning up to eight or so beautiful Resplendent Quetzals would fly about and over us among the large trees surrounding the camp. What a delightful and memorable experience! During this expedition Al Gilbert found many opportunities to observe bird behavior, paint from collected and mist-netted specimens, and make notes and sketches for future work. He was able to watch a Horned Guan's foraging behavior for some time. Later, he generously gave me his original painting of the Horned Guan postures used in my paper on the species (Andrle 1967a) and also a head portrait of an adult male Highland Guan (*Penelopina nigra*) that he painted at camp from a specimen I secured. I admire them now as I write.

One day a botanical collector named Thomas MacDougall walked into camp. He was securing plant specimens for various institutions, such as the New York Botanical Society. MacDougall had planned to ask a Mexican family

Figure 2.4. Horned Guan (*Oreophasis derbianus*) expedition members at El Triunfo camp at 6,068 feet (1,850 m) in the Sierra Madre de Chiapas, March 22, 1965. *Left to right:* Jorge, Bonifacio, R. F. Andrle, Ron Andrews, Rodrigo, Angel, and Miguel Álvarez del Toro. Photo by R. F. Andrle.

living near camp at the edge of the cloud forest whether he could have dinner with them, expecting tortillas and beans or similar fare. I invited him to eat with our group, and he was suitably surprised and pleased to enjoy a complete Swiss steak dinner from our supply of freeze-dried food.

Those pleasant weeks at El Triunfo were unforgettable—with Al, Ron, Miguel, and his men, our daily excursions into the magnificent cloud forest, and the excitement of watching a Horned Guan forage low in the trees at the edge of camp. We enjoyed the bird life and other sights and sounds of this great forest, which fortunately has been preserved. Among the bird species we found there were Spotted Nightingale-Thrush (*Catharus dryas*), Tawny-throated Leaftosser (*Sclerurus mexicanus*), Spotted Woodcreeper (*Xiphorhynchus erythropygius*), Black-throated Jay (*Cyanolyca pumilo*), Unicolored Jay (*Aphelocoma unicolor*), Amethyst-throated Hummingbird (*Lampornis amethystinus*), Scaled Antpitta (*Grallaria guatimalensis*), Barred Forest-Falcon, Mountain Thrush (*Turdus plebejus*), Slate-throated Redstart (*Myioborus miniatus*), Golden-browed Warbler (*Basileuterus belli*), Emerald Toucanet, White-naped Brush-Finch (*Atlapetes albinucha*), and Brown-backed Solitaire (*Myadestes occidentalis*).

Figure 2.5. Robert Andrle making observations on a trail in the understory of cloud forest southeast of El Triunfo, Sierra Madre de Chiapas, March 19, 1965. Photo by R. F. Andrle.

The Mexicans living at El Triunfo at that time had a few cattle that foraged through the forest, obviously finding little sustenance and damaging the vegetation. Ascending one of the ridges to the southeast of camp through dense elfin forest, which at times required crawling on hands and knees through the moss-draped limbs, I reached the ridge crest and was amazed to see the skeletal remains of a cow, which had apparently become entangled among the branches and been unable to extricate itself. In March it grew chilly at night; one morning I broke a thin sheet of ice from the washbowl. Sometimes clouds would move in during the afternoon from the Pacific and envelop the camp in a cool, damp layer, so that we had to suspend fieldwork temporarily except for tending the mist nets or working on specimens. It was an eerie experience, with only the voices of birds heard from the thick mist.

Miguel was a fine field companion and a close friend. I miss him. His remarkable, pioneering work on the wildlife of Chiapas will long be remembered. A modest and retiring man, in some ways he was like a voice crying in the fast-diminishing wilderness. I remember his pleasure when he won the Getty prize for his accomplishments. The remarkable zoo that now exists in his name (ZOOMAT) in Tuxtla Gutiérrez stemmed from his initial efforts with a few cages many years before. Later, ecotour guru Victor Emanuel told me that Rodrigo, one of Miguel's men who was with our party, was leading groups to see the Horned Guan and other birds on nature tours over the Sierra Madre trail through El Triunfo and down to Mapastepec.

Guatemalan and Costa Rican Adventures

During my expeditions to study the Horned Guan in Mexico in the Sierra Madre de Chiapas and in the mountains of Guatemala, I had several experiences that proved to be interesting and rather exciting. One fine, clear morning I drove to the airport at Tapachula, on the Pacific coast of Chiapas. I wanted to rent an aircraft for an aerial survey of the southeastern end of the Sierra Madre, particularly Volcán Tacaná on the Mexican-Guatemalan border, to determine the extent of forest habitat there that might be suitable for the guan. Driving about the small airport and seeing no aircraft that might serve my purpose, I noticed a man on the tarmac near a Stearman, a two-seater, single-engine biplane with an open cockpit. He was working on a large number of oily engine parts strewn about in front of the plane. I asked whether he knew of an aircraft that I could rent for the flight. He said there were none available just then but that he would fly me around in an hour or so, as soon as he had reassembled his engine. Looking at the quarter-century-old plane and thinking about Tacaná's 13,425-foot (4,093 m) height, the rugged Sierra Madre, and photographing from an open cockpit, I decided against this, although it certainly would have been an exhilarating experience! I really prefer a two-engined aircraft in such situations.

Later, on April 3, 1965, while taking off from the Guatemala City airport and ensconced comfortably in the copilot's seat of my friend Manfredo Lippmann's Aero Commander for aerial surveillance of habitat for the Horned Guan, I thought of the Stearman incident and what a contrast this was. The twin-engined, high-winged Commander is an excellent aircraft for aerial survey and photography, providing good viewing and a stable platform. I used a later model, the Shrike Commander, in my aerial survey of potential Whistling Warbler (*Catharopeza bishopi*) habitat on St. Vincent Island in the West Indies, particularly of the Soufrière volcano, where the forests had been destroyed in a 1902 eruption and were in the process of regrowth. Even in the stable Commander and on a clear day, we were buffeted by moderate turbulence from the northeast trade winds while observing and photographing along the lee side of the volcano.

On this dry season flight over the great chain of volcanoes in southern Guatemala I could see a pall of smoke over the countryside from burning fields and forests. It was an interesting experience to fly through intermittent clouds beginning to billow up among the volcanoes from the Pacific slope, wondering if there was a lofty peak within those clouds. During this reconnaissance flight I had excellent opportunities to view these giant volcanoes, move in at close range over their forests and craters, and photograph them from different angles. Particularly fascinating was the view straight downward about 10,000 feet (3,048 m) into one of the deep gorges on the Pacific side of Volcán Tajumulco, the highest peak in Central America at 13,845 feet (4,220 m). On the steep slope of one of its gorges I could see large trees lying like jackstraws, apparently the result of human action. Clearing for cultivation extended up the steep slopes of many of the volcanoes, in some places exceeding 6,000 feet (1,829 m) elevation.

Also in April 1965, Manfredo flew us to a dirt airstrip at about 3,000 feet (914 m) on the south slope of Volcán Tajumulco, from which we transferred our equipment to vehicles and drove upward to his coffee plantation, Finca Waldemar, at about 5,200 feet (1585 m). This was our base of operations for research on the Horned Guan on this volcano. I employed coffee plantation workers to assist us in transporting our equipment.

As we reached a small opening in the forest high on one of the knifelike ridges above the finca, we saw two Resplendent Quetzals perched near each other high on the horizontal branch of a tall tree. I was watching and admiring them when Alvaro Quesada, in charge of my Guatemalan assistants, said, "Quick, shoot them." I asked him why, and he replied that they were good to eat! I told him a little about the bird and explained why I would not kill them.

During another ascent on this volcano, on April 8, 1965, we set up camp for the night in the cloud forest at a small, relatively level place on a steep ridge. Our assistant placed his opaque plastic shelter a short distance from our small canvas tent. During the night I was awakened by a snuffling sound and other noises close by the tent.

Our assistant called softly from his shelter, *"Tigre, tigre,"* in a somewhat alarmed tone.

Thinking from the sound that it was probably an ocelot or margay (*Felis wiedii*), I called softly, "*¿Tigrillo?*"

He replied in a strained and now excited voice, *"¡No, Roberto, tigre grande, tigre grande!"*

We had a visiting jaguar. Making sure that I knew where my guns were, I thought of him with only his machete and understood his concern. But there were no more sounds, and the rest of the night passed peacefully.

While at the finca I prepared a Horned Guan specimen as a study skin. I had secured it so Albert Gilbert could have color photographs of the soft parts and the fresh skin to use for his subsequent painting of the species for a

Figure 2.6. The Quesada family at their home near Finca Waldemar, at about 5,500 feet (1,676 m) above sea level on the Pacific slope of Volcán Tajumulco, Guatemala, April 7, 1965. Alvaro *(fourth from the left with cap)* worked at the finca and ably assisted Andrle in his research on the mountain. Photo by R. F. Andrle.

paper I planned to write and for his illustration of it in a forthcoming book by Delacour and Amadon on the curassows, guans, and chachalacas. Fascinated finca personnel gathered around me as I prepared the skin, but I eventually understood that their curiosity did not involve the species or the preparation technique. They were more interested in having the body of the guan to eat.

On April 11 I awakened early in the morning in the heavy cloud forest at about 8,300 feet (2,530 m) on one of the volcano's narrow ridges. It had been difficult to find a camping place, because deep wooded gorges fell off close by on both sides. Hearing rustling and wing flapping above me in the dense canopy, I searched carefully and in a few minutes was thrilled to see an adult male Horned Guan peering down at me. I will always treasure that moment on this wilderness volcano. Later, as we reached about 10,000 feet (3,048 m), I glimpsed the bare rock faces on the peak of the mountain glistening in the sun. I wanted to climb to the peak, but our purpose and limited time did not allow that.

On our return to Guatemala City from the narrow dirt airstrip below Finca Waldemar we had to lift the tail of the Aero Commander by hand and turn it for takeoff, then wait while some cows were shooed off the other end of the strip. Just after leaving the ground we entered heavy clouds and did not emerge into the clear until we reached about 10,000 feet. Although I knew we had taken off to the south over the Pacific, I could not help thinking, in that dense cloud, of the tall volcanoes thrusting upward just behind us.

The long-continuing political turmoil in Guatemala at that time sometimes affected my studies there. One year I crossed the border at Puente Talismán, beyond Tapachula, on the Pacific coast of Chiapas. My station wagon was heavily loaded with equipment, including a large overhead rack with several duffel bags and other items. At the customs station I immediately perceived that all was not well. A number of officials gathered around my vehicle, and there were several soldiers nearby carrying automatic weapons. The tension among these men was palpable. I learned that a so-called "state of siege" had just been declared in the country. After showing the customs officials my credentials, explaining my purpose, and telling them generally what I was carrying, I waited for their reaction. They looked over the equipment. Then what I feared happened. They wanted me to take down all the things in the overhead rack for them to examine. I had spent a good deal of time packing, and this delay was the last thing I wanted. By talking faster, further explaining my connection with the Museo Nacional de Historia Natural in Guatemala City, and then adding a judicious distribution of gratuities, I managed to change their minds and proceed on my way.

At another time, the German ambassador was murdered while I was in Guatemala City. As a consequence, things in the city were in somewhat of an uproar. Police and military patrols were much in evidence, and I decided it was best to head for the mountains. Through the generosity of James Greenway, Jr., and the good offices of Dean Amadon at the American Museum of Natural History, I had the use of a jeep, which was stationed at the Museo Nacional under the jurisdiction of its director, Professor Jorge Ibarra. As we drove through the city past a large military establishment, a young soldier with his finger on the trigger of an automatic rifle laughingly pointed his weapon at our vehicle and swung it to follow us as we passed. Despite the Museum logo and name on the jeep's doors we were stopped by military patrols at several roadblocks before reaching the comparative peace and quiet of the rural highlands.

Field equipment can certainly attract attention. When carrying out field studies in remote areas where considerable walking or climbing is necessary, I attach my spotting scope to a rifle-type stock slung over my shoulder. One day in February 1987 I was carrying this rig through the streets of San José, Costa Rica, for a short distance from a parking area to a hotel, and I noticed that people in the crowded streets were staring at me. I was unaware that the day before, the national chief of police had been assassinated by two men on a motorcycle, which had caused alarm and created a sensation in the capital of this normally peaceful country. After that I made sure that the scope and stock were concealed.

Also in Costa Rica, the manager of Braulio Carrillo National Park told me that tourists had recently been accosted and robbed on one of the trails. Hence I was not surprised one rainy morning to see a policeman with an automatic rifle standing at a trail head where, he told me, the incident had occurred. Such vicissitudes of research and travel in Latin America sometimes make for tense occurrences and tend to sharpen your awareness of things happening around you.

Professor Ibarra was always very hospitable and helpful to us on our trips to Guatemala. At the time, he had been furthering wildlife and habitat conservation in Guatemala for many years and had received national recognition for his efforts. On one trip we were pleased to have his young son, Jorge Jr., accompany us. On March 22, 1970, Dick Byron, Bert Wright, Art Clark, and I were in a jeep and Land Rover ascending an old road on the northern side of Zunil Ridge, which culminates in two massive peaks, Zunil and Santo Tomás, each reaching above 11,500 feet (3,506 m). The road deteriorated as we climbed, and sometimes we had to cut or remove trees and branches that had fallen across it. To the west we could glimpse another locality inhabited by the Horned Guan—the beautiful, almost symmetrical cone of Volcán Santa María, rising to 12,372 feet (3,772 m). After reaching a small clearing at about 9,000 feet (2,743 m), we could get the vehicles no farther.

We camped at this place and listened during the moonlit night to Fulvous Owls (*Strix fulvescens*) hooting. At dawn the clear, ascending whistles of Highland Guans issued from the surrounding forest, accompanied by their distinctive rattling, crashing sound, which is similar to that of a tree falling. Early the following morning Dick and I set out southward on the ridge, ascending through forest following a trail that sometimes became rather precarious and narrow above precipitous slopes. However, our search here for the Horned Guan was to no avail. We finally reached a place at about 11,000 feet (3,352 m) where we had an awe-inspiring view of the almost sheer, forest-covered wall of Pico Zunil and of the impressive row of great volcanoes stretching for over fifty miles to the east, silhouetted in the morning sun and mist. As we stood there absorbing this beautiful and humbling scene, we could feel slight earth tremors, possibly originating from Volcán Pacaya to the east, which was then active. We turned back, disappointed at not finding a guan but fully satisfied with our experience.

From the picturesque town of Zunil, on March 23, 1970, we drove upward on the steep western side of the Zunil Ridge to a large gate. It was eventually opened for us, enabling us to continue to ascend along the forested slope to about 8,000 feet (2,439 m). Here the road ended with a row of bungalows and, at the mountain wall, a large pool and a bar. This was Fuentes Georginas. Heated water came directly from the mountain and was piped down through the bungalows' baths, so that one could luxuriate and loosen tense muscles with a hot bath, just adding the right amount of cool water.

Above Fuentes Georginas we climbed the steep forested slope and eventually reached a trail on Zunil Ridge where we found a Horned Guan feather. Later on the trail we met a small group of local people who were traveling along the ridge from the south. These people knew the Horned Guan and said they sometimes saw the birds while on the trail. Fuentes Georginas is a beautiful place that I would recommend to weary travelers after a hard day in the field. Near here we also attempted to enter a large sulphur cave, but we were driven out by the powerful fumes.

At times, a vast layer of clouds forms late in the afternoon through the condensation of humid air being uplifted as it moves northward from the Pacific Ocean through the gap where the Río Samalá flows between Volcán Santa María and the Zunil Ridge along the great chain of Guatemalan volcanoes. Sometimes this layer extends over the town of Zunil and reaches the city of Quetzaltenango. A traveler can then look down from high points along the Pan-American Highway onto a dense blanket of clouds with Volcán Santa María thrusting several thousand feet above it, an impressive sight. During our March 1970 visit, we found that a large section of the winding highway along a steep mountain slope had collapsed from the center outward. A lone tree had been stuck into the edge of the vanished section and was the only warning to anyone driving fast around the bend. I would not want to be driving here at night, or in cloud or fog. Landslides are not uncommon along the Pan-American Highway—we had been delayed in April 1965 while one of several landslides was cleared from the highway just east of the Mexican border.

The road from Panajachel to San Lucas Tolimán around the eastern shore of Lago Atitlán provides some fine views of this beautiful lake and the volcanoes Atitlán, Tolimán, and San Pedro. We visited Edgar Bauer in April 1970 at his home on the lake near Santiago Atitlán. In this area we saw the Atitlán Grebe (*Podilymbus gigas*), now extinct, which Anne LaBastille, with Edgar's assistance, had worked so hard to save. Tragically, Edgar was killed by unknown assailants some years later in the civil strife that plagued Guatemala for so long. Around the south side of the lake, near Cerro de Oro, there were piles of coffee bean skins and pulp covered with black flies. Much later, after returning to the United States, Dick Byron and I had the usual chigger and tick bites. But when two of his did not disappear I suggested that he have a medical check. Local medical personnel were at first unable to tell what the bumps were, but eventually it was determined that they were from the parasite *Onchocerca volvulus*, a filarial worm transmitted by black flies (Simuliidae). The microfilaria in this species sometimes migrate through the lymph system in humans. Eventually, if untreated, they can cause blindness. During my investigations in Mexico and Guatemala I saw some coffee plantation workers affected by this parasite. We were all greatly relieved when Dick's two were treated with antibiotics in time to prevent any further problems.

Birds and Ancient Ruins

Reading John Stephens's accounts of exploring some of the renowned archaeological sites in the Neotropics, and studying the superb illustrations of them by his companion, Frederick Catherwood (Stephens 1841), stimulated my desire to see them. My all too brief explorations of the great ruins at Palenque and Tikal are vivid in my mind.

Those at Palenque always fascinated me, so my visits to this impressive place fulfilled a long-standing wish. It was very exciting to wander around and inside the buildings, to look for birds in the humid forest behind them, and especially to ascend the Temple of the Inscriptions, from which one obtains an exhilarating, panoramic view of much of the site. To watch a Bat Falcon (*Falco rufigularis*) fly about and perch on the tall tower of the Palacio and to observe a White Hawk (*Leucopternis albicollis*) soaring over the ruins and standing out sharply against the green forest background were satisfying, enduring moments.

In April 1970 my wife and I took a few days during research on the Horned Guan to fly from Guatemala City to Tikal. Our aircraft was a somewhat battered but sturdy old Douglas DC-3, renowned throughout the world for its versatility and reliability. Warm, humid air permeated the plane's cabin as we cruised low over the vast El Petén forest, occasionally seeing an egret flying over the canopy.

Our first view of the tallest temple thrusting above the forest was thrilling. As we banked on approach, the narrow airstrip was not visible until the last minute, screened by the tall forest trees close by on each side. It was a delight to walk among Tikal's many structures, usually in the shade of the forest, and to enjoy the many birds that inhabit this national park. The bird highlight of our visit was when we focused our scope on a rare and beautiful Orange-breasted Falcon (*Falco deiroleucus*) perched high on one of the temples. The color plate of this species in Smithe's book on Tikal's birds (Smithe 1966) and its recorded nesting in the temples had always intrigued me, and here it was, a fitting climax for us.

When storms over Guatemala City prevented our return flight, we traveled the short distance by road to Flores on Lago Petén Itzá for the night, where the roaring of howler monkeys issued from the nearby forest. This impressive sound seems the essence of the American tropics, never failing to stir deep emotions.

Ivan Sanderson said it well in *Living Treasure* (1941): "Once you have lived under the sound of the howler's roar, the echoes of the slumbering, silent rain forest will have entered your soul. You will wake up on a quiet night in some horrible northern place with a ghostly echo of it in your ears; when you are tired and lonely and sick of the world, it will suddenly come flooding into your mind, a forerunner of visions of long, still rivers winding between towering walls of greenery, of stately palm groves breathing in the platinum light of the moon, of inky pools of shadow moving silently on a leaf-strewn floor."

The next day the weather had cleared at the capital. At the airport was a Curtiss C-46, the famed old workhorse Commando; like the trusty DC-3s, many of these had found their way to Latin America. After assorted cargo had been unloaded from the aircraft, we entered the cavernous interior to sit on fold-down seats along the sides of the fuselage. As soon as a young boy had checked the levels in the wing fuel tanks with an old stick and then chased some cows off the runway, we took off for an uneventful flight that ended a brief interlude we will always remember with great pleasure and satisfaction.

3

Studying Birds in the Sonoran Desert

JOHN M. BATES

John M. Bates began his ornithological career as the son of an avid birdwatcher in Arizona. Lured early to the northern Neotropics, he completed a master of science degree at the University of Arizona on birds in the Sonoran Desert and his Ph.D. at Louisiana State University on birds in South America. The studies related here were part of his master's thesis, the scientific results of which were reported in Bates (1992a, 1992b). He is chairman and associate curator of birds in the Department of Zoology at the Field Museum in Chicago.

I was lucky. Tucson, Arizona, where I grew up, was less than two hours from the Mexican border. Being the son of an avid birder, I was able to travel in Mexico on a number of birding trips. For water-starved inhabitants of the Old Pueblo, as Tucson is often called, a trip to the closest ocean beach meant hopping into the car and driving through Organ Pipe Cactus National Monument down to Puerto Peñasco, Sonora, on the Gulf of California. Thus, while to most people Mexico conjures up visions of Aztec pyramids near snow-covered volcanoes, Mayan ruins emerging out of the jungle, or snow-white beaches below tropical thorn forest hillsides, I think first about the wonderfully sparse northern deserts and the Sea of Cortez. For me, Mexico was a place to see not only tropical birds but oceanic birds.

Long before the birding community's promulgation of "Big Day" rules specified a 24-hour period beginning at midnight for those crazy attempts to see all the birds you can in a day, my dad, brother, and I did one trip starting at 4 p.m. in Puerto Peñasco. As the sun set, we tallied up loons, Brown Pelicans (*Pelecanus occidentalis*), boobies, gulls, terns, Black Skimmers (*Rynchops niger*), Wilson's Plovers (*Charadrius wilsonia*), and other shorebirds. When it grew too dark to see birds, we climbed into our Dodge Dart station wagon and sped north through the Mexican desert. I was pretty young then, and what I remember most was all the kangaroo rats (*Dipodomys* sp.) and pocket mice (*Perognathus* sp.) hopping across the highway that night. At dawn we were on the top of Mount Lemmon, north of Tucson, hearing the first Steller's Jays (*Cyanocitta stelleri*) and Red-breasted Nuthatches (*Sitta canadensis*) call.

Figure 3.1. Birding at The Point (low tide), always the first stop on arriving at Puerto Lobos, Sonora, December 11, 1986. The shrimp boats have dropped anchor in the harbor for the day. The large opening between the cutaway hills in the distance is the mouth of Arroyo San Lorenzo, a Gray Vireo wintering site. Photo by R. B. Bates.

Our Mexican birding trips were always quick, with an emphasis on seeing as many species as possible. Later, as an undergraduate at the University of Arizona, I was lucky enough to make a number of trips to Mexico with Steve Russell during his research along the back roads of Sonora for his book on the state's birds (Russell and Monson 1998). With Russell we covered large distances and moved camp often, but we would also spend several days at more interesting places. My favorite of these was Lo de Campo, an ungrazed little ranch between the Río Yaqui and Hermosillo. One fall, in a mist net line through the ungrazed pasture and adjacent thorn scrub hillside, we recorded fifteen species of sparrows and towhees. I still doubt that there is another place in the world where this is possible.

These trips whetted my appetite for more work in Sonora. When we visited one of Russell's study sites along the Sonoran coast with his ornithology class in 1985, he let us in on a project that had interested him for some time: the wintering behavior of the Gray Vireo (*Vireo vicinior*). I maintain that this species is still among the most poorly known North American birds. However, Russell had found them to be fairly common in winter in the desert arroyos bordering the Gulf of California. The area he had chosen to study the species included several desert arroyos on the coast near a tiny Seri Indian village called Puerto Lobos, about 60 km south of Puerto Peñasco. In January 1986 I returned to Puerto Lobos with Rick Bowers to commence master's degree research under Russell at the University of Arizona.

Rick, later a successful bird tour leader, was at the time finishing his undergraduate degree, but he already had extensive netting experience. He also had more energy than any other field ornithologist I knew. This combination of skills was exactly what I needed, because our goal was to return to Russell's study areas to catch and color band as many Gray Vireos as possible. Russell had banded some individuals at one of the sites in previous years, and the banded birds would form the basis for my research on the species' winter behavior.

On the first two trips we took Rick's old Datsun pickup, but later our chariot was my own. After some searching through the used car ads in the Tucson newspaper, I realized that for a lowly graduate student, "affordable and dependable" were nonsequiturs when describing used four-wheel-drive vehicles. Instead of that Ford pickup I had always thought I wanted, I bought a red 1968 Volkswagen bus from a Californian friend of one of my officemates. It was one of the best things I have ever done. This vehicle got me back and forth to Lobos with almost no problems. (I eventually ran it into the ground and sold it for two hundred dollars the morning I left for my first South American field season with Louisiana State University.) I could keep my mist net poles and other field gear inside, and thus it was always ready to leave at a moment's notice. In camp I opened the rear doors and slept on the built-in bed in the back. It had great clearance; I got it stuck only once in some sand on its maiden voyage when I was by myself. But in minutes I was out again.

The VW bus had only two drawbacks. On the two-lane Mexican highways it only had enough pickup to pass the ubiquitous slow Mexican trucks with a running, downhill start. And it seemed to say "drug smuggler" to law officers on both sides of the border. As regards this last character flaw, I was always most worried that the previous owners might have left in it something I did not know about. But the several dogs that sniffed their way through the vehicle never found anything more than one of my own stowaway Mexican limes, to the visible consternation of at least one diligent U.S. customs agent. I suppose my explanation that the purpose of my trip was to study birds in the middle of the Mexican desert was a little difficult to believe.

My memories of Mexico are always tied to its roads. No one who has gotten to know any part of the country well has not come to love the wondrously varied though sometimes maddening Mexican roads. Few routes give you a better picture of the variety of plant communities lumped into the classification "Sonoran Desert" than a trip from Tucson to Puerto Lobos. With a few stops to eat, it is a seven- to eight-hour journey; one lunch spot was great for Rufous-winged Sparrows (*Aimophila carpalis*). The first two-thirds of the trip, to the agricultural town of Caborca, can be done two ways. One is through the large border crossing in Nogales, down to Santana, and then west on Mexico Highway 2. This is a route for those wanting to introduce themselves to the desert slowly. It is the paved, civilized route, following much the same path the missionaries used as far back as 1600. The second route, more scenic, goes west from Tucson toward the Tohono-O'odham Indian Reservation, turning south at Three Points in the Avra Valley to cross the border at Sasabe (pop. 200). This route passes east of Baboquivari, which gets my vote for the most striking mountain in Arizona and is the dwelling of I'itoi, the Elder Brother, a God.

From Sasabe there is a dirt road of variable quality, depending on the severity of the last rains and when the road was last graded. It runs through large desert ranches, reaching Mexican Highway 2 just east of Caborca. In Caborca you always get gas and the last items of food for your trip. Supplied with appropriate amounts of Tecate beer, limes, and other essentials (including all the water you will need and a full auxiliary gas can, if you are smart), you head west out of Caborca, following the faded signs. The paved road heads straight west to El Desemboque, a coastal town with a government-operated power plant.

For Puerto Lobos one turns south onto a dirt road that passes through several families' front yards and then along agricultural fields. When the fields end—like dropping off the edge of the earth—one enters the desert on a dusty road that appears to lead nowhere at all. This road crosses a low set of hills and enters a wide desert valley. The roadbed is deep sand with occasional cattle guards. With experience, one can slip and slide along this road at sixty miles an hour, but the several cattle guards are guaranteed to send the inexperienced through the roof—or through the floor boards from stomping on the brakes. Maximum speed over the cattle guards is 1 mph. This section of the road is 30 km long, and the only structures along it are an abandoned one-room school and several corrals. The road runs as straight as an arrow across the valley, through creosote bush (*Larrea tridentata*), mesquite (*Prosopis glandulosa* and *P. velutina*), and the occasional organ pipe (*Cereus thurberi*), senita (*Cereus schottii*), or cardón cactus (*Pachycereus pringlei*). A few tracks leave it, heading for several small cattle ranches, and a high-tension power line from the Desemboque power plant runs down the middle of the valley, but in all directions there is essentially unpeopled Lower Sonoran Desert.

After what seems an eternity in the creosote and mesquite, you reach hills on the far side of the valley. Climbing out of the valley, the roadbed turns corrugated and hard; ocotillos (*Fouquieria splendens*) and brittlebush (*Encelia farinosa*) dominate the hillsides. Desert bighorn sheep (*Ovis canadensis*) live in these hills—animals that seem much too big to survive in this arid land. I saw a herd of seven one morning on a return trip. Although one is only 10 km from the coast, there is no hint of anything but desert. The road climbs and falls over low, sparsely vegetated ridges, until suddenly at the top of one ridge the Gulf appears, like a blue mirage in the distance. After you top the hill it disappears, leaving only the desert again. You are tantalized like this as you crest several more rises before finally crossing the last saddle and beginning the descent on the hard road sloping down to the coast. Along this stretch is a sign advertising a hotel back in Caborca. I have always wondered about this sign—wondered if anyone having come this far out into the desert on these empty roads ever saw this sign and turned back, thinking there would be nothing worthwhile at the end of the road. What a mistake that would have been.

The people of Puerto Lobos live in small brick or adobe houses and fishing shacks. They are generally disinterested in the occasional visitors who come here. The town is always half empty. Some houses are owned by residents of Caborca, who must use them when wanting to visit the ocean. The two study sites for Gray Vireos were north and south of the town, but after the long trek through the desert the first stop was always The Point, a lava hump sticking into the Gulf, to gaze at the Sea of Cortez and marvel at the birds—so different from those in the place left that morning. On a rocky island in the bay, boobies (*Sula* sp.), Brown Pelicans, and cormorants (*Phalacrocorax* sp.) roost. There are loons (*Gavia* sp.) and mergansers (*Mergus* sp.) in the bay, and on the sand on either side of the point are skimmers, Elegant Terns (*Thalasseus elegans*), and various wintering shorebirds. All along the coast are Yellow-footed, Heermann's, Ring-billed, and Herring gulls (*Larus livens, L. heermanni, delawarensis,* and *argentatus*).

The sounds of seabirds in the dry, salty air takes a little getting used to after kicking up dust in the desert to reach this spot. They just don't sound right at first. Wintering on the Point are usually a small flock of Black Turnstones (*Arenaria melanocephala*), Surfbirds (*Aphriza virgata*), and one or two Wandering Tattlers (*Tringa incana*). Several hours are needed for a census of this coastal outpost. It includes a tiny *estero* (estuary), with the northernmost mangroves in the Gulf of California—a tough little cluster, all under two meters tall, sandwiched between a sandy beach and the Seri Indian houses. Bird-wise, there is almost always some additional reward here—perhaps a Red Phalarope (*Phalaropus fulicarius*), a Tricolored Heron (*Egretta tricolor*), or some Magnificent Frigatebirds (*Fregata magnificens*). We further justified the stop because even in winter there would be little avian activity in the deserts, so the change here was welcomed. And as much as anything, we were drawn to the sea.

After wetting our minds by gazing at the Gulf, we would turn our focus back to the desert, where the Gray Vireos winter. The two study sites differed in their proximity to the coast. The Arroyo San Lorenzo site south of Puerto Lobos was several kilometers into hills that the Gulf is slowly cutting away. The Cerro Prieto site was in a smaller arroyo, north of town, closer to the Gulf, and named for the isolated volcanic hill that forms the north side of the arroyo. At San Lorenzo you are again surrounded by desert, with little evidence that you are so close to the coast until you climb to the arroyo's rim. The road here is nothing more than the arroyo itself; a truck passes through only once or twice a week, so the wash has that clean and tidy look that I love about undisturbed desert. There is no grass carpet, only bare ground between the hardy shrubs, trees, and cacti.

The vegetation is spaced, ideal for moving through, except for the frequency of cholla cactus (*Opuntia* spp.), with their detachable balls of spines just waiting to latch onto you with the slightest brush of a pant leg or boot. The plants in this community have distinctive personalities. Ironwood (*Olneya tesota*), despite its name, has a soft, fuzzy look from a distance. The ocotillos remind you how dry the area is, or has been, by having green leaves for only days following rains. You might think that there would be little color here, but everything takes advantage of any winter rain. Each plant provides unique shades and textures of muted greens and browns, and there is more. In the canyons are two-meter-tall *Solanum* with purple flowers, and tumbleweed-shaped *Justicia* with their red flowers on which the Costa's Hummingbirds (*Calypte costae*) depend. Even on the hillsides, there can be color in the yellow flowers of *Encelia*, or brittlebush. Non-nectar-feeding birds eat the tiny reddish purple fruits of the desert mistletoe (*Phoradendron californicum*) that parasitizes the mesquites, ironwoods, and palo verdes (*Cercidium* spp.); there are also purple and red fruits on the two species of elephant trees (*Bursera* spp.).

In these deserts the strongest plant personalities belong to the cacti. There are the chollas that can grow in large, impenetrable patches. There are senitas, "old man" cacti, with arms that are star-shaped when viewed from above. These plants grow in candelabra fashion, putting numerous arms up from the ground. Their arms sport a dense set of thorns, giving them a shaggy, ancient look. Dominating everything else are the incredible cardóns. The cacti of stereotype are the tall, statuesque saguaros (*Carnegiea gigantea*) of the upper Sonoran zone, but in these coastal deserts they give way to their cousins, the cardóns. Saguaros may be more pleasing in an aesthetic sense, but cardóns are behemoths. Large ones weigh as much as two large saguaros. The cardóns branch at about a meter and send mighty arms straight up from there. These arms—and there may be eight or more—can each have the girth of the base of a saguaro. If saguaros are natural apartment houses for many birds, cardóns offer the potential for small cities. In the Lobos area they are colonized first by woodpeckers, then by a host of other species: American Kestrels (*Falco sparverius*), Elf Owls (*Micrathene whitneyi*), and even such surprising species as the Violet-green Swallows (*Tachycineta thalassina*) that breed here. Several cardóns have even become the dwellings of House Sparrows (*Passer domesticus*) and European Starlings (*Sturnus vulgaris*), which, in their quest to blanket the New World, have managed to establish small colonies even here. Presumably they moved in from one of the larger coastal towns to the north or south. Luckily, they occupy only cacti that hug the coast and are within sight of town. Finally, the cardóns provide roosting and nesting sites for the area's large birds of prey: Great Horned Owls (*Bubo virginianus*), Red-tailed Hawks (*Buteo jamaicensis*), and Ospreys (*Pandion haliaetus*).

Every evening as the sun sets, one certainty at both sites would be the high, yelping calls of the Ospreys coming in to roost on their favorite cardóns. They would leave again at dawn to begin the day's fishing, but their favorite cardóns could be found at any time. All one had to do was look for a ring of white excrement for a radius of two meters around the cacti. I guess it is probably a result of repositioning on windy nights, but Ospreys do not seem to exhibit much preference for the direction in which they shoot their droppings from their desert roosts. Inside the circle of whitewash are fish bones, a reminder of how close you are to the sea.

I confess I have never been to Puerto Lobos between the months of May and August. The Seri Indians are here then, and so are many of the birds: the Ospreys; a hardy, large-billed subspecies of Savannah Sparrow (*Passerculus sandwichensis*) that lives in the *Salicornia* mats along the coast; LeConte's Thrashers (*Toxostoma lecontei*) in the coastal dunes; and many of the desert birds. However, some of the desert birds leave. Costa's Hummingbirds, Phainopeplas (*Phainopepla nitens*), and Northern Mockingbirds (*Mimus polyglottos*) may breed here as early as February and then move north, possibly to breed again with the summer rains in southern Arizona.

Those species that stay in the desert must deal with daily heat stress and a lack of fresh water for weeks or months at a time. It can get hot even in the spring and fall, when the migrants appear. Some individuals moving north in spring or south in fall have to pause here in their travels. To my mind, Lobos must be as different from their breeding or wintering grounds as it can get, and I wonder, if they survive, whether they repeat this route. In fall the Olive-sided Flycatcher (*Contopus cooperi*) and Western Wood-Pewee (*Contopus sordidulus*) have appeared. In spring I have mist netted a male Common Yellowthroat (*Geothlypis trichas*) in the arroyo and a Lucy's Warbler (*Vermivora luciae*) at Cerro Prieto. Northern and Scott's orioles (*Icterus galbula* and *I. parisorum*) and Black-headed Grosbeaks (*Pheucticus melanocephalus*) also pass though. The migrants add a spark to the desert, but it was the winter bird community, and arguably its most unusual member, that I had come to learn about. Most species present during the winter in these coastal deserts also nest in deserts, either here or farther north: Gambel's Quail (*Callipepla gambelii*), Ladder-backed Woodpecker (*Picoides scalaris*), Gila Woodpecker (*Melanerpes uropygialus*), Ash-throated Flycatcher (*Myiarchus cinerascens*), Verdin (*Auriparus flaviceps*), Curve-billed Thrasher (*Toxostoma curvirostre*), Northern Mockingbird, Phainopepla, Black-tailed Gnatcatcher (*Polioptila melanura*), Cactus Wren (*Campylorhynchus brunneicapillus*), Rock Wren (*Salpinctes obsoletus*), Black-throated Sparrow (*Amphispiza bilineata*), Northern Cardinal (*Cardinalis cardinalis*), and House Finch (*Carpodacus mexicanus*). Exceptions are the Gray Vireo, Ruby-crowned Kinglet (*Regulus calendula*), and White-crowned Sparrow (*Zonotrichia leucophrys*).

The vireos spend up to seven months of the year on these wintering grounds; thus they are more than just "snowbirds," and as I would learn, their behavior is much more like that of residents than of other winter visitors like the White-crowned Sparrows, which move in their small winter flocks. The vireos set up individual territories that they defend from conspecifics throughout the winter. They also return to these territories year after year. Establishing a territory carries with it the connotation that there is something worth defending, and as I wandered through these desert arroyos following color-banded birds, I would see them forage almost exclusively in the smaller and more common of the two elephant trees, *Bursera microphyllum*. These small trees produce a crop of a thousand or more fruits that ripen slowly over the winter months; when ripe, the fruits split to reveal bright orange arils covering seeds. It is these arils that I believe provide much of the vireos' winter food supply. Calorically speaking, they are as rich as any fruit eaten by birds. One possible explanation for winter territoriality in these birds is that they are defending a seasonally sufficient supply of these fruits. This is only a hypothesis, and two years were hardly enough time to understand a situation that has evolved over thousands of years, but my work provided baseline data for future studies.

That migration occurs each year is one of the wonders of the bird world, but we still know little of the behavior of these migrants once they reach their destinations. Slowly this is changing. I marvel at the variety of these destinations—from Swainson's Hawks (*Buteo swainsoni*) and Mississippi Kites (*Ictinia mississippiensis*) on the pampas of Argentina to Wood Thrushes (*Hylocichla mustelina*) in the rainforests of Veracruz and Gray Vireos in these lowland deserts. It is only one's point of view that defines what these birds really call home. The vireos are clearly as at home in the Mexican deserts as they are in the foothills of the western United States. Studying them during those Mexican winters allowed me to get to know an incredible community and region that people, even today, have affected little.

The pyramids built by the mighty civilizations of southern Mexico are amazing, and the views from the tops of the Mexican volcanoes are spectacular. However, for me, no less spectacular are the many sights of the northern Sonoran deserts, like a flock of White Pelicans (*Pelecanus erythrorhynchos*) with breeding knobs on their bills moving north in majestic synchrony. For someone standing in the desert, the backdrop for these northward-bound flying fortresses is the shimmering Sea of Cortez, with the sun setting in the west behind the peaks of the San Pedro Martir on the Baja Peninsula. Soon the Ospreys will come back to roost in their cardóns, and the Common Poorwills (*Phalaenoptilus nuttallii*) and coyotes (*Canis latrans*) will offer an evening chorus. Then the millions of stars will come out and you can go to sleep knowing that another beautiful desert day will dawn tomorrow.

4

Back Roads with Ben

LULA C. COFFEY

Lula C. Coffey and her husband, Ben B. Coffey, Jr., both now deceased, were tireless amateur ornithologists who made important scientific contributions to our knowledge of night birds, swifts, and bird sounds. Among their published works were Coffey (1943) and Coffey and Coffey (1984, 1989). In this chapter, Lula relates some of the adventures she shared with Ben. In a note accompanying her essay, Lula wrote of her late husband: "We were together for nearly 65 years, and *all* my precious memories include him." More about Lula and Ben can be found in Jackson (1994).

Ben came home in 1946 from four years in the military. It was a memorable year! Making plans for a special vacation to celebrate, we decided on a birding trip to Mexico. It took some months to get a car, though, because the waiting lines were long. In the meantime, we studied all we could about Mexican birds. There was no field guide. Dr. George Sutton's articles "At a Bend in a Mexican River," published in *Audubon* magazine, were fascinating. Ben secured all the checklists available and everything else he could find on Mexican birds.

Our First Trip

After several months we got a little new Nash. We started out on November 16, 1946. Frank and Ginny McCamey went with us. Dr. George Lowery, of Louisiana State University, arranged for Robert Tucker to meet us at the museum there and to let us examine the Mexican bird collection. We spent a busy three hours making notes, then we were off again—next stop Laredo, Texas.

As we drove along into Mexico we made frequent stops to look at birds new to us. Parrots, motmots, and trogons were at the Río Corona, just north of Ciudad Victoria. We had a schedule to keep, as Dr. Lowery had also arranged for Bob and Marcy Newman and David Shaw to meet us at Antigua Morelos. They were doing fieldwork in the state of San Luis Potosí. They were great people, and this was the beginning of a forty-year friendship. Two days and nights were spent with them, camping at night. A Mottled Owl (*Ciccaba*

Figure 4.1. Ben and Lula Coffey at the Tropic of Cancer on their first trip to Mexico, 1946. Photo courtesy L. Coffey.

virgata) called regularly nearby, and with flashlights we were able to see it plainly. By candlelight, with insects buzzing constantly around the flame, Bob told us a lot about birds and about Mexico in general. Our notebooks were getting rather thick. But how helpful this all was. After we returned home, we found that we had been able to identify 90 percent of the birds we saw on the trip, even though some of the females were very difficult.

Heading south again, we went to Mexico City, took a side trip to Morelia, went back to Mexico City and then on south through Cuernavaca, Tasco, and down to Chilpancingo. We covered a lot of territory, as we wanted to see Mexico and thought this might be our only trip. It was not, though—over the years we made about twenty more, covering every state by car.

As we were driving north, we stopped again at Antigua Morelos. We had only two days left on our vacation, but *Power's Guide* mentioned a 900-foot waterfall, El Salto, just off the highway to the city of San Luis Potosí. This would mean a detour of some thirty miles. The last seven miles were rough. It was a poorly graveled road with many potholes, but we made it. Birding was great, though time was short. Two Military Macaws (*Ara militaris*) perched near the falls, and we saw motmots and a trogon (*Trogon* sp.). Near dusk, a flock of about fifteen hundred White-collared Swifts (*Streptoprocne zonaris*) came in to roost behind the falls. A falcon (*Falco* sp.) swiftly dove into the flock and picked one up for supper.

As we neared the car to leave, we smelled gas. A fine stream of gasoline was coming from the gas tank. The men tried to stop it up with a rag, then with soap, but still it leaked. One called out, "Is anyone chewing gum?"

"Yes!" Ginny and I answered. They applied the gum to the leak and it stopped. We still had some five gallons of gas left, and we hoped to get back to the main highway. At Antigua Morelos we got more gas—the gum was holding the leak. On to El Mante, Ciudad Victoria, Monterrey, and then Laredo. No leaking. We decided to keep driving—we did not dare stop at a motel to sleep. When we were about 150 miles from Memphis, in Arkansas, the gauge showed that we were losing gasoline again. Another stop, another wad of gum applied, and we made it on home. Not on the proverbial wing and prayer, but on a wad of Dentine gum.

The Blasted Bottle

Between us, only one gunshot was fired in Mexico. Ben hated guns. The only time he had fired one was when he was in Officer Candidate School in WWII. In the Mexican case we had parked our car by a swift-flowing river, remarking that the place looked good for a picnic. After we had birded for a few hours we returned, and a *big* picnic was in progress—the Lions Club picnic from the nearby town. The ladies were putting food on temporary tables, and the men were staying close to the tubs of ice, which held a lot of beer cans. They were having a competitive rifle shoot—shooting at empty Coca-Cola bottles thrown into the river.

They greeted us warmly. The beer was cold and quenched a big thirst. Ben was offered the rifle and invited to join in the competition. He politely declined. Out of courtesy, I suppose, I was offered the rifle too. I had not held a gun in twenty-five years and had no intention of shooting, but the rifle felt good in my hands.

Raising it to my shoulder just to test the weight and the sights, I heard Ben say, very softly, "Be sure you hit the river."

That was the wrong thing to say. I suddenly felt like a thirteen-year-old girl again, with my dad standing beside me saying, "All you have to do is stand steady, get the target in your sights, and pull the trigger."

I called out for the fellow upstream to throw the bottle. Here it came. With only four inches of the neck showing, it was bobbing and traveling pretty fast. I pulled the trigger, and the bottle was blasted. Luck—just pure luck. A shout went up from the crowd. The rifle was quickly reloaded, and I was told I must shoot three times to stay in the competition. I whispered to Ben, "Please get me out of here *quick*." He did.

The Stray Road

To escape traffic noise when Ben was recording bird songs, we traveled a lot of back roads. Dirt roads, little roads—sometimes they were no more than a double cowpath. I was often skeptical. Would we get stuck? Would we have to back out? I composed a little verse that I often said aloud—it made me feel better:

> Stray roads lead to romance,
> We must take a chance
> On a road that leads to nowhere
> To see the chachalacas dance.

We never saw the Plain Chachalacas (*Ortalis vetula*) *dance*, but we often saw them walking around on the lower branches of small trees giving their raucous calls. Irby Davis said the male was calling "*Slap her back, slap her back,*" and that the females were answering "*Keep it up, keep it up.*"

One of these roads ended at a small thatch-roofed house. The *señora* and her four children were standing out front, watching our big white car come bumping down the road to stop in their yard. It was lunchtime, and the big shade tree was an inviting spot for our picnic. I asked if we might park there and eat. The señora give a big smile and answered, "*Si, si.*" A Spot-breasted Wren (*Thryothorus maculipectus*) was singing from a small clump of bushes nearby. Ben took out his recorder and big parabolic reflector and went to tape it, while I started making lunch. When he returned, he played the bird song for the children. They quickly asked if the bird was in the black box. I don't know just how Ben explained tape recorders, but the children giggled and seemed satisfied. I opened a can of Vienna sausage and a can of fruit cocktail, sliced some tomatoes, and served lunch on bright blue plastic plates.

The señora eyed the plates carefully. As I was cleaning up, she came shyly over, touched one of the plates, and said softly, *"Muy bonito."*

I had been wondering how I was going to express our thanks for her hospitality, and she had given me the answer. I dug into the trunk of the car and came out with four of the colorful plates, which I handed them to her, saying "Thank you."

She stroked them gently and said over and over, *"Muy bonito."*

Then she called out an order to the children. They rushed to the back yard and started chasing chickens. Soon she pushed a live, squawking chicken into my hands, saying, *"Por su comida."*

I certainly did not want a live chicken for my dinner—not now, not ever. But it would be ungracious to refuse her generous gift. What could I do? I gave Ben my helpless look, which he could easily interpret as "Help me, help me. Get this chicken out of my hands!"

Ben was always my Knight in Shining Armor, and he came to my rescue then, as he always did. He gently took the bird from my arms and handed it back to the señora, telling her that he could not let me accept it—that we were going back to the city to stay in a hotel, and that he did not think the hotel would let us cook a chicken in our room. She smiled, understandingly.

Midnight Melodies

We were always on the lookout for a place to stay that was not in a city. We liked to be where we could start birding early in the morning without having to drive miles out to the country. On returning from a lengthy stay in southern Veracruz, and with only a few days of vacation time left, we could not make stops for birding. At a poor country road we saw a new handmade sign declaring: "Resort and Motel, 7 miles." We went bumping along the seven miles and came to a very small lake. New cabins were spaced around it. The proprietor was genial and welcomed us warmly. He hoped to get families there for vacations, just to enjoy the out-of-doors. He said the hunting was fine. We told him we could not stay right then, but that on our next trip we would probably stay with him for several days.

Some six months later we headed for this small resort. The sign was still there—weathered but intact. But the road was different. It was wider, with deep ruts, mudholes, and small detours. We reached the cabin area at about dark. Only one small light was showing in the building called the office. A caretaker came out to greet us. He said the place had been bought by a big lumber company—the trees were being cut down and workers lived in the cabins. So back we went, in the dark. And we got stuck in the mud. Really stuck. We thought we might have to sleep in the car and wait for a truck the next morning to pull us out. But we worked on it, using our spade and some tree limbs and much pushing and struggling. It was about midnight when we got back to the highway.

We were exhausted, and muddy all over. After driving about ten miles, we saw a *beautiful* sign: "Motel—Vacancy." We turned into the driveway and found about ten widely separated cabins. I asked to see one. The smiling clerk got into our car and took us to a cabin. I dashed in to check the bed and the bathroom. They were very neat and clean, so I called back for Ben to take it, and I headed for the shower.

When Ben came in he asked if I really wanted to stay; the clerk had charged him an hourly rate. I suggested that this must be a new custom in this area. Then he asked how carefully I had looked at the room. I took a close look. Pink taffeta spread on the bed, small lamps with pink shades, no closet, no luggage rack, just one big chair and a small table. "Look, there isn't even a dresser or mirror," I said.

Ben pointed to the ceiling. There was the mirror—a big one. I groaned. "We are exhausted, I've washed my hair, I am cleaned up. Let's just get in that clean bed and we will be asleep in ten minutes."

We were, but not for long. Soon we were awakened by the strains of "Moonlight and Roses" coming to us through the loudspeaker right over our heads. This was no Muzak; it was a very scratchy record being played at the office. It finally ended, and we dozed off—only to be awakened again in about ten minutes by "Moonlight and Roses." When I turned in the key the next morning, the grinning clerk said, "We hope you enjoyed your stay." I grinned right back and told him we could have done without the music.

Bridges, Fords, and Ferries

Bridges are very necessary. They get you from one side of the river to the other, but they are impersonal. The people who built the structure are long gone. You just swish across the river without even slackening your speed. Fords, on the other hand, are challenging. You must stop and look over the depth of the water—has there been rain upstream, and do you need to wait until the water level is okay? Just where is the rocky stone bed? Sometimes I would wade across in front of the car, showing Ben where to put the wheels.

A ferry is personal. The operator shows how to get aboard. He often likes conversation—asking to see the engine, how much the car cost, and such.

Ben took care of the conversation, because I had an important chore to do. In the early days it was almost impossible to find ice for our little ice-box. The pineapple juice, orange juice, and Cokes that we carried with us were always warm—very warm—because we had no air conditioning in the car. When we were settled on a ferry, I would put two drinks in a long sock, lie flat on the deck, and drag them across the river. The drinks did not get cold exactly, but they were cooler, and that was nice.

The Vigil

For decades we pursued a special interest in night birds. In West Tennessee, Arkansas, and Mississippi we would drive back roads all night long on moon-lit nights during the breeding season. We would stop every seven-tenths of a mile to listen for three minutes, making notes of all the sounds we heard. We were checking on the Whip-poor-will (*Caprimulgus vociferus*) as it extended its range to the south and west. This night riding with my guy was beautiful. In addition to the Chuck-will's-widow (*Caprimulgus carolinensis*), Whip-poor-will, and owls, we often heard the Yellow-breasted Chat (*Icteria virens*) and Yellow-billed Cuckoo (*Coccyzus americanus*) give a few notes. The Northern Mockingbird (*Mimus polyglottos*) was usually in full song. We listened to the frogs and the toads at the little ponds. Night animals such as skunks (*Mephitis mephitis*), opossums (*Didelphis virginiana*), raccoons (*Procyon lotor*), and cottontail rabbits (*Sylvilagus floridanus*) dashed across the road, and Polyphemus, Io, and Luna moths (*Telea polyphemus, Automeris io,* and *Actias luna*) came to our car headlights. In some places, myriads of fireflies twinkled over meadows. It was a different world at night.

We also did a lot of this night riding in Mexico. When Irby Davis told us of finding the Spot-tailed Nightjar (*Caprimulgus maculicaudus*) in southern Mexico, we went there as soon as it was practical. In a large field near Minatitlán, Veracruz, we heard several birds giving the high-pitched *pit-sweet* call. We went out into the field with our big spotlight and recorder. Ben taped the call, and upon playback the bird came in close enough for us to identify it. Ben wanted to work the field thoroughly to count the birds and to get a perfect recording of this unusual nightjar song. There was no reason for me to trek along, so I went back to the car, rolled up the windows, locked the doors, and began writing up my notes by flashlight.

Some ten minutes later a truck stopped, and the driver asked if I had trouble. I told him there was no trouble and that everything was okay. My Spanish was so poor that I knew I could never make him understand our activity. Night birding is difficult to explain. We had difficulty explaining it in Arkansas, and

Figure 4.2. Lula Coffey and the new Nash at the end of the Pan-American Highway south of Comitán, near the Guatemala border, ca. 1948. Photo courtesy L. Coffey.

we speak "Arkansas" very well. Even so, a local sheriff once came up and asked us why we were doing all this stopping on country roads at 3 a.m. Ben politely explained—even pulling out the recorder and playing a few Whip-poor-will songs for him.

The sheriff did not buy it. He ordered Ben out of the car, smelled his breath, then made him walk a straight line and touch his nose. The sheriff then said, "Well, you're not drunk. You must just be a weirdo," and he drove off in a huff.

The helpful truck driver evidently went on into town and reported to the police that a lone Americana was sitting in a car on a back road. Shortly after he left, two uniformed policemen arrived and tapped on my window. I lowered it a bit and they asked, "Trouble?"

Again, I attempted to explain that there was no trouble. They sat down on the roadside and smoked a few cigarettes, while I continued writing. Then again came the tap on the window. "*Gasolina* okay?" they asked.

"Yes," I told them, "*gasolina* okay."

More time passed; more cigarettes were smoked. Then came another tap. "Carburetor okay?" was the question this time.

Just then I saw Ben's big spotlight over in the field. I called their attention to it and explained that it was my husband with the spotlight and that he would be back for me soon. They stayed on, smoking more cigarettes. Suddenly they jumped up and pointed down the road to where Ben was swinging his spotlight—the signal for me to pick him up. "Su esposo, su esposo," they cried.

They were right, it was my husband. I reached back into my goodie bag, found two packs of Chesterfield cigarettes, and gave them to the fellows with my thanks for watching over me. I would have liked to have seen the official report of their midnight vigil.

Much Ado about a Fan

In the years B.A. (before air-conditioning), it was hot, hot, *hot* in the small motel rooms in southern Mexico. At most places we could rent a small electric fan (a six- or eight-inch model) for about fifty cents extra. These little fans did not cool the rooms, but they served a most useful purpose—they let me get some sleep. I would drape a soaking wet towel over myself and turn the fan on it, and I would be cool and sleep well until the towel dried out. This meant getting up seven or eight times a night, but interrupted sleep was much better than no sleep at all.

At Pijijiapan, Chiapas, we stopped at the PijijiHilton motel. It was no Hilton. We paid the fifty cents extra for a fan. While we were unpacking in the room, the little fan rattled and whirred, faintly stirring the hot air.

We had a couple of daylight hours left, so we decided to drive out into the country and find a good birding place for the next morning. When we returned, the fan was gone! We dashed over to the office to get it back. First the clerk told us that the fan was not working and that he had picked it up to get it repaired.

"It was working perfectly two hours ago," Ben said, and he wanted it back. After another lame excuse, the clerk leaned over and whispered in a confidential tone that a *político* had registered and wanted a fan, and ours was the only one he had that was working; he knew we would understand, since políticos were *muy importante*.

Ben did not understand, and he told the clerk so in rather strong language, adding, "My wife has a physical disability, and the fan is *muy importante* to me."

This startled me, as Ben was so honest and truthful that he never, never told even a tiny white social lie. But he had definitely said that I had a disability, so I thought this was no time for me to be standing there looking in robust health. I walked over to a chair, sat down, leaned forward, put my head in my hands, and delivered myself of a great sigh. The clerk quickly said, "*Un momento, señor*," and took off almost at a sprint.

When we were back in our room with the little fan whirring and rattling, I asked, "What *is* my disability?"

Ben leaned over, kissed me, and softly said, "You can't sleep in hot motel rooms without a wet towel and a fan."

I slept well that night in the PijijiHilton in Pijijiapan.

The Butterfly Net

We headed west for the state of Jalisco. The Eared Poorwill (*Nyctiphrynus mcleodii*) had been rediscovered by Allan Phillips and William Schaldach, and we wanted to tape-record its song. We were late in getting away on our vacation, and by the time we reached the Pacific slope the nights were quiet. No nightjars, except for the Common Pauraque (*Nyctidromus albicollis*), and it sang only intermittently. We started our driving and listening south and west of Autlan. The woods were quiet. A nightjar flew across the road, and in the bright headlights we saw it for only a split second, but we felt sure it was a new one for us. We made a special note of the locality and drove on. After two nights of work, we gave up, thinking better luck next year.

The following spring, Dr. Wendell Whittemore, an orthopedic surgeon, and his fifteen-year-old son Bobby went with us. Bobby had only a mild interest in birds—his passion was butterflies. He kept his net at the ready, and when we were birding he was catching butterflies. He was good at it, and his collection grew rapidly.

We started our night driving and listening west of Autlan. It was a clear, moonlit night, and the birds were active. After some ten or twelve stops, we came to the place where we had seen the strange bird the year before. As soon as we stopped the car, we heard it! *Fig-a-ro, Fig-a-ro*—the Eared Poorwill. Howell and Webb (1995) describe the song as *preeOO*, or *wheeOO*, but I like *Figaro* better. The bird sounded for all the world like a boisterous Figaro calling his name. Ben taped the song, and on playback the bird flew to the middle of the road.

We turned on the headlights, and our avian visitor was temporarily blinded—for about a minute. We walked to within some ten feet of the Eared Poorwill before it flew to a ledge on the roadside. Quick as a flash, Bobby grabbed his butterfly net and with a big swoosh netted the bird. We handled it gently as we took measurements, made notes about the plumage, and photographed our prize. We knew some of our museum friends would have been very happy to have this bird their collection, but it was too beautiful and had been so cooperative that we could not bring ourselves to turn it into a dried museum skin.

We gave Bobby the privilege of letting the poorwill go. It sat for a second in Bobby's open hand, then flew to a nearby tree and gave two loud *Figaros*.

Bobby asked his dad, "Do you think he's scolding me because I netted him?"

His dad answered, "Maybe he is just glad to be free again, free to call his name in his own scrub oak forest."

Howler Monkeys

Howler monkeys (*Alouatta palliata*) are big, and they have big voices. The loud, stentorian call of the adult male can be heard for almost a mile in dense forest. They may call occasionally during the day, but the whole tribe seems to join in a chorus at sunrise and sunset. I liked these sunset calls, and while working at Palenque I learned to find them useful. When we were in the forest under a dense canopy it was not easy to know when sundown was upon us. There was little twilight; it just seemed to be daytime one moment, then dark the next. The sunset howling told us it was time to get back out into the open. We saw these monkeys rarely, but when a big male spotted us he would often give a few grunts and perhaps a short call. If Ben taped these sounds and played them back, the male usually came in a bit closer, looked us over, and then scampered away, getting out of sight in a hurry.

Howler monkeys are very interesting, and they can be quite clever. I learned this through an intimate encounter with one while staying at a small lodge on the edge of the jungle in Peru. The proprietor's wife kept pets: parrots, macaws, and a half-grown howler monkey (*Alouatta seniculus*) called Monolito. The activity room of the lodge was rather large—a few tables for dining, sofas, card tables, a ping-pong table, and stacks of reading material were scattered about the place. Monolito was allowed to run free in this room, and we became friends. I could coax him to me with a banana, and he would jump up on my lap for a split second, grab the banana, and dash away. Sometimes he would climb up on the back of my chair and groom my hair—I did not mind; he was very gentle.

When it was time for Monolito to go to bed, the señora would bring out his leash, coax him to her, and lead him off to his cage. One night he did not want to go to bed, so he hid from her. He was not very good at hiding, but he tried. He would get under a chair, hide behind the sofa, or just put a newspaper over his head. Suddenly, he seemed to think of a new hiding place. He raced across the room, jumped up on my lap, and went up under my T-shirt as far as he could go. When a young howler monkey has a firm grip on your body it is not wise to pull him out forcefully. We coaxed and coaxed, and finally a bit of a Hershey bar made him relax and back out. After that experience I kept my T-shirt firmly tucked into my pants.

Angels on a Third-Class Bus

The new secondary road did not have many pull-offs—places we could park for a while to bird an area. When we did find a spot to park, Ben would walk ahead and I would pick him up in about thirty minutes, after I had birded around the car. I would blow the horn and he would come to the roadside. Once, after I had driven a long distance with no sign of Ben, I felt I should go to the next parking place and wait. Suddenly, at a curve in the road I saw a

Figure 4.3. Ben and Lula Coffey at their home in Memphis, Tennessee, 1980s. Photo courtesy L. Coffey.

fine-looking pull-out—it was even graveled. I turned off the road at a pretty good clip onto the gravel—mistake!—*into* the gravel. It was a rather level *pile* of gravel left there by the road crew. The car sank to its floorboards and was hopelessly stuck. I waited a few minutes, but there was no sign of Ben. What if he had passed this place and was still walking ahead? I had to stop him, so I started the distress signal on the horn: *dit-dit-dit, da-da-da, dit-dit-dit*. No response from Ben. After what seemed an hour, though it could not have been more than fifteen minutes, I started worrying about the battery. Would it go dead with all this horn blowing?

There was little traffic, but I decided to stand by the roadside, flag a car, and ask its occupants to look for a tall Americano down the road and tell him to come back to the gravel pile. Soon a third-class bus came rattling down the road and stopped beside me. The driver called out, "Trouble?"

"*Mucho* trouble," I answered.

He turned to the passengers and asked them if they wanted to help me. They were all laughing uproariously, no doubt at the stupid woman driver who had sunk her car in the gravel pile. About ten men descended from the bus. They looked the situation over carefully. Then they circled the car and picked it up as if it were a toy, and they put it back on the road, still laughing. About this time Ben walked up. He pulled out his wallet and put some pesos in the driver's hand, suggesting he buy beer for all the fellows at the next cantina.

The men all shouted, "No, no," as they climbed back aboard the bus. As they drove away, they leaned out of the windows to shout *"¡Buena suerte!"* (good luck).

I had already had my good luck—they had stopped and lifted the car up onto the road—and they had lifted my spirits even higher.

5

A Collecting Expedition to the Isthmus of Tehuantepec

WALTER W. DALQUEST

Walter W. Dalquest (1917–2000) was a distinguished naturalist with a long and productive scientific career spanning disciplines as diverse as mammalogy, paleontology, geology, herpetology, and ornithology. After working under E. Raymond Hall at the University of Kansas and ultimately receiving his Ph.D. under George Lowery at Louisiana State University in 1951, he spent his academic career at Midwestern State University in Wichita, Texas. The scientific results of most of the fieldwork included here appeared in Lowery and Dalquest (1951). For more details, see Horner and Stangl (2001).

I was determined to become an ornithologist when I was in high school. In those days of the Great Depression, no one objected to a boy collecting birds if it was for a reason, and I built up a collection of some five hundred well-prepared skins. Many I shot, and many were DORs (the museum abbreviation for "dead on the road") mostly given to me by people aware of my work. Dr. Robert C. Miller, who taught ornithology and other vertebrate classes at the University of Washington and later became director of the California Academy of Sciences complex at Golden Gate Park in San Francisco, paid me to prepare bird skins for him. When I entered the University of Washington in 1936, ornithology was an advanced course by "permission of instructor." I was able to con Dr. Miller into admitting me into his class, even though I was just a freshman.

Classes had been in session for about a month when Dr. Miller took us on a field trip to the countryside. At the first stop he gathered everyone around and said, "Now listen to that song," pointing to a nearby tree. Everyone listened and nodded. "That," said Dr. Miller, "is a Traill Flycatcher" (*Empidonax traillii*). "Now, listen to that song," he said, pointing in another direction. "That is a Least Flycatcher" (*Empidonax minimus*). Everyone nodded and smiled happily, except me. I could not hear either of the birds. I had known that my hearing was funny. I could hear a Dusky Grouse (*Dendragapus obscurus*) hoot-

Figure 5.1. Meat for camp on the Río Solosuchil, Isthmus of Tehuantepec: Guans (*Penelope purpurascens*), 1948. Strong black Mexican cigarettes helped keep the *rododores* and mosquitoes away. Photo courtesy W. W. Dalquest.

ing when others could not, but I could not hear the lizards moving through the leaves. How could I be an ornithologist?

I was, however, very good with a shotgun and began to study and collect bats. Among the first few bats I shot were new distributional records, and bats proved every bit as interesting as birds. From studying bats it was a short step to working with other native mammals, and by the time I graduated with an MS degree in zoology in 1940, I was publishing papers on mammals. But I still prepared bird skins and gave them to whoever could use them.

In 1945 Dr. E. Raymond Hall, director of the Museum of Natural History of the University of Kansas, offered me an opportunity to collect vertebrates in Mexico for the university. I accepted, but it was not until February 1946 that permits and other paperwork were obtained and I could leave for Mexico. We had decided that the most promising Mexican state for the planned work would be Veracruz. On February 9 I arrived at Potrero Viejo, home of Dyfrig McHattie Forbes and his family. The Forbes family had been host to numerous scientists over the preceding years, and they made me welcome at their home for the next three collecting seasons (until the end of April 1949). I was in Veracruz almost continuously, except during the summer months (the rainy season), when roads to the back country were impassable and specimens did not dry in the high humidity.

When the rainy seasons approached I took accumulated specimens to Kansas and spent my time preparing an extensive report on the mammals of Veracruz. During this time Dr. George H. Lowery, later director of the Museum of Zoology at Louisiana State University, was at the University of Kansas and encouraged my bird collecting in Veracruz. George also pressed me to collect skeletons of birds, for none were available for many species of tropical birds. The total number of birds I collected in Veracruz was 1,007 skins and skeletons. For a detailed listing, see Lowery and Dalquest (1951).

Although birds were collected from many sites in Veracruz, the specimens most interesting to me, and events concerning which are still freshest in my memory, were found in southern and eastern Veracruz, in the tropical zones.

One of the first tropical birds I collected was a common Lesson's Motmot (*Momotus momota lessonii*). Dyfrig Forbes was showing me around a limestone hill that supported many tall, vine-clad trees a few kilometers from his home in Potrero Viejo, a site called Esmeralda. I heard a low *hoot-hoot* sound, somewhat like the call of an owl. This was well within my range of hearing. Dyfrig said that it was not an owl but a small bird, but he could not come up with the name. I followed the sounds to a beautiful, vine-hung dell at the base of a limestone cliff and shot the calling motmot, a lovely blue, green, and russet bird with two long central tail feathers with racquet-tips. We returned proudly to the hacienda, and I placed the bird on the floor of the kitchen while we went to lunch. A short time later we heard a scream from Marianna, Dyfrig's older daughter. We rushed to the kitchen to find the family cat devouring my motmot. Dyfrig assured me that the motmots were quite common, and indeed they were—usually in dense, dark, beautiful niches near limestone cliffs.

Another kind, the Keel-billed Motmot (*Electron carinatum*), proved not common and very difficult to find. It was located only east of the Río Coatzacoalcos where the tributary rivers flow cool and clear, like mountain trout streams, and steep hillsides of limestone border the streams. On numerous occasions, from the tops of the hillsides we heard a chickenlike *cut-cut-cadack*. Locally employed assistants Castulo Gregorio and his half-brother Chico and I literally ran up the hills on several occasions, but the birds ceased calling when we were still some distance away. Castulo was of the opinion that the caller was a kind of tinamou. Chico favored a kind of pigeon. I suspected a kind of jungle quail. During the first season on the Coatzacoalcos we probably heard a dozen of the odd "chickens," and tried for every one of them, but did not even get a glimpse. The next year results were identical until one afternoon, after scrambling up the hill to find a "chicken," we sat down to rest and have a cigarette. We had given up hope of ever getting the bird. Suddenly one called from a tall tree overhead. Sharp-eyed Chico saw it, and a shot brought it down. It was a beautiful motmot, smaller than Lesson's, with a large, serrated bill.

Before leaving motmots I must mention another species, the little Tody Motmot (*Hylomanes momotula*). I took one of these in 1948 and two in 1949 in the dense jungle southeast of Jesús Carranza. All were seen while pushing through areas of cane or slender trees at night, where the pale green color of the birds made them stand out in the beam of my headlight. The birds were caught by hand. I never saw one in the daytime.

Birds of prey were numerous and varied in the Tehuantepec jungle area. Along the Río Coatzacoalcos the common vulture was the Black Vulture (*Coragyps atratus*), and I never saw a King Vulture (*Sarcoramphus papa*) there. However, to the east, along the Río Solosuchil and Río Chalchijapa, the King Vulture was common. They are gorgeous birds, with pure white bodies and black wings. The lappets and fleshy areas of the head are brilliant, almost enameled red, gold, and blue. For all their beauty they are still vultures, and they stink like vultures. I shot one for a specimen, a nice adult male, which had a partly decomposed foot-long section of a large snake, *Spilotes*, in its crop. I shot another for a skeleton, but had one of my assistants clean it.

A beautiful hawk of the rivers east of the Coatzacoalcos is the White Hawk (*Leucopternis albicollis ghiesbreghti*). This hawk, slightly smaller than the Red-tailed Hawk (*Buteo jamaicensis*), soars endlessly in circles, avoiding sand bars or clearings. I obtained two males and found them to smell almost as bad as a King Vulture.

The most memorable bird I found on the eastern tributaries of the Coatzacoalcos was the Harpy Eagle (*Harpia harpyja*). I saw one or two of these flying ahead of us as we pushed our dugout up the Río Chalchijapa and Río Solosuchil. I got a hasty shot at one that flushed from a large limb of a tall tree beside the river. It flew about a hundred meters, sinking steadily lower, to crash into a thicket beside the river. I went to see what the eagle had been feeding on, and found a half-devoured iguana under the branch where the bird had been perched. Chico had run to get the eagle but called to Castulo. I heard them giggling and talking, and I in turn called to ask if they had found the bird.

They answered, "Yes."

"So bring it here," I ordered.

"It doesn't want to go," Chico called.

I pushed through the trail they had cut and found them. The eagle lay on its back, feet and claws (almost the size of my fingers) stretched, and beak gaping. Indeed, it did not want to go. Castulo got one wing tip and Chico held the other while I pressed my foot on its chest until it died. I never killed or wanted to kill another Harpy Eagle. The single specimen I shot is probably the only one from Veracruz in scientific collections, and there are probably none left alive in the state.

One more hawk story: on March 4, 1947, Gerardo Mazza, my field assistant at that time, and I went by train to Jimba, a village on the railway south of the point where the railway spur to San Andrés Tuxtla leaves the main line. Here we met Gerardo's uncle, who arranged a hunting trip to wild areas to the southwest. Our party of six left at dawn the next morning and rode to the *rincón* where we were to hunt. We arrived at about 1 p.m. and found that a party of hunters had apparently been camped there for a week or more. The game, including tapir and peccary, had been killed or frightened away. We found a large pile of turkey feathers at their old camp, the only evidence of turkeys I ever found in Veracruz. Circling over the forest were several large hawks the size of the northern Red-tailed Hawk. The birds emitted harsh, unpleasant screams as they circled. I shot one, a rather brownish, purplish, bird with bright red face and neck. I had no idea what it might be. The men of the party urged me to throw it away and did not even want me to carry it on my horse. Its feathers were said to have a dust that was deadly poison. However, I prepared the skin with no ill effects. When I unpacked in Lawrence several months later, George Lowery became quite excited. The bird was a

Figure 5.2. The bird that did not want to go, a Harpy Eagle (*Harpia harpyja*), with field assistants Castulo Gregorio *(left)* and Chico Gregorio, 39 km southeast of Jesús Carranza, Isthmus of Tehuantepec, April 9, 1948. Photo by W. W. Dalquest.

Red-throated Caracara (*Ibycter americanus*), probably the first record from Mexico.

The little Ferruginous Pygmy-Owl (*Glaucidium brasilianum*) occurs in the southwestern United States, but it is probably the most common owl in Veracruz. I was unaware of this until Gerardo taught me to listen for its call. The low, whistled *wheet-wheet-wheet* goes on and on, but it is difficult for me to trace. Apparently children follow up the sound, but I doubt that they catch many owls. The birds call most in the morning and evening but may call at any time. It is easy to imitate the call and start an owl calling. The tiny owls perch in bushes and lower parts of dense trees and are difficult to see, even when one knows almost exactly where they are.

The common, more typical owl of the tropics is the Mottled Owl (*Ciccaba virgata*), which reminds one of the Barred and Spotted owls of the United States (*Strix varia* and *S. occidentalis*). It lacks horns, but it hoots. Larger and much rarer are the odd-colored Spectacled Owl (*Pulsatrix perspicillata*) and the Striped Owl (*Pseudoscops clamator*). I saw only two of the former, and obtained one. I collected two Striped Owls in Veracruz. Examination of them led to a study of the species and description of a new race named for Dyfrig Forbes (Lowery and Dalquest 1951: 576).

Because I spent much time hunting mammals at night wearing a headlight, I had unusual opportunities to observe owls. I also saw many potoos. These curious birds of the family Nyctibiidae are related to the whip-poor-will family, Caprimulgidae. The Mexican species, the Northern Potoo (*Nyctibius jamaicensis*), is a large bird with relatively enormous eyes that shine brilliantly in the beam of a headlight; they can be seen for a hundred yards or more. The first one I saw was across a large cleared area, and I mistook its eyes for those of a carnivore. It seemed we scrambled forever through the brush of the clearing, keeping the eyes in sight. When I shot the bird I took it for a relative of the Common Pauraque (*Nyctidromus albicollis*), but pauraques look at a light with only one eye. Further, the bird was sitting crossways on a branch; the caprimulgids sit parallel to branches. My assistant Gerardo called it a *lechusa* and said killing one produced bad luck. He told me that the next time I fired my shotgun, I must hold two sticks under the barrel in the form of a cross. I found the potoos very difficult to prepare. The skin was like wet tissue paper, the feathers so loosely attached that they would stick to a damp finger and be pulled free almost by a breath. I collected two more potoos but saved them as skeletons.

On the Río Coatzacoalcos I heard another pauraque story. A man who had never hunted brought a gun and went hunting with a headlight, an acetylene lamp held on the forehead with a cloth band. A short time later he came panting to a nearby house to ask for help. He said he had shot a *tigre* (jaguar), but it had only been wounded. Several heavily armed men accompanied him to the site where he had fired, where they found the feathers and shot bits of a pauraque. "See," said the man, "the tiger was eating the *tapacamino* when I fired." At close range the eye of a pauraque really does glare. If one keeps the light on the eye, it is often possible to ease up close enough to seize a pauraque by hand.

Crested Guans (*Penelope purpurascens*) and Great Curassows (*Crax rubra*) are large game birds, the size of small turkeys, and their meat was an important part of our diet in the Isthmus jungle. However, they tended to be tough. Much more desirable, even if smaller, were the tinamous. The Great Tinamou (*Tinamus major*) was not found west of the Río Coatzacoalcos. The smaller Slaty-breasted Tinamou (*Crypturellus boucardi*) and Thicket Tinamou (*Crypturellus cinnamomeus*) were more widespread. Their flesh is tender and flavorful but has a pale green color. One must accept that it is not partly decomposed. The cooked meat is pure white. I put a bit of tinamou flesh in fixing fluid and later prepared microscope slides to see what caused the greenish color. The striated muscle was strongly cross-banded and the numerous veinules were prominent. Apparently the color results from a scarcity of myosin in the muscle and an abundance of blood in the small veins. Tinamous fly readily and strongly, but only for relatively short distances, because of their low myosin and energy reserves.

Tinamous have an eerie call, often heard at night. This leads to the conviction among local people that they feed on fireflies and glow worms. There is also a children's legend in which Pavo Real, an Ocellated Turkey (*Agriocharis ocellata*) wanted to enter a contest to determine which bird had the most beautiful feathers. The tinamou had the most beautiful plumage, but Pavo Real persuaded the tinamou to lend him its feathers, with the understanding that they would be returned that night. Meanwhile, the now dull-colored tinamou hid in dense brush, ashamed of its ugly coat. Pavo Real, however, decided to cheat and keep the bright plumes. Forever after, the tinamou has hidden in dark places and called for the turkey, *Pavo Real, Pavo Real*.

Glow worms can seem like a special kind of magic, as we once saw on the Río Chalchijapa. I was hunting bats until almost complete darkness. Camp was just across a small stream, where narrow channels formed a network on a sand and gravel bottom before joining the river. The overhead cover was dense. As I entered the deltalike area I found it to be lighted by pale bluish fire. The running water appeared black, but the damp ground was carpeted with millions of tiny glow worms. I stood watching the sight for some time, until my men became concerned at my delay. I called to them, and they were as enchanted by the sight as I was.

Doves and pigeons are abundant and varied in Veracruz, most kinds being common and widespread. One species, the Short-billed Pigeon (*Patagioenas nigrirostris*) gave me some trouble for a while. The birds called from the tops of tall trees in the jungle, *best, bost-a-whey*. I could hear them, but I spent hours before shooting one. As with other pigeons, the fall from their high perches caused them to break open and lose large areas of feathers. Once I got one and identified it, I found that the species was relatively abundant and that specimens could readily be collected when they came to drink at the river in the afternoons. They did not drink from bare areas of sand or gravel, but only where limbs or vines close to the surface allowed them to drink while perched. Less common is the Scaled Pigeon (*Patagioenas speciosa*), another resident of high trees. I obtained only two of these in all my time in Veracruz.

I never liked to prepare skins of waterbirds. They are usually fat and have long legs, or big floppy feet, and take up a lot of room in the collecting chest. Nevertheless, they are interesting and diverse in the tropics. The Sungrebe (*Heliornis fulica*) is called "little widow" by the Indians of the Coatzacoalcos. It did not live in the swift, clear water of the tributaries but in the lower parts of the main river. It belongs to a family of its own, Heliornithidae, but resembles a grebe in life. If wounded or approached closely by a canoe it swims to shore and hides in the reeds, rather than escaping by diving, as do other waterbirds. I took one specimen of this little bird for a skin and two for skeletons, though I could have shot many more.

Ducks were virtually nonexistent east of the Coatzacoalcos. I saw a big black Muscovy Duck (*Cairina moschata*) on several occasions, but was unable to get a shot at it. An Indian gave me the leg band from a duck he had speared while fishing, and I sent it to the U.S. Fish and Wildlife Service. It was from a Blue-winged Teal (*Anas discors*) banded in North Dakota, if I remember correctly.

The Gray-necked Wood-Rail (*Aramides cajanea*) is locally common in central and southern Veracruz. It is usually inconspicuous, but it does have a loud call, *poposcala, poposcala*, and is usually known by this name. One was seen to perch in a small tree at dusk, but I do not know if the species usually perches in trees. It has an alarm note like the growl of a carnivore. This bird is best hunted in the early morning along the river's edge, where the reeds make a thin margin along the shore. I collected two skins and one skeleton for the KU Museum.

Boat-billed Heron (*Cochlearius cochlearius*) colonies of twenty to thirty birds were common along the shores of the clearwater tributaries of the

Río Coatzacoalcos. The birds perched ten to twenty feet above the ground in low, dense trees. The vegetation beneath their roosts was whitewashed by their droppings. The boat-bills seem entirely nocturnal. They were common at their roosts but were never seen fishing as we traveled the rivers by dugout. They seemed to be the only herons to live in the swift, clearwater rivers. Downstream on the Coatzacoalcos the pretty Bare-throated Tiger-Herons (*Tigrisoma mexicanum*), usually solitary fishers, flew ahead of our dugout until six or eight would be concentrated. Then some would circle inland and back, while others continued to be herded ahead.

Kingfishers were also herded ahead of the canoe on occasion. I found four species in Veracruz, and the size of the birds somewhat followed the size of the water they occupied. The little American Pygmy Kingfisher (*Chloroceryle aenea*) I found in ponds and small streams. The larger Green Kingfisher (*Chloroceryle americana*) preferred medium-sized streams, and the big Ringed Kingfisher (*Megaceryle torquata*) was found mostly in the larger rivers. I found the Amazon Kingfisher (*Chloroceryle amazona*) only twice, in the broader, lower parts of large rivers.

The trogons are surely among the most beautiful of American birds. They are also among the most difficult birds to prepare as study skins. Their skin is incredibly thin and delicate, and the feathers are loosely fixed in the skin. The birds are sedentary and are most often found perched on branches near trees with ripe berries, such as *jobo* plums. I had hoped to find the quetzal in the Tehuantepec jungle but never did. The nearest thing is the Slaty-tailed Trogon (*Trogon massena*), a large trogon with bright green head, chest, and back, and scarlet underparts. I found it only south of the Río Coatzacoalcos, where I saved six specimens, two as skeletons. Next in size is the Citreoline Trogon (*Trogon citreolus*), a bird of the more arid coastal plain region of Veracruz. This is a duller bird, with green back, blackish head and chest, and yellow underparts. The Collared Trogon (*Trogon collaris*) is the common red-bellied trogon of Veracruz. It is of medium size and has a white line separating the dark head from the red belly. The little Violaceous Trogon (*Trogon violaceus*) is a neat trogon with green back, almost black head and chest, and bright yellow underparts. It is probably the most common trogon in Veracruz.

The hummingbirds in the Mexican tropics are so varied that their identification in the field is hopeless. My collection from Veracruz included eighteen species. I did notice that when near an intended perch, the big *Campylopterus*, the Wedge-tailed Sabrewing (*C. curvipennis*), sometimes stopped its "humming" flight and maneuvered to the perch by a slower, normal "bird flight." The tiny Stripe-throated Hermit (*Phaethornis striigularis*) is rather dull colored for a hummingbird, being reddish brown except for the slightly iridescent green back and the black "mask." Its body is almost round, ball-like. It spends much of its time over the surface of small pools, skimming the surface and plunging briefly into the water. I could never discover if it was drinking, bathing, or taking small insects from the surface film.

The parrots are well represented in Veracruz, mostly by common and widespread species. On almost any afternoon, pairs of the large Red-crowned, Yellow-crowned, and Red-lored parrots (*Amazona viridigenalis*, *A. ochrocephala*, and *A. autumnalis*) are seen as they fly to their roosts. Their flight is reminiscent of that of ducks, but the birds usually call as they fly. On the coastal plain and in the more arid tropics of northern Veracruz the small White-crowned Parrot (*Pionus senilis*) is rare to moderately common. Flocks of Green Parakeets (*Aratinga holochlora*), with long, pointed tails, and Aztec Parakeets (*Aratinga astec*), with shorter, squared-off tails, are found where there are forests. In the jungles east of the Río Coatzacoalcos pairs of the gaudy Scarlet Macaw (*Ara macao*) are present, but they are not common. I found them difficult to obtain, usually flying high and keeping well out of shotgun range over our dugout. The macaw and the larger *Amazona* parrots are eaten in Veracruz, and their flesh is as good as that of any game bird except tinamous.

The only unusual parrot I obtained was a Mealy Parrot (*Amazona farinosa*). In the jungle near Zapotal, on the Río Coatzacoalcos, my field assistant Castulo Gregorio saw two parrots land in some tall, dense trees. Search as I would, I could not see the birds until one moved. It was only about fifty feet from me, but in spite of its bright colors it was almost invisible. I shot one of the pair. It was a female, distinctly larger than the common Red-lored, Red-crowned, or Yellow-crowned species. So far as I know, this bird remains the northernmost record of the species.

I observed and collected many smaller birds, such as toucans, woodpeckers, woodhewers, and assorted perching birds. The antbirds and other forms that are dull-colored and hide in vegetation on the jungle floor are best hunted by waiting silently until they reveal themselves by movement. Some of the most colorful Passeriformes live in the jungle crown, and they are difficult to see or identify from the ground. It is hard on the back of the neck, but if one looks long enough at the treetops, birds can be seen moving around. A shot may bring one or more down, but the collector usually has no idea what they are until they fall. Sometimes a lucky shot yields an oriole, a tanager, or some other fine specimen. More commonly it is a Masked Tityra (*Tityra semifasciata*) or a flycatcher. It is also possible to get some of the treetop species by watching alertly along the edges the forest, where the dense thickets wall in the jungle. Here the light lets the vegetation form a niche equivalent to the treetops, and some birds that usually dwell in the forest crown come to lower elevations.

I am proud of the more than a thousand birds collected in Veracruz. Many species are probably gone from the state, if not from Mexico. Mexican authorities transported large numbers of men from Mexico City and other population centers with orders to clear the land and plant corn. One man who wanted to preserve some land for wildlife was told: "If you don't want to clear that land we will give it to somebody who will."

In 1974 two of my students drove to Veracruz and the Isthmus. They found a pall of smoke from burning jungle over the land east of the Coatzacoalcos. They found the village of Boca Chalchijapa, but not Zapotal, my headquarters on the Coatzacoalcos a few kilometers downstream from the mouth of the Chalchijapa. No one could tell them anything of Castulo or Chico Gregorio, who had lived there.

The new owners of the land east of the Coatzacoalcos will have no tradition of preservation of wildlife. The existence of a bird or mammal will depend on its value as meat, and will be compared to the cost of the shotgun shell used to shoot it. My specimens and notes may soon be the only evidence that some species of birds and mammals ever lived on the Isthmus of Tehuantepec.

6

Some Mexican Experiences

ROBERT W. DICKERMAN

Robert W. Dickerman is one of the preeminent avian taxonomists of the latter half of the twentieth century and also one of the most experienced bird collectors the world has seen. After receiving his Ph.D. from the University of Minnesota (1961), he went on to a long career at the Cornell University Medical College in New York (with an office at the American Museum of Natural History). After retiring he began a second career as curatorial associate in birds at the Museum of Southwestern Biology and research associate professor in the Department of Biology at the University of New Mexico in Albuquerque. The scientific results of the fieldwork related here varied from descriptions of new subspecies (Dickerman 1961, 1974) to increasing our knowledge of Venezuelan encephalitis virus (Scherer et al. 1985).

When I finished my master's degree at the University of Arizona in the spring of 1953, I dropped out of academe. Professor Chuck Lowe, a member of my committee, admitted that I deserved the degree, but then he set about letting me know what I didn't know. He so devastated me during my orals that I could not even think of going on, so I took a job with an educational supply company in Phoenix. All went well until some time in the fall, when I got a phone call out of the blue from mammalogist E. Raymond Hall at the University of Kansas in Lawrence. He wondered if I would consider working for him as a collector in Mexico. I would indeed, and I drove home to Ithaca, New York. Dad was a Dodge car salesman. They had a small stake truck on which he built me a traveling cabin, with a hinged bunk bed that let down over a body-long, hinged-topped storage chest. The rest was just empty space. And I was off to Lawrence and thence to Coahuila with a list of localities and of mammals to collect for various graduate students.

Tabasco, 1950s

I had a letter of introduction to Robert Spence III in Sabinas. Bob was a rancher, originally from English stock, but he sounded more like a Texan. His

Figure 6.1. Robert Dickerman with only a hummingbird to show for an exhausting collecting effort, Tabasco, 1955. Photo courtesy R. W. Dickerman.

family had ranched around the world before he ended up in Mexico. But at the time I met Bob and Elizabeth and their children, Bobby and Chavela, they had a huge ranch in northern Coahuila, Las Margaritas, and a smaller ranch, La Gotcha, not too far from Sabinas, where they had a house. They took me in like family. Rollin Baker, then also at the University of Kansas, thought Bob might know of a field man for me to hire, and he did. We drove out to La Gotcha, where that year's calves were being castrated and branded, and we had real fresh mountain oysters grilled on the branding fire. I met and hired a fellow named Manuel, who had been around English speakers enough to be able to communicate, more or less.

So we set off. There were a lot of places to hit in Coahuila. Manuel soon learned the routine. We would reach a camping place, Manuel would pull out gear and gather wood, and I would decide how many traps to set out. He would go in one direction and I in another, then he would build a fire and get supper. He made pan-bread every few days in the Dutch oven. He would make a pot (teakettle) of coffee, and I would sit in my director's chair with a skinning plywood across the arms and write notes, or perhaps do some skinning if we had something early. Almost invariably some local man would show up out of the darkness, to whom Manuel would offer a cup of coffee, a piece of bread and perhaps jam, and the same conversation would be repeated every night—Who is the gringo? What are you doing? Is he married?—etc., etc. By that repetition I learned Spanish.

No wonder, then, that months later in Mexico City, Señora Villa, Bernardo Villa's wife, said to me, "Bob, you speak like a campesino." She did not mean this as a compliment, but I have had only one other more flattering comment in my whole life.

Manuel did not work out, and when he did not show up after Christmas and New Year—(which I spent with the Spences, where I learned the tradition of moonshine and black-eyed peas just after the New Year was rung in)—I was not sorry. I took off alone for Torreón, and in the hotel where I stayed there

Figure 6.2. The Dodge stake truck with the traveling cabin built on the back, being loaded onto a Pemex barge at Coatzacoalcos, Veracruz, April 22, 1955. The truck was christened El Topo Verde (the green gopher). Photo by R. W. Dickerman.

was a Mexican American. We buddied about a bit—went swimming in a local pool—and I met Jesús Sefuentes Baron, a young man recovering from a stab wound to the stomach. He became my companion for the next year and several months. We could not have made a better pair. My Spanish was usually sufficient to get along, and Chuy (the standard nickname for Jesús) turned out to be a better cook—he made flour tortillas—better trapper, and better company than my former helper. We had a great time and saw a lot of Mexico together.

One of our last joint adventures—before we joined Rollin Baker and a crew of students from KU on a summer field trip—was to go via barge to Tabasco, an area of Mexico not accessible by auto; no connections to the main Mexican highway system existed at that time. I had been introduced to a Pemex engineer in Celaya, Guanajuato. He wrote a letter to a Pemex official in Mexico City, and via a letter from the second official to a local Pemex man in Coatzacoalcos, we arranged for Pemex to load my truck on a barge taking supplies to their people in Tabasco. Of course nothing happened on schedule; we spent a week waiting to load the truck, from April 16 to 22, 1955. This provided a chance for some local collecting, and there were wonderful expanses of marshes just inland from Coatzacoalcos. The truck was loaded on the 22nd, but the barge was not ready to sail. On the 23rd they took the barge downriver to the city and tied up, and on the 24th the weather was bad, but we got off on the 25th. We were then towed down the Coatzacoalcos River and out to sea, thence eastward along the coast, and finally up the Grijalva/Usumacinta River to El Bayo, a Pemex dock and warehouse area serving Fortuna Nacional, the Pemex headquarters in Tabasco. Note that neither of those names is on a *Caminos de Mexico* map of 1964, just nine years later. But Fortuna Nacional is only a few miles from Macuspana, and on the 1964 map there is a "Pemex City" at about the same locality.

At Fortuna Nacional my truck was lifted off the barge and set down on an independent road system—largely built by Pemex in Tabasco—and we spent until May 26 collecting in a region not available at that time to most biologists. Because Tabasco was isolated, it was underpopulated, especially east and south of Villahermosa. For the same reason, wildlife was abundant—and people were welcoming to outsiders. We had unstinting help from Pemex. Before we left the office on our first visit we had a guide, who proved to be a fine hunter, and also a live baby river otter (*Lutra longicaudis*) as a companion! We arranged for the office in Villahermosa to pick up our mail, and they offered to fly us there to save time.

There were wonderful large marshes that we hunted from the roads and from a Pemex boat. On May 9, traveling by boat, we saw at least fifteen Pin-

Figure 6.3. Women washing clothes in a small stream that emerges from a cave near Teapa, Tabasco, May 1955. In this cool-air drainage bat nets were set at night. Photo by R. W. Dickerman.

nated Bitterns (*Botaurus pinnatus*), and we collected one; on May 17 we collected two more near Villahermosa. The first became the type specimen of *B. p. caribaeus* (Dickerman 1961), with a colored plate by Walter J. Breckenridge. When Breck was doing the painting I suggested that he add an Altamira Yellowthroat (*Geothlypis flavovelata*), another species not illustrated in the North American literature until then.

With all of the low country and abundant water supply came, of course, abundant mosquitoes. Fortunately, Ray Alcorn, the renowned collector, had given me a giant mosquito net, to which had been added a *yarda* of heavier material sewed around the edge (I later used blue denim for the same thing). Thus it could be hung from branches, yielding a tall, mosquito-proof space in which to set up a card table and chairs with lots of room for equipment, notebooks, etc. It made life enjoyable. Inland, the coastal plain abuts rugged, heavily forested karst topography. Howler monkeys (*Alouatta palliata*) and spider monkeys (*Ateles geoffroyi*) were abundant, and as the trees were not very high, these monkeys were too easy to shoot, for us and for other hunters—we at least saved ours. We took six howlers one day; there were three of us shooting, and no controls applied. They were the last primates I ever collected. But I know they have been useful; an anthropologist from the University of New Mexico studied their fingerprints!

Figure 6.4. First camp near Teapa, Tabasco, May 1955. Note the mosquito-net tent for skinning and five long guns leaning against the rock. Photo by R. W. Dickerman.

The best feature of the karst was the abundance of caves and cool streams that came out of them, not to mention the bat populations. We explored several caves, collecting in them and netting just outside them. From my journal I can identify obvious *Noctilio* among the bats we netted, and I remember taking two huge *Chrotopterus* (Peter's False Vampire Bat) in a cave.

I flew to Mexico City on May 25, and from there I went to Ciudad Juárez for my younger brother's wedding in El Paso. Chuy remained in Tabasco. A Pemex driver took him to collect birds locally until the 28th, when they loaded the truck on a barge. In doing so they were sloppy with the rope, and they dropped the right front end of the truck on some empty barrels, damaging it "slightly." Chuy commuted from Macuspana to El Bayo daily until June 1, when he slept in the truck on the barge. They left at 7:20 a.m. on the 2nd, getting as far as Frontera, near the mouth of the river. Finally, on the morning of June 3 they left, arriving at Coatzacoalcos at about 8 that evening, having had a rough passage. Both Chuy and his baby spider monkey were seasick. It was his second and last sea voyage. I was not sorry to see him sell the monkey for fifteen pesos. It was a clammy little tyke that would rather ride on my shoulder than Chuy's.

We headed back across the Isthmus and to Ciudad Oaxaca, one of my favorite cities in Mexico.

A Zip Trip, 1968

The distinguished ornithologist Allan R. Phillips (1914–1996) had many useful insights on the study of geographic variation in birds. I am a strong believer in Phillip's Law, "If a species is strongly dimorphic, females are more useful taxonomically," and in Allan's dogma of the use of fresh plumages, which represent the genetically controlled characteristics of feathers before dirt, wear, and fading have their effects. The Red-winged Blackbird (*Agelaius phoeniceus*) is a prime example: males are collected only as collateral damage, useful only for measurements, while females vary greatly in coloration (but note that the Yellow Warbler, *Dendroica petechia*, is the exception; almost all systematic studies have been done on the alternate-plumaged male).

During the five years that my family resided in Mexico City, I had accumulated nice series of the Mexican populations of Red-wings, but those of Central America were sparsely represented in North American collections, and most of those specimens were in worn plumages. Thus when the Pan American Health Organization asked me to fly to Panama to take part in a site visit in February 1968, I jumped at the opportunity and routed my return via Honduras and Guatemala. I packed my .410/.22 and ammunition in my suitcase. I was traveling on a U.N. passport, and at that time little attention was paid to luggage. Although I was planning on looking at birds, I forgot to pack binoculars, but fortunately they were available in the tax-free zone in Panama City.

One morning during my stay, Dr. Karl Johnson, then director of the Middle American Research Unit in the Canal Zone, loaned me a car so that I could visit a nearby marsh. I saw and collected my first Gray-breasted Crake (*Laterallus exilis*); my first red-bellied, tropical meadowlarks—Red-breasted Blackbird (*Sturnella militaris*); and what I catalogued as "*Agelaius*" (= *A. icterocephalus*??). If that was what they were, I would have thought Bob Ridgely would have found them, but there were none in his *Birds of Panama*. I had a good time, getting plastered with mud in the process, as one does around a marsh. For comfort on the drive back into Panama City, I shed my muddy pants. As a result, when I came to a police check-point that had not been in place in the morning, lying on the floor of the car were an illegal gun, several poached birds, and my pants. What to do? Presuming the officials would not shoot at a U.S. government car, and since they did not seem to have a vehicle, I decided it would be wisest just to keep driving. Karl later reported that in due time he got a letter complaining about this, which he placed in the round file.

Figure 6.5. Robert Dickerman and Allan Phillips collecting birds along the Santa Cruz River on the way to Sonora, March 22, 1958. Photo by B. J. Hayward.

The rest of the trip, however, went like clockwork. At the end of the site visit I flew to San Pedro Sula, Honduras, where we had earlier done some exploratory work looking for mosquito-transmitted viruses, namely Venezuelan Encephalitis virus. We had an acquaintance there from whom I borrowed a car. And on February 11, within hours, I got lucky and collected a nice series of seventeen female Red-wings, plus two males. Before returning the car I stopped at a clear stream to take a bath—and lost the car keys. I had to hitch a ride back, and the car owners fortunately had another set of keys.

The next stop was Guatemala, where a vehicle, permits, and a 12-gauge shotgun awaited me. On February 15 I drove down to La Avellana on the Pacific coast east of Escuintla. Hugh Land (author of *Birds of Guatemala*, 1970) had recommended the marshes there to me, and when we wanted an area to study arboviruses we explored it and found the town ideal: a hamster exposed to mosquitoes would last less than a week, yielding any of three abundant endemic viruses, so I knew the marshes well. I collected a total of twenty-three females and eighteen males, plus two Boat-billed Herons.

I then drove to San Salvador, where on the 17th I first collected at Laguna de San Juan, getting only a Striped Cuckoo (*Tapera naevia*). But at Laguna Jocotal I collected a male and three female Red-wings in the afternoon. On the morning of the 18th I hired a boatman, and we hunted birds feeding in water hyacinth. I got another male and eight females, and also a Pinnated Bittern, Pied-billed Grebe (*Podilymbus podiceps*), and Least Grebe (*Tachybaptus dominicus*).

That afternoon I drove back to Guatemala City, stopping briefly at La Avellana again and taking two more Boat-billed Herons. I spent the night, and on the morning of February 19 flew to Flores on Lago Petén Itzá at the base of the Yucatán Peninsula. Again I hired a boat. That afternoon we collected seven female Red-wings and a Least Bittern (*Ixobrychus exilis*), and the next morning we got seventeen more female Red-wings and seven males as well as a nice adult Great Blue Heron (*Ardea herodias*); I believe this was the first specimen from Guatemala. In this case I did not mind the male Red-wings, for that population proved to be a new subspecies, and one of the females was destined to become the type specimen of *Agelaius phoeniceus aurthuralleni*.

After this it was back to Guatemala City, with one final stop on the 21st at San Antonio Agua Caliente in Sacatepequez Department, where I collected a few highland Red-wings, two females and three males. The next day I flew to Mexico City with my overflowing box, which I left the with my field assistants Santos Farfan B. and Juan Nava S. They prepared the specimens over the next several months, and I picked them up the following field season. This rapid and by no means traditional collecting trip yielded a large enough series in good plumages to complete a revision of the Red-wings.

7

Sabbatical Trip to Panama, 1970

STEPHEN W. EATON

Stephen W. Eaton received his master of science and Ph.D. degrees from Cornell University in 1942 and 1949, respectively, spending 1942–46 in military service, including a year and a half in China. In 1946 he joined Ernest P. Edwards on a ten-week expedition to Mexico financed by terminal-leave pay. In 1970, on his first sabbatical, he and his wife, Betty, drove to Panama in a Volkswagen camper to study birds, especially warblers. His career spanned thirty-five years teaching biology at St. Bonaventure University. His scientific contributions range from the botanical (Eaton and Schrot 1987) to the life histories of birds (Eaton 1992, 1995); the latter no doubt benefited from behavioral insights obtained during the trip related below.

By 1968 St. Bonaventure University had inaugurated a sabbatical year program for faculty who had served full time at the university for seven years or more. I jumped at the chance in 1970 when the program was put into effect. In my application I proposed to study the warblers of Mexico and Central America and the Ocellated Turkey (*Meleagris ocellata*) of the Yucatán and Guatemala—an overly ambitious attempt. I was starved for some fieldwork after twenty years of teaching everything from taxonomic botany and comparative anatomy to ichthyology and ornithology.

My wife, Betty, and I left our place in the woods of western New York on February 3 in a Volkswagen camper and headed to New Jersey to see Betty's parents. We stayed there for two days while I looked at warbler and Ocellated Turkey skins and skeletons at the American Museum of Natural History. Then we headed south, stopping at Sweet Briar, Virginia, to see Buck and Mabel Edwards. By February 13 we were looking at skins in the Louisiana State University collection and saying hello to George Lowery and Bob Newman. It was interesting to see the hybrid warbler that Ken Parkes had identified as a Black-and-white × Cerulean (*Mniotilta varia* × *Dendroica cerulea*). On February 15 we arrived at the gate to the Rob and Bessie Welder Wildlife Foundation near Sinton, Texas, where we were greeted by Clarence Cottam. We spent three days at their graduate student facilities and while there were able to see the

Figure 7.1. Eaton camp on Padre Island, February 17, 1970. Photo by S. W. Eaton.

Wild Turkey subspecies *Meleagris gallopavo intermedia*, listen to the coyotes at dawn being answered by turkey gobbling, and see birds that winter in the area. From Welder we headed for Padre Island National Seashore. Here we spent our first night in the camper to the sound of breakers rolling in along the flat sandy beaches. A half moon lit up the sand and dunes with moonglow. In the afternoon (February 18) we drove to Brownsville and prepared to enter Mexico. The next morning we dropped into the AAA office and picked up seventy-five dollars' worth of Mexican insurance and a form to help with a vehicle permit. From there we drove to the Mexican consul to get our multiple entry visas and then on to the border. Cameras and tape recorders were declared, but the U.S. border guard suggested that I smuggle the .22 rifle across. At Matamoros our visa was stamped, and we were off for a month and a half in Mexico and a trip down Central America to Panama. I had previously arranged for a collecting permit, which we picked up with some other mail in Mexico City.

As we drove toward Ciudad Victoria in Tamaulipas, the mesquite-grassland country was quite showy. In some areas the ground was cultivated and planted, and the crop was just beginning to show (Corpus Christi and Sinton had still been fallow). Great-tailed Grackles (*Quiscalus mexicanus*) seemed to be somewhat affected by spring; a few were in pairs, and one near Victoria was doing "bill-up" displays. As we drove along we saw American Kestrels

(*Falco sparverius*) in several places, Inca Doves (*Columbina inca*), Common Ground-Doves (*C. passerina*), Northern Harriers (*Circus cyaneus*), and Loggerhead Shrikes (*Lanius ludovicianus*). Loose horses and cows posed a danger to driving, particularly at night. At about 5 p.m. we saw large flocks of blackbirds headed toward the coast, and a Great Kiskadee (*Pitangus sulphuratus*) flew across the road and landed on a post. It seemed strange to see such a tropical bird in the cool of the *norte* (a weather system from the north) we were experiencing. Meadowlarks (*Sturnella* spp.) were common until we hit the rolling country toward Ciudad Victoria. At a place along the road about fifty miles north of Victoria we pulled off the road to eat a light supper, and while eating we watched a couple of Common Black-Hawks (*Buteogallus anthracinus*). We drove on through Victoria, and at the top of the hill to the south we stopped for the night at Bella Vista Courts. Every wall of our room was of a different bright color, reminding us that we had entered a different culture. In the morning (February 20) we had breakfast in the café, where a group of jolly school girls and boys came in to have *desayuno*. They appeared to enjoy listening to a couple of gringos.

The *norte* was still with us as we started off for Tamazunchale, San Luis Potosí, in a cold rain. A little south of Victoria we crossed the Tropic of Cancer, and the place where Buck Edwards and I had camped overnight on the Mesa de Llera in 1946 was still recognizable. It brought back a wave of nostalgia that lasted after dropping into the lowlands and crossing the Río Sabinas. At a lunch stop south of Monte I saw a flock of five or six Olive Sparrows (*Arremonops rufivirgatus*) and collected one. When I skinned it that night I found it showed two cerebellar windows, probably a hatching-year bird. Near Valles the country changed into what A. Starker Leopold called tropical evergreen forest. Here there were many orange groves, and the trees were in fruit and blossom at the same time. The bald cypress along the rivers we passed had their new leaves.

As we came into Tamazunchale, only a remnant shell of El Sol Courts showed through the gathering jungle. Buck and I had stayed there in 1946, and this was where I had received a telegram from the girl I was to marry in less than a year. We stayed in Tamazunchale a couple of days at the San Antonio Hotel, which was run by the Holingsworths, and we had the chance to see some more tropical birds. On a hike down the road from town I saw a pair of Yellow-winged Tanagers (*Thraupis abbas*) eating small fruits. Along the flats of the Río Moctezuma was a gathering of vultures and a Green Heron (*Butorides virescens*), Great-tailed Grackles, a Vermilion Flycatcher (*Pyrocephalus rubinus*), a small flock of Northern Rough-winged Swallows (*Stelgidopteryx serripennis*), a Say's Phoebe (*Sayornis saya*), and a House Wren (*Troglodytes aedon*). No warblers appeared along this stretch of habitat. We got into the swing of Mexican living by trying tequila, salt, and lime before *cena*.

After gassing up with Gasso Mex on February 22, we started the big climb up the Sierra Madre Oriental, often being slowed by trucks belching out dark fumes. Leaving the orange groves on the lower slopes, we passed through a cloud forest with tree ferns, air plants, lichens, and bryophytes. Soon we entered the state of Hidalgo, and at 2,500 feet (we carried a P-40 altimeter) we saw two pairs of White-crowned Parrots (*Pionus senilis*). At about 5,000 feet we had glimpses of hummingbirds, euphonias, and a pair of Red-crowned Ant-Tanagers (*Habia rubica*).

An amentiferous tree appeared in blossom at 5,500 feet. We came to pine and juniper at 5,600 feet near Sierra Colorado, and at a flat place where roads led back into the forest, we pulled off the highway and I looked the area over for birds while Betty made lunch. Soon a bunch came along, including an *Elaenia*, two Blue-headed Vireos (*Vireo solitarius*), and a Hermit Warbler (*Dendroica occidentalis*) and Townsend's Warbler (*D. townsendi*), both brightly colored. These fellows were almost at eye level, because they were working about twenty feet up in juniper, pine, and oak on a slope below. Soon I noted a Crescent-chested Warbler (*Parula superciliosa*) in high plumage and a pair of Steller's Jays (*Cyanocitta stelleri*). I was about to collect the warbler when a big *toro* appeared, so I made a quick exit to the camper. A trio of human characters came along in a pickup truck and parked behind our camper. It was time to leave this interesting spot. Farther on we saw a headed-out field of grain and what appeared to be redbud in blossom. Soon we were looking down the valley toward Jacala, Hidalgo. At 6,000 feet we saw three Turkey Vultures (*Cathartes aura*), which appeared to be the vulture of the highlands in this area, as the Black Vulture (*Coragyps atratus*) had been in the lowlands.

From Jacala to Zimapan, Hidalgo, the country was what Leopold called mesquite-grassland of the central desert. In Zimapan we took in the market, where Betty bought a *jorongo* (weaving) and I picked up from the ground a few small corn cobs that were only two inches long, not having gone through the long process of artificial selection. We got a room at the Hotel Fundación, formerly the home of a silver-mine owner, and while there I found a Nashville Warbler (*Vermivora ruficapilla*) dead under the windows; after supper I prepared it as a skeleton. The next day (February 23), we drove out to the Pan-American Highway and then south through desert country, winding up through a range of the Sierras. At a crossing of the Tula River we stopped to enjoy the view of the great cleft in the mountains caused by the river. It was lined by bald cypress that was just starting to green, quite a bit behind the cypress of the lowlands, as was a large cypress tree planted in Zimapan. Of course we watched birds as we drove along the Pan-American Highway in the high desert country. Stopping for lunch above Pachuca, we watched some ants chewing up a shrub. The soldiers along the route to and from their nest were big-headed, cutting blossoms and carrying them home.

At the highest point on the Pan-American Highway in Mexico (8,209 feet), at Hacienda de la Concepción, we stopped to photograph a domestic tom turkey with four hens. The tom was little bigger than the hens, and when I imitated a series of yelps he puffed, strutted, and gobbled. There was one dominant hen that led the group down to us. These birds were of the bronze color type, but they were much darker than the wild type. The hens looked me over and then picked up bugs and seeds, went over to a water hole where some rain water stood, and drank, then went feeding right along the highway. Domestic turkeys are seen all through Tamaulipas, San Luis Potosí, and Hidalgo and are a common bird of the farmyards, where they are allowed to roam free. They must be resistant to black-head disease. Perhaps these domestics in the high country north of Mexico City are fairly close descendants of *Meleagris gallopavo gallopavo*.

We passed irrigated areas as we drove south toward Mexico City, and in these places there were many Vermilion Flycatchers (*Pyrocephalus rubinus*). Soon we entered Mexico City and hit Avenida Insurgentes, then we turned onto Paseo de la Reforma, went into Chapultepec Park, retracked a bit, and after a merry-go-round and some help from some people, made it to the Park Villa motel, where a Military Macaw (*Ara militaris*), a solitaire (*Myadestes* sp.), Inca Doves (*Columbina inca*), and House Sparrows (*Passer domesticus*) hammed it up for the guests. There were two other VW campers there like ours, both from California. After getting a late start the next morning (February 24), we took a cab downtown and visited the United States Embassy, where we picked up some mail. Back at the Park Villa we called Allan Phillips, who asked us to come out and see him at the university (Universidad Nacional Autónoma de México, UNAM). Allan looked well. He had crowded quarters on the top floor, but he seemed happy surrounded by his skins and skeletons. He showed us a malformed turkey hip and other bones from Pleistocene diggings in the Mexico City area that he and Pierce Brodkorb were working up. He was also working with Bob Dickerman and Ken Parkes on the birds of the Yucatán, saying that Paynter (1955) needed considerable revision. There was a lot to be learned on the Yucatán.

In town the next morning we picked up an El Salvador visa and bought a Goodrich atlas of Mexico, a string hammock, and eight 1:500,000 topographic maps of the Yucatán Peninsula (dated 1958) for thirty pesos per map. After supper, Betty and I visited Allan out at his home on Aguilas, off Centrales. At the motel clerk's suggestion we had taken the Periferico, one of those circles about cities intended to increase the flow of traffic, and we succeeded, but it made for an exciting ride. Allan had a charming wife, Juana, and they had three boys of their own as well as two girls and a boy from Juana's previous marriage. We arranged a 6:30 a.m. meeting the next day to hit the highlands along the road to Cuernavaca.

Accordingly, Allan and I left his house early for a day of collecting in the highlands to the south. The sun was just rising over the snow-covered outline of Iztaccihuatl, visible through the haze of Mexico City. Allan said people were starting to worry about air pollution in the valley. He pointed out Lago de Texcoco as we climbed almost 10,000 feet to the pass to Cuernavaca. At about 9,500 feet, near a small restaurant at Tres Cumbres where we stopped to buy tacos and coffee, we saw Cedar Waxwings (*Bombycilla cedrorum*) and Striped Sparrows (*Oriturus superciliosus*). Frost still covered the ground, but it would soon burn off. Here we took a side road that went off to the west toward Huitzilac, and we parked along the roadside about a mile and a half from the turnoff. We hunted singly from 9:00 to 12:15. Allan collected a series of Cactus Wrens (*Campylorhynchus brunneicapillus*), a Golden-browed Warbler (*Basileuterus belli*), a Red Warbler (*Ergaticus ruber*), a Gray Silky-flycatcher (*Ptilogonys cinereus*), and some other specimens. I collected a Red Warbler, an Olive Warbler (*Peucedramis taeniatus*, which I traded with Allan for a Slate-throated Redstart, *Myioborus miniatus*), an Orange-crowned Warbler (*Vermivora celata*), and two MacGillivray's Warblers (*Oporornis tolmiei*). I set up a mist net that was empty when we left at 12:15, and I left it there to pick up the next day. Other birds seen in this pine-oak scrub were Steller's Jay, vireos, Ruby-crowned Kinglets (*Regulus calendula*), and both Turkey and Black vultures.

I returned the next day by 7 a.m. The mist net was still empty, so I began hunting and observing birds. There seemed to be less activity than the day before, but I saw Ruby-crowned Kinglets, Gray Silky-flycatchers, Blue Mockingbirds (*Melanotis caerulescens*), and a flock of six Hooded Grosbeaks (*Coccothraustes abeillei*). I collected a Warbling Vireo (*Vireo gilvus*) and a Chestnut-capped Brush-Finch (*Arremon brunneinucha*), which I gave to Allan for the university collection. Black and Turkey vultures circled along the ridges. I saw a Slate-throated Redstart and collected a Golden-browed Warbler that was with one other bird, calling *chee—chee, chee—chee*. The *Basileuterus* was quite deliberate in its actions, yet warblerlike. One was seen to jump to the ground once to feed, but most of the time it kept from two to ten feet above the ground as it fed through the scrub. In contrast, the *Myioborus* were very jumpy and often fanned their tails very broadly and the wings slightly, behaviors that were much more accented than in the genus *Setophaga*, the American Redstart (*S. ruticilla*).

I came down off the highlands after eating lunch in the camper and met Allan at his bird range (the collection and where it was housed). There he allowed me to look at his excellent collection and to record data. There were many observations recorded on the labels indicating progress of skull ossification in the immature warblers, which I was very interested in assembling. Before returning to the Park Villa I recorded skull ossification data up through *Basileuterus culicivorus*. All *Basileuterus* immatures showed their distinctive posterior skull roof closure.

The next morning, the last day of February, Allan and I and his two boys Robert and Eddy left again for Tres Cumbres and the road to Huitzilac, where we collected in the same area of the previous two days. I collected a Golden-browed Warbler that was paired, saw another pair, and collected two Warbling Vireos, which Allan thought might be residents. He collected a Hooded Grosbeak, a Chestnut-sided Shrike-Vireo (*Vireolanius melitophrys*), and a Crescent-chested Warbler (*Parula superciliosa*). We also saw a siskin of some species (*Carduelis* sp.), Red-shafted Flickers (*Colaptes auratus cafer*), a dendrocopid woodpecker (*Picoides* sp.), Mexican Chickadees (*Poecile sclateri*), a flock of Bushtits (*Psaltriparus minimus*), and a White-eared Hummingbird (*Hylocharis leucotis*). I was beginning to get to know and appreciate again the importance of the southern pine-oak forests of Mexico.

On March 1, after skinning the Golden-browed Warbler, we went downtown and Betty went to the thieves' market while I watched the camper and read about the Mayan Indians of the Yucatán lowlands. Then we visited the pyramids of the sun and moon at Teotihuacán, north of the city, where a Canyon Wren enhanced our view from the side of the pyramid to the sun.

I worked on the ARP (Allan R. Phillips) skin collection the next day and mined a wealth of data from the specimen labels of the warblers I examined. The only thing to desire might have been that they were complete skeletons and not just skins with excellent data on labels.

On March 3 Allan showed me the habitat of the Rufous-capped Warbler (*Basileuterus rufifrons*) and the Hooded Yellowthroat (*Geothlypis nelsoni*) in the Barranca del Muerte not far from his house. This habitat is cut by many erosion trenches. Between and in the shallower ones are shrubs and thorn scrub with occasional cactus and agave. The Hooded Yellowthroat was extremely wary and difficult to collect. We took three shots (Allan two, Steve one) and got no birds. Later in the morning we went to the university, where I finished collecting data from the warbler specimens and said good-bye to

Allan. The next time we met was on my next sabbatical year in 1979, when he was at the Denver Museum.

On March 5 we left the Park Villa and headed east up the volcanic ridge to Río Frio, where there was a national park in the shadow of Iztaccihuatl at about 10,000 feet. We spent two days here learning more about the birds of these pine-oak woodlands. After finding a nice camping spot under pine I looked around a bit. There were two flocks of Western Bluebirds (*Sialia mexicana*; of five and six individuals). Perching on mounds thrown up by gophers, they did much feeding in an open field closely cropped by a flock of sheep. Here too were American Robins (*Turdus migratorius*), running in typical robin fashion while the bluebirds hopped. There were also large flocks of Yellow-eyed Juncos (*Junco phaeonotus*) feeding in the short, cropped grass, and nearby were siskins and Audubon's Warbler (*Dendroica coronata auduboni*). We cooked up a nice stew for supper and had a small campfire. We were joined by a couple of visitors from the park headquarters, who seemed genuinely interested in our company, but we had difficulty communicating with little more than half sentences and hand signals. At about 9 p.m. when we went to bed the thermometer read 6° C, as it also read at 7 a.m. when I got up to examine the forest behind camp.

There I watched a couple of Red Warblers feeding. They did much hovering, kingletlike, and very little gleaning of foliage. They also made a few aerial pursuits after flying insects. One chase of one by another was also seen, accompanied by some chatter. The two birds looked to be in basic plumage; they foraged from about six to twenty-five feet from the ground, mostly in oaks that were in blossom. I watched two different Slate-throated Redstarts foraging also. Both the Red Warblers and Slate-throated Redstart were singing from 7 to 8 a.m. as I observed them. The Slate-throated Redstarts, when feeding, seemed tamer than those observed at Tres Cumbres, south of Mexico City. When perched with head down watching for prey, body below the horizontal, they rotated the body side to side by foot action, spreading the tail feathers and partially opening the wings. If successful in flushing prey there would be a chase, then to a perch. There were also many Olive Warblers calling and singing. They worked the pine needles mostly twenty to forty feet from the ground, generally above the Red Warblers. The Olive Warblers' plumage varied from yellow to rufous around the head and neck. Many other species were seen about our camp.

At 7 a.m. on March 7 it was −3° C. I had a glass of Tang and headed up into the woods for a couple hours of collecting. With the cooler temperature, birds were quieter, but I was finally able to collect a Slate-throated Redstart with light tips to the greater coverts and an Olive Warbler. After breakfast, as I was skinning the birds, a bunch of fellows from the park headquarters came over to see if we had anything with which to watch the eclipse of the sun. We were only about a hundred miles from the total eclipse path. We rigged up something with three pairs of sunglasses and a pin-hole in paper and could just see the moon starting to line up with the sun. At full eclipse in our area, though the sky was clear, there were extensive shadows and songs of the birds increased.

From March 9 to 12 we traveled to Puebla, Catemaco, and Veracruz and then took Route 185 across the Isthmus of Tehuantepec and turned onto Route 190 headed east to Tuxtla Gutiérrez, Chiapas. We found Miguel Álvarez del Toro at his museum, and he graciously invited us down to his office at the Botanik Building. He showed us a topographic map of the area where he had seen the Ocellated Turkey along the valley of the Río Lacantun near the Guatemalan border. He said he had seen the bird perhaps five times in the wild—fewer times than even the Horned Guan. We bought a copy of his *Lista de las Aves de Chiapas*, and he told us where we could get ice and *agua purificado*. He also told us where we could find the Seventh Day Adventists and their clinic near Pueblo Nuevo Solistahaucan on Route 195 north of Tuxtla, in Chamula Indian country; these Indians were reputed to be unpredictable. We arrived there at about 5:45 p.m. and met Dr. Elwin Norton, who was very hospitable. He showed us where we might park the camper near a water faucet. Later we met two sisters, Olive and Nancy Mason from Ontario, New York. In the gathering darkness we cooked supper next to the prettiest pine woods, with bromeliads and Spanish moss, oaks in blossom, and sweetgum that was in early leaf. After dark we heard a burry Whip-poor-will, probably *Caprimulgus vociferus chiapensis*.

I woke up at about 6 a.m. to the crowing of a nearby rooster, and by 6:30 I was off for a hike in the woods of what Leopold refers to as tropical deciduous forest. What a fascinating place—a haven for resident and migrant warblers from eastern and western North America. I saw many interesting birds, including a Red-faced Warbler. This bird sat quite still and upright for a warbler, and I could see all the field marks well. I wished for my .22 with dust shot, which I had decided not to bring along for fear of offending our hosts. The Nortons had asked me not to collect birds, because many ornithologists had come by and taken so many. The Red-faced Warbler soon started feeding, jumping rather perkily from small twig to small twig and peering. It did not keep its body horizontal as many of the crown-gleaners do. The bird fed fifteen to twenty-five feet up in oaks and pine, and after about two minutes of observation it flew out of sight. The light patch on the nape was very distinctive. A Painted Redstart (*Myioborus pictus*) came by feeding with none of the flourish of the Slate-throated Redstarts seen recently. Over a stretch of twenty seconds while it was in my view, it moved without spreading wings and tail to capture food. Perhaps it is closer to the American Redstart (genus *Setophaga*) than the genus *Myioborus*.

At about 10 a.m. we set off north to Villahermosa, Tabasco, after saying good-bye to Dr. Norton. The scenery was beautiful as we made our way through the highlands and down through the tropical evergreen forest to the lowlands. We arrived at Villahermosa at about 5 p.m., got a room at the María Dolores Hotel, arranged for a 6,000-mile check-up on the camper, had a supper of fish, and walked around the *zócalo* before writing notes. The next morning (March 13), while a mechanic worked on the camper, we visited the park where there were artifacts from La Venta. I was more interested in the warblers that came in to my squeak and Northern Saw-whet Owl (*Aegolius acadicus*) imitation. These included an American Redstart, which did not move like *Myioborus* but rather more like a Painted Redstart, and a Northern Waterthrush (*Seiurus noveboracensis*) that shared water with a kinkajou (*Potos flavus*) and a gray fox (*Urocyon cinereoargenteus*); the waterthrush was acting as a winter resident, walking through the netting that contained the animals without a flaw to eat flies near the feces of the animals. We had entered a disturbed area that had once been "rain forest," according to Leopold. We left Villahermosa that afternoon, after gassing up and shopping for food and ice, to head east—our destination was the ruins at Palenque. Along the pools and mud flats on either side of the road we saw more interesting birds. It started to rain as we got toward Palenque and the rather dismal, partially renovated Palenque Hotel.

At the parking area near the ruins the next morning we dug out the primus stove and boiled water for coffee and boiled eggs, watching three Wood Thrushes (*Hylocichla mustelina*) sprinting around the parking lot. There were Melodious Blackbirds (*Dives dives*) about, and a Louisiana Waterthrush (*Seiurus motacilla*) fed along the beautiful freshwater stream below the souvenir shop. We climbed the Temple of the Inscriptions, went down into its depths (opened in 1949), and glanced at the closed tomb. The rain eased up a bit, and we enjoyed seeing the palace with its Moorish-looking sculpture and the jaguar with its beautiful hieroglyph. As we walked about the ruins, we saw several good birds, including one Louisiana Waterthrush that gave a weak song. We met an English couple, the David Stevensons, on their honeymoon. They were seeing Mexico on five dollars a day, and they hitched a ride with us to Campeche in the afternoon. In the lowlands along the road to Escarsega there were Cattle Egrets (*Bubulcus ibis*) feeding near the cattle and Great and Snowy egrets (*Ardea alba* and *Egretta thula*) feeding in ditches filled with water along the roadsides. Along this stretch we also saw three immature White Hawks (*Leucopternis albicollis*) sitting on the telephone wires. The Brown Jay (*Cyanocorax morio*) had been the jay of the lowlands along the gulf; the White-throated Magpie-Jay (*Calocitta formosa*) was the jay of the dry lowlands of Oaxaca and Chiapas.

South of Escarsega a Gray-crowned Yellowthroat (*Geothlypis poliocephala*) crashed into the camper; we saved it later as a trunk skeleton and skin. The land in this area was cattle country, and later, north of Escarsega, the country changed into dune and coral reef–type topography. In Campeche we pulled into the López Hotel, two blocks from the Gulf, had dinner on the Stevensons, and celebrated with a bottle of champagne that our dean had given us at the beginning of our trip. As we had breakfast (March 15), a group of six Gray-breasted Martins (*Progne chalybea*) sat on a wire above the street, and they did a bit of "nest demonstration" around two holes in a wall, but their main pursuit seemed to be resting in the sun. Two Rough-winged Swallows (*Stelgidopteryx* sp.) joined them soon on the wire. We walked over to the nearby Sunday market, which was interesting. Large, live sea turtles had been placed on their backs and showed occasional slow movement of legs. Fresh fish such as *pámpano* and skipjack were for sale. People walked around with live chickens and turkeys, tied by wings and feet, having bought them at the market. There were nice-looking papayas, mangoes, oranges, bananas, and many kinds of vegetables.

We set off for the ruins at Uxmal and then on to Mérida the next morning (March 16). Leaving Campeche, we drove east on Route 180 through dry country for a while, then north. Occasionally we saw flat areas of perhaps a hundred acres, where soils were reddish and looked fairly rich. These were interspersed with rocky coral hillocks covered with dry scrub, often burned. At Uxmal we stopped to see the buildings and temples. The temple of the turtle and dove seemed particularly appropriate to the country. There were many iguanas up to about thirty inches in length. Along the road to Mérida we picked up two DOR Gray-crowned Yellowthroats. These were the only two of several seen killed that looked salvageable for specimens.

As we entered a town just south of Mérida, a flock of Black-throated Bobwhite (*Colinus nigrogularis*) flew across the road in front of us. We got a nice room in this city of windmills in the Hotel Toledo, run by Dr. Guerro, who had turned his twelve rooms into a guesthouse. The rooms were cool, with ceiling fans and hammock hooks, as in all the hotels in this fiercely hot country. For a couple of days we took care of business. In the process of buying more traveler's checks Betty met a Miss Barbachano, whose family was prominent in the affairs of the area. She took us to see her beautiful mansion on Avenida Majorca. Many of the materials for its construction had been brought from France, including huge marble columns in the foyer. We took a side trip up to the Gulf and Progreso in the hottest part of the day. As we approached the Gulf we noted its moderating effect on the temperature. Soon we saw mangroves and many herons—Little Blue, Tricolored, and Great Blue (*Egretta caerulea, E. tricolor*, and *Ardea herodias*). East of town in short scrubby growth we saw more migrant and resident birds.

The next day (March 20) we set out east to Chichén Itzá and looked down into the great *cenote*, where many interesting artifacts are said to lie hidden. We found refuge from the fierce sun at the Hotel Chichén Itzá, which was new and nice at 350 pesos for two, American plan. In the morning before breakfast I took a short hike from the hotel into the adjacent scrub to watch birds. Among other species I saw a flock of six to eight Yucatan Jays (*Cyanocorax yucatanicus*), one with a yellow bill (an immature) and the rest with black bills (adults). It was great birding in the cool of the morning. Next we took off for Puerto Juárez, Quintana Roo. This town was on the coast of the Caribbean about opposite the island of Cancun, which was not yet transformed. The country around Chichén Itzá and on to Valladolid was quite dry, except where water influenced the soil, but as we drove east the climate became more humid. About five or ten miles east of Valladolid we picked up a colubrid snake DOR, and by the time we were about twenty miles from the sea on Route 180 the jungle seemed in fair shape—except where it had been burned to open it up for some new venture. As we drove along we could not help but feel that this country would soon be changed from a gentle Mayan way of life to some rowdy playground for the gringos. It looked pretty crowded at Puerto Juárez, so we took the road south to a smaller village called Puerto Morelos. Here we found a place to camp back from the beach in a kind of a trailer park where some power was available from outlets mounted on two or three palm trees. The only other visitors were a couple in a trailer who had just come into Mexico from Guatemala: we were interested in sounding them out on things to the south. As we set up camp for a couple of days we saw about fifty Lesser Scaup (*Aythya affinis*) flying north up the coast; we saw five more flocks the next day and still more on the 22nd.

On an early morning hike down the beach (March 22), Palm Warblers (*Dendroica palmarum*) were feeding from the sand and low vegetation, and after moving into a coconut plantation back from the beach, I saw a Prothonotary Warbler (*Protonotaria citrea*), a Yellow-throated Warbler (*Dendroica dominica*, apparently subsp. *albilora*), and several Common Yellowthroats (*Geothlypis trichas*). A Yellow-rumped Warbler (*Dendroica coronata coronata*)

I watched for some time acted territorial, flying from five coconut palms then down to the beach, where there were grasses in a dune. Birds seen that day included a Yellow-crowned Night-Heron (*Nycticorax violaceus*) feeding on hermit crabs and land snails in the coconut grove.

I took in the sun on the beach the next day and went out on the pier, where a boat, the *Cozumel*, had come in from the island to pick up vegetables, eggs, and a few passengers. The fee was twenty pesos out, twenty pesos back. A roustabout from the boat swam from the dock with snorkel, goggles, and harpoon getting small fish for bait. Then he swam out farther, speared a small tunalike fish, placed it on his holding chain, and continued fishing. All of a sudden he reacted to a disturbance; a four-foot barracuda had severed the tuna he had been trailing on his chain. He got the barracuda and brought it and what was left of the tuna in to the dock.

I got up at dawn the next day and hiked the road leading west across the swamp from Puerto Morelos. Beyond the barrier beach, with its coconuts and grasses, was a zone of mangroves followed by cattails and rushes, then jungle. In this area between the barrier beach and jungle I saw numerous birds and two raccoons (*Procyon lotor*) that crossed the road. On the telephone wires were two adult male Purple Martins (*Progne subis*) with two females, appearing paired, and two more females seemingly unpaired. These were obviously migrants and showed no interest in holes, as did the martins in Campeche and Mérida. I heard a sweet buntinglike song, which was the only passerine singing in the area of cattail, rushes, and scattered mangroves. Soon I identified the songster as the Gray-crowned Yellowthroat as he sang, six songs per minute; he was obviously maintaining a territory. He sang from exposed perches in mangroves about twelve feet from the surface of the water.

We packed up on March 24, as we were feeling the pressure of time. We had a reservation at Barro Colorado, Panama, for the week of April 14—only three weeks off and about two thousand miles to go. We had originally hoped to drive south from Puerto Morelos to Chetumal, into Belize, then into Guatemala to Tikal and on to Guatemala City, but information we got along the way argued against this, so we backtracked to Mérida, Campeche, and Villahermosa. On the way we picked up a road-killed Plain Chachalaca (*Ortalis vetula*) near Leona Vicario, Quintana Roo, with soft part colors pinkish red. I fleshed out the DOR bird as a skeleton, noticing with interest the exposed loop in the trachea extending to the back of the sternum. As we drove west to Chichén Itzá we saw two groups of the beautiful Yucatan Jay and a flock of Brown Jays with white in the tail. I put out the chachalaca to dry in the sun as we ate lunch, and a Mayan who recognized it volunteered that the *pavo de monte* (Ocellated Turkey) was quite common in the region about Chichén Itzá. We left Chichén Itzá on March 25 and noted as we drove west that the country became drier and much henequen was grown, particularly as we got toward Mérida. The plant from which sisal is derived for cordage was starting to give way to the synthetics, so another change would be coming to this country. We continued to backtrack through Campeche on Route 180 on March 26. Along one breakwall east of Lerma, where the shrimp boats were made and wharfed, there were several Royal Terns (*Thalasseus maximus*).

The road from Campeche to Compoton winds through the old coral beach, but south of town as we headed away from the coast the air got hotter and drier; then from Escarsega westward it grew more humid. The road west of Escarsega yielded several DORs—a Yellow-billed Cacique (*Amblycercus holosericeus*), an Indigo Bunting (*Passerina cyanea*) with brown "freckles," a Gray-crowed Yellowthroat, a Common Yellowthroat, and a Least Flycatcher (*Empidonax minimus*). Farther west were pools of water in borrow pits along the road, where we saw many Great Egrets. The country north of Palenque was savannah, pasture for Brahma cattle. We stayed again at the María Dolores Hotel in Villahermosa, where the manager helped us arrange a room for the following night at Mrs. Blom's in San Cristóbal de Las Casas, Chiapas. On March 27 we drove south toward Teapa and soon noted that the Brown Jays had lost the white in the tail and, four miles out, we collected a DOR female Gray-crowned Yellowthroat in which the ovary showed signs of activity. Eventually we pulled into the Seventh Day Adventist camp, again feeling more secure there. A Mrs. Butler told us of a bright "comet" visible low in the east, and she woke us at 5 a.m. on March 28 to see it. Perhaps it was a satellite, but it was very spectacular. I went birding in the forest again and found the Red-faced Warbler in the same area as on March 12. It moved its tail medium-fast sideways, like a *Wilsonia*, but it remained more upright than a *Dendroica* as it did much peering for insects. It was not a particularly active warbler. We saw a large woodcreeper (probably *Xiphocolaptes*) pecking into a bromeliad and watched a Mountain Trogon (*Trogon mexicanus*).

After breakfast we got going to drive to San Cristóbal de las Casas, and about two miles east of Jitotol we came upon a five-foot, five-inch bull snake (*Pituophis deppei*) hit by a car. It was still in reasonable condition, so I pickled it with a handy bottle of tequila. It had recently eaten and only slightly digested a female weasel, 300 mm in length, tail 110 mm. In the same general area a Common Raven (*Corvus corax*) flew over. We drove onto the Pan-American Highway east of Tuxtla Gutiérrez and headed for San Cristóbal, and we arrived at the door and compound of Casa Na Bolom at about 3 p.m. Mrs. Blom (Gertrude Duby) was all that the literature had indicated and more. She was an accomplished gardener, linguist, archaeologist, horsewoman, general scholar, and excellent host. We wanted to return and go with her to her *selva* of the Lacondon Indians near the Guatemala border along the headwaters of the Río Usumacinta.

On Easter Sunday we spent an interesting hour at the village of Chamula, where the Indians were celebrating a combination of Indian-Christian Easter. We looked in the door of the church, which was crowded with people and difficult to see into because of the smoke from hundreds of candles. Outside, men were holding pieces of iron with holes that held black powder, and they were lighting the powder while still holding the irons in their hands. The noise was about like that of a cherry bomb firecracker. On March 30 we drove to the lagunas east of Comitán, Chiapas, through a dry pine-oak forest. In the pine-oak woods around the lagunas was a flock of Band-backed Wrens (*Campylorhynchus zonatus*) feeding in the bromeliad-covered oaks. We heard and saw *tengofrio grande*, a much more euphonious name than Greater Pewee (*Contopus pertinax*), and a couple of Least Grebes (*Tachybaptus dominicus*) in the lagunas. In the evening Gertrude showed us an interesting jaguar call. It was a round gourd with a leather diaphragm over the opening at the top and a stick protruding from the diaphragm. When the stick was pulled slowly, out came the call of a jaguar.

We left Gertrude Duby's wonderfully relaxing house at about 7:30 a.m. on March 31 and headed down Route 190 to the Guatemala border. To save possible grief at the border, I had sold my .22 rifle to another visitor who was going to the Lacondon country, so we were now without a firearm. There had been no problem at the Mexican border, but the Guatemalans had us take out most of our bags and then put them right back in. We gave them a fifty-peso note and gave the fellow who moved the bags a U.S. dollar bill. Then we drove through the famous slide area of the Río San Gregoria, called the El Tapan landslide area. The high country was pine-oak as in Chiapas, but it got much drier as we passed to lower elevations. The Indians, particularly the men, wore more colorful clothes than in Chiapas, particularly reds and less black. In the high country were many Unicolored Jays (*Aphelocoma unicolor*), and in the afternoon we reached the Pan-American Highway a little east of Quetzaltenango, Guatemala. After traveling a few miles, we came to the road down to Lake Atitlán and Santiago Atitlán. While Betty did some shopping, I remained in the camper and enjoyed watching a Rufous-collared Sparrow (*Zonotrichia capensis*). He came and sang from a post six feet from the camper, then flew to another post and sang again; he was vocally mapping out his territory. The Boat-tailed Grackles (*Quiscalus major*) were nest building and giving pre-copulatory displays to females, yet with no response. The nesting season seemed a little further along. When Betty returned from shopping we

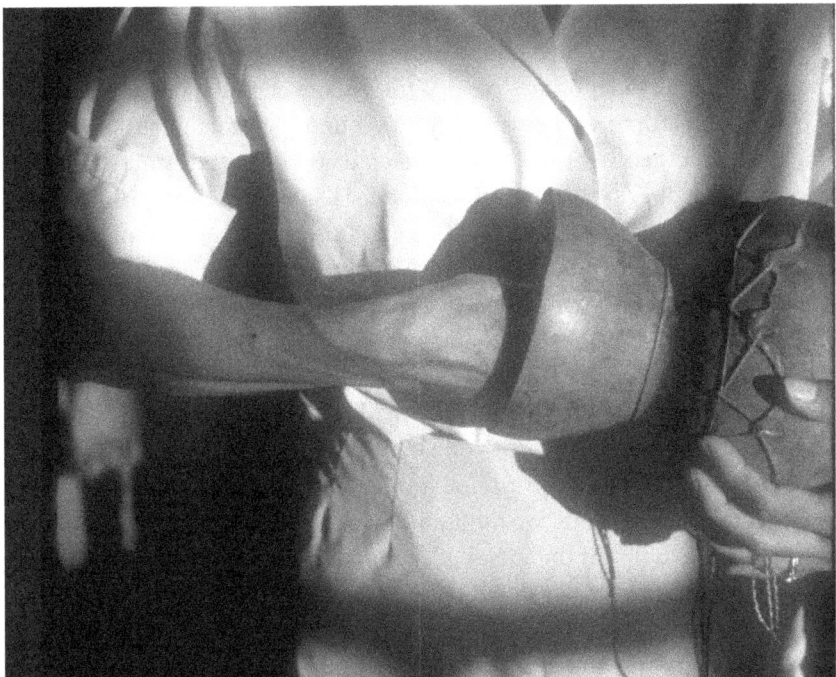

Figure 7.2. Betty Eaton calling jaguars at Casa Na Bolom, March 29, 1970. Photo by S. W. Eaton.

drove down to the beach of Lake Atitlán and parked for the night. A Brown Pelican (*Pelecanus occidentalis*) fished in the lake as we watched the sun drop behind the volcanic rim. The water of the lake was a most wonderful blue and absolutely calm, a sight that Aldous Huxley had said was "more beautiful than Lake Como."

We started for Guatemala City at about 10 a.m. and began the steep climb up out of the lake basin, stopping at Solota to buy film and exchange Mexican pesos for Guatemalan quetzals. We met an interesting Hollander who asked for a ride to the Pan-American Highway. He was bound for the famous Thursday market at Chichicastenango. We gave him a sandwich and a beer and dropped him off with his pack and drinking cup at Los Encuentros. He said he generally liked Guatemalans better than Mexicans and had been traveling for three months in the Yucatán to Tulum and on down to Belize. That stretch of road was good but required three ferries, and the road from Belize City west to the Guatemalan border was very rough but passable. He had gone up to see Tikal, then traveled south to Puerto Barrios on the coast, then up to Guatemala City.

Traveling through the high pine-oak forest we saw Black-capped Swallows (*Notiochelidon pileata*) flying up to holes in an exposed bank along the road. In several places slides of the volcanic soil had taken out about half the road. We drove down into Guatemala City and found the Motel Plaza on 7a, had a shower, and then went out to buy fifteen days of Central American insurance for forty-one dollars; it was not good for Panama. Between 5:30 and 6:30 p.m. we saw Great-tailed Grackles (*Quiscalus mexicanus*) and Giant Cowbirds (*Molothrus oryzivorus*) both going through precopulatory displays, given on the ground in front of their respective females.

Betty finally had a touch of the *turista*, so I nursed her in the Motel Plaza all day, then took a taxi for two quetzals to pick up our Central American insurance and mail a letter home. Our mail, which we had hoped to pick up at Clarke's Tours, was not there—apparently held up by a postal strike in the United States. We asked for it to be forwarded to Barro Colorado. At about dusk a large flock of about two thousand Great-tailed Grackles came into trees across the avenue from the motel. Planes landing at the Guatemala International Airport occasionally scared them up, and they would look for new trees for roosting, like European Starlings (*Sturnus vulgaris*) in the United States. Several attempts were made to scare them off with firecrackers at about dawn, but with little success.

I got up at about 6:30 a.m., and Betty was feeling better, so we decided to push on. We got ice from the bar in the motel, paid up, and drove to the Bank of Guatemala, where we cashed in more Mexican pesos for Guatemalan quetzals. Then we headed southeast out of the city and climbed up to the volcanic rim. At the top we were stopped by an army patrol for some unknown reason. An army officer looked us over, opened our glove compartment to have a look, and motioned us to go on, probably realizing that we were just gringos. When we got to Costa Rica later on, we found out that the German ambassador to Guatemala had been killed by reactionaries in an aborted attempt to extort 700,000 quetzals in ransom and the release of twenty-four political prisoners. From the rim there was a fine panorama of the city, which, like most cities in Central America, was located in a flattened basin of volcanic activity. The temperature was hot, cooling down in late afternoon, but then it became quite warm at night.

As we continued southeast and dropped to 2,000 feet, the country grew drier and hotter as we approached the El Salvador border. We took the new road through Oratorio and Jalpatagua to the frontier at the Río de Paz and arrived at 1:35 p.m., while officials were having a siesta, so we waited about twenty minutes until business started up again. The routine at borders was fairly standardized. First, you went to *imigración* with passports for stamping,

Figure 7.3. Typical scene on the Pan-American Highway in El Salvador, April 3, 1970. Photo by S. W. Eaton.

then you were directed, either by a small boy as guide or by a wave of the hand, to the *policia*, who made out a small slip of paper on which the car license number was printed. This was handed to you, and a boy guide or a wave of the hand directed you to *aduana* (customs), where a car permit was made out. In El Salvador and Guatemala we were given tags to put over the rear view mirror. The personnel at the border usually asked for our car registration or operator's license to obtain certain numbers to fill out their daily log. At the El Salvador border with Guatemala we first ran into the tangled money problems of Central America. Starting at the north with U.S. dollars one changes to Mexican pesos, then to Guatemalan quetzals, to Salvadoran *colones*, to Honduran *lempiras*, to Nicaraguan *córdobas*, to Costa Rican *colones*, and finally to Panamanian *balboas*, each with a different exchange rate. Betty exchanged a few quetzals into colones to have a little cash to deal with the locals along the Pan-American Highway.

Along the El Salvador part of the highway we saw people toting round metal water containers, and we also saw many ox carts with solid wheels. The ox yokes were interesting, as there were at least three places for oxen on the yoke. The land along the Pan-American Highway was dry, hot lowland through El Salvador, Honduras, and Nicaragua. After a long drive we stayed at the Motel Mijiana in San Miguel, El Salvador. At about midnight the night man at the motel knocked on our door and asked us to park our camper closer to our room. At the café where we had registered, there was a man who was drunk, and he must have given the night man an indication that our camper was worth stealing. We left San Miguel at about 6:30 a.m. (April 4) and took the Ruta Militar, which was a good road until close to the Honduran border, where great chuckholes made the driving much slower. The land had been made over into Brahma cattle country, as has happened in Florida and the West Indies. Along the last four miles of road in El Salvador there were many troops along the highway, but few were seen in Honduras.

As we drove along through the dry, hot Honduran lowlands we saw many iguanas on the road or crossing it, and there was a short stretch where painted pottery was being sold. We stopped and bought a turtle and a fish for $1.25 lempiras. Along the highway was a milkweed six to eight feet tall, in flower near the top, and with round fruits farther down the stem, probably *Asclepias pellucida*. We stopped between San Lorenzo and Chouteca and took a picture of a fellow's bee yard. He had about fifty active hives, and the bees were busy collecting nectar from a pink-flowering acacia. It seemed to be a good harvesting period. The owner said he had problems with ants and birds. At 2,700 feet along the highway we first noted pine trees in the southern part of Honduras, where the trees were rapidly being cut adjacent to a mill along the Pan-American Highway. At the border between Honduras and Nicaragua we were held up for only forty minutes, including officialdom on both sides, a record time at border crossings. We pulled into the Estrella Hotel in Managua, Nicaragua, at about 4 p.m. and, getting further into the spirit of the tropics, we took a siesta. This is tropical lowland country, very hot, and Managua is the only large Central American capital not in the highlands. We left the Estrella Hotel leisurely at about 9:30 a.m. (April 5), headed toward Lake Managua. On the way we passed a recent lava flow that entered Lake Nicaragua from a volcano southeast of the city. Then we headed southeast, skirting Lake Nicaragua, and saw the old Spanish town of Grenada, captured by the scoundrel Henry Morgan in about 1850. There were many large toads, probably *Bufo marinus*, DOR along the road through a resort area along the lakeshore.

It was Sunday, and many Nicaraguans were down along the lake cooling off and enjoying a swim, shaded from the fierce sun by thatch-roofed cabanas. We drove on south along the lake and stopped for lunch near a place called La Virgen. Here in a stretch along the lake were thousands of Barn Swallows (*Hirundo rustica*), mixed with perhaps 10 percent Bank Swallows (*Riparia*

Figure 7.4. Border between Nicaragua and Costa Rica, April 5, 1970. Photo by S. W. Eaton.

riparia), feeding on insects blown inland from the lake by easterly winds. Every fence line and every bit of vegetation suitable for perching harbored swallows sitting, as swallows do, side by side. In an area estimated to be 200 to 300 acres there were at least 5,000 Barn Swallows and smaller numbers of Bank Swallows. As we drove twenty miles farther east toward the border with Costa Rica, we saw an almost continuous line of swallows perched and flying; certainly there were millions of birds. We had witnessed a huge staging area for swallows headed north from wintering areas in Costa Rica, Panama, and South America. This area should be recognized as an important staging area and protected from future development. The aquatic insects hatching from Lake Nicaragua must form an important food source for swallows migrating north, and perhaps south, through the area. In this area, in the lee of the trade winds blowing over Lake Nicaragua, the vegetation was more luxuriant, and we saw Brown Jays with white-tipped tails; but in the dry country of the lowlands north of Lake Nicaragua the White-throated Magpie-Jay was common. In the area of the highway along the lake were many Cattle Egrets near the Brahma cattle, and in areas where the cattle were not pastured a pink acacia was in flower.

We had to pay thirty córdobas to check out of Nicaragua on Sunday (*servicio extraordinario*), and we also had to wait until 2 p.m. because the border was closed between noon and 2 for siesta. Costa Rica was most gracious and asked no fees, even on Sunday afternoon. All the way to Alajuela a few miles north of San José, the Pan-American Highway was in poor condition, but soon we came to a four-lane section leading right into the capital. We saw a kinkajou DOR about five miles south of La Cruz and stopped to examine an apiary near Esparta. We pulled into the Motel Bemus at about 8 p.m. and for twelve dollars obtained a suite with a kitchen, including a refrigerator. During the next two days (April 6–7) we got the camper serviced and had our passports stamped. About the city wherever there was vegetation, such as in parks and gardens, the Rufous-collared Sparrow added much character with its pleasing song, reminiscent of its relatives in the north, such as the White-throated Sparrow (*Zonotrichia albicollis*). About the motel were Clay-colored Thrushes (*Turdus grayi*) and a swallow with white breast, blue back, and emarginate tail, appropriately called the Blue-and-white Swallow (*Pygochelidon cyanoleuca*). These were going in and out of a ventilator under the eaves, where their nest was hidden. The voice was not unlike that of our Tree Swallow (*Tachycineta bicolor*).

On a visit to the Museo Nacional we saw an interesting display of gold items dating back to the sixteenth century, reminding us of the source of the country's name. The next day we were on the Pan-American Highway by 8 a.m.; to the northeast it was clear, but to the southeast, over Cartago in the direction we were headed, things looked overcast and wet. We drove rapidly to just outside Cartago on a good highway and then turned southwest to San Isidro, where the pavement ended and we started our climb up Cerro de la Muerte. At 7,400 feet we were still being serenaded by the Rufous-collared Sparrow. Except for an occasional gap where the wind blew the mist away, visibility was only 50–200 yards until we started down on the south side of la Muerte. Many plants typical of the north were noted along the road in the higher openings, such as clover, plantain, *Rubus* (some in fruit), many mosses, *Lycopodium clavatum*, *L. annotinum*, ferns of all kinds—from lianas to trees to simple swords—a large thistle, and an orange-and-yellow orchid, which I first thought was *Asclepias tuberosa*, seen in the highlands of Chiapas and Guatemala. I picked one for Betty, and she wore it in her buttonhole (poor conservation). At 8,200 feet we saw a Rufous-collared Sparrow and a beautiful white-to-pink *Digitalis*. At 9,200 feet, as we sat eating lunch in the camper alongside the road, we were serenaded by a Black-faced Solitaire (*Myadestes melanops*), which sang a few short phrases, and I got a quick look at him before he vanished. Soon I saw a dark, plump, wrenlike bird. It had a reddish brown topknot and was reddish in the wings but was otherwise all dark brown. He came to look at me a second or two after my squeaking and Northern Saw-whet Owl calling. This was my first and only encounter with the interesting warbler now incorrectly called the Wrenthrush (*Zeledonia coronata*). The commonest bird along the roadside along this high misty part of the mountain, above about 8,000 feet, was the Sooty Thrush (*Turdus nigrescens*), black with yellow bill and feet.

It was cold at these heights, and we used our car heater, which coughed out the dust collected from Llanos Grande in Pueblo, Mexico, through the Yucatán, and south through Central America. We had not used it since the plateau country of northern Mexico during the *nortes*. The road peaked at 3,350 meters (10,800 feet), and the sign identifying the area said that this was the highest point on the Pan-American Highway. At 9,600 feet on the southeast side of the mountain we saw a swallow and at 9,000 feet a gull was circling just below the mist. At 8,600 feet on our altimeter it had started to clear, and we again saw the Rufous-collared Sparrow, which appeared to be missing from the top 2,000 feet of the mountain. At 5,000 feet we stopped for lunch in the rain forest, where there was almost no wind, but it was overcast. The masses of vegetation in this still-forested region were staggering. It is difficult to see how the big trees can stand under the great weight of the water-soaked epiphytes. We came down through San Isidro del General, wishing with all our hearts that we had made arrangements to meet the man who had lived in this country most of his life and had written so beautifully of its natural history. But we did not know of Alexander Skutch's whereabouts and needed to press on. Here we saw several beautiful Passerini's Tanagers (*Ramphocelus passerinii*), which Skutch told us in his inimical style were what he rather called the Song Tanager. This subspecies, *Ramphocelus passerinii costaricensis*, occurs on the Pacific side of Costa Rica and has a more beautiful song than its relative on the Carribean side of the cordillera. The females may be distinguished in the field but not the brightly colored males, which Skutch reminded us in his almost poetic prose was an example of heterogynism.

The road deteriorated rapidly about sixteen miles beyond San Isidro and crossed tributaries of Río General as we descended. At one of these crossings we made a photo stop and saw a Green Kingfisher (*Chloroceryle americana*) and a pair of Scarlet-rumped Tanagers, noting the more colorful female of those seen on the Carribean side of the cordillera. We came to a short section of paved road, but it soon degenerated into a rough and unpaved passage, not what one would expect of the Pan-American Highway. In this country they use a short machete, probably to cut banana bunches, nicely sheathed in worked and decorated leather. We stopped to take a picture of a waterfall and watched a fight between a Common Ground–Dove (*Columbina passerina*) and a Tropical Kingbird (*Tyrannus melancholicus*) trying to live up to its scientific name.

When we arrived at the border of Costa Rica and Panama at 6:45 p.m. (7:45 on the Panama side), they were on some kind of break but opened at 7. We crossed through Costa Rican customs in ten minutes but were held up a considerable time on the Panamanian side by a bus traveling ahead of us. The Panamanians looked us over more than anyone in Central America, though even then not really seriously, simply looking quickly through about four bags. It had started raining hard at about 5 p.m. (Costa Rican time) and continued through the night. As we drove on through the early evening we saw many frogs and small snakes crossing the road before we arrived at the Rocio Hotel in Concepción, Panama, at about 9 p.m.

In the morning of April 9 we heard on the radio that there had been a flash flood at Boquete and at Cerro Punta in the area where we were headed. We called Capt. Horace Loftin at Albrook Air Force Base to check on the Florida State University Camp, and he said we might not be able to get there but to give it a try—so off we went. We climbed gradually up from Concepción, and on the road we picked up a DOR Pale-breasted Spinetail (*Synallaxis albescens*) nine miles north of Concepción. I skeletonized it, noting that it lacked central ossification in the skull roof but seemed near breeding condition. Loftin had told us to stop at Mr. Leonard Butz's house on the road up to Cerro Punta and inquire about conditions at the camp. At the road leading to Volcán the local police stopped us from climbing higher, so we turned and headed for the Dos Ríos Hotel in Volcán, which had been recommended by Horace Loftin. The Rufous-collared Sparrows were here with us, as they had been in the highlands since Chiapas. A pair of Blue-and-white Swallows was nesting under the eaves. Here we learned that two North Americans who had been living at Cerro Punta had been swept away in the flood and at least one other person had been swept away near Boquete.

I woke up early (April 10), anxious to see what birds were in the area. The Rufous-collared Sparrow and Mountain Wren (*Troglodytes solstitialis*) were singing as I hiked west along the road toward the Río Chiriquí Viejo. It felt good to be out walking again and enjoying a fascinating new area. I hiked rapidly to the river, where the force of the great flood was evident: the bridge and its approaches had been carried away. On the way back I watched a pair of Slate-throated Redstarts (yellow-breasted *Myioborus miniatus*) as they foraged in trees used as fencing around a cow pasture. They twisted the feet and fanned the tail like the red-breasted form seen in Chiapas and Morelos. Along a clear-running tributary of the Río Chiriquí Viejo I watched an American Pygmy Kingfisher (*Chloroceryle aenea*) capture its early breakfast and then a large jay went screeching over, a Black-chested Jay (*Cyanocorax affinis*), our ninth species of jay since leaving home.

Figure 7.5. Flooded road near Bambito, Panama, April 11, 1970. Photo by S. W. Eaton.

After breakfast we drove up the road as far as possible toward Cerro Punta to find Mr. Butz's house. Where we stopped for lunch the woods began, and we were treated to the singing of several Swainson's Thrushes (*Catharus ustulatus*). From our lunch spot I walked up the road and met a fellow who had had about one-third of his coffee plantation washed away in the flood. He told me where Mr. Butz's house was, and I was able to go back, get the camper, and drive up to the house. He graciously met me at the door and gave me the keys to the Florida State University and Audubon Society Camp. I planned to hike up there the next day, two miles beyond where we had gotten to today at about 5,700 feet.

I got up early, drove up to just below the bridge at Bambito, and parked the camper alongside the road where other cars and trucks were parked. With backpack, poncho, binocs, camera, and a little food I began the hike up to the camp along the road. The flood had come down through the town of Bambito, wiping out most of the houses on the east side of the stream, and just above the town it had taken all of the road out, but there was just enough room to walk around the edge of the hard volcanic rock. About three hundred yards upstream another wash had taken out the entire road. But the road from a low white ranch-style house up to the camp was still intact. I arrived there at about 9 a.m., opened three shuttered windows for light, and looked at the literature available and the guest book. The only person listed who had been there recently and whom I knew well was Henry Stevenson. After walking across a nearby creek and up a ridge behind the camp, I came to a dirt road leading up to a small finca, where there were many flowers. Along the road was a border of trees and an open pasture.

Here I saw my first pair of Collared Redstarts (*Myioborus torquatus*). This pair of beautiful warblers was hawking and peering for flying insects in the trees adjacent to the road. They depressed and laterally spread their tail feathers before launching out after their prey. It looked as though they were using tail action to flush the insects into the air for capture, but perhaps it was just an intention movement to flee, or to indicate to its partner "that's my bug." The depression of the tail was almost continuous and was followed by lateral extension of the tail feathers. The movement seemed quite different from that of the Slate-throated Redstart. In two minutes of observation I saw one scratch its head indirectly (over the wing). In the foraging of three pairs of Slate-throated Redstarts, seen nearby, only one showed much tail depression; the other two pairs tail-fanned and did little wing-flicking but no tail depression. This last behavior may indicate a stage in the reproductive cycle.

When I eventually returned to the camper, workers were making progress on restoring the road. It would probably be several weeks before even one lane of traffic could get to Bambito, but power was restored to lower Bambito. When I stopped by to return the key to Mr. Butz, he discovered that I had bees up north, and he told me about bees in his area. He said there was a species here that lived in the ground and produced honey, but they would not box and were ornery. There were two other species in Panama, there was always a honey flow, and the bees worked even in the rainy season.

The next day (April 12) I took a short hike before breakfast down the road to the west. Many birds were feeding in two fruit trees and a flowering tree, along with many butterflies. I also saw a pair of Elegant Euphonias (*Euphonia elegantissima*) building a nest. They visited a tent caterpillar's nest twice. Along the bank of the Río Chiriquí Viejo was a pair of gray birds with black caps that regularly held up their tails at an angle. This Tropical Gnatcatcher (*Polioptila plumbea*) seemed to prefer walking on logs, quite a different habitat than that of our northern species. Back at the Dos Ríos Hotel I retired to the upstairs porch overlooking some trees and a small stream to write up some notes. There were many interruptions as more birds appeared. The Blue-and-white Swallow nesting under the eaves flew from its nesting place with a large fecal sac, giving away its carefully guarded secret. And I looked up to see my first Buff-rumped Warbler (*Phaeothlypis fulvicauda*) on the ground near some rocks along the stream. It wagged its tail down and sideways like the Louisiana Waterthrush and, when on rocks and other flat, solid things, it seemed to run as the waterthrushes do. The rump patch was so obvious, perhaps another feature to accent its position, like the tail wagging. The tail movement was remarkably *Seiurus*-like, but then, when the bird got to an area where there were insects in the air and no good perch beneath, it gave its generic status away. It captured insects in the air four or five times in a row without touching the ground, and after about five minutes departed downstream.

We left the Dos Ríos Hotel the next morning (April 13) and drove down to Concepción and then southeast toward the Canal Zone. The usual roadside birds were seen as we traveled through open country. Just before leaving Chiriquí Province we saw a domestic turkey strutting in a farmyard, the first since Guatemala. We pulled into Mu Mu Diggings Motel on the Pacific Ocean at about 4 p.m., where among other birds a pair of Fork-tailed Flycatchers (*Tyrannus savana*) were feeding stub-tailed young, and some fruit-eating bats shared our bungalow, up in the rafters.

The drive to the Canal Zone was a short two hours, but before entering, in La Chorrera, Panama, we cashed an American Express traveler's check because our Costa Rican money was not accepted. Along the road to Balboa we saw flocks of Barn Swallows, perhaps fifty in a flock, still on the way north. At the border a fellow reluctantly took information from our car permit and we entered the Canal Zone. After Betty got our card number from the Smithsonian Tropical Research Institute headquarters, we got a room at the Tivoli Hotel and arranged for a one-week stay at Barro Colorado Island. We were required to get a permit to import the camper into Panama, and then we arranged for its export and booked passage home. After visiting several offices we decided to take passage on the Grace Line's *Santa Mariana* leaving on April 25 or thereabouts. The cost to Port Newark for shipping the camper was a little over four hundred dollars, probably less than the cost of driving it back.

We boarded the last daily train going east to Frijoles, where we got off and boarded the launch for Barro Colorado. We were soon climbing the two hundred steps up to the famous station. At the top, J. Hayden, the resident manager, was making maniacal comments about all the mail we had waiting. We had a nice supper and flopped into good digs, with a refrigerator and three other rooms, and, to the tune of several species of frogs, fell asleep in the very hot, humid tropics.

At about 5:15 a.m. on April 16 we awoke to a strange howling, which I assured Betty was not a jaguar but a couple of troops of howler monkeys (*Alouatta palliata*) establishing territory. After breakfast I went off on one of the many trails to look around. A Red-capped Manakin (*Pipra mentalis*) perched on a horizontal limb, and soon I became aware of army ants coming along a log in two large columns attended by antbirds—Spotted Antbird (*Hylophylax naevioides*), Dot-winged Antwren (*Microrhopias quixensis*), Ocellated Antbird (*Phaenostictus mcleannani*), and Plain Antvireo (*Dysithamnus mentalis*). On the side of a large tree trunk was a small dendrocolaptid hitching up the tree like a Brown Creeper (*Certhia americana*)—an Olivaceous Woodcreeper (*Sittasomus griseicapillus*). All the trails were labeled and numbered, usually with the name of a famous naturalist. I went out along Snyder Moline, to Ramon Shannon, then across AMNH to William Norton Wheeler, up to Tower, and down from Tower on Wheeler.

After lunch I looked over the library and met John and Lisa Oppenheimer, he a recent Ph.D. who worked on white-faced monkeys at the University of Illinois. Later I met Robin Foster from Duke University, who was working on seed distribution in tropical trees. He became an important link in Conservation International's Rapid Assessment Program. The next day (April 17), Robin invited us to circumnavigate the island in a motor boat to see the blooming of *Tabebuia guayacan*. Neal Smith had recorded the activity of the yellow-flowering tree for five years and had predicted this show to the very day. As we motored around the island, the beautiful show was particularly striking along the margin of Gatún Lake. Robin said the chances were that the flowers would all be gone in two or three days. He pointed out an epiphytic bromeliad about twenty feet up, and adjacent to it were two orchids, a yellow and a blue one. These orchids are usually found near the bromeliads, which have stinging ant colonies, so it is difficult to collect both the orchids and the bromeliad. We also saw numerous bird species, including Black Terns (*Chlidonias niger*) in a flock following a tarpon. About halfway around the island, after we had gone ashore, the motor failed to start. It was a great opportunity for us to benefit from a walking field trip back to headquarters with Robin, who was so well acquainted with the flora and such an excellent teacher. We learned much about the trees, their seeds, and the animals that fed on them.

I hiked to Fuertes House the next day (April 18), and on the way a beautiful morpho butterfly went wobbling through the forest. About fifty feet up in the forest a Canada Warbler (*Wilsonia canadensis*) foraged with antbirds and treecreepers. The warbler laterally flicked its tail with some slight depression of tail feathers. The leaf-cutting ant colony off Latham Trail, pointed out by Robin the day before, was working industriously. It had been photographed recently by the Time-Life people. Two peccaries (*Tayassu* sp.) crossed the trail ahead near F. Miller, and I heard a troop of howler monkeys calling to the north along the lake. A beautiful Keel-billed Toucan (*Ramphastos sulfuratus*) foraged above on fruits and gave its froglike call. I made it to the Fuertes House, then went back to headquarters. In the afternoon I read in the library about the snakes and flora of the island. The next day as I walked the trails I disturbed an anteater, which hissed as I approached to get a look. It climbed up a vine and then hid behind a palm frond. At Balboa 5 a large, spotted rodent ran across the trail, my first look at an agouti (*Dasyprocta*). At S. Molino 2.5 six to eight Red-capped Manakins were displaying at a lek, snapping their wings and giving *whee-whee whee-wheeing* notes. In the afternoon it started to rain, a clear start to the rainy season, so I looked over the bird skin collection, the herptile specimens, mammal skins, and the herbarium, handy reference collections of the American humid tropics.

Dee Bonker and I went canoeing the next afternoon. She was the wife of a retired colonel who had come to try to increase the strength of the transmitter. Along the edge of Gatún Lake a troop of white-faced monkeys foraged in a large tree that produced a green fruit with orange rind inside. John Oppenheimer said he had written about this in *Science* the previous July. While climbing up the bank of the lake to retrieve the fruit dropped by the monkeys, I saw a beautiful small frog, black with a blue cross on its back, sitting on the leaves of the forest floor. A semi-aquatic lizard with dorsal and caudal fins splashed ashore and then looked back at us. As darkness descended in the evening all sorts of animals showed up at the door of the kitchen, where the cook left bread—tapirs (*Tapirus bairdii*, which looked to be in the 300- to 400-pound range), agouti, coatimundi (*Nasua nasua*), kinkajou, a big woolly spider, and a giant toad.

We said good-bye to Barro Colorado on April 21 and took the train at Frijoles back to Balboa and the Tivoli Guest House. The next day we paid our bill for our stay at Barro Colorado and bought some clothes for going back to civilization. In the evening we went to a seminar presided over by M. Moynihan and given by Henry Hespenheider on foraging by swifts, swallows, and flycatchers. The next day (April 23) I went out to Madden Forest, where Eugene Morton said there were several Buff-rumped Warblers. I was interested in collecting a couple to determine the type of skull roof closing in this group of warblers. I parked at the stream near a green monument and soon located one. As I followed it upstream about three hundred yards it stayed along the stream, ran after a bug, and jumped up to a rock, and in thirty continuous minutes of observation, I saw it scratch indirectly (over the wing) twice. It sang one weak song during this period. From an elevated position the tail was depressed and the feathers spread slightly to the accompaniment of a side to side movement of the body, which was done by pivoting at the intertarsal and tarsometatarsal joints. When running, this tail pumping was absent, as in waterthrushes, but when the bird stopped, the pumping resumed. Before leaving the area I set a mist net in hopes of catching the Buff-rumped Warbler.

That evening there was a farewell dinner for the Oppenheimers, with guests including Robin Foster, Eugene Morton, a Polish couple, a girl from the University of Illinois studying fiddler crabs, and a fellow from Johns Hopkins on a predoc. The dinner was at the Panamar Restaurant down on the Pacific Ocean, and believe it or not, we watched the moon rise up over the Pacific Ocean. Robin had been collecting in highlands west of the Canal Zone and was excited about having discovered a new species of *Symphonia* (a tree or large shrub that was in flower and fruit).

After breakfast the next day, I drove out to Madden Forest to check the mist net. There were two Buff-rumped Warblers, a Cinnamon Becard (*Pachyramphus cinnamomeus*), two vampire bats, and two smaller leaf-nosed bats in the net. As I took it down and processed the specimens, another Buff-rumped Warbler was heard singing, so there were at least three individuals in the area. The warblers were a male and female and both showed the typical basileuteran skull roof closing. Windows remained in the parietal bone, and the second layer of bone was being added from an anterior to a posterior position on the parietal bone. The female appeared to have two postovulatory follicles, and the skeletal muscle in the male was superficially covered with small, light-colored parasites. The becard was a female with an egg in the enlarged ovary.

For the next three days (April 25–27) we explored areas in the Canal Zone and prepared for our journey home. One of the interesting sights from the Tivoli Hotel occurred after an afternoon shower, when about fifty Magnificent Frigatebirds (*Fregata magnificens*) and seventy-five Black Vultures located a thermal over Old Panama and circled upward, the frigatebirds above and the vultures below.

The *Santa Mariana* arrived and we boarded, found our room, and watched the dockhands load our camper in a seatainer and haul it aboard. We went through the Panama Canal, then up through the Yucatan Channel, and, following the Gulf Stream, pulled into Jacksonville, Florida, on past Cape Hatteras and into Norfolk, then up Chesapeake Bay to Baltimore, and from there we transited the canal across the Delmarva Peninsula and eventually pulled into Port Newark. And so our journey ended. On our long trip we had been able to observe and study most of the Central American warblers and we had learned of areas where, in the future, we might study the Ocellated Turkey. As we arrived off Norfolk, a Barn Swallow flew along with us for a while on its way north; this migratory species had been with us since the Yucatán. When the Barn Swallow returned to western New York later that spring, we appreciated more than ever the remarkable nature of bird migration.

8

My Early Mexican Travels

ERNEST P. EDWARDS

After receiving his Ph.D. from Cornell University (1949), Ernest P. Edwards taught at the University of Kentucky and the University of the Pacific. He then he went on to a long career as a faculty member at Sweet Briar College, Virginia, where he is professor emeritus. The trips reported here were part of the research that went into multiple books on birds and bird watching in Mexico (e.g., Edwards 1955, 1972, 1998).

With the surrender of Germany on May 8, 1945, and the surrender of Japan on August 14, 1945, World War II came to a close, and the eagerly awaited demobilization of the citizen-army of the United States began. Although some of us who had left the Laboratory of Ornithology at Cornell University in 1941 or 1942 to enter the armed forces would not be mustered out until another six months to a year had passed, we began to plan for the day when we could return to our studies. Those who had served the longest were mustered out most quickly, and some were able to return to Cornell as early as the spring semester of 1946. Others, including me, were not released from the armed forces until that semester was nearly over, and consequently we planned to wait until the fall semester to resume coursework and research projects after a four-year hiatus.

Ithaca, New York, to McAllen, Texas

Thus it was that with our newfound freedom from the regimentation of life in the armed forces, with an open summer ahead, and with some money saved from our service pay, Steve Eaton and I planned to follow the footsteps of other Cornellians into northern Mexico and then test the limits of passable roads southward on an opportunistic ornithological expedition.

Stephen W. Eaton had come to the Ornithology "Grad Lab" in the autumn of 1941 to work toward an advanced degree under the direction of Dr. Arthur A. Allen. Steve had graduated that spring from Hobart College in his

Figure 8.1. Some of the students in the Laboratory of Ornithology, Cornell University, 1940–41. *Back row (left to right):* William Montagna, Lloyd Hulbert, Henry Stevenson, J. Southgate Hoyt, Ernest (Buck) Edwards. Middle: John Wannamaker, Dwain Warner, Steve Eaton. *Front:* Robert Lea, Oliver Hewitt, Allan Phillips. Photo courtesy D. W. Warner.

hometown of Geneva, New York, and he was already keenly interested in, and knowledgeable about, the birds of the Finger Lakes Region. His father, Elon Howard Eaton, had taught in the Biology Department at Hobart College and had written the definitive book on the birds of New York State, a two-volume work entitled *The Birds of New York*, published in 1910 by the New York State Museum. Steve would resume his formal ornithological studies at Cornell in the fall of 1946, going on to write his doctoral dissertation on the life history of the Louisiana Waterthrush (*Seiurus motacilla*), and then accepting a teaching position at St. Bonaventure College in western New York State.

I had come to Cornell to begin graduate work in the summer of 1940, about a month after graduating from the University of Virginia, not far from my home in Sweet Briar, Virginia, where my father was a professor at Sweet Briar College. Not being certain whether I could scrape up the funds needed to continue at Cornell in the autumn, I took all three of the summer-school courses in ornithology then available with Dr. Allen and Dr. Peter Paul Kellogg, a total immersion in ornithology for about sixteen to eighteen hours each day. I was able to continue there in the fall, and I was soon a member of the Grad Lab, working with Dr. Kellogg on the hearing capabilities of birds. My plans for the doctoral dissertation would change, however, after the war and after my trip to Mexico, and when I resumed my studies at Cornell in the fall of 1946 my coursework was combined with an ecological and distributional study of the birds of the Lake Pátzcuaro basin in central Mexico. When that was completed in the fall of 1949, I accepted a teaching position at the University of Kentucky.

Our preparations for the trip to Mexico consisted mainly of assembling basic camping equipment and supplies, field clothing (mostly our army khakis and boots), and what books we could find for reference material. The first field guides to Mexican birds and bird finding would not be published until the mid-1950s. Transportation was our big problem, because none of us had enough money to buy an automobile, and we would have had to wait months on a long waiting list even if we had had the money. But Steve's mother was very generous and willing to let us use her car for the summer. If we could have imagined the pounding the car would suffer we might not have asked to borrow it, but with the help of numerous Mexican mechanics and tire repairmen, we did manage to bring it back two and a half months later still in drivable condition, albeit much the worse for wear. My discharge from the army (after about a month of accumulated terminal leave) was effective on May 28, and on June 1 we left Ithaca, New York, driving south to Virginia and on to the Gulf Coast, and then westward and southward toward the Mexican border.

I was reminded of my southern heritage during a brief stopover at my home in Virginia, when we not only heard and saw some birds that were not common around Ithaca but also found that in the nearby small town of Amherst, the bank was closed on June 3 because that was the anniversary of Jefferson Davis's birthday, and I was unable to cash a check.

Leaving Sweet Briar with less money in our pockets than we would have liked, we nevertheless savored our leisurely exploration of the territory between Virginia and the Mexican border. We allowed ourselves nine full days to reach south Texas, "birding" the most interesting places along the way (the term did not exist in 1946). There were many memorable moments before we even reached the border, but the events of a forty-eight-hour period in coastal and near-coastal areas of western Louisiana and eastern Texas stood out.

Near Crowley, Louisiana, where the highway led through flat, wet fields planted with rice, we found a Purple Gallinule (*Porphyrio martinica*) that had recently been killed by an automobile. The bird was beautiful, with its glossy olive green back, purple breast, white undertail coverts, and bright red bill yellow-tipped. The blue casque on the forehead was still colored as in life.

Over a distance of several miles through the rice fields, we saw recently killed Purple Gallinules and King Rails (*Rallus elegans*) on the highway at the rate of two or three birds per mile in some places. A family of rails that we saw later illustrated why they were at great risk. They all ran about halfway across the road, then turned back as we approached more closely, then after we passed and stopped they all started across the road again; then, as we backed up slowly to get a better view, two of the young ones broke away from the group and returned to their starting point while the others finally reached the other side.

The next day we encountered a somewhat similar situation in the marshes along the highway in the vicinity of Sabine Pass, Texas, where we saw two or three dead Least Bitterns (*Ixobrychus exilis*) per mile. This seemed strange, because we felt that the bitterns, not likely to walk or run across the highway as did the rails and gallinules, might not be threatened by highway traffic. However, one individual that flew across in front of us (safely this time), appeared to fly closely enough to the surface of the raised highway, and slowly enough, to be at great risk, especially from large, fast-moving trucks.

Later that same day we drove through intermittent heavy showers as we approached Bay City. During the heaviest downpours our tires sent great showers of water up and off to the side, and as we drove through some of the lower-lying streets of the city the car was up to its hubcaps in water. Farther along, as we drove toward Port Lavaca, we saw our first Scissor-tailed Flycatcher (*Tyrannus forficatus*) perched on a telephone wire along the highway in the rain. Then the sun came out just before setting and made a beautiful rainbow in the east. The bow was a complete semicircle and arched high toward the zenith, because the sun was so low in the west. Within the circle of the rainbow the clouds were lit up, while the clouds immediately outside the circle were still dark. Soon some blue sky appeared ahead and, as the rainbow gradually faded, a beautiful sunset lit up the western skies.

Driving late into the night again, we checked several "tourist courts" in Corpus Christi and other towns along the highway but found no suitable accommodations. Finally, when we saw only "No Vacancy" signs in Kingsville, we drove on out of town up a side road near a large emergency landing field with a beacon and put our cots out on the ground. We covered ourselves with a mosquito net and went to sleep at about 1 a.m., not lulled by frequent flashes of lightning.

We woke up at about 3 and had not yet gone back to sleep again when it started raining. We had to retreat to the car. We left everything but the sleeping bags outside, because it was raining so hard that we would have gotten soaked if we had stayed outside to retrieve the cots, etc. We slept in the car for about two hours, then decided we might as well drive on to Brownsville. We got out and folded the cots during a lull in the rain and set off for Brownsville at about 6 a.m.

We had gone only about five miles when we came upon a woman by herself trying to push an incredibly muddy car, so we stopped to help. Steve learned that she was just trying to push it off the road to leave it because it was out of gas. We took her to a filling station, where she woke up the man and bought a bucket of gas. Back at the car, Steve poured most of the gas into the tank and a little into the carburetor, and after a few tries the motor caught and everything seemed to be alright. The woman was grateful, and we headed southward.

We arrived in Brownsville at about 9:30 a.m., found a pleasant room with twin beds at the Charro Courts for three dollars per night and reserved it for two nights. After sleeping for about three hours we commenced two days of birding in the Lower Rio Grande Valley, buying additional supplies and preparing to enter Mexico south of McAllen. (We could have crossed the bridge from Brownsville to Matamoros, but at that time there was no highway south from Matamoros.)

When the day came to cross the border, we drove south from McAllen to the small Texas town of Hidalgo, where we passed through American customs and then across the bridge to the outskirts of Reynosa, where we passed through Mexican customs. We encountered little difficulty on either side of the border, having already obtained Mexican car insurance and tourist cards, and having filled out the various forms and affidavits in various offices in Brownsville.

Then, with the proper seals on our suitcases and our tourist cards stamped and signed, we drove into Reynosa, which at that time was a little town with adobe houses and dirt streets—very rough. There were no road signs or other indications of the road to Monterrey, but we soon found a paved highway leading out of town and were on our way.

The Lowlands of Northeastern Mexico

There was no mistaking the fact that we had come into a different country. It seemed completely strange and exciting and interesting. In terms of bird life and plant associations, it is true that the change was not dramatic. Here in northeastern Mexico the great expanses of arid terrain closely resembled the undisturbed areas just north of the border in Texas, where we had already seen the Inca Dove (*Columbina inca*), Golden-fronted Woodpecker (*Melanerpes aurifrons*), and White-tailed Hawk (*Buteo albicaudatus*). But the people and the human environment seemed entirely different, even from what we had seen for the first time in the Lower Rio Grande Valley in Texas, where many highway signs were printed in both English and Spanish.

Reynosa, Tamaulipas, to Linares, Nuevo León

West of Reynosa we drove through a flat, semidesert land, seldom turning a curve and seldom ascending or descending a hill. It might have seemed monotonous had we not been so interested in the thick, scrubby growth that extended with little change for miles. In this great expanse of sagebrush, cactus, and assorted small thorny shrubs and dry grasses were many Greater Roadrunners (*Geococcyx californianus*), White-winged Doves (*Zenaida asiatica*), Pyrrhuloxias (*Cardinalis sinuatus*), Black-throated Sparrows (*Amphispiza bilineata*), and other species that we had seen previously only in south Texas or that were completely new to us.

Passing through the small towns of General Bravo and China (pronounced "chee-na") we began a gradual climb toward the approximately 1,800 feet elevation of Mexico's great northern metropolis, the city of Monterrey. As the highway turned and ascended, and occasionally descended, it was still flanked by generally the same scrubby, thorny vegetation characteristic of the broad, low-lying plains through which we had just passed.

Before long, the impressive buildings of northern Mexico's largest city materialized in the distance, and soon we were driving along admiring the beautiful avenues connecting the suburbs with the main business section of Monterrey. One of our first concerns was to find a gasoline station and top off our tank (at twenty cents a gallon, full service); there we received detailed instructions from the attendant on how to find the highway south to Linares and Victoria. In the process of following these instructions we made more than our share of wrong turns, but with the help of numerous traffic policemen and friendly pedestrians we finally made the right choice and got on the highway leading southeastward into a verdant valley carpeted with groves of citrus trees. The peak of Cerro de la Silla (Saddle Hill or Mountain) rose to our left, and the rugged peaks and ridges of the northeasternmost ranges of the Sierra Madre Oriental flanked the highway on the right.

Reaching Linares at dusk, we obtained accommodations in a pleasant motel—the Canada Courts, operated by Mr. and Mrs. Colin Hardwicke, originally from Canada. We had been alerted to the presence of this delightful motel by Dr. George Miksch Sutton, Dwain Warner, and Bob Lea, fellow Cornellians who had stayed at the Canada Courts briefly en route to and from the Rancho Rinconada in southern Tamaulipas. It was too late to get supper at the Canada Courts, so we went up town to the café in the hotel and had steak for four pesos (about eighty cents).

We had scheduled a three-and-a-half-day sojourn at the Canada Courts, and even though we could have seen some of the same birds as far north as southern Texas, it was in Linares that we really began to savor the newness of the bird life of Mexico. In groves of pecan trees we saw Rose-throated Becards (*Pachyramphus aglaiae*) at their bulky nests; watched a pair of Social Flycatchers (*Myiozetetes similis*) and a Great Kiskadee (*Pitangus sulphuratus*); heard for the first time the raucous scolding of Brown Jays (*Cyanocorax morio*) when we trespassed into their territory; and found an occupied nest of the Audubon's Oriole (*Icterus graduacauda*). There, too, were the Tufted (Black-crested) Titmouse (*Baeolophus bicolor*), the Tropical Parula (*Parula pitiayumi*), and the familiar Yellow-breasted Chat (*Icteria virens*) and Blue Grosbeak (*Passerina caerulea*).

On our first "working" afternoon in Linares we made a side trip up a canyon that led into the range of magnificent mountains that we had seen lying off to the west ever since we had left Monterrey. These mountains were rugged and arid, with jagged peaks, steep rocky slopes, and only the barest covering of cactus and other thorny vegetation. But in the stream-cut canyons the trees were taller and greener, and the woodlands seemed almost luxuriant in comparison with the parched, open slopes. There we saw the red and iridescent green Elegant Trogon (*Trogon elegans*), while Brown Jays scolded and the loud calls of the Plain Chachalaca (*Ortalis vetula*) echoed up and down the canyon. There too, late in the afternoon, we heard the incomparable song of the Brown-backed Solitaire (*Myadestes occidentalis*), completely new to us, its medley of notes seeming to cascade down the canyon toward us. Turning back toward Linares we saw high overhead a small flock of Band-tailed Pigeons (*Patagioenas fasciata*) sweeping across the canyon, hinting that pine woodlands might be hidden somewhere on the higher slopes of the mountains. As we emerged from the mouth of the canyon we saw a brilliant Vermilion Flycatcher (*Pyrocephalus rubinus*), perfectly at home in the semidesert at the foot of the mountains.

At night, on those same semidesert flatlands between Linares and the mountain slopes, we found the exciting night birds of northern Mexico. The Chip-willow, or Buff-collared Nightjar (*Caprimulgus ridgwayi*), voiced its name, a clear, persistently repeated *chip-willo*, while the Common Pauraque (*Nyctidromus albicollis*) called a buzzy *per-wee-er*. The latter species was abundant there, and on a night walk down a desert path we frightened one from the ground and watched it flutter away, its wings and tail flashing patches of white in the moonlight. Sometimes a Common Pauraque would rest in the middle of the gravel road, its eyes glowing a fiery orange, reflecting the beams of the automobile headlights as we drove toward it. Not until the automobile approached within a few yards of the bird would it fly up and away, often coming back to rest on the road farther along.

In the early morning, along the Río Camacho, we found another rewarding place to look for birds. We saw our first Green Kingfisher (*Chloroceryle americana*) there. It was a diminutive bird that perched quietly for a time and then plunged into the water to catch a small fish. Soon it flew purposefully upstream to search another pool.

Although there were four of us working through the undergrowth along the river (the two Hardwicke sons, Norman and Gerald, had joined us), the group was soon split up by the lure of different bird voices and different flashes of color. I moved upstream, following the call of the Elegant Trogon, always hoping to get a better view of it. One of the others, who had seen the trogon well the previous day, was more interested in following an owl that had flown a short distance downstream. It proved to be a Mottled Owl (*Ciccaba virgata*), much more likely to be heard at night than to be seen in the daytime. Another of our group wanted to get a good look at the chachalacas, which were making a racket in the thickets across the river. Finally we converged at a point where a small, colorful bird was singing a very musical, complicated series of phrases in the top of a small tree at the water's edge. With its yellow underparts and rich brown, black, and white around the head, it turned out that it was a distinctively tropical warbler, the Rufous-capped Warbler (*Basileuterus rufifrons*).

Tent Camp on the Mesa de Llera

When we left Linares after our first few days in Mexico, we drove southward through arid country cut by dry arroyos. About twenty miles south of Victoria and at about the point where the highway crossed the Tropic of Cancer, the road began to twist and turn and climb, up over a series of flat-topped mesas and buttes and down into the valleys between them, and we began to watch for signs that might mark the Mesa de la Angostura, a scenic spot that Dwain Warner and Bob Mengel had recommended after they had visited Mexico briefly in the early 1940s.

We soon came to a sign for Puerto de la Angostura and then shortly after that, on the same mesa, a sign saying Mesa de Llera. We picked out a beautiful camping site at the south side of the mesa, where there is an overlook about a hundred yards off the road from the point where it begins to swing down and around off the mesa to the valley below. The outlook was spectacular, with other mesas far off in the distance and a couple of buttes sticking up, just as Bob Mengel had depicted them in a drawing he had made when he camped there in 1941. Later we saw the evening flights of parrots, which had figured prominently in the drawing.

The flat top of the Mesa de Llera, several hundred hectares in extent, was covered mainly by a relatively dense growth of prickly-pear cactus (*Opuntia*), thorny shrubs, and much tall grass with scattered, small, thorny trees. The steep rocky sides of the mesa were more sparsely covered by similar vegetation. The grass was brown and appeared lifeless, and the branches of most of the trees and shrubs had just begun to show touches of green in response to the first sporadic rains of the summer rainy season. We set up our tent and cots close to the rim of the mesa, where we looked out over the lowlands to the southeast. We put up mosquito nets as a precautionary measure, but it proved to be unnecessary.

That night we were occasionally awakened by the soon-to-be familiar sound of heavy trucks grinding ever-so-slowly up the steep grade on the side of the mesa, or grinding down the grade only a little more rapidly with screeching or hissing brakes and rhythmic backfiring. These trucks, along with buses of all sizes and mostly venerable ages, were the undisputed masters of the roads throughout the country, from city streets and paved highways to nearly impassable country roads. Whenever the drivers had to stop to mend a blown-out tire or make other repairs, or simply to sleep after long hours of driving, they might pull off partly or completely onto the shoulder, but as often as not, in those years, they would park fully in the right-hand lane of a two-lane road. We frequently encountered a truck parked in that manner, whether close beyond a blind curve or far out on a long straightaway, with only a few big rocks placed at intervals on the road behind it to warn of the danger. Here at the Mesa de Llera, with mesquite grassland stretching for miles around, and with only widely scattered small ranchitos and the small village of Llera a few miles away, the slow, noisy passage of an occasional heavy truck seemed oddly more reassuring than annoying, particularly at night.

Early on the first morning of our sojourn on the mesa we spent an hour or so sitting in front of our tent watching the birds that were flying below us and listening to their peculiar calls. Most of the songs and calls were unfamiliar, although we could place some of them in a general way, as probably wrens or jays or sparrows or doves. We could gradually make more definitive identifications as a singing bird would come to the edge of a nearby thicket or move into view in the bare branches of a small tree a short distance below us. In that manner we watched and identified our first Botteri's Sparrow (*Aimophila botterii*), singing its short, tinkling song atop a small yucca a few dozen yards away. We heard and saw Yellow-billed Cuckoos (*Coccyzus americanus*) in the valley and on the edge of the mesa, then were amazed that another cuckoo song we heard, much like that of the Yellow-billed but ending in several much deeper, more guttural notes, proved once we saw the bird to be that of the Mangrove Cuckoo (*Coccyzus minor*), seeming completely out of place in these thorny, scrubby thickets on dry, rocky terrain. While this individual remained nearby we heard another one in the valley just off the mesa to the east.

Dwain Warner had described and imitated the call of the Rufescent (Thicket) Tinamou (*Crypturellus cinnamomeus*) before we left Cornell and had alerted us to the possibility that we might hear tinamous calling from the base of the steep sides of the mesa. Consequently, when we heard a loud, clear, oft-repeated whistle we linked it in our minds with that species—correctly, as it turned out.

Other birds were more readily identified by visual cues. Occasionally we caught sight of Red-crowned Parrots (*Amazona viridigenalis*) flying down the ravine to the east of us, and once a pair of Green Parakeets (*Aratinga holochlora*) flew past our vantage point. By far the most common bird was the White-winged Dove (*Zenaida asiatica*), which flew in flocks as large as thirty birds down the valley beneath us and sometimes just over our heads, coming to within ten feet of us at times. Turkey Vultures (*Cathartes aura*) and Black Vultures (*Coragyps atratus*) often soared close to us also, as did the small Tamaulipas Crow (*Corvus imparatus*) and the White-necked (Chihuahuan) Raven (*Corvus cryptoleucus*).

Venturing farther afield, we made our way northeastward, away from the highway and through the thickets bordering the mesa, until we came to a more gently sloping portion of the generally steep-sided mesa. There we clambered down the rocky slopes through the dense vegetation, stopping occasionally to search more intensively for a singing bird or to rest on a large rock while picking off some of the many ticks of various sizes that clung to our trousers. A tiny larval tick, called a *pinolillo*, about one-tenth the size of a pin head or smaller, would be brushed off a plant onto our trousers, along with several or many dozens of its siblings in a small clump, which then seemed to spread like a drop of water on a paper towel as the ticks crawled away from the center. We could easily brush them off with a leafy switch if we discovered them soon enough. The adult ticks, called *garrapatas*, could be effectively removed also, when discovered, but had to be picked off individually. In most cases we would eventually find that one or two or a few individuals of assorted sizes had escaped detection long enough to begin feasting on our blood.

Near the foot of the slope I heard the now familiar call of a Thicket Tinamou nearby, and I clambered atop a small boulder and sat down to search the undergrowth more carefully. In the hope of luring the bird into view, I began imitating its whistle at intervals. The bird continued to call in response to my imitation and to move toward the slightly more open space surrounding "my" boulder. Although the tinamou finally stood not more than ten feet away and continued to trade calls with me for a few suspenseful minutes, it never emerged from the denser undergrowth, and it soon moved gradually farther and farther away, still calling. (Later, using this same method, I was frequently able to attract a tinamou to nearby thickets, and was finally able to lure one close enough for a good view on two occasions, once even for some hurried motion pictures, in the scrubby woodlands and *huapilla* thickets near the Río Sabinas and in the cloud forests near the Rancho del Cielo.)

Farther down the side of the mesa, where the terrain leveled off somewhat and where more moisture could accumulate, birds were more active and more readily visible than on the steeper slopes. Among them were three of the brightly colored species of the area and a counterbalancing three with plain, rather drab plumage. The Green Jay (*Cyanocorax yncas*) was the most colorful, with its bright yellows, yellowish greens, blue, and black; its eye color was brown, the same as that of the Green Jay in the Lower Rio Grande Valley of Texas. We were to confirm later that the eye color of this jay's southern counterparts, for example those in central and southern Veracruz, was bright yellow. The Fan-tailed Warbler (*Euthlypis lachrymosa*) was not only dapper in its dark bluish gray, bright yellow, tawny, and white but also intrigued us by its behavior, moving about mainly on the ground or in small shrubs, frequently spreading its black tail and displaying the white tail-corners prominently. The green, blue, and rich rufous Blue-crowned Motmot (*Momotus momota*) was notable for its call, reminiscent of that of a dove, and its racket-tipped tail, which it sometimes swung abruptly from side to side, especially when alarmed, sometimes voicing a clucking alarm note at the same time. Some Mexicans have called the bird *pájaro reloj* (the clock bird), likening its tail motion to that of a clock pendulum.

Much less conspicuous in behavior and plumage colors, but each with notable songs or calls, were the White-tipped Dove (*Leptotila verreauxi*), Clay-colored Thrush (*Turdus grayi*), and White-bellied Wren (*Uropsila leucogastra*). We found the frail twig nest, about ten feet above the ground in a small dead tree, and heard the mournful *oo-ooo* of the dove, but we caught only fleeting glimpses of it as it flew from the nest and walked ahead of us. In later years its call would become a familiar sound in the tropical forests and thorny woodlands where we worked, but we seldom saw the bird well unless we came upon it feeding along a small dirt road or track. Then it would display its only prominent markings, the white tips of the tail feathers, when it flew up with tail spread.

The Clay-colored Thrush, common in the less arid pockets of vegetation on the slopes, was even more plainly colored than the White-tipped Dove, being almost entirely buffy brown, with darker wings and tail and obscure streaks on the pale throat. Its song was pleasant, somewhat like that of the American Robin, and one of its calls was very unusual, a loud, musical, somewhat petulant *pee-u-u-woot*, voiced mainly when it was agitated, particularly just before going to roost.

The rarest among these plainly colored birds, somewhat brighter in plumage and also perhaps the most fascinating, was the White-bellied Wren. It is smaller than a House Wren (*Troglodytes aedon*) and has a much shorter and more staccato song—*chip-it-ti-pee*—which it sometimes shortened to *tuwit-yu*. Its mostly white underparts and superciliary line contrasted with the reddish brown of its upperparts, wings, and tail. When John Boehm, Robert B. Lea, and I stopped at the Mesa de Llera the following spring, we saw and heard a White-bellied Wren and were able to find its nest. Because not much was known at that time about its nesting habits or the color of its eggs, Dr. Sutton, who had joined that expedition for a couple of weeks, reached carefully into the small tubular entrance and extracted an egg. Although the nest is basically a neater version of the retort-shaped, completely enclosed nest of the Banded Wren (*Thryothorus pleurostictus*) and some other tropical *Thryothorus* wrens, its eggs were blue, unlike the white eggs of most birds that nest in cavities or in completely enclosed nests.

When it was time for Steve and me to break camp and leave the Mesa de Llera to continue our southward journey, we packed up all our belongings, drove northward first to Victoria to pick up mail and supplies, and then retraced our path southward to the mesa. Continuing past our campsite, we immediately began the long, winding, steep descent that we had heard so many trucks make from the top of the mesa southward to the valley of the Río Guayalejo.

Pano Ayuctle and the Río Sabinas

We crossed the broad floodplain of the Río Guayalejo on a long bridge that spanned much more than the few small channels where there was a shallow but steady flow of water. The flowing water was bright blue, not completely transparent, but seemingly carrying some tiny particles producing a translucent powder-blue tone that we saw in several of the small rivers of northeastern Mexico, particularly during the dry season. We surmised that at the height of the rainy season the river would be filled with rushing muddy water from bank to bank, because all the way across the wide river bed we could see that the rocks, even those as large as basketballs or larger, were smooth and rounded as a result of much tumbling in swift currents.

Beyond the Río Guayalejo we entered a more luxuriant region. In the low-lying flatlands, mostly east of the highway, we saw fields of sugar cane, corn, and pineapples, and vast groves of palm trees. Close at hand, to the west of the highway, the lower foothills of the Sierra Madre Oriental supported a dense growth of medium-sized forest rather than scrubby, thorny woodland and chaparral, while the successively higher mountain slopes farther to the west were covered with tall tropical forest. Occasionally parrots flew in pairs over the highway, while along the borders of the woodlands (and even on some telephone wires and power lines along the highway) the hanging nests of the Altamira Oriole (*Icterus gularis*) swayed in the warm breeze.

By this time we were checking the small side roads and ranches along the highway in the hope of finding the Rancho Rinconada, a small ranch in southern Tamaulipas on the Río Sabinas later made famous by George Sutton in his book *At a Bend in a Mexican River* (1972). Dr. Sutton, Dwain Warner, and Robert B. Lea had spent some weeks there in the spring of 1941 along with Dr. Olin Sewall Pettingill before going into military service in World War II. At Cornell, Sutton, Warner, and Lea had regaled us with details of their ornithological experiences there, and after the war Dwain had provided us with a sketch map to help us find the ranch.

When we reached the highway crossing of the Río Sabinas, about 100 km south of Victoria, having gone beyond the side road that would have led us to the Rancho Rinconada, according to the sketch map, we turned around and began to retrace our path and intensify our search by following some of the side roads and making numerous inquiries at a filling station and at ranch houses; one house was owned by a Frenchman who said he had lived there thirty-six years. We finally narrowed our choices to two ranches, one owned by a General Gonzales, and one owned by an American named Everts Storms. We decided to try the Storms ranch first.

And so it was that we finally left the highway about five miles north of where it crossed the Río Sabinas and drove westward toward the base of the mountains along a rough, rutted, dirt and rock road through sugar cane fields and thorny woodlands. After a couple of miles this road led to a small ranch known in the Huastecan language as Pano Ayuctle, and in Spanish as Paso Calabasas, the home of Everts Storms. We learned later that Don Everisto, as he was known locally, had grown up mostly in Mexico, the son of the American consul in Victoria, and had then settled on this small ranch close to the banks of the beautiful blue Río Sabinas, where he would live for the rest of his life. This place, as it turned out, was not the Rancho Rinconada renamed. That distinction belonged to the property now owned by General Gonzales and now called the Rancho Pico de Oro.

It soon became apparent, however, that even if the fabled Rancho Rinconada could have been reincarnated in all its past glory, it could hardly have been a more exhilarating and rewarding setting for our first experiences in the humid tropics than this place called Pano Ayuctle. Complete strangers though we were, and without mutual friends or even acquaintances, we nevertheless received a warm welcome and were urged to make the ranch our home for as long as we wished. When we expressed our desire to camp for a few days beside the Río Sabinas, Mr. Storms was cordial in showing us the way to the river, and later he sent a boy down with us to show us a good place to camp at another spot on the river. We chose the latter place to camp, and after a while we drove down and set up our tent, cots, and mosquito nets. The Río Sabinas is beautiful. The first sight we had of it was much as it has been pictured at the Rancho Rinconada. We saw blue water swinging around a right-angled turn under huge cypress trees draped with Spanish moss. We heard Red-crowned Parrots and saw them flying and screaming about the big cypresses down the river.

We camped in a small clearing that had originally been prepared for sugar cane processing, situated in the narrow strip of woodland atop the east bank of the river and about ten feet above the normal water level. Our tent was sheltered by towering cypress trees, and we could look down upon a deep, quiet section of the river and watch the giant Ringed Kingfisher (*Megaceryle torquata*) and the tiny Green Kingfisher flash past, and follow the progress of the Neotropic Cormorant (*Phalacrocorax brasilianus*) even when it swam beneath the surface in its quest for fish. Occasionally we plunged into the cold, greenish blue waters of the river to bathe or swim after the exertions of hours in the field. When we swam at night, the deep pools at times seemed dark and forbidding, and I would feel the odd sensation of not wanting to let my feet sink far below the surface toward the dark depths. On other nights the river seemed cool and inviting, sparkling with moonlight filtered through the lacy cypress leaves and branches.

Camping there at a point barely three hundred highway miles south of the border, and much less than that in a straight line, we learned that the entire aspect of the vegetation and animal life was richly tropical, from the broad valley of the Río Sabinas to the 3,500-foot crest of the first big mountain ridge to the west. With the first light of dawn, parrots and parakeets milled around by the hundreds among and over the upper branches of the cypress trees for which the river was named, and they flew back and forth between the riverside and the forests that bordered the fertile river valley.

Several times a trim Bat Falcon (*Falco rufigularis*) raced across the tops of the very trees under which we camped, sending Red-crowned Parrots and Red-lored Parrots (*Amazona autumnalis*) screaming in all directions. Then it would alight and perch among the topmost branches, apparently without making any real effort to catch one of the big, tough parrots. Although the falcon appeared at first glance to perch quietly, more careful observation showed that it was almost constantly moving its head, scanning the air above and below and on all sides, ever alert for potential prey of the proper size. Once we watched the Bat Falcon make a picture-perfect, sweeping, sailing dive toward a large insect in the air below, miss its mark, then recover and fly rapidly back to capture the prey successfully in a more mundane manner.

Within a few hours, working on field notes beside our tent or ranging only a few dozen feet into the nearby cultivated fields and patches of low woodland, we became acquainted with many tropical birds completely new to us. The concept of "life birds," or adding new birds to our life list, would have seemed strange to us there in the summer of 1946. And the first field guide to the birds of Mexico was still at least seven years in the future. We simply savored each new bird, observing distinctive features of its plumage, noting its habitat preferences, learning its song and call notes, studying its behavior and interactions with other birds in the vicinity, and finally making a tentative identification with the help of the few reference books and journal articles we had brought with us. We might have been able to see a few of these birds during our first week in Linares or at the Mesa de Llera, or even in south Texas, but most were at or very near the northern ends of their normal ranges here in the valley of this tropical river.

One of the first of these to approach our camp site, emerging from a bordering thicket where it had been scolding and chattering almost as if in a panic, was a bird with a heavy black bill and mostly black head, looking like some overgrown, ungainly grosbeak. As it flew low from branch to branch around the edge of the small clearing along with a few others of its kind, we could see that it had a white throat bordered with black and a distinctive yellowish green back, wings and tail. We tentatively identified it as a saltator, and looking through our references, found that the Black-headed Saltator (*Saltator atriceps*) was indeed to be expected in this part of Mexico.

Familiar with the songs of the Northern Parula (*Parula americana*) and the Red-eyed Vireo (*Vireo olivaceus*) in the eastern United States, we easily detected the presence of numerous Tropical Parulas (*Parula pitiayumi*; which we called

Figure 8.2. Tent camp and skins drying, eight miles west of Tehuantepec, July 16, 1946. Photo by S. W. Eaton.

Sennett's Warbler in those days) and Yellow-green Vireos (*Vireo flavoviridis*), which sang frequently from the upper branches of the cypress trees along the river. We could seldom see the vireos well in spite of their abundance, but we were able to follow family groups of the Tropical Parula with our binoculars and note that some individuals (immature birds, no doubt) were much duller and grayer above and duller yellow below than the others. The Spanish moss, which hung in great abundance from the cypress branches, provided nesting material and nest sites not only for the Tropical Parula but also for the Social Flycatcher (*Myiozetetes similis*), the Yellow-throated Euphonia (*Euphonia hirundinacea*), and the Scrub Euphonia (*Euphonia affinis*), among others, and we sometimes had difficulty determining whether these birds were entering a particular clump of Spanish moss to gather nesting material, get something to eat, build a nest in the clump, or tend an existing nest.

The Social Flycatcher, with its bright yellow belly and black-and-white head, although common and conspicuous in the scrubby woodlands and scattered trees throughout the region, seemed to have a particular affinity for tree branches growing out over a river or small pond. Pairs or small groups of these flycatchers were almost always in evidence directly over the waters of the Río Sabinas, even where only a few trees lined the banks. The birds perched or fluttered "nervously" around the clumps of epiphytes, and though seldom seen alone, they frequently seemed to be petulant and antagonistic toward any bird that happened to be nearby, scolding persistently and spreading their wings and fluttering even when perched. The roughly globular nests of the Social Flycatcher were conspicuous in the sparse foliage of the small, thorny trees away from the river, but we had much greater difficulty pinpointing a nest among the many clumps of Spanish moss and other epiphytes over the river.

Close at hand we found Blue-crowned Motmots nesting in holes dug into the dirt banks along the river and in the clay banks of the small arroyos that drained into the river. From our camp we could hear their unobtrusive *hoot-hoot* call notes and occasionally watch as an individual switched its racket-tipped tail spasmodically from side to side.

Among the orchids and other massed epiphytes of the riparian woodland we saw both Yellow-throated and Scrub euphonias for the first time, tiny yellow and steel-blue-black tanagers that fed on the sticky-pulped fruit of the tropical mistletoe and nested in dense clumps of epiphytes. The males were almost identical in size and in their patterns of the blacks and yellows in the plumage, but the Scrub Euphonia was slightly the smaller of the two and had a black throat. The females were even more nearly alike, and the slightly whiter belly of the Yellow-throated Euphonia and the slightly grayer crown and yellower rump of the Scrub Euphonia were sometimes not apparent. We almost never saw a female without its mate, however.

A pair of Elegant Trogons calmly and deliberately investigated tree cavities along the nearby river banks, cavities originally excavated by woodpeckers or formed by the rotting out of the stump of a large, dead limb. We assumed the birds were seeking a suitable nesting site, but we found no active nests on this occasion. When we talked with the Mexicans about the trogon, which they called *coa*, they would sometimes compare the colors of the male's plumage to the red, white, and green of the Mexican flag.

A hard rain on the second day of our sojourn at Pano Ayuctle and an even harder downpour and thunderstorm the second night brought us back to the reality of the onset of the rainy season and of our plans for visiting many other parts of Mexico. We had no formal schedule to follow, but if we were to see El Salto, Tamazunchale, Mexico City, Popocatepetl, Paricutín, Oaxaca, and the Isthmus of Tehuantepec, we would soon have to leave the Río Sabinas. The longer we waited, the more rain would fall, and the more difficult the passage would be over the mud road that led to the highway.

The morning after that hard downpour of our second night at the Río Sabinas, therefore, having already decided to leave later that day, we walked up to the ranch house to talk with Mr. Storms about our planned departure and a possible second visit as we returned from southern Mexico in August. Before we left we wanted to learn as much as we could about the history of the ranch and about the Río Sabinas and the surrounding area, especially the mountains to the west. Mr. Storms, having lived at Pano Ayuctle for many years, and having crisscrossed the area many times on foot and horseback and local buses, had accumulated a great store of knowledge, some recorded on paper in file boxes but most of it simply stored in his memory.

He enjoyed answering our questions at length, about the origin of the Río Sabinas, about the wild animals and luxuriant plants of the cloud forests across the first mountain ridge to the west, and about a clear lake and a small village in a high mountain valley beyond the ridge. Because he had worked for many years as an advocate for the local villagers and campesinos, helping them with all sorts of legal, social, and even medical problems, he was extremely well informed about the political and military history of the region, and the stories he recounted were full of details about things he had personally observed or encountered.

We were much interested in his tales of hunting far up in the mountains, up to a peak that reaches 7,000 feet and a lake at 5,000 feet. He spoke of having seen tigers and lions up there, and black bear, as well as plenty of deer, and ducks on the lake. The tigers we assumed were *el tigre*, the jaguar (*Panthera onca*), and the lions must have been mountain lions (*Puma concolor*). He spoke of a Canadian who lived up in the mountains alone and had quite an establishment, and also a German. We thought more and more that we would like to come back and spend a week or two there.

The river had risen two or three feet after the hard rain of the night before and seemed to be still rising as we returned to our camp. We folded our tent and cots, packed all our belongings into the car, and drove out toward the highway. When we stopped at the ranch house briefly to say "*adios*," Mr. Storms gave us each a *piloncillo* (not to be confused with the small ticks, *pinolillos*), a six-inch-long truncated cone of brown sugar, wrapped and tied neatly in corn shucks. It was originally prepared at our camp site by the river by boiling the sweet sap of the sugar cane, then pouring the thickened material into flowerpot-shaped molds to solidify. The *piloncillos* we received had been made more like candy by adding sesame seeds (*ajonjolillo*) and pecan halves to the thick liquid in the molds before it hardened.

Bearing these gifts, and reassured when Mr. Storms said he had asked a neighbor to have a yoke of oxen and some men ready to help pull us through the worst of the mud, we were about to face the first of many tests of strength and endurance that we and some of our friends and assorted oxen and tractors would encounter over the years along this road, now deep, soft, sticky mud, though at other times rough, rocky, hard-packed dry clay.

In a similar situation years later in the Sierra de Los Tuxtlas in Veracruz when I was traveling with Richard Tashian, a team of oxen, working along

Figure 8.3. E. P. Edwards and Señor Doria talking at Mr. Storms's ranch, Rancho Pano Ayuctle, Gómez Farías, Tamaulipas, June 21, 1946. Photo by S. W. Eaton.

with the engine of our pickup truck, was unable to pull us more than a few feet forward when we tried to leave our camp and drive through a long stretch of deep mud toward the highway. The oxen could pull us out and back to the camp site, however, so we parked the pickup and most of our equipment inside a nearby mineral-water bottling plant and hitched a ride to town on a powerful two-and-a-half-ton truck with dual rear tires. Even then we barely got through a series of extended mudholes en route. We rode the bus from Catemaco to Coatzacoalcos, took the train to the Yucatán for two weeks, then retraced our journey by train and bus to Catemaco, rode in a regular city taxi-cab over a now perfectly dry, almost dusty road back to the warehouse where we had left our vehicle. Everything was just as we had left it, and within an hour we were back on the paved highway in our pickup truck and heading for Mexico City.

Approaching the first long stretch of deep mud about halfway between Mr. Storms's house and the highway, we stopped and got out to chart the best course through the mud, while two oxen were yoked and hitched to the car. Then, with the combined efforts of men, machine, and oxen, we fought our way through about seventy-five yards of the worst of it before bogging down, unable to move forward. Somehow the oxen were able to pull us back to somewhat more solid ground, where we could prepare for another attempt along a slightly different track. With this effort we almost reached the higher, drier portion of the road before becoming stuck tight, unable to budge the car in any direction, no matter how valiantly the men and animals worked—digging, putting brush under the wheels, pulling, and pushing, all in vain.

Soon another plan was devised. Señor Doria, the neighbor who owned the oxen, would ride his horse up to the highway about a mile away and borrow a tractor. Tinamous were calling in the low thorny woodland alongside the road on this hot, humid afternoon, and as I walked up toward higher ground and sat in the shade of a taller tree to await the tractor, the tinamous seemed to exchange whistled notes with me as they had at the Mesa de Llera. A pair of Crimson-collared Grosbeaks (*Rhodothraupis celaeno*) came into view as I sat quietly, the male striking black and crimson and the similarly patterned female black and olive-green.

One of the helpers from the ranch walked past me and on up toward the highway, hoping to encounter Señor Doria and the tractor, but he returned in a few minutes to report that they were nowhere to be seen. With nothing much left to do, I walked toward the highway and soon met Señor Doria, now accompanied by his son, the two of them riding the same horse. The bad news was that the motor oil had been drained out of the tractor, and no more was to be had. They now appeared to be resigned to leaving the car in the mudhole until the next dry day when the road might be passable again. I walked on up to the highway and was able to confirm, even with my limited knowledge of Spanish, that the tractor was indeed inoperative.

Meanwhile, Steve, back at the car, had received the same discouraging report from Señor Doria, and by the time I returned and a light rain began falling, we were both mentally prepared to walk back to Pano Ayuctle with our cots and some supplies and ask if we could sleep on the front porch and regroup for a greater effort the next day. As it turned out, however, Señor Doria and his son had not given up, and before we could begin retrieving some of our equipment from the car, we saw them approaching in an ox-drawn wagon laden with the dried remains of sugar cane stalks and leaves.

Their plan was to use the wagon somehow as a sort of primitive wedge and jack, to lift the rear wheels, and then jam the dried cane stalks underneath the wheels and into the ruts ahead. After an hour or so of work in the sticky mud, we hitched the oxen to the wagon and the wagon to the car, and with everyone straining, the car miraculously came out. Several more times as we proceeded toward the highway there was considerable danger of getting stuck, but the oxen pulled us through. Not until the car was on solid ground near the highway and moving along smoothly under its own power did we all feel triumphant. Only two of the men were willing to accept any remuneration at

Figure 8.4. Oxen inspanned to pull out the stuck car, Rancho Pano Ayuctle, Gómez Farías, Tamaulipas, June 21, 1946. Señor Doria's son was doing the hard work. Photo by S. W. Eaton.

all for their efforts—the others were more interested in having a photograph of the struggle. The best of intentions to send copies of photographs taken in distant places often came to naught, at least before the Polaroid camera was invented, but in this case Steve had brought a small developing tank and contact printer and was able to make up some prints before we revisited Pano Ayuctle on our way back from southern Mexico.

Muddy, wet, hot, and weary, we stopped in El Limón for refreshing soft drinks and bananas, then drove on to a small hotel in Mante for a shower, a delicious steak dinner, and our first long night's sleep in large, clean, soft beds since we had left the Canada Courts in Linares nearly a week earlier.

9

Adventure Is Where You Find It

JOHN T. EMLEN, JR.

John T. Emlen, Jr. (1908–1997) was a naturalist, scholar, and teacher who had a long, productive career. He received his Ph.D. under Arthur Allen at Cornell University (1934) and began his academic career at the College of Agriculture in Davis, California. After World War II he began his long second academic appointment as professor at the University of Wisconsin–Madison. For more details, see Lanyon et al. (2000). The fieldwork related here, the specimens and insights gained, and the groundwork laid resulted in scientific publications varying from the description of new subspecies (Stone 1931) to the herpetofauna of Honduras (Dunn and Emlen 1932) and methods of observing animal behavior and assessing their densities (e.g., Emlen 1950, 1979). Excerpts from his self-published autobiography (Emlen 1996) are included with permission.

The summer of 1929 was to be different, a break from adventures in the field and an exposure to the world of birds in the world's largest collection of bird specimens at the American Museum of Natural History in New York City. I had been introduced to the Neotropical avifauna in the West Indies and to the Palearctic avifauna in England and Europe, and I was anxious to broaden those revelations to an overview of the birds of the world.

My Aunt Bessie and Uncle Con would provide a bed at their wonderful Liberty Corner farmhouse where I would sleep with their two sons on the sleeping porch. Staying there provided a base from which I could reach New York each morning before standard working hours. I would simply ride my bicycle to the Lyons Station on the Erie Railroad, chain the bike under the station platform where it would be safely hidden from view, and catch the early commuter train to Jersey City. Here I would transfer to the tube train that would zoom me under the Hudson River to a subway car that would whisk me up to the 81st Street station and the museum. This daily commute provided its amusing adventures and educational experiences strictly with one species, the human species, which I am considering beyond the scope of this narrative.

The American Museum in New York, 1929

My job at the museum was to catalogue a large and valuable collection of Brazilian specimens, the Kaempfer collection, an assignment that I initiated by spilling a bottle of India ink over the handsome catalogue book. Dr. Chapman, director of the Bird Department, came in to assure me that this mishap was not fatal. In fact, thereafter he was even more tolerant of my boyish enthusiasms.

The cataloguing was monotonous but fascinating nevertheless. I learned the names and characteristics of the many species and of the Brazilian provinces from Bahia to Pernambuco and Maranhao. I also had a chance to chat with the world-famous ornithologists whom I met and had lunch with every day. I was particularly enchanted with Dr. James P. Chapin, a specialist on African birds. He had fascinating stories to tell of his experiences while collecting specimens and of tracking down rare and elusive species, such as the African peacock (now Congo Peafowl, *Afropavo congensis*), a remarkable pheasantlike bird. Before it was ever known in the field, he had found a specimen in the Belgian Museum in Antwerp.

My closest contact, however, was with a shy, retiring, ornithologist, Dr. Waldron DeWitt Miller, who, I found, was the final authority for all questions on specimen identification. Dr. Chapman and Dr. Robert Cushman Murphy—the big names on the staff—would drop by at least once or twice a week to ask him a question and would almost always get an answer or a helpful steer. On my first day he had an Ostrich (*Struthio camelus*) intestine from a zoo specimen stretched out, back and forth along the corridors between the specimen cases, to examine its structure and measure its length.

I often had my sandwich with Dr. Miller at noon. He had a four-cylinder motorcycle that he loved to take out to New Jersey birding localities on weekends, a hobby that led to tragedy before the summer was over. On a trip to Spring Lake one Sunday he was killed in a traffic accident. This shy, retiring gentleman had made a big impression on my young life during those few weeks I had with him at the museum.

Honduras, 1930

Despite having what I considered a profitable summer at the American Museum in 1929, I was anxious to get back into the field when the summer of 1930 rolled around. Thanks again to my father and his behind-scenes maneuvering with Witmer Stone, a new opportunity emerged. Dr. James A. G. Rehn was planning to travel to Honduras to collect Orthoptera (grasshoppers, crickets, etc.) that summer and could shepherd a couple of young ornithologists who could pay their basic travel expenses. Father found the few hundred dollars required, the parents of my friend Brooke Worth at Swarthmore managed a similar arrangement, and the expedition was launched. Brooke and I were to collect as many birds, reptiles, amphibians, and fish as possible along routes selected by Dr. Rehn and were to deliver them to the Academy of Natural Sciences of Philadelphia. It was hoped that we might also contribute to or directly author several scientific papers on our results. Using our field notes to supplement his report on the bird collection of 569 specimens, Dr. Stone published on the birds and named a supposedly new pewee in my honor (Stone 1931). Meanwhile I teamed up with Dr. Dunn, my biology professor at Haverford, to publish on the reptiles and amphibians. This article apparently added nine species of amphibians and twenty-six reptile species to the known herpetofauna of the country.

After a ten-day trip with visits in Santiago de Cuba, Kingston, and Puerto Castillo on the United Fruit Company liner called the USS *Carillon* headed to Puerto Barrios, Guatemala, our first adventure began. Our train to Guatemala City had just left, and the next train would not leave until the following day. No problem. A Mr. Gaylord from our boat happened to be general manager of the International Railways of Central America. Seeing our plight and complications, he invited us to join him on his personal rail car, a luxurious unit with running water, showers, and a bar. Furthermore he ordered a special car to be added to the next day's train to be sure our equipment reached Amapala, the Honduran port, before our scheduled arrival there. Within a half hour we caught up with the train we had missed, and with a blast of our train's horn it moved over onto a side track that allowed us to pass. Such is the life for those with authority in Central America.

The next day, between Guatemala and San Salvador, the track and railroad equipment being rather decrepit due to termite damage, our car suddenly started to *thud-thud-thud*. One wheel had slipped off the track. The train came to a screeching halt, and the crew, well prepared for such emergencies, leaped out with a four-foot segment of arched track that they placed against the main track. After a signal to the engineer and a few loud puffs of the steam engine up front, and with the assistance of the crew and several dozen volunteering passengers, our car was back on the rails and ready to proceed. The scene was repeated a half hour later, and again after several jerky pulls and pushes, we were ready to move on. Such derailments were obviously not healthy for the roadbed, the ties of which were heavily splintered from many such incidents. But such, apparently, was the way of the Central American Railway.

After a comfortable night in Guatemala City and another in San Salvador, with its volcano-cracked streets and a noisy and colorful local circus show, we were up at daybreak for another long railroad trip to the Honduras border at La Union, a little island town in the Gulf of Fonseca. The scenery along this route was spectacularly beautiful, especially the symmetrical cone of Volcán San Miguel, periodically puffing great clouds of volcanic smoke from its peak. Near San Miguel we crossed a large lava flow, incredibly rugged, with huge volcanic rocks tumbled helter-skelter over the plain. We then passed an area of lakes and marshes, peppered with Northern Jacanas (*Jacana spinosa*) and grebes, and came into La Union and a night on army cots at the Hotel America.

From La Union a clumsy three-cylinder motor launch took us across the Gulf of Fonseca, the entry port and customs station of Honduras at Amapala, where we picked up our *equipaje* (equipment), safely transported under the supervision of our benefactor, Mr. Gaylord. Two uniformed gentlemen, asking if we were the "Commission de Philadelphia," then escorted us to a special launch in which we were whisked across the truly beautiful Gulf, surrounded by volcanic cones on all sides, and on to the little settlement of San Lorenzo. Here we hired a car to take us to Tegucigalpa and sent our luggage up by truck. The road to Tegucigalpa, although hard-surfaced, was incredibly rough, steep, and winding. Climbing to 5,000 feet it apparently passed through stretches of dense forest, but most of our trip was in darkness. Our arrival at the Ritz was to the thrilling musical strains of a full band of marimbas, xylophonelike instruments played by half a dozen accomplished and colorful musicians distributed around banks of keyboards, mostly of wood.

Our first field base was at the field camp of the American Rosario Silver Mine Company, an encampment on a steep mountain slope at an altitude of 5,100 feet. Here we were offered basic food and lodging facilities within a few miles of extensive stands of cloud forests, brushlands, and pine forests—habitats where we particularly wanted to focus our exploring and collecting activities. A mule train would be coming to Tegucigalpa in a few days, and we could join them on their return trip. There would be plenty of mules for us and our luggage. The road was impassable for any sort of wheeled vehicle. It was essentially a trail cut into the steep mountainsides, used primarily by native villagers traveling or transporting goods in mulepacks, on small horses, or, if these were not available, piled on the heads of women.

The camp was a simple cluster of about a dozen bunkhouses with an attractive mess hall and social hall for the fifteen or so mine bosses and their families. The area surrounding the buildings had been largely cleared of vegetation to discourage bandits, who had over the years made several raids on the administrators' homes and families. Beyond this clearing and down for several thousand feet was dense brushland, from which wood materials were constantly stripped to feed the charcoal pits maintained by the local natives for their fuel requirements. Foot trails in the area were characteristically very steep, although the larger trail leading down to the tiny villages of San Juancito at 3,800 feet and Cantarranas at 2,200 feet, where we camped for a week, were roughly graded for mule and horse travel. Pine forests—open pure stands or with patches of scrub oak—were found in the less disturbed areas up to 4,500 feet and in earlier times probably to 6,000 feet, where the cloud belt and its distinctive flora and fauna abruptly replaced all other vegetation.

The cloud forest densely covering the mountain peaks was the most readily reached about two miles west of the mine buildings at a point where the principal mine shaft plunged horizontally into the hillside. Here a high white limestone wall, lit up at night with brilliant floodlights to discourage trespassers and bandits, functioned wonderfully for our purposes by attracting thousands of spectacular moths and nocturnal insects. Night after night we walked the four-mile round trip to this point to collect specimens for the Academy or for our own show boxes at home.

From this point the Tegucigalpa road plunged into the cloud forest, providing access to many square miles of largely undisturbed wonderland ranging up to over 7,000 feet in elevation. Standing and gazing upward into the forest overhead, we could not but be overwhelmed by the scale and somberness of the scene. Tree trunks, buttressed with flanges like great walled partitions, towered upward into mists that hid their crowns. Massive branches, often fifty or even a hundred feet above my head, projected horizontally into great misty spaces, heavily loaded with bromeliads, orchids, ferns, and mosses, dripping with the heavy moisture that permeated the atmosphere everywhere.

Birds? The silence of the scene suggested they were scarce, and we spent many hours waiting for just a peep or a cheep to give us a suggestion of at least a few. They were there, but they were lost in the scope and magnitude of their habitat. The bird life was dominated by large species of ground foragers and by treetop gleaners far overhead; their calls were simply occasional loud wails, shrill screams, or the sharp barks of tinamous, parrots, or trogons rather than the drips and twitters we associate with small insect or seed feeders in our familiar temperate woodlands.

With no identification guides and no list of likely encounters, we were constantly perplexed and challenged by strange sounds and strange forms flashing across our visual fields. Our limited knowledge and memory of museum specimens back home only aggravated this confusion and led to much wild speculation: An owl? A trogon? A new species? How different this was from the modern tropical bird tour with its illustrated reference books and colored plates, recorded song tapes, and trained guides experienced in the local geography and local avifauna! It was doubtless less efficient, but was it less challenging and fun? I doubt it.

It was in these magic cloud forests that I encountered my first white-lipped peccaries (*Tayassu pecari*), my first tayra (*Eira barbara*, a large fisherlike member of the weasel family), and my first mountain lion (*Puma concolor*). I had seen footprints that suggested mountain lions were present, but my first encounter was as I was walking up the Tegucigalpa road near the summit when a huge tawny creature, the size of a Great Dane but with a long tail, streaked across the road and down a narrow game trail into the forest. As I rushed forward for another look, a local boy coming toward me from the opposite direction also saw it. When he saw me running in apparent pursuit, he shouted warnings: "¡*Leona, leona! Le comé, le comé!*"—(it will eat you).

Wondering whether the boy might know more about such creatures than I did, I hesitated, and the animal disappeared into the forest. I found more footprints to convince me that I had not been dreaming, but that was all. The animal was indeed a mountain lion. I wished I could have seen more of it.

At Cantarranas we were fascinated by what the local people referred to as four-eyed fish. These fish abounded here in several swift-flowing streams, revealing their presence by two small bumps about an inch apart, protruding above the surface like a pair of little bubbles. If the surface of the water were disturbed by throwing in a stick or pebble, the bubbles moved, drifting along the surface but maintaining their even spacing. With further disturbance they would vanish or, if really disturbed, the fish would skitter along the water on their tails, much like the pipefishes or flying fishes in the Caribbean. After collecting several specimens with a .22 rifle aimed at drifting bubble pairs, we saw the fish's trick. The lens of the creature eye, placed at the dorsolateral angle of the head, was divided by a horizontal partition into two parts, an upwardly directed lens for aerial vision and a ventrolateral lens for aquatic vision. The fish were insect eaters and could search for prey or scan for enemies in either medium at the same time.

Tropical ants were also sources of fascination. We saw long columns composed of thousands of individuals, each carrying a flag, a neatly cut fragment of leaf over its back. Though we did not know it then, the columns were marching to an underground fungus garden, where the bed of leaves to which they were contributing would be inoculated with special fungus spores, creating the food supply for the colony queen's new brood of young.

One day I found a large rock over which millions—yes, I'm sure it was millions—of small black ants swarmed in a complex system of branching and re-branching trails to some destination that I could not locate. Several sizes were present. The smaller ones carried insect fragments, and the larger ones apparently served as policemen, patrolling the never-ending columns as though maintaining order. Having heard that such colonial ants follow scent trails, I broke the flow in one column by rubbing the sole of my shoe in it. The visible trail system was promptly interrupted as hundreds of individuals crisscrossed back and forth in confusion. At another point where a column was following the contours of a deep crevice, down then up on the other side, I constructed a bridge. With a bit of coaxing and training to scent trail fragments, I got the column to adopt a new and more efficient trail across the crevice.

Our last week in Honduras was spent at the Lancetillas Experiment Station of the United Fruit Company near Tela on the Caribbean coast. Here, while collecting my quota of bird specimens one day, I spotted a small, strange, tentlike structure in the forest, something resembling the bird blinds I had seen years before at Cornell. Then I saw that it was placed near a large, bulky bird nest and realized that it must indeed be a bird blind. Presently a young man appeared to ask what I, a complete stranger, might want, and we fell into conversation. His name, he said, was Alexander Skutch. Although he was a plant pathologist with a recent Ph.D. degree from Johns Hopkins University in Baltimore, his real interest was in bird behavior. Having completed his routine chores for the United Fruit Company for the day, he was spending the afternoon studying the nesting behavior of a Rufous-breasted Spinetail (*Synallaxis erythrothorax*) at its nest by the blind. I introduced myself and explained my interest in birds and my mission with the Philadelphia Academy.

Skutch invited me into his blind, and I was utterly fascinated with what he showed me. Behavior was what had really intrigued me about birds all along, but to this point I had scarcely recognized it as a legitimate aspect of ornithology. Skutch had inserted a small paintbrush, dipped in yellow paint, into the roof of the tunnel-like entrance to the bird's nest. As we watched, the female came, incubated the two eggs, and left with a neat yellow stripe down her back, a readily distinguishable marker for future individual recognition.

I was thrilled and returned to the experiment station determined to see more of this strange man and his work. Dr. Rehn was dubious and reminded me of my intention to collect and prepare six specimens each day. With that accomplished, he said, I could see more of Skutch and his research. This meshed well with Skutch's daily routine, and I returned for a few hours of behavior watching on each of the remaining two days before our scheduled departure from Honduras.

This accidental encounter, I now believe, was a turning point in my developing career. It convinced me that I should think more seriously about what

I wanted to do with my life. I have had few opportunities to visit Alexander Skutch since those few days in Honduras, but to this day, I have remained a devoted fan of his extensive research and writings on Central American birds.

The Tres Marias Porpoises, 1964

My adventures in 1964 occurred before my illness and its associated restrictions.[1] With the arrival of a new grad student interested in marine mammals, our destination was Mazatlán and the Tres Marias Islands, some sixty miles off Guadalajara in the Pacific Ocean. Intrigued with what these marine mammals might reveal in terms of social behavior, I and the student had arranged with friends from the University of California–Los Angeles (UCLA) to join forces for a four-day cruise on the high seas. We were to leave from Mazatlán harbor on these friends' recently acquired thirty-foot *Yaqui Queen*, a war surplus submarine chaser.

A Cruise Vessel

We arrived by plane in Mazatlán on the morning of July 14, primed to set off in the afternoon. But at noon the skies threatened a brisk storm, and by late afternoon, when our captain was still in town downing his last beer, that storm hit with full force. It was what the Mexicans call a *chabasco*, a localized but full-force hurricane.

Within a half hour the harbor of Mazatlán was in turmoil. Fishing boats, yachts, and a half-dozen sixty-ton, rust-encrusted shrimp trawlers were adrift, torn from their moorings by the strength of the gale. The student and I and one unseasoned crewman from the *Yaqui Queen*, all unfamiliar with the workings of the vessel, tried to start the engine but found ourselves unable even to get it turning. Boats of all types, from sleek, expensive yachts to those rusty shrimpers were being tossed and buffeted across the harbor. Crashes were occurring every few minutes, including two hits to our *Yaqui Queen*. In only an hour the peak of the turmoil was over—as we had been told it might be. However, grave damage had been done. Captain Will showed up dismayed and angry, but it was too late. The damage was not as bad as it could have been, he agreed, but it was sufficient to cancel any possibility of continuing with our cruising plan. Knowing the town, Will had his beloved craft in drydock for repairs in less than an hour. Furthermore, he had started negotiating with the owner of one of the trawlers for a four-day rental of the *David C.* for our cruise. Those coming aboard would have to join the existing crew, who would remain on the trawler.

Where could four biologists bed down at night? We took a quick look at the bunks down below with their myriad cockroaches and lice crawling over filthy blankets and conceded that we would prefer the hard-floored decks, even with the possibility that we might have a soaking shower or two before we made it back to Mazatlán. I had my eye on a coiled rope up in the bow that I knew from experience might provide a semblance of comfort.

Pacific Sights

The Tres Marias Islands are a cluster of three small islets, each five to ten miles in diameter, lying some two hundred miles off the tip of the Baja Peninsula and some sixty miles off the west Mexican coast at the latitude of Guadalajara. Used as a penal colony by the Mexican government, the islands rose no more than twenty feet above the high-tide line, their land surfaces sparsely covered with low desert scrub. The porpoises and dolphins that constituted its primary inhabitants swarmed in the shallow seas offshore where we would be cruising for them in our antique shrimper, or dashing out in a Boston Whaler, a speedy rubber-bottomed skiff in which we would follow them along the beaches and out into the shallow offshore waters.

Besides their intriguing social behavior, porpoises and dolphins have a complex vocabulary of grunts, whistles, and clicks that would be a major focus for my student's research. In our brief contact with them on that July voyage we would simply try to obtain an introduction to what he presumably would be focusing on. We also hoped to find an answer to why schools of these beautiful creatures occasionally dashed ashore in mass strandings to die in what appeared to be meaningless self-destruction.

Those few days of adventuring in the tropical Pacific also provided me with a few marvelous opportunities to witness hundred-pound sea turtles floating on the pitching waves; marlin leaping high into the air along the horizon; sailfish cruising along the surface, their sails raised high above their backs; and flocks of Brown Boobies (*Sula leucogaster*) plunging into panicking schools of mackerel.

My sleeping accommodation aboard the boat indeed turned out to be the staked-out coil of rope in the bow of the *David C.* The rain held off until the final night, when I was wakened before dawn with a few sprinkles, while the waves pitched me rudely back and forth on my coiled-rope couch.

Mexico's Northeastern Province—Tamaulipas, 1967

After correcting my students' exam papers for the fall semester of 1966, my wife Jinny and I headed south for Texas and the Welder Wildlife Foundation's research ranch, where we had made arrangements to spend the spring months of 1967. The 30,000-acre ranch with its large populations of collared peccaries (*Tayassu tajacu*), deer (*Odocoileus virginianus*), and waterfowl was a wonderful haven for my recuperation. But where were our adventures?

As the spring flowers started bursting forth, we became restless, and realizing that the Rio Grande was only a hundred miles to the south, we flipped a coin and decided not to return to Madison directly but to head south and see what we could find over in Tamaulipas, Mexico's northeastern province.

Within a couple of hours we were in the town of Matamoros on the south bank of the Río Bravo, as the Mexicans call that international boundary river. Suddenly everyone was speaking Spanish, and the countryside had changed from a land of extensive ranches and country estates to one of small plots and adobe shacks.

Speeding down Mexican Highway 101 through gently rolling country dominated by sisal and sugar cane with an occasional *ejido* (collective farm), we arrived at Ciudad Victoria. Here, after a delicious lunch of tortillas and enchiladas, we took off for the neighboring countryside for a bit of birding. Even the crows here spoke a Spanish dialect, barking out a croaking *Irb* in an excellent imitation of the first name of Irby Davis, the prominent Mexican ornithologist and author of the popular Mexican bird guide that we had right there on the car seat.

In Ciudad Mante we entered a mountainous region with many lovely little waterfalls and a dense oak forest, alive with big blue morpho butterflies. A green-backed Elegant Trogon (*Trogon elegans*) was perched silently on a low branch, while a tinamou called from the ground below with its strange, guttural whistle. Here was our first post-illness adventure!

At Ciudad Valles, a few miles farther into the forest, we turned off on a small branch road to the town of Xilitla (pronounced "Hee-leet'-la"). The town was a quaint little Indian village with steep, rocky streets, often becoming stone steps where the grade rose sharply. The residents of Xilitla were colorfully dressed. None apparently spoke either Spanish or English; they never responded when we tried to speak with them in those languages.

On a high hill a few miles to the north of Xilitla rose a truly remarkable stone palace, a completely incongruous structure of towers, columns, spires, balconies, and spiral staircases leading up to essentially nothing at the top. Who could possibly have built or wanted to build this monstrosity out there on an empty hill? The citizens of Xilitla could tell us nothing. Asking a Mexican farmer, we learned that it had been built in the 1920s by a crazy Englishman, probably a remittance man who had millions and no way to spend it. No one knew who the builder might have been or where he really came from, but rumor had it that he was the "bastard son of the King of England."

My bird list for seven days in northeastern Mexico was 135 species. Of these, forty-five were strictly Mexican birds not found north of the U.S. boundary except as accidentals. These Mexican species included such spectaculars as the Thicket Tinamou (*Crypturellus cinnamomeus*), Muscovy Duck (*Cairina moschata*), Roadside Hawk (*Buteo magnirostris*), Red-billed Pigeon (*Patagioenas flavirostris*), and Red-crowned Parrot (*Amazona viridigenalis*). Yes, this little excursion was a genuine adventure.

Baja California and Western Mexico, 1972

As late as 1970, a naturalist asked the name of the least disturbed major natural area in the western hemisphere south of the Arctic Circle might have responded: Baja California. No hard-surfaced road for auto traffic had been pushed south of the U.S.-Mexican border onto that 800-mile peninsula until 1972. The peninsula had, of course, been accessible by sea since the sixteenth century, permitting modest aspects of modern civilization to become well established down to the tip of Baja California long before San Francisco and Los Angeles were settled. The first capital of California was not Sacramento but Loreto in Baja California, a little Mexican town established by Father Kino and his Spanish pioneers some three hundred years before the forty-niners pushed their exploratory frontiers across the Sierra Nevadas of Alta California.

Trip Plans

This remarkable peninsula would obviously have to be on our adventure docket before modern civilization destroyed its natural beauty. Accordingly, in early January of 1972, with that awful highway already under construction on the upper part of the peninsula, Jinny and I crossed the international border at Nogales and headed down into Mexico on the Sonora (mainland) Highway. Passing through the rich, irrigated farmlands around Hermosillo and Guaymas, we continued on to Los Moches at the mouth of the Fuerte River. This river brought irrigation water down through hardwood-forested foothills from the high mountain ranges of the Sierra Madre Occidental a hundred miles to the east.

Another day brought us into Mazatlán, the coastal city to which I had flown eight years before on my first trip to Mexico to visit the Tres Marias Islands and their exciting colonies of porpoises. In 1972, however, our adventure would be across the mouth of the two-hundred-mile-wide Gulf of California to the town of La Paz near the tip of the Baja Peninsula.

The Gulf, with its mouth facing the open sea, was clearly not the calmest body of sea water in the world; that night's passage had its ups and downs as well as its intended forward progress. I managed to keep my supper down, but Jinny had her usual spells of discomfort until we had safely docked at La Paz's peaceful landing pier. On arrival in that quiet little peninsula town we drove south a few miles to our motel, the Guayacura. There the manager and his jolly assistant Jesús showed us to our pleasant bedroom, assuring us that we had been totally misinformed by our Tucson friends, who had warned us that we should not leave our door unlocked anywhere in Mexico.

An Unexpected Detour

In Mazatlán while Jinny was taking a shower she discovered what felt like a little lump in her breast. On arriving in La Paz and learning that there was a "good doctor" in town, we made an appointment. The doc (who spoke English) agreed that indeed there was a small lump there and advised that we fly immediately to Mexico City to have it professionally diagnosed and removed. With the language complications we decided instead to call our friendly English-speaking physician, Dr. Taylor, back in Tucson and immediately phoned him for an appointment then phoned the Aerowaves airline for two tickets to Tucson. Jesús helped us find a vacant lot where we could park our car for an indefinite period, and we took a taxi to the La Paz airport, which up to that moment we had not realized existed.

The flight to Mazatlán took only half an hour, but there our troubles began. After plunking down our money for the ticket to Tucson, we were asked by the agent if we had registered our car. After asking what he meant by that, we were told that no foreigners were allowed to leave Mexico without first registering their car and leaving it in an official government lot. "Why?" we asked. "So if your car is stolen, as it might well be, the Mexican government can be sure it is safe." Reasonable enough, we agreed; but this of course would mean that Jinny would have to proceed alone to Tucson. Meanwhile, I would have to take our car out of Jesús's lot, find the proper government office, register the car, move it to the indicated spot, tip a half dozen officials (a familiar custom in every Mexican city), and then get back to Tucson and Jinny. By that time she would probably be under the knife in the operating room.

I pleaded with the agent, but those were the laws of the land. Dejected and bewildered, I walked out to the plane and boarded it with Jinny, knowing full well that if she was going to go on to meet her doctor's appointment, I could not go with her.

After ten minutes the engines were started, and I walked back to the exit door and descended the stairway. Standing there at the foot of that stairway with the engines roaring, I saw Jinny's head suddenly reappear at a window in the doorway. She waved frantically. I wondered what she was doing, then the stewardess slowly opened the door, and Jinny started to descend. "Hey, Johnny," she shouted, holding up a little box in her hand. I had forgotten my camoquin pills on which my very life depended, and at the last second Jinny had remembered them. What a wife! And what an occasion to be waving her on to an unknown fate in the Tucson doctor's hands.

Dejected and worried, I walked back to the airport building, where two small lights indicated that at least someone was still around. The two air attendants, just closing their books, greeted me with questioning looks on their faces as I asked if they might take me back to town in their car. At that moment I realized that if they couldn't, or did not wish to, I would have to walk the ten miles to town. Seeing my depressed condition, however, and although they did not know my full story, they obligingly took me back to Mazatlán and a hotel where I could catch my breath and consider my fate.

The next morning I caught a biplane flight back to the La Paz airstrip and walked the five miles to the Guayacura where Jesús met me with his cheerful, "Emlens! Ha-Ha-Ha," his special salute for Jinny and me. It was Sunday, and no one was at any of the government offices in town. Under the circumstances, however, this was good news for me, for that day I did not want to do anything but sleep. Wending my way back and forth through endless government offices on Monday was a nightmare of Latin American red tape. At one office, as an example, the agent listened carefully in the Mexican way as I gave my detailed explanation of why and how I had parked my car in an unofficial parking lot. The agent painstakingly wrote my story down in pencil on a sheet of ruled paper. After this he called in another agent and dictated a memo to agent number two, who typed it on a clean sheet of paper, after which agent number one crumpled the handwritten sheet and threw it into the waste basket. He presented his typed copy to a superior agent, number three, to file away. Eventually I was freed to retrieve my car, still safely parked where Jesús had unwittingly (and illegally) told me two days earlier to park it.

On Monday afternoon, as soon as I had my car securely parked in the official but unofficially undesignated government lot behind a broken-down family truck, I caught an Aerowaves Mexico flight to Los Angeles. From here an evening flight took me on to Tucson, where Dr. Taylor had left me a message that Jinny was in St. Mary's Hospital, having had a successful operation, and was completely OK! The lump, a benign tumor, had been removed, and I could see her the next morning. I checked in at a Motel Six, and in the morning was in Jinny's hospital room.

Back to Baja

After a few days of rest and recuperation Jinny was released, a cured woman. Together we headed back south to Mazatlán, taking the ferry across the Gulf again to La Paz. We relaxed there for several days, then we took off for Cabo San Lucas at the tip of the Baja Peninsula with that frightening experience all but forgotten.

Three days later we were again on the road, this time heading north up the track that led toward the international border. People told us that the new highway was already pushing south far into Mexican territory and that all roads north of mid-peninsula were in bad disrepair. This would, however, be our last chance ever to see the Baja Peninsula in anything like pristine condition.

We proceeded slowly northward, driving only fifty to a hundred miles each day, picking our camp sites leisurely so as to take in as much of the scenic desert beauty as possible. In this wilderness country we could choose camp sites simply by driving our car off the road for a hundred feet or so to duck down behind a palo verde for privacy in the unlikely event that a car should happen along during the night.

Every morning at dawn I would be out making bird counts while Jinny tended camp and cooked breakfast. Local sheepherders, detecting her presence, would occasionally drop in with their flocks and a sheep dog to two to pass the time of day with her. Friendly and curious, they would often engage Jinny in conversation, but her Spanish was limited and those conversations never got very far. One goatherder, however, became quite insistent that he wanted to buy our car, a deal that of course would be illegal; she had little trouble turning him down.

To the west of Santa Rosalia on the Pacific slope of the peninsula lies the broad, shallow Bahía Visciano, the breeding grounds of a population of gray whales (*Eschrichtius robustus*) that annually migrate thousands of miles south to this sheltered bay from the arctic seas. We contacted a local airplane pilot in the town of Loreto, the capital city of Baja California. The pilot owned a Cessna-170 plane, and for forty-five dollars he offered to fly us over the bay and give us an opportunity to view the rugged central mountain ranges of the peninsula. The day happened to be a windy one, and the whitecaps on the bay limited the quality of our viewing. But we saw at least half a dozen of these great marine beasts plus a recently born infant that was swimming close to its mother while she maneuvered back and forth in the shallow water.

Crossover to the Mainland

From Loreto we continued our slow exploration north into the upper part of the peninsula. North of Santa Rosalia on the Gulf coast, the road deteriorated rapidly and soon became impassable. We therefore decided to return to Santa Rosalia and take a ferry across the Gulf to Guaymas. On arriving on the mainland, we drove north past Tiburón Island with its thousands of Heermann's Gulls (*Larus heermanni*) to the tiny village of Puerto de la Libertad. There we were told we would find a gas station, an item of which we were sorely in need. Spotting a small two-room shack that appeared to resemble the building that had been described to us, we drove up and banged on the door. A man appeared and told us, yes, he had *gasolina verde* and would serve us in just a minute.

Lifting the bottom strand of a barbed-wire enclosure where several fifty-five-gallon drums filled with gasoline were standing, he ducked under and unlocked a padlock. Taking out a three-foot length of garden hose, he dipped one end into an open drum and started sucking with his lips on the other end to get the liquid flowing. Hastily spitting out a mouthful of the green stuff, he transferred the flowing end of that hose to a rusty bucket, which he then handed to me through the fence. After repeating the process several times, I had my gas tank approximately full and was ready to move on. I noticed two fresh coyote carcasses hanging in that gasoline enclosure and a dozen or so raw pelts lying on a box. "Last night's catch," the attendant proudly commented on the carcasses. He told me he sold about a dozen pelts each week at eighty cents each.

Before heading for home, we made one other short side trip. We had been searching without luck on the Baja Peninsula for specimens of the boojum tree (*Fouquieria columnaris*), a strange, twenty- to thirty-foot member of the ocotillo family found only on the Baja Peninsula except for one small colony on the Sonora mainland. With instructions from a man on the Guaymas ferry we thought we might be fortunate enough to find that mainland colony, and we did. The boojum, named after Lewis Carol's imaginary creation, resembles a giant, upside-down carrot root rising thirty feet into the air with hundreds of short, sticklike twigs and blossoms spraying out in all possible horizontal directions. There were a thousand or more of these strange trees in a strip perhaps a half mile long and a few hundred yards wide, situated about five miles south of Puerto de la Libertad. Here we had our picnic lunch in the only boojum grove on the American continent.

Note

1. Editor's note: While at the South Pole in 1965, John T. Emlen, Jr., began having symptoms later diagnosed as serious heart disease. This condition necessitated dramatic lifestyle changes until surgical techniques had improved sufficiently for (and continued life demanded) multiple bypasses in 1974.

10

An Ornithological Expedition to the Lowland Tropical Rain Forest of the Sierra de Los Tuxtlas, Southern Veracruz, Mexico

PAUL D. HAEMIG

Paul D. Haemig is a Swedish ecologist and ornithologist working at Linnaeus University in Kalmar. The experiences related here began a career in ornithology from the Neotropics (e.g., Haemig 1978) to the Palearctic (e.g., Haemig 1999, Haemig et al. 2008).

Preamble

The tropical forests of Mexico's Gulf coast are an important overwintering area for millions of songbirds from the United States and Canada, with some species spending as much as nine months of each year there. Until the 1970s almost nothing was known of these birds' ecology in this crucial wintering area, a deficiency that prompted Dwain W. Warner (1917–2005) and his students at the University of Minnesota to begin investigations there to determine whether these tropical forests were important to the survival of wintering songbirds. They chose as their study site the Sierra de Los Tuxtlas region of southern Veracruz. This region, part of the ancient Olmec heartland, attracted Warner and his research group because it held the largest remaining rain forest on Mexico's Gulf coast. Years earlier, Warner's doctoral student Byron Harrell had hiked through this spectacular forest and described it in a letter to Warner. Although much of it had been destroyed by the 1970s, large tracts still remained that were ideal for research. Warner led a team that subsequently conducted intensive ornithological studies in the Tuxtla rain forest, and they became the first to show the importance of pristine lowland tropical forests to the ecology and survival of migrant songbirds—both those from North America and those from higher elevations in tropical mountains. Dr. Paul D. Haemig, then

Figure 10.1. Paul Haemig in the mountains southwest of Ciudad Victoria, Tamaulipas, October 1988. Photo by K. Winker.

an undergraduate student at the University of Minnesota, accompanied Warner and John Rappole on the first expedition to study migrant bird ecology in the Tuxtla rain forest. This expedition left Minneapolis on January 24, 1973, and, after brief fieldwork in Texas, entered Mexico eleven days later. Haemig's narrative begins with the expedition's border crossing at the southern tip of Texas and is based on a journal he kept at that time.

We arrived in Brownsville, Texas, on a warm, bright, winter day, February 4, 1973. There were four in our party: Dwain Warner, John Rappole, Dick Oehlenschlager, and myself. I was many years younger than the others, being only in my first year of biological studies at the University of Minnesota. Warner was a professor of zoology at that university and curator of birds at its Bell Museum of Natural History. Rappole was a doctoral student working under Warner's supervision, and Oehlenschlager was a curatorial assistant in birds at the museum.

The purpose of our expedition was to begin a study of bird life in the vanishing tropical forests of Mexico's Gulf coast. We wanted to know if migratory birds from North America, as well as the resident tropical birds, were dependent on this vegetation for their survival, or if they could survive equally well in the man-made habitats that arose after humans destroyed the forest. Our goal for this trip was to find a suitable tropical forest to conduct research on this topic and to begin scientific collections to document these studies. This research would cover a span of many years, involve dozens of other workers, and result in a score of important publications.[1] We four thus comprised the vanguard of what would be a much larger enterprise, the full-scale operations of which would begin six months later.

On February 6 we crossed the frontier, driving over the Rio Grande and into the Mexican city of Heroica Matamoros. As we passed the garbage dump at the south end of the city, we saw several thousand Tamaulipas Crows (*Corvus imparatus*)—an impressive sight—and heard their unique vocalizations.

Driving south from Matamoros, we crossed through flat and monotonous land devoted almost entirely to agriculture, but just before reaching the town of San Fernando we entered hilly country. Here the land was covered with tropical thorn forest, which became even more extensive as we proceeded south, where the country was considerably wilder and less populated than that through which we had already passed. This part of the road, from San Fernando to the Río Corona, was the most exciting we had encountered since entering Mexico. An abundance and diversity of raptors could be seen along it, feeding on road kills and soaring over the highway and adjacent landscape. Characteristic roadside species included the Gray Hawk (*Buteo nitidus*), White-tailed Hawk (*Buteo albicaudatus*), Harris's Hawk (*Parabuteo unicinctus*), Crested Caracara (*Caracara cheriway*), Turkey Vulture (*Cathartes aura*), Black Vulture (*Coragyps atratus*), White-necked Raven (*Corvus cryptoleucus*), Common Raven (*Corvus corax*), and Tamaulipas Crow.

After driving for two hours through this elegant thorn forest, we crossed the Río Corona, with its tall gallery forest of Montezuma bald cypress (*Taxodium mucronatum*) and shortly thereafter arrived in Ciudad Victoria, at the base of the massive mountain range known as the Sierra Madre Oriental. Being the capital of the state of Tamaulipas, this city was quite handsome; its streets were kept clean, and the shrubbery planted along its avenues was nicely trimmed. However, we did not tarry but hastened southward, hoping to travel much farther before darkness fell.

Between Victoria and Ciudad Mante the highway crossed the Tropic of Cancer, descending into humid lowland tropics. Warner always maintained that it was along the big escarpment here that the boundary between the Nearctic and Neotropical zoogeographic regions occurred. He told us, for example, of camping on the top of this escarpment and waking up in the morning to the sounds of singing birds. In one ear, he heard Nearctic birds singing from the vegetation surrounding his camp and, in the other ear, Neotropical birds singing from the valley below. Of course, many today do not believe that zoogeographic realms exist, and still others insist that the Neotropical region extends even farther north. But I was then a young student who had not yet heard these dissenting viewpoints, so as we drove south from Victoria I looked forward with eager anticipation to crossing that legendary boundary into the most species-rich bird region of the world: the Neotropical realm. Unfortunately, night came before we crossed the line, so I was not able to see the transition. We descended the escarpment in darkness and drove on to Ciudad Mante, where we rented hotel rooms for the night.

The following morning we awoke to the sound of tropical birds singing in a fig tree outside our rooms. Rappole looked out of the window and excitingly reported that he saw a tanager. Warner hurried us down to the restaurant to eat breakfast, then we packed our things into the car and drove south out of town. Entering the foothills, we soon came to a small remnant tract of tropical deciduous forest. Because it was still the dry season, most of the trees were completely bare of leaves. Here we saw Neotropical species such as the Elegant Trogon (*Trogon elegans*), Plain Chachalaca (*Ortalis vetula*), and Great Kiskadee (*Pitangus sulphuratus*), all new to me. After returning to our car, we drove down the road to nearby San Luis Potosí. There we were disappointed to find that a tropical forest Warner once knew in this area had been destroyed. Retracing our route to Mante, we drove east toward the coast and then south toward Tuxpan.

Passing through many small towns and settlements, we were forced to reduce the speed of our car. However, this was not all bad, because it allowed us to get a closer look at the people inhabiting the region. Seeing an attractive young woman emerge from a shack, Warner turned to Rappole and exclaimed,

"The amazing thing is that no matter how poor and shabby the homes look where these girls live, they always come out of them looking fresh, clean, and well-groomed."

Years later, when I personally experienced the unemployment and poverty that often comes to those who attempt to make a profession of ornithology and ecology, I remembered those economically impoverished people we saw in Mexico and tried to emulate them by keeping myself fresh, clean, and well-groomed. I found that in the face of adversity it helped bring dignity to my life.

At Tuxpan, in the state of Veracruz, we checked into a hotel and went upstairs to a large room that had been assigned to us. Upon entering the room, Warner took a quick survey of its fauna. Motioning for us to be silent and follow him, he walked quietly to the closet door and opened it quickly. The sudden entry of light into the dark closet revealed two gigantic tropical cockroaches sitting on the shelf meant for our hats. In a flash they disappeared into the cracks and crevices of the wall, with a speed that amazed me. Warner laughed and said, "Some of these are so fast that the only way to hit them is with a shotgun. They're hiding now, but as soon as we turn off the lights tonight they'll come out and roam around the room."

The following morning we drove south out of Tuxpan. As we crossed the bridge spanning the Río Tuxpan and saw an impressive view of that peaceful tropical river city, Rappole remarked that the sight reminded him of Vietnam, where he had recently served in the U.S. military. During the rest of the day we visited the ruins of El Tajín and the coastal town of Tecolutla, and then we drove west into the mountains. Over our entire route we found that most of the forest of both the lowlands and highlands had been cleared for cattle and crops. No suitable tracts of forest remained for our studies. In the fields where cattle grazed, only a few of the old forest trees still stood, left as shade trees for cattle. The result was a savannah-like habitat replacing the forest that once covered the area. As we traveled this route, Warner frequently expressed his sorrow and disappointment that the tropical forests he once knew in this area were now gone. He spoke to us often that day, and throughout our time in Veracruz, about how much the land had changed in only a few years. It was not until we reached the Sierra de Los Tuxtlas area, in the southern part of the state, that we found a lowland tropical forest matching the size and splendor of those where he had previously worked, and which he regarded as suitable for our research. When the rest of us saw that spectacular forest and compared it to the dismal cutover lands we had passed through earlier, we at last understood the great tragedy that had befallen Veracruz with the destruction of so many of its tropical forests.

Driving westward, we ascended into the mists of a cloud forest. Here at Xicotepec, in the heart of coffee country, we found only a few bird species, for the land had been converted to the cultivation of this important crop. Among the few birds we did see were the Yellow-winged Tanager (*Thraupis abbas*), Acorn Woodpecker (*Melanerpes formicivorus*), Yellow-bellied Sapsucker (*Sphyrapicus varius*), Black-throated Green Warbler (*Dendroica virens*), Wilson's Warbler (*Wilsonia pusilla*), and Green Kingfisher (*Chloroceryle americana*). About two weeks before our arrival, a frost had struck and damaged the forest. The trees seemed to have survived, but many of the understory plants, including the coffee, had been killed. We had hoped to set up mist nets in the forest, but there were so few living bushes left that we decided not to.

The next day we continued driving westward through the thick fog of the cloud forest. Suddenly the road emerged into sunlight and clear skies. Here the vegetation was pine-oak forest. We saw cattle grazing in these forests and suspected that they were preventing the forests from regenerating, because we saw no seedlings growing beneath the trees. Soon these forests ended, and we entered the high altiplano of the Mesa Central, where most of the land was under cultivation. After a few more hours of driving, we arrived in Mexico City and checked in at the Hotel Escargot.

Our sojourn in that city lasted several days. Sometimes, as we drove down the streets between buildings, we heard the unmistakable song of the Canyon Wren (*Catherpes mexicanus*) singing above the roar and horns of automobile traffic. In the late afternoon of our second day in Mexico City, we paid a visit to the home of Dr. Allan R. Phillips (1914–96), an ornithologist and avian taxonomist who had been one of Warner's classmates at Cornell in the 1940s. Phillips was a conservative and traditional ornithologist who rejected newer approaches to the study of birds, preferring instead the old methods used by ornithologists in the 1800s. He especially venerated and emulated the work of Robert Ridgway (1850–1929), whom he called "the greatest ornithologist who ever lived." Phillips believed that the most important task awaiting modern ornithologists was to update Ridgway's classic multivolume work *The Birds of North and Middle America* (Ridgway and Friedmann 1901–50), and consequently he concentrated his own research around this task. Hence, when we entered Dr. Phillips's presence, it was as though we had traveled back in time a hundred years to the nineteenth century and were meeting an associate of Robert Ridgway, for this man kept alive all the old traditions and methodologies of that bygone era.

Phillips greeted us warmly and motioned for us to sit down in his living room, while his wife Juana prepared coffee for us. We told him about our proposed field studies and the difficulties we would face identifying some of the birds we found. The area we had chosen for our research, the tropical Gulf coast of Mexico, was the wintering ground of migratory birds from both eastern and western North America. Hence many taxa we would encounter there would be similar in appearance to each other, particularly in the female and immature forms. Phillips had lived in Mexico for many years and had much experience identifying these birds, so we asked him for assistance. He kindly agreed to identify any specimens that we could not identify.

When Warner explained our plans to catch birds in Veracruz using large numbers of mist nets, Phillips sighed and said he wished that he too had a team of mist-netting students like Rappole, Oehlenschlager, and me. If he did, he added, he would send them to a site in western Mexico where he had recently observed what he believed to be a new species of bird. By covering that locality with large numbers of mist nets, he reasoned that he could eventually collect a specimen of the bird. The thought of discovering a new bird taxon excited me, and I hoped Warner would volunteer our help to Phillips, but he did not. Our own work awaited us in Veracruz, and so far we had not even found a suitable site for our research. We simply did not have the time to help anyone else.

We passed the evening in conversation with Phillips. All of us enjoyed talking with him because he was so enthusiastic, opinionated, and passionate about ornithology. For Phillips, ornithology was not just a job but a way of life. He seemed always to talk about ornithology and little else. Sadly, few scientists in Mexico at that time were as interested in birds as Allan Phillips was, so he sometimes had no one to talk to who appreciated and valued his specialized knowledge of birds.

We conversed for several hours. At that time Phillips was working as a researcher and teacher at the Universidad Nacional Autónoma de México (UNAM), but he told us he would soon be moving his family to Monterrey in Nuevo León to escape the air pollution of Mexico City. There, he would work at another university. What Phillips thought would be a simple move, however, had created unforeseen problems. He complained bitterly to us that when the administrators at UNAM found out he was moving, they told him his bird collection must stay with them in Mexico City. This collection, which Phillips had built up largely at his own expense, contained thousands of specimens that carefully documented the distribution and systematics of Mexican birds. It also contained a large number of specimens from the United States that Phillips had collected before moving to Mexico. His administrators, however, coveted the entire collection. Phillips wanted to take it with him, not only because he planned to continue using it in his research but because he feared that the collection might someday be destroyed by rioting students if he left it at UNAM. Although such a danger seems exaggerated to us now, Phillips believed it a real possibility then because of violent political demonstrations that had occurred during preceding years, and because the university's autonomous status reduced the probability that federal and municipal security forces would enter the campus to quell riots and vandalism.

Phillips wanted future generations of ornithologists, including of course Mexicans, to be able to use his collection, so when the university's administrators expressed their intention to take it over, an alarmed Phillips decided to assert his own control over it. He did this in two ways. First, he replaced the original labels on some of his specimens with new labels that carried no information except a code number. This meant that anyone interested in a given specimen would have to see him if they wanted to know any information about it (such as where it was collected, date of collection, weight, sex, etc.). He would then provide all this information after looking up the code number in his notebooks. Putting such labels on his specimens was a clever move on Phillips's part, for as every first-year zoology student knows, a specimen without data is valueless. By keeping the data in his possession, Phillips became the one who gave his collection value. If anyone tried to separate him from his collection, they would consequently destroy its value.

A second way in which Phillips asserted control over his collection was by secretly moving his most important specimens from UNAM to his home. At the time we visited him, he told us that he was in the process of doing this. Warner asked how he could accomplish such a feat if the university planned to take possession of his collection. Surely, Warner reasoned, they would notice him moving it. Phillips replied that he still worked with the collection, and that every day when he left his office, he hid a few specimens in his briefcase or clothes and simply walked out of the building with them. Over a span of months he had moved out large numbers of his specimens this way. The thought of a world-famous scientist like Phillips walking out of his workplace everyday with bird specimens concealed in his clothing and briefcase, like a spy smuggling secret documents over a guarded border, was too much for us. We broke into laughter. I wondered if Phillips was some sort of fanatic, but as I got to know him better in the following years and learned of his many struggles with animal rightists and U.S. government bureaucrats, I came to see him as a heroic figure. Phillips was a simple person who only wanted to study birds. Yet, like many other professional ornithologists, he felt harassed by administrators, bureaucrats, and extremists who had little knowledge or understanding of what it takes to conduct serious scientific research. One thing that made Phillips different from other ornithologists was that he was not afraid to criticize these authoritarian forces in his writings (see, e.g., Phillips et al. 1986,

1991). And he sometimes devised ways to defy and circumvent their unwise and unfair decisions.

Before we left the house that night, Phillips told us about a new paper he was writing on loop migrations in hummingbirds (Phillips 1975).[2] He also gave Rappole a reprint of a recent paper he had authored entitled, "An ornithological comedy of errors: *Catharus occidentalis* and *C. frantzii*" (Phillips 1969; see also Phillips et al. 1991). This paper reported his discovery that a large number of thrush specimens from Mexico had been misidentified by researchers, with the result that one species' supposed geographic variation was based to a significant degree on specimens of another species. I remember Rappole reading the paper when we returned to the hotel and finding its facts and writing style quite amusing. Tossing it on the table after reading it, he laughed admiringly, "A typical Allan Phillips paper!"[3]

Two days later we visited UNAM to see the distinguished mammalogist and professor Bernardo Villa (1911–2006), reputed to be a direct descendent of several Aztec emperors, including Auitzotl and Cuahtemoc. Dr. Villa was another old friend of Warner's, and we sought his advice on our proposed research. After listening to us tell about our recent experiences in Veracruz, Tamaulipas, and San Luis Potosí, Villa told us about the problems that Mexican conservationists were having trying to save tropical ecosystems and recommended that we do our studies in the Tuxtla rain forest of southern Veracruz if we could not find any sizable tropical forests in the northern part of that state. I enjoyed very much meeting this man.

During our discussions with Villa, Warner mentioned that I was interested in learning Spanish. A smile crossed Villa's face and he spoke something in Spanish that caused Warner to laugh. When I asked what Villa had said, Warner told me, "He said that if you want to learn the Spanish language, you ought to get yourself a long-haired dictionary [i.e., a Mexican girlfriend]. You will learn faster that way."

Before we left the office, Warner gave Villa a gift of a few dozen mammal specimens from the United States for UNAM's collection. I cannot remember the identities of all the specimens, but I do remember that one was a mountain beaver (*Aplodontia rufa*).

One afternoon during our stay in Mexico City, we went to a bullfight at an arena near our hotel. It was the first bullfight I had ever seen, and I did not like it, but two amusing incidents happened while we were there. The first occurred when the bull knocked the matador down. The crowd cheered, and the embarrassed matador then finished off the bull quickly to save face and regain his dignity. The second humorous incident occurred when suddenly, during the fight, Warner started laughing.

"What's so funny?" I asked him.

"I'm thinking of poor Parmelee in the Antarctic!" he roared, and we all burst into laughter. Dr. David Parmelee (1924–98) was another professor who worked at the Bell Museum, but unlike Warner, who studied temperate and tropical birds, Parmelee specialized in polar birds and was at that very minute doing fieldwork in the Antarctic (see Winker 1999; Pietz 2000). Although we admired this man and his research, we laughed because we could not imagine how anyone in the cold Antarctic could be having as much fun as we were having in warm and sunny Mexico.

Another day during our stay in Mexico City, I returned to the hotel one afternoon to find Warner intently studying Blake's (1953) *Birds of Mexico: A Guide for Field Identification*.[4] I asked what he was looking at, and he said he was looking up all the new bird species we might encounter in southern Veracruz when we visited there. He further explained that some Neotropical birds reached their northernmost distribution in the tropical rain forests of that area, and, because he had done most of his research in other parts of Mexico, he had never seen some of these species.

"Look here," he said, pointing to a page on furnariids, "aren't these names ridiculous?" I looked at where Warner was pointing, as he read the names out loud: "Rufous-breasted Spinetail, Scaly-throated Foliage-gleaner, Ruddy Foliage-gleaner, Buff-throated Foliage-gleaner, Tawny-throated Leafscraper, Scaly-throated Leafscraper."

He laughed. "Now look at this one. After all those long elaborate names that I just read, this last furnariid is simply called the Plain Xenops."

He laughed again and said he found that short name quite amusing, adding that he hoped we would find the Plain Xenops (*Xenops minutus*) when we visited southern Veracruz, for he had never encountered it before.

We were delayed a few more days in Mexico City waiting for our revised collecting permits from the government. Finally one day they were ready. The following morning, on Friday, February 16, we arose at 6 a.m., packed, ate breakfast, and drove east. During our passage through the mountains near Río Frio, we saw Steller's Jays (*Cyanocitta stelleri*) foraging along the edge of the pine-oak forest.[5]

We descended into the Valley of Puebla and soon arrived in Cholula, one of the most ancient cities in the western hemisphere. A short distance from its massive pyramid lay the campus of the University of the Americas, a private bilingual college with a student body then composed of approximately equal numbers of American and Mexican students. When Warner invited me to accompany him on this expedition to Mexico, I decided that it would not be enough Mexico for me, so I made plans to enroll as a guest student at the University of the Americas during the spring term, which would start a week or so after Warner's expedition ended. I told Warner about this shortly before we left Minneapolis, and he said he thought it was a great idea. Hence, when we arrived in Cholula both Dwain and I were curious to see the university where I would begin studies in a few weeks.[6]

We visited the campus and found the Loggerhead Shrike (*Lanius ludovicianus*), Vermilion Flycatcher (*Pyrocephalus rubinus*), Cassin's Kingbird (*Tyrannus vociferans*), and Curve-billed Thrasher (*Toxostoma curvirostre*) common there. A colony of Great-tailed Grackles (*Quiscalus mexicanus*) resided in the trees near a small pool of water, and large flocks of wintering American Pipits (*Anthus rubescens*) foraged on the lawns. To the west, the high volcanoes Popocatepetl and Iztaccihuatl and the historic Paso de Cortés between them could be clearly seen. To the north another volcano, Malinche, towered above the hills of Tlaxcala, and to the east the dim outlines of Mt. Orizaba, the highest peak in North America outside Alaska, were faintly visible through the haze hanging over the city of Puebla. The university's location at one of Mexico's important archaeological sites, in an area of traditional Nahua Indian communities yet near the major city of Puebla, made it seem like an interesting place to study, and I felt glad to think I would be taking classes there soon.[7]

After finishing our informal tour of the campus, we continued eastward to Perote. Upon arriving there we drove north out of town on the ominously numbered Highway 13. Just after leaving town the road entered a thick bank of clouds, and shortly thereafter it started to rain. At the same moment the vegetation changed abruptly to cloud forest, with oaks (*Quercus*), sweetgums (*Liquidambar*), a profusion of ferns, and wet pine (*Pinus*) groves. We stopped briefly at a remnant tract of cloud forest between Teziutlan and Tlapacoyan. Here we saw the Common Bush-Tanager (*Chlorospingus ophthalmicus*), Tufted Flycatcher (*Mitrephanes phaeocercus*), Wilson's Warbler, Townsend's Warbler (*Dendroica townsendi*), Black-throated Green Warbler, Blue-headed Vireo (*Vireo solitarius*), and Ruby-Crowned Kinglet (*Regulus calendula*). At Tlapacoyan, below the cloud forest, it was still raining, so we stopped at a restaurant for a cup of coffee.

Proceeding to the next city, Martínez de la Torre, we secured lodging for the night at the Hotel Central, located across the street from the town square or *zócalo*. This square had many tall coconut palms (*Cocos nucifera*), which served as a nightly roost for thousands of noisy Great-tailed Grackles.[8]

In the morning as we prepared to leave the hotel, we watched the grackles depart from their roost. Some left singly, others in flocks. They flew in all directions. We also observed the Social Flycatcher (*Myiozetetes similis*) in the town square before leaving to spend the day exploring many sites between the mountains and the coast. We drove over back roads and made many stops but were continually disappointed at not finding any good tracts of tropical forest. Most of the land had been converted to agriculture and ranching, and most birds we saw were those of open or second-growth habitats. Among the more interesting species we saw that day were the Roadside Hawk (*Buteo magnirostris*), Common Black-Hawk (*Buteogallus anthracinus*), White-tailed Kite (*Elanus leucurus*), Brown Jay (*Cyanocorax morio*), Green Jay (*Cyanocorax yncas*), Vermilion Flycatcher, Melodious Blackbird (*Dives dives*), White-collared Seedeater (*Sporophila torqueola*), Yellow-winged Tanager, Tropical Kingbird (*Tyrannus melancholicus*), Black-cheeked Woodpecker (*Melanerpes pucherani*), Great Kiskadee, and Band-backed Wren (*Campylorhynchus zonatus*). Occasionally we saw a pair or small flock of parrots, but they were scarce.

At about 11 a.m. we passed through Misantla. After entering the countryside again, we reduced our speed to about ten miles per hour and cruised slowly down a dirt road. We were in our usual positions: Warner was driving, Rappole was sitting next to him in the front passenger seat, and Oehlenschlager and I occupied the back seats: he on the left, I on the right. Suddenly, a roof rat (*Rattus rattus*) ran out on the road in front of us, chased by a tropical long-tailed weasel (*Mustela frenata tropicalis*). As Warner hit the brakes, we watched with fascination as the weasel boldly attacked and killed the rat right in the middle of the road, just a few meters from us. Our box seat view of this seldom-witnessed predation event, however, was interrupted by Rappole, who swiftly jumped out of the car and stole the dead rat away from the weasel. Returning to the car, Rappole explained that he had stolen the rat because he wanted to make a study skin of it for the museum collection. The Bell Museum, he added, did not have many specimens of *Rattus rattus* from this part of Mexico.

Along the coast that day we stopped at a mangrove swamp right below Punta Villa Rica and observed the following species: Boat-billed Flycatcher (*Megarynchus pitangua*), Little Blue Heron (*Egretta caerulea*), Green Heron (*Butorides virescens*), Great Egret (*Ardea alba*), Yellow-crowned Night-Heron (*Nycticorax violaceus*), Varied Bunting (*Passerina versicolor*), Painted Bunting (*Passerina ciris*), Black-necked Stilt (*Himantopus mexicanus*), Long-billed Curlew (*Numenius americanus*), Whimbrel (*Numenius phaeopus*), and Spotted Sandpiper (*Actitis macularius*). We also saw the White-tailed Kite foraging over the coastal grasslands there and observed a large kettle of approximately two hundred Black Vultures and Turkey Vultures soaring in the vicinity.

That night when we returned to the hotel in Martínez de la Torre, Rappole skinned the rat he had snatched from the weasel and prepared it as a museum specimen. When he finished, he showed me the label he had written for it. The label contained the usual information (scientific name, date, location, sex, weight, etc.) and noted that the specimen had been prepared by John Rappole. However, it listed the collector as "*Mustela frenata*."

The next morning, we left the Hotel Central and drove west along the road we had come in on two days before. The sky was overcast, and a light rain fell. We stopped at the cloud forest tract between Teziutlan and Tlapacoyan that we had visited two days before. This forest contained a few large trees but was largely second growth. Additional disturbance came from a few cattle that grazed there. However, several areas of dense vegetation remained, and in these we hacked out six mist net lanes with our machetes. After setting up the nets, we left the area for a short while.

Upon our return, we found the nets filled with birds and so decided to stay at this forest the rest of the day, tending the nets and collecting the birds that flew into them. We caught the following species: Common Bush-Tanager, Gray-breasted Wood-Wren (*Henicorhina leucophrys*), Wilson's Warbler, Ruby-crowned Kinglet, Golden-browed Warbler (*Basileuterus belli*), Black-headed Siskin (*Spinus notatus*), Brown-backed Solitaire (*Myadestes occidentalis*), and Ivory-billed Woodcreeper (*Xiphorhynchus flavigaster*). We also observed the Black-throated Green Warbler, Townsend's Warbler, and Cattle Egret (*Bubulcus ibis*). There was a small mountain stream running through the site, and we saw an American Dipper (*Cinclus mexicanus*) foraging in it. Along this stream Warner and I searched for the relict salamander species known to exist in this part of Mexico but found none. However, we did find many small crayfish.

As evening approached, the clouds thickened and descended on us. We took down our mist nets and hiked back to the car. As we stowed our specimens and gear, the clouds closed in even more and it began to rain lightly. Pausing briefly before getting into the car, Oehlenschlager mentioned one of the bird species we had found that day and said that he was glad we had encountered it because he had never seen it before. He quickly added with great seriousness that he was not a life lister but that he always enjoyed seeing a new species of bird. We agreed.[9] Driving back to our hotel in Martínez de la Torre, we ate supper and then prepared the specimens of birds we had collected that day before going to sleep.

The next morning we checked out of the hotel and drove east on Highway 125, then south on 180. This road followed the coast and passed beautiful palmetto savannahs, freshwater marshes, and a few mangrove swamps. We saw many Northern Jacanas (*Jacana spinosa*) in the wetlands along the road but were again disappointed to find most of the land devoted to cattle raising. By this time, Warner realized that we were not going to find any large and accessible tropical forests remaining in this part of Veracruz, so we decided to go south to the Tuxtla rain forest that Bernardo Villa had recommended for our studies. We drove south the rest of the day, passing the city of Veracruz, the beautiful Río Papaloapan, and eventually arrived in San Andrés Tuxtla during the early evening.

The following morning, February 20, we continued south on Highway 180, driving through still more lands that were cut over. At Sihuapan we stopped at the offices of the Estación de Biología Tropical "Los Tuxtlas," which, as I understood it, was owned and managed by UNAM. Here we obtained permission to visit a tract of rain forest that the university had preserved and to study the bird populations there. On our way out of town we passed a garbage dump and noticed a Black Vulture and a Groove-billed Ani (*Crotophaga sulcirostris*) loitering there.

At Catemaco we stopped at a Pemex station and filled our gas tank. Continuing on our way, we drove through landscapes of cutover and second-growth rain forest until, some miles after leaving Catemaco, the road at last entered primeval rain forest. The joy and excitement we felt upon arriving at this spectacular forest was tempered only by the sadness of our realization that the cutover lands through which we had passed had, until recently, been splendid forests such as the one in which we now found ourselves. Yet this sad fact soon vanished from my mind as I looked around in wonder at the first tropical rain forest I had ever seen. Its elegance, beauty, great height, and complexity fascinated me. In the giant trees near where we stopped our car, a small group of Collared Aracaris (*Pteroglossus torquatus*) foraged in the trees, and every few minutes a flock of parrots flew overhead screaming loudly. I looked in the distance and saw the rain forest extending seemingly forever. Two hundred meters away, an elegant whitish-colored hawk resembling a *Buteo* soared back and forth a few meters above the canopy of the unbroken rain forest. I pointed to it and asked Warner its name. He replied that it was called the White Hawk (*Leucopternis albicollis*), and that it was found wherever there was primeval rain forest. He added that as soon as the forest disappeared, the White Hawk also disappeared.

I could tell from Warner's happy mood that he was pleased with this forest, and in a few minutes he proclaimed it suitable for our studies. To make final preparations for our investigations of the birds inhabiting this area, we secured lodging at a small, primitive hotel located a few miles away on the coast. This hotel, with the alluring name Playa Escondida, was situated in virtually undisturbed coastal rain forest on a cliff overlooking a sandy beach on the Gulf of Mexico. When we arrived, the owner had just recently started to graze a few cattle in the forest around the hotel, and the disturbance caused by these domestic ungulates was still minimal. The building with our rooms was a small, one-story structure. The hotel rooms had floors and walls made of cement, no curtains on the windows, no toilet seats, and no hot water. However, they were kept very clean by the maids. Neither the hotel nor any people living in the surrounding area had telephones. Of course, other luxuries like televisions were also lacking. The hotel served excellent Mexican food in a primitive but clean restaurant. Oehlenschlager, who had traveled extensively around the world, said the coffee served at Playa Escondida was the best he had ever tasted.

On February 20, our first day at Playa Escondida, we arrived late in the afternoon. After renting our rooms (at an incredibly low price), Warner, Rappole, and I walked down to the beach to cut mist net poles from the vegetation there. Then, in the evening, we set up mist nets in the forest near our rooms. While setting up the nets, we observed a White Hawk fly into a nearby tree and perch there for several minutes. A short while later, Oehlenschlager returned, having collected a Wood Thrush (*Hylocichla mustelina*) with his shotgun. At dusk we observed many parrots flying overhead in pairs toward the south.

When we awoke the next morning it was raining heavily. At about 9 a.m. the rain stopped, but the sky remained overcast. Venturing out of the hotel, we saw a Masked Tityra (*Tityra semifasciata*) and a Squirrel Cuckoo (*Piaya cayana*) in the trees near our rooms. In the following days we would observe still more Neotropical birds in and around these trees, including the Keel-billed Toucan (*Ramphastos sulfuratus*), Collared Aracari, Montezuma's Oropendola (*Psarocolius montezuma*), Yellow-throated Euphonia (*Euphonia hirundinacea*), Gray-headed Tanager (*Eucometis penicillata*), Spot-breasted Wren (*Thryothorus maculipectus*), Northern Barred Woodcreeper (*Dendrocolaptes sanctithomae*), Ivory-billed Woodcreeper, Band-backed Wren, Aztec Parakeet (*Aratinga astec*), Violet Sabrewing (*Campylopterus hemileucurus*), and Lovely Cotinga (*Cotinga amabilis*).

Before lunch we set up three more mist nets in the forest by the hotel. In the afternoon, while Rappole and Oehlenschlager collected birds, Warner and I drove into Catemaco to buy more groceries and supplies. While there, Warner also called Bernardo Villa on the telephone. During the drive back to the hotel a heavy rain began to fall. At one of the bus stops along the road I noticed several people holding sheets of plastic over their heads to stay dry. A few kilometers down the road, we passed another bus stop. Here a lone man stood in the rain. Unlike the people at the earlier bus stop, however, he had no sheet of plastic or raincoat. Instead, he held the immense leaf of an elephant ear plant over his head, using it as an umbrella. The leaf did a good job of keeping his head and upper body dry.

Warner, Rappole, and Oehlenschlager visited the biology station the next day, and there they hacked out mist net lanes in the rain forest with their machetes. While they were gone I tended the mist nets in the forest at Playa Escondida. During a pause, I took a short hike down to the beach and saw a flock of six Brown Pelicans (*Pelecanus occidentalis*) fly by. I also observed a kiskadeelike flycatcher (*Pitangus* or *Megarynchus*) sitting low in a tree by the beach with a small crab in its beak. Upon my approach, it disappeared into the forest.

The following morning we took down all the mist nets at Playa Escondida, packed them into our car, and drove over to that part of the rain forest near the biology station. We spent the rest of the morning and early afternoon setting up approximately twenty mist nets there. Later that day, while checking our nets, we found a number of interesting species, such as the Blue-crowned Motmot (*Momotus momota*) and Red-capped Manakin (*Pipra mentalis*). We also observed large flocks of parrots flying south. Apparently they were flying to a roost, for we observed this spectacle every afternoon at the biology station and at Playa Escondida.

Warner and I tended the mist nets in the forest at the biology station the next morning while Oehlenschlager and Rappole prepared bird specimens back at the hotel. Warner and I also repaired the car's muffler, which had taken a serious beating from the primitive roads we had driven over during the past few days. At 2 p.m. Warner and I returned to Playa Escondida for lunch but afterward drove back immediately to the biology station. We were delighted to find a diversity of birds in the nets, including many hummingbirds.

It was late in the day when we checked the nets for the last time. Those that were my responsibility had more birds than Warner's nets, so he finished before I did and came over to help me as I took birds out of my last net. Usually when I found a bird in a net I identified it immediately before removing it from the net. But now, because it had started to rain heavily and Warner was waiting, I did not waste time trying to identify any of the birds we caught. I intended to do that when we got back to the car. As I removed one of the last birds from the net, Warner's eyes lit up.

"What's that you've got there?" he asked.

Before I could answer his question, or even examine the bird, he took it from my hands and excitedly cried, "You've found it, you've found it: the Plain Xenops!"

I looked down into his hands and saw that he held the bird we had laughed about in Mexico City, the bird with the funny name. When we arrived back at the hotel, Warner proudly showed John and Dick the Plain Xenops, and they also seemed glad to see this denizen of the rain forest for the first time.

That evening, as we examined our complete bird collection from Playa Escondida, our attention was drawn to the specimens of three species which, according to the literature, were not supposed to occur at the low elevation where we were working: the Blue-crowned Chlorophonia (*Chlorophonia occipitalis*), Common Bush-Tanager, and Violet Sabrewing. Because these birds were typically found at higher elevations in the adjacent Tuxtla Mountains, we hypothesized that they had descended to sea level for several days to avoid spells of cold or inclement weather at the higher elevations. Warner later told me he believed this was common behavior for many birds living in the mountains here, including many migrants from North America.[10]

During the next few days we continued to work in the rain forest near the biology station. One afternoon I wore a wool shirt as I walked through the forest to check the mist nets. The shirt was bright red, and it soon attracted a male Violet Sabrewing. This elegant hummingbird approached me curiously several times and hovered a few centimeters in front of my shirt, perhaps wondering if I might be a giant red flower.

We continued to catch many birds in our mist nets, including the Olivaceous Woodcreeper (*Sittasomus griseicapillus*), Wedge-billed Woodcreeper (*Glyphorynchus spirurus*), Barred Woodcreeper (*Dendrocolaptes certhia*), White-throated Spadebill (*Platyrinchus mystaceus*), White-breasted Wood-Wren (*Henicorhina leucosticta*), Red-crowned Ant-Tanager (*Habia rubica*), Red-throated Ant-Tanager (*Habia fuscicauda*), Gray-headed Tanager, Hooded Warbler (*Wilsonia citrina*), Kentucky Warbler (*Oporornis formosus*), Wilson's Warbler, Golden-crowned Warbler (*Basileuterus culicivorus*), Wood Thrush, Slate-colored Solitaire (*Myadestes unicolor*), Golden-fronted Woodpecker (*Melanerpes aurifrons*), Bright-rumped Attila (*Attila spadiceus*), Scaled Antpitta (*Grallaria guatimalensis*), and Long-tailed Hermit (*Phaethornis superciliosus*).

I was amazed and fascinated by many of the bird species we caught in the rain forest. They came in a diversity of colors and shapes, and many had strange names. Some looked quite silly, and of course these drew comments from the ever comic Oehlenschlager. As I gently picked up a White-throated Spadebill to examine, Dick shook his head and laughed, "Stupid-looking little farts aren't they?"

A few moments later, he picked up a Scaled Antpitta and started chanting, "antpittas, prune pittas, peach pittas, apricot pittas..."

In addition to catching birds, we also caught many different species of bats, because we kept the mist nets open at night. These bats represented a hazard to our research group, because some carried rabies, and they were also an annoyance because they were difficult to untangle from the nets. One day, while taking bats out of the nets, I told Warner that I was tired of bats and wished we did not have to handle so many of them.

In reply, Warner picked up one of the bats, gently stroked its fur, and then spoke to me kindly and philosophically: "You can't learn everything about animals by reading about them or looking at them with binoculars. You also need to hold them, touch them, and feel them. This helps you understand them better as well as remember features of their morphology and anatomy. The kind of education that you are getting on this expedition is very special. Not many students these days receive such training."

On the morning of February 27, Rappole and I checked the mist nets for birds while Warner and Oehlenschlager stayed at the hotel and prepared specimens. As I approached one of the mist nets I saw a hideous-looking, yet strangely beautiful bat struggling in the mesh. I instantly recognized it as a vampire bat, for I had seen pictures of them in books, including one by Bernardo Villa. I called out to Rappole and excitedly told him we had caught our first vampire.

That day turned out to be a great one for mammals. A few hours later Rappole and I saw our first jaguarundi (*Felis yagouaroundi*). The sight of this dark brown, secretive cat running across the road in front of our car thrilled us. That evening at the hotel we worked again preparing bird specimens. We had caught only a few birds that day and attributed this poor catch to the weather. The entire day had been overcast, with intermittent heavy rain. We could now expect such rain to increase in frequency and volume, because the rainy season was approaching, and this did not bode well for our fieldwork. The trails in the forest were now muddy and slippery, and the dirt road leading to the hotel was becoming more difficult to drive with each rain. Fortunately, our work was almost finished.

The next day Rappole and I collected birds from the mist nets and then took down all the nets. We finished this task and were back at Playa Escondida for lunch by 2 p.m. Oehlenschlager and Warner had stayed at the hotel preparing specimens. In the afternoon, the sky cleared and the sun came out. The weather was so beautiful that we relaxed by hiking down to the beach and along a road. After supper we prepared the birds we had already collected.

The next morning we remained at the hotel and continued this work. During a pause, Oehlenschlager took his shotgun out into the surrounding forest and collected a Black-cheeked Woodpecker. He also attempted to down the Magnificent Frigatebird (*Fregata magnificens*) that soared daily above the cliff overlooking the beach, but he was unsuccessful.

In the afternoon Warner, Oehlenschlager, and Rappole drove over to the biology station to look for new sites to put up mist nets in August. They were gone the whole afternoon. While they were away I continued preparing specimens, and when they returned at 5 p.m. they joined me to complete the task.

On Friday March 2, we packed up our car and left Playa Escondida, driving first to San Andrés Tuxtla and then up the coast. In the city of Veracruz we checked the post office for mail, but we were disappointed to find no letters waiting for us.

After lunch we left town, and as we drove west we discussed some ideas regarding the migratory birds we had been studying. Warner told us a story about how, many years before, when he had been doing research at another site in Veracruz, he had pointed out a wintering Wood Thrush to a Mexican peasant and said, "Do you see that bird over there? That is one of *our* birds. It nests in the United States." To Warner's surprise, the peasant vigorously disagreed. Shaking his finger back and forth, he told Warner, "No *señor*, that is one of *our* birds!"

After telling us this story, Warner reminded us that the Wood Thrush spent nine to ten months of each year residing in the tropical rain forest of Mexico, and it would not be unreasonable for us to adopt the Mexican peasant's view and consider the Wood Thrush a tropical rain forest bird that flies north for a short period each year to breed. Traditional views of this species always emphasized its role as a breeding species in the temperate forests of North America; that is, as an "eastern woodland bird." Yet this completely ignored its role as a tropical rain forest bird. Because the bird spent most of its life in the tropical rain forest, Warner suggested to us that these forest communities might play a greater role in its evolution and ecology than did temperate forest communities.[11] At the very least, he added, it must be recognized that what happens on the wintering grounds is much more important than previously thought. Warner also pointed out that the same could be said for many other migratory birds that wintered in the tropical forests of Mexico. At the time he spoke these words to us, I thought his ideas were an exciting new way of thinking about the migratory birds we had been studying.[12]

That day we also discussed one of Allan Phillips's opinions expressed to us during our visit in Mexico City. When he heard of our disappointment at finding so many of Mexico's tropical forests destroyed, Phillips told us not to worry about the forests being cut down. "They'll grow back," he assured us.

Now, as this topic came up again, we were passing a cutover forest where cattle grazed in a grassy, savannah-like setting, composed of a few old surviving rainforest trees in a pasture. With one hand on the car's steering wheel,

Warner motioned with his free hand toward the ranch and skeptically exclaimed, "Hell, I don't see how the forest can grow back. They won't let it!"

Warner's point was well taken. The question of whether tropical rainforests could fully regenerate was academic. They could do so only if humans permitted it. If people decided to use the cutover lands for something else, all the regenerative abilities of the forests were to no avail. Intense economic pressures and human population increases in Mexico were simply not allowing most cutover forests to grow back.

We spent that night in Córdoba and then drove west the next day to Mexico City, where in the early afternoon we arrived back at the Hotel Escargot. After checking in we went to eat lunch, and then Warner sent me downtown to pick up photographs and slides at a film store. The taxi drivers, seeing I was an American, tried to charge me thirty pesos for a one-way trip downtown. But I was by then wise to their ways and paid them only five pesos each way, the normal rate. When I returned to the hotel, I heard Warner talking on the telephone to Bernardo Villa and Allan Phillips.

On our last day we drove to Teotihuacán and climbed one of the pyramids. When we returned to the hotel, I began packing my things for the University of the Americas. In the late afternoon, Allan Phillips came over to the hotel to look at the bird specimens we had collected in Veracruz and help us identify our series of *Empidonax* flycatchers. He also walked to a restaurant with us that evening for dinner, and once again I remember enjoying his conversation.

We checked out of the hotel after breakfast. Warner and the others now intended to drive back to Minneapolis by way of Puebla, Tamaulipas, and Texas. Spring term would soon start at the University of Minnesota, and all three had teaching responsibilities in the ornithology course there. On their way through the Valley of Puebla they would drop me off in Cholula, where the spring term at the University of the Americas would also soon begin.

We drove east over the same route we had traveled before and in two hours arrived at the University of the Americas. Parking where we had done so during our previous visit, Warner helped me gather my belongings from the car and paused to shake my hand and say good-bye. As he did so, he smiled and said that he wished he too could remain in Mexico for the spring term and study at the University of the Americas. He also wished me luck in my upcoming studies and urged me to learn as much as I could about Mexico. As I said good-bye to him, Rappole, and Oehlenschlager, I thanked them for the great times we had had together in the Tuxtla rain forest and told them I would see them all again in a few months in Minneapolis.

I watched their car depart until it was out of sight. Suddenly, I felt alone, for I had not yet met anyone at the university and could not yet speak Spanish. My adventure with Warner and Rappole's expedition had ended so abruptly. Yet, a new adventure for me was now beginning. Gathering up my bags, I walked to the building that housed the university's registration office and opened the door.

Notes

1. Some of the important publications emanating from this research program by Warner and his students in southern Veracruz were Rappole and Warner (1980), Ramos and Warner (1980), Rappole and Morton (1985), Ramos (1989), Ramos and Rappole (1994), Rappole et al. (1989), Winker et al. (1990a, 1990b, 1992, 1995, 1997) and Winker (1995). A great many Mexican biologists have also done important research in the Sierra de Los Tuxtlas area, and their numerous contributions have made the tropical rain forest of Los Tuxtlas "the best-studied forest site in Mexico, and one of the best-studied tropical forests in the world" (Dirzo and Garcia 1992). For details, see sources such as Rodríguez-Yañez et al. (1994) and the ISI Web of Science.

2. This hummingbird paper (Phillips 1975) has become a classic, as evidenced by its citation one-third of a century later in Newton (2008).

3. For a complete list of publications by Allan Phillips and a summary of his life and contributions to ornithology, see Dickerman (1997).

4. Blake (1953) was the first field guide ever published on Mexican birds and an important contribution to Mexican ornithology because it made field identification of birds easier. Before it was published, researchers such as Warner relied on museum specimens and faunal lists to identify Mexican birds. During my time on the Warner and Rappole expedition, we used the newly published field guide by Edwards (1972) to identify birds, which we generally felt was an improvement over Blake's because it had color paintings of the birds. The field guide by Peterson and Chalif (1973) was not yet available.

5. A few weeks later, when I revisited this locality, I found many other species there, including the Red Warbler (*Ergaticus ruber*), Slate-throated Redstart (*Myioborus miniatus*), Black-eared Bushtit (*Psaltriparus minimus melanotis*), Mexican Chickadee (*Poecile sclateri*), White-breasted Nuthatch (*Sitta carolinensis*), Yellow-eyed Junco (*Junco phaeonotus*), and Green-striped Brush-Finch (*Arremon virenticeps*). During my days as a student at the University of the Americas in Cholula (1973–74), the forest surrounding Río Frio was one of my favorite areas to visit because of its diverse pine-oak forest avifauna and the fact that it was easily accessible by bus from our campus. My first scientific paper originated from this locality (Haemig 1977).

6. Dennis Puleston (1940–78), who along with Warner served as one of the two official supervisors to my Baccalaureate studies at the University of Minnesota, was the person who first directed my attention to the University of the Americas and rec-

ommended that I study there for two terms as a guest student. Puleston was a gifted young Maya archaeologist, whose promising career ended prematurely one day in the Yucatán when he was struck and killed by a bolt of lightning while standing on top of the big pyramid at Chichén Itzá. See Flannery (1982).

7. One exciting feature of the University of the Americas at that time was its three-day weekend. Classes met on Monday, Tuesday, Wednesday, and Thursday for extended periods (usually eighty minutes), but then students were free to do as they pleased on Friday, Saturday, and Sunday. Teachers and administrators there believed that it was not enough to study Mexico in the classroom. Fieldwork and travel were also an important part of the educational experience. Hence the three-day weekend, which allowed students to travel more easily and see the rest of Mexico.

We students typically went to the bus or railroad station on Thursday afternoon right after classes and left immediately for Oaxaca, Veracruz, Nayarit, and other remote locations. We took homework with us and usually returned on Sunday night or Monday morning. In addition, classes often took field trips on the three-day weekends, or teachers required students to do a project in some remote part of Mexico. For example, in my anthropology course Modern Indian Mexico, we were required to spend several weekends living in a remote Indian village and then write a report on the culture of the Indians we studied, based not only on literature studies but also on our own fieldwork.

I believe that the concept of the three-day weekend is a sound one for education. Not only does it give students more time for field studies and educational travel experiences, but it also has a very positive effect on student morale and enthusiasm. My fellow students at the University of the Americas were not the most gifted with whom I have studied, for that university did not have an elite admissions policy. Yet as a group, they seemed the happiest, most optimistic and adventurous students I have ever known. During lunch hours and between classes they passionately discussed their travels of the past weekend and planned new journeys for the coming weekend. It was thrilling to live in such an exciting part of the world, to study it in our classes, and then learn even more about it on weekend travels.

8. Great-tailed Grackles from this part of Mexico were introduced into the Mexico City area by Aztec emperor Auitzotl, who reigned during the years 1486–1502 A.D. For details of this exotic introduction of a bird in pre-Hispanic times, see Haemig (1978).

9. Like most professional ornithologists, Oehlenschlager disdained the practice of keeping a "life list" (i.e., a list of all bird species observed during one's lifetime). When I first met him during my initial few months at the University of Minnesota and learned that he had traveled extensively around the world in the navy and on scientific expeditions, I naively asked if he kept a life list. Oehlenschlager laughed and replied that he did not, but that he did keep a "death list." When I asked what that was, he answered that it was a list of all the bird species he had collected for museums. Because Oehlenschlager had an extraordinary sense of humor and constantly joked about all kinds of subjects, I never found out if he really did keep such a list, or if he was only kidding.

10. For more information about these elevational movements and their impor-

tance to the ecology of birds in the tropics, see Ramos (1989) and Winker et al. (1997, 1999).

11. Several of Warner's students subsequently conducted detailed studies of the Wood Thrush on its wintering grounds in the Tuxtla rain forest. For details, see Rappole et al. (1989) and Winker et al. (1990a, 1990b, 1995).

12. Rappole (1995) has further developed this perspective on the ecology of migratory birds.

II

The Rancho del Cielo

JOYCE HECK

After earning a master of science degree in ornithology at the University of Minnesota in 1959, Joyce Heck, D.D.S., M.S.D., went on to a highly successful career as a pioneering woman in dentistry. She served on the faculty of the University of Minnesota Dental School as director of Dental Clinics, director of the Periodontics Hospital graduate program, and professor of periodontics. She went into private practice for six years before retirement to Prescott, Arizona.

I had wanted to do avian research in the northern tundra, but my advisor at the University of Minnesota, Dwain W. Warner, thought that funding research there would be too expensive. He suggested that the grant from the American Museum of Natural History would stretch farther in the opposite direction, toward Mexico. When I received the small grant, I sadly realized that it would not get me to the Arctic. Another Minnesota graduate student, Byron E. Harrell, who was almost finished with his research, confirmed that the funds could be adequate in Mexico, especially if I were able to set up my headquarters at the Rancho del Cielo in Tamaulipas, the home of Frank Harrison. Byron would be returning to Mexico to tie up loose ends for his intended work on the birds of Tamaulipas, and he planned to visit the Rancho del Cielo occasionally. Paul Martin, a graduate student from the University of Michigan, was completing his work on the herpetology of that region, and he also planned to visit the rancho. In addition, a fellow student, Eugene (Gene) LeFebvre, planned to headquarter at the Rancho del Cielo to study the tinamou and Singing Quail (*Dactylortyx thoracicus*).

I thought, "Great, one big happy research group." I went to Mexico.

Mr. Harrison indicated in his letters that he had one building available for shelter. Byron said he had used the same building, and that it should be adequate. Ever notice how sparse on details some men can be? Thus the big adventure began. It was April 1953.

Gene LeFebvre and I rushed through final exams and then drove almost nonstop to Mexico. We had field equipment on loan from the Minnesota Mu-

Figure 11.1. Joyce Heck cutting Frank Harrison's hair—"spring shearing," Rancho del Cielo, Tamaulipas, 1953. Photo courtesy J. Heck.

seum of Natural History (later known as the Bell Museum of Natural History). We had binoculars, pencils, and notebooks; but we had no experience setting up research projects in the field. We did not even have field guides; there were none. En route, we made one stop in Norman, Oklahoma, and met George Miksch Sutton, who graciously showed us his Mexican collections, especially those made from the Sierra Madre Oriental. For one short afternoon we memorized and took notes.

I did not even know the results of the exams for my first quarter of graduate studies, but I had confidence that I would know what to look for in the field and that my notes would miraculously become a thesis. I had studied Margaret Nice's work on the Song Sparrow (Nice 1937). With the naiveté of youth, I thought I was prepared.

What I was not prepared for was the border at Matamoros, our port of entry. Just prior to leaving Minnesota we had received official documents from the bureaucracy in Mexico City permitting us to collect birds, mammals, and plants. Permits to transport firearms had been denied. Gene's old Dodge had big, wide, curved, honest-to-goodness bumpers. We covered these with cardboard bumper advertisements that were in fashion in the early fifties. Behind "Visit Mt. Rushmore," "See the Badlands, South Dakota," and "Minnesota State Fair," we concealed rifles and shotguns. We removed inside panels in the doors to store handguns and ammunition. I was very apprehensive. I knew these were simplistic methods to slip contraband into Mexico. As we crossed the border, we decided that I would stay with the car and that Gene would handle the details in the immigration office.

I was alarmed when one uniformed official walked around the car several times. I crossed my fingers and hoped he was reading about Mt. Rushmore and not looking for guns. Gene was in the office a long time, while I had anxiety pains in the parking lot. After more than an hour he remembered someone's advice to hand a few dollar bills to the official, and with that the man resoundingly stamped the papers. As Gene left the office I heard him say, "*Danke schön.*" His two years of high school Spanish had been forgotten, but his almost nonexistent German was remembered. He was visibly shaking.

When we reached Ciudad Victoria we were exhausted. The road from Matamoros to Victoria was in terrible shape. Some small streams had to be forded. At larger rivers, serviced by primitive one-car ferries, the banks were steeply pitched because the water levels were low. There was a danger of overshooting the ferry when going down, or of rolling back onto it when trying to get up the other side. Parts of the road had been washed out, and there were more burros and livestock on the road than cars. We never saw a service station. We limped into Victoria on an empty tank.

We thought we had made arrangements to store the car and rent some burros from Everts Storms, who lived on the Río Sabinas fifty miles south of Ciudad Victoria, but Mr. Storms was not home. The ranch personnel knew no English, and our high school Spanish was a failure. We were shown a thick-walled adobe building. There were beds, a chair or two, a small window, and, if I remember, a dirt floor. It was dark inside but pleasantly cool. After many days of hectic activity, it looked very inviting.

At meal times we were escorted to an outdoor kitchen and given wonderful tortillas, some scrambled eggs, chicory coffee, and a chile sauce that would ignite wet paper. Chickens roamed underfoot, and small children stared at us from the doorway. In the afternoons, women led me to the Río Sabinas and a great place to bathe. The women had their bathing spot upstream; the men bathed downstream. As we bathed, they pointed to a large boa constrictor, a habitué, on a cypress limb stretched out over the river. We were awakened at dawn by singing as the Mexicans passed on their way to cultivate the fields. We did not know then that this was a labor of futility, because in 1953 the crops failed for yet another year. It was so dry in 1953 that the Rio Grande was reduced to a trickle, and Mexicans were called "dry hicks" as they illegally crossed the riverbed into the United States.

In two or three days Everts Storms arrived from Texas. I cannot remember why we had the timing confusion. He told us about the ranch and showed us several bullet holes in the adobe walls of our sleeping quarters: the ranch had experienced the Revolution of 1910. He made arrangements for burros, and the next morning we had our gear strapped to these pack animals and set off for the cloud forest and the Rancho del Cielo—the Sky Ranch.

We crossed the Río Sabinas, and as we approached the mountain trail I was preoccupied by the *no hope* calls of Inca Doves (*Columbina inca*). My experiences thus far had not been encouraging, and I was hungry. It had all been interesting, and in some cases dramatic, but I was starved for food; most any kind of food would do, but I wanted lots of it.

As we started to climb, I wondered where the trail was. Perhaps cows or other animals had passed this way, but they left little trace. It was rugged; the rocks were loose; the trail went straight up "as the crow flies," and there was evidence that water (when there was water) flowed down this way. It was more a waterfall than a trail. This eastern wall of the Sierra Madre Oriental is very steep, and it was slow going. Our cumbersome metal specimen case had to be retied many times, and the plant presses got caught in the vegetation. It was hot, but I did not sweat; I was too dehydrated. We had long ago emptied our small canteens containing the last of our "safe" water. After 3,500 vertical feet we reached the oak-sweetgum (*Quercus-Liquidambar*) cloud forest, and I remember feeling it before I was otherwise aware of being in it. It was cool, wet, and fragrant, and the ground was leveling off. The trees were very tall, and festooned with Spanish mosses, epiphytes, bromeliads, and lianas.

Meeting Frank Harrison was an experience. Beyond the very firm handshake, he was shorter than I was (five feet, eight inches at the time). He had a large head, made bigger by a thick thatch of black hair sprinkled with gray, and a leathery, weathered face. He was bone, skin, and muscle, and he had just enough of a French-Canadian accent to be interesting. He proudly showed us his new bilevel, one-room house, constructed of rough-sawn lumber and topped with a metal roof. He was most proud of the attached plant house, which was crowded with African violets, gloxinias, and tuberous begonias, all growing in rusty cans. A foot or two higher, on the upper level, he had a bed in one corner, a cot not far away for his employee Lucas, a rough plank table surrounded with benches, two interesting chairs of his design, a wood-burning cook stove, a bookcase filled with *McLean's* magazines sent to him by his sister in Canada, and a rough cupboard that was his pantry. Nails on the walls near his bed held what little extra clothing he had, and a wooden box under the bed held small items.

If I have missed anything, it is not much of an oversight. His house was a necessary arrangement to get out of the rain, a place to sleep, cook, and eat, and nothing more. Frank's more important installations were his outdoor plant nursery, his plum, peach, pear, and apple orchards, his lily fields, and his many acres of flowers and fruit trees. It was in these places that Frank did his living. A corral less than fifty feet from the corner of his house sheltered his milk cows. He used the milk to supplement his mostly vegetarian diet, and he sold the excess to women who hiked long distances from the lumber camps farther to the west and higher up the mountain. He once kept chickens because he loved eggs, but their scratching habits were not compatible with his flowers.

Frank casually indicated the outhouse and the open rock cistern for water. The outhouse looked normal (it even had a door), but the side facing away from the other buildings had no wall. Later I came to appreciate the view from this perch, but initially my visits were ultra brief and I ignored the view. The cistern was about two hundred feet from the outhouse—downslope, naturally.

Frank then took us to our cabin, about twenty-five feet from his new house. It looked very old. Little of the log structure could be seen under an enormous roof. I had to stoop low to get under the six- to eight-foot overhang. Once inside the cabin it took some time for my eyes to focus in the dark interior. Fortunately, the lack of light covered my disappointment; actually, it was more like panic. At that moment I had had enough adventure. I wished I had followed some sage's advice to consider being a secretary, nurse, primary teacher, or whatever. I wanted to forget about a science career. I wanted to go home.

I felt I had been grossly misled, though I also realized that Dr. Warner had never been to the Rancho del Cielo, and that Byron Harrell was not into houses. Byron was not into creature comforts. In all the times he was in this building he probably never saw the holes in the roof, the discarded junk too good to throw away but no longer realistically usable, the lack of springs or mattresses on the two rusty bed frames, the rough planks that topped the bed frames, or the cobwebs and small-animal feces everywhere—or even noticed the smell of bat guano. The lack of windows was not important, because any view would only have been of the underside of the extensive overhang. The logs were not chinked, and it was more a matter of what the walls kept in than what they kept out. The cabin was dark and grimy. It smelled badly. It had been two years since Frank had moved out of this building, after living there for at least fifteen years.

Panic led to action. There was no time to throw a tantrum or even to cry. With what daylight remained, we moved stuff into one corner, swept cobwebs, swept floors, pushed out the guano, suspended mosquito nets from the rafters, managed some privacy screens, filled containers with water, treated the water with iodine tablets, set up candles in strategic places, and unpacked our sleeping bags. There was not much conversation.

Meals were to be with Frank and Lucas. When Frank called early that evening it was dark enough for a kerosene lantern. This was not the most illuminating light, but it was enough to give me another shock: the plates were badly chipped enamelware, with what appeared to be dried food from past meals covering enamel and rust. The utensils were also coated, rusty, and so weakened by rust that I thought they would bend maneuvering through the rice and raisin supper. I was starved, but I could not eat. I was the closest to the light, and I detected maggots in the rice. Everyone else ate, and Gene cleaned my plate and saved us both from an embarrassing situation. Later I asked if he knew there were maggots. He said he thought so but was not sure and rationalized that since they were cooked, they provided added protein—and he was very hungry. He was much more practical about such things. No thought had been given to taking food on this trip. That night I lay in bed lamenting that all the extra space had been packed with equipment and a few items of clothing. There was not a can of food or a snack to be had.

Lying there in the dark on wooden planks, I heard the bats. They were flying in and out of the cabin. I realized that the bat guano seen earlier had been fresh, and that the bats were roosting in the rafters. I carefully tucked the mosquito net around my sleeping bag. The next morning Frank said they were vampire bats, but they would not harm us. They fed on his cows in the corral. Whenever the wounds would not heal Frank would apply a hot tar poultice. Ouch. One night we collected several bats. We hit them with sticks as they perched on the backs of the cows. As the days and weeks went on, I somehow adjusted to sleeping on boards, and to the bats, but I constantly dreamt of food—especially ice cream.

The next morning I volunteered to do the dishes. Initially it was a challenge to find the enamel or rusty metal. Frank's dishwasher was a big kettle of water that was always kept warm-to-hot on the back of the stove. I had the feeling that Frank was careful to clear the table after meals, but he did not rinse, scrape, or wash. When the kettle boiled dry, the food got baked onto the dishes. I scraped and managed to substitute rusty metal for the baked-on rice and oatmeal, which were the mealtime staples. It was not much of an improvement, and was probably less sanitary than the "super-boil" method, but it looked better.

Later I learned that the supplies of rice, which Lucas packed up from El Limón down below, were infested and in short supply. The drought of several years was being felt everywhere, especially in the country. People had no corn or bean crops; they had little food and no money. Merchants in the small vil-

Figure 11.2. Frank and Lucas on the stoop of the new house, Rancho del Cielo, Tamaulipas, 1953. Photo by J. Heck.

lages were keeping only small food inventories, but even these were not moving, and they easily became infested. The people of Mexico had experienced all this before, including Frank. It was not pleasant, but nor was it considered catastrophic to have maggots in the rice.

In time I discovered a deep cast-iron kettle under the stove, and using blackberries I found in the orchard, I made deep-dish cobblers. I managed cobblers with green peaches. I picked green pears to go with the usual lunch of big heavy muffins that were Frank's specialty. When we craved meat, we shot squirrels in the name of science, and although they were small, I made a sort of stew. With the rest we made study skins for the museum. The squirrels were easy targets. They ran along the tops of the stone walls surrounding the orchard and they often had a green pear or peach in their mouths, so we aimed for the fruit and usually made clean head shots. I thought a tinamou or Singing Quail would be especially nice, but my colleague was having mediocre results locating the elusive birds and was not about to sacrifice the very few he had located. We both lost weight and became almost wiry. But neither of us was as thin as Frank or Lucas, who daily worked in the orchards and fields of flowers with hoes and machetes.

The fruits and flowers were sold to Mexican vendors from the markets in the valley. It was a long journey for the men and burros using the trail from Gómez Farías. Frank had for years been haphazardly storing the pesos from these sales in tin cans and in the pages of *McLean's* magazines. We went through all the back issues and did an accounting for him, and convinced Frank that he should take the time and make the effort to travel to the border to open a bank account. This he did a few months after we left.

I had some success in my fieldwork with the four local thrushes, the Clay-colored and White-throated thrushes (*Turdus grayi* and *T. assimilis*), the Brown-backed Solitaire (*Myadestes occidentalis*), and the Black-headed Nightingale-Thrush (*Catharus mexicanus*). But the breeding season of these and other birds was much delayed. In fact, *Turdus grayi* did not begin nesting until the very end of May, when we had a few brief showers, making mud available. This thrush uses mud in the construction of the nest. I was working in the northernmost extension of the Middle American cloud forest, but there were no clouds in the spring of 1953. It was sunny, dry, and very warm. Frank could not recall such a lack of clouds, fog, or rain in his eighteen years here.

Although this was not the cloud forest I had expected, I enjoyed being out in the oak-sweetgum forest. I lived in that forest for ten to twelve hours almost every day. I was reluctant to return to camp, not because of the living conditions but because I was captivated by this beautiful forest, where both tropical and temperate plants intermingled. Everywhere I looked so much was new, including both the smells and the sounds. I became very sensitive to sounds, and because the forest floor was dry, there was much to be heard. Once, energetic sounds led me to a scene of frenzied activity. Noisy birds were feasting on insects that were crawling and jumping away from the path of army ants on the move. I had read about just such a scene in the work of William Beebe. It was wonderful. Frank did not think a marching column of army ants was wonderful. He had been evicted several times by army ants when they moved through his house.

We were warned about the many sinkholes and caverns in the area; if we got lost it was prudent not to move after dark. Occasionally Frank would leave his work and take us to special haunts of his. He had quite a good rope, and he lowered us down past beautiful walls covered with ferns, mosses, and delicate orchids. All the up and down movement was accomplished by hand-over-hand rope climbing. For many years this rough terrain of limestone boulders and sinkholes had contributed to maintaining the relatively primeval condition of America's northernmost cloud forest. However, in step with technical knowledge had come improved power equipment, and the forest in this once inaccessible area started to be exploited in 1951. By 1953 there were new lumber roads dissecting this 1,500-acre forest. Fortunately, because of the rugged topography, the roads did not penetrate everywhere, and pockets of virgin timber still remained in the area for study sites.

After many weeks I was surprised to hear laughter and conversation as I returned to camp one day. Byron Harrell and Paul Martin had arrived for an overnight stay. They had managed the rough, newly constructed logging road from Gómez Farías in Paul's jeep. As I approached I was surprised when they got up and offered me the choice seat, the top step to Frank's house. In a split second I was airborne and projected several feet from the stoop. Big joke. They had planted a newly killed rattlesnake under the steps, hoping its paroxysmal rattles would occur when I sat down. It was an impressive specimen, probably three to four feet long, though in memory it grew to more like six feet long. I was even more cautious in the forest thereafter. Poisonous snakes were in the forest, but with the usual precautions I avoided any incidents.

The drought was affecting the water supply, and such water as there was in the cistern looked awful. As water became scarcer and scarcer, the tracks of large cats, probably pumas, were often seen around the cistern. We had been rationing water religiously. Frank boiled it, and in addition we doubled the iodine in our canteens. At some point I was careless and contracted severe dysentery, with fevers, chills, and delirium. Frank boiled several concoctions, but none was effective. I was so weak that I needed help to the outhouse. After many days I woke to a fetid odor and realized that it was me and my sleeping bag. Days of sweating, diarrhea, and no baths were an ugly combination. I felt fully awake, and needed a bath, but a small basin with limited water would have to do.

In June the shortened breeding season was nearing its end, and it was necessary to return to the University of Minnesota to attend required classes at the Itasca Biological Station in northern Minnesota. I was concerned about the limited information I had collected, but I was also salivating at the thought of hot baths, lots of food, cool, clean drinking water, and ice cream.

In 1954 Dr. Warner and I both knew that I needed to return to Mexico for more data. When I explained my dilemma to Frank, he urged me to return. Because I was coming alone, he requested that I bring a handgun and holster. In less than one year there had been increased logging activity, and he would be more comfortable about my roaming the forest if I were wearing a visible gun. He also had exciting news. He had leased land to Mr. and Mrs. Frank Blesse from Harlingen, Texas, and there was a new cabin for me to use, since the Blesses would not need it until July. What a relief—no more vampire bats. I sent care packages ahead and packed nonperishable food, vitamins, and calcium supplements. As a consequence, I was healthier and felt better in 1954.

This time I felt like a pro confronting the officials at the border in Matamoros. I had no delays, but it took me a long day to reach Ciudad Victoria. The road was fantastically terrible, and it was deserted. I was pretty shaky when I pulled into a service station in Ciudad Victoria. The attendant knew some English. He wanted to know where Minnesota was; how many kilometers away was it? Where had I come from? When I told him I had driven from Matamoros, he was mystified. Did I not see the sign in Matamoros indicating that the road was closed? I decided that this country could be dangerous without knowledge of Spanish. I thanked my old 1938 Chevy for not breaking down and counted my blessings. On the return trip I used the Pan-American Highway and exited the country at Reynosa.

This time at Rancho del Cielo the oak-sweetgum forest was truly a cloud forest. It rained; it was wet; birds responded; and there was lots of activity in the April-May breeding season. The forest had changed. More sweetgum had been cut for railroad ties. To the west of the ranch there were more roads, and more sounds from the lumber camps. There were also more people from the lumber camps, and Frank had visitors from the United States.

Among these visitors were Ernest Edwards and friends of his who managed to get there on the lumber road from Gómez Farías. They were amused at my holstered handgun. I had become rather oblivious to its presence on my hip. It was just something I put on every morning, like my boots; and when questioned about it I was at a loss to explain it. It seemed rather unnecessary, although I did on occasion collect a specimen with it. I usually reserved my Sundays for collecting specimens and preparing skins. Frank had suggested that I avoid the roads and camps, but once I had wandered too close. Too late, I saw a group of men approaching and I felt sure they had seen me also. My normal reaction would have been to greet them and continue my search, but Frank had very pointedly told me to avoid such a situation. They were quiet as they approached. I saw a small bird, and I slowly raised the gun and fired. I calmly picked up the bird, put it into my creel, and said, "*Buenos días.*" The men were talking excitedly, but the only word I could understand was *caramba*, which translates roughly as "yikes" or "good grief." They did not know that my ammunition was birdshot, making for an easy shot. Several days later Frank asked me about the incident. One of the women who came for milk had told him the story. He thought I had handled the situation just right.

On occasion, the mayor from the second ridge over from La Joya de Salas would drift down to the rancho to work for extra cash. I had missed him the previous year. One day he was clearing undergrowth near the Blesses' cabin. He beckoned me over to a stump to show me his .22 caliber rifle. After much sign language and a few words of simple Spanish, I returned it to him. From his pocket he extracted a small spent fuse, probably from a lumber truck, and indicated that we should shoot at it. He was challenging me to a duel. This was

Figure 11.3. Joyce Heck going after nests, Rancho del Cielo, Tamaulipas, 1953. Photo by Frank Harrison.

not a comfortable situation. He placed the fuse on the stump and handed me the rifle, but I indicated that he should shoot first. He paced off a reasonable distance, fired, and missed. I added ten more paces, fired, and shattered the fuse. I could not see it very clearly from where I was, but I had memorized the location and the placement, and that was where I aimed. Again there came lots of gestures, and lots of rapid-fire Spanish. At lunch he told Frank about the target practice. Frank said he was not going to be worried about me in the forest, because I was the Mexican equivalent of Annie Oakley.

In July, at the end of my research, I returned to Mr. Storms's ranch on the Río Sabinas, and it turned out he knew all about my shooting exploits. The news had traveled down the mountain. I felt I had never really been in any danger, but that was a statistic I was happy not to challenge. I had respected Frank's advice to be careful.

Frank Harrison was a most kind man. He left cold Canada in the 1920s and gradually migrated southward. His story of how he came to Mexico and the Rancho del Cielo is most interesting. Between Canada and Mexico he had labored on the aqueduct for Los Angeles, had been an extra in Hollywood films, and had even taught school. He was always looking for a suitable place to grow flowers—lots of flowers. Eventually he found the rancho. He was a member of several horticultural societies, and he had developed several varieties of gloxinias, African violets, begonias, amaryllises, and others. One of his goals was to cultivate a pure black amaryllis. He had given me some counter space in his plant room to prepare study skins. It was a wonderful place for the task. I was surrounded by his beautiful flowers. One day, though, my tranquility was shattered. Frank hit me between the shoulder blades and I fell off the three-legged stool. What a shock. He calmly bent over and picked up a black widow spider. I kept it in a vial to remind me of the incident.

My research was much more productive in 1954. I left the rancho with much sadness, knowing it would be a long time before I would be able to return. In January 1957 Frank wrote, "I am figuring on tearing down the old house and building a lumber one as it isn't worthwhile fixing it up." I agreed. In May 1957 he wrote, "I finally got the new house built. It isn't furnished and lacks two windows, but it is a big improvement over the old one, 12 × 20 ft. with a seven-foot porch on the south and north sides, . . . built of pine lumber by the loquat and avocado trees, with the big early plum trees touching the porch on the north side, I invite you down to read and rest while you enjoy the scenery." I made a very brief visit in 1959. It was indeed wonderful.

In 1966 I was planning a long stay over several summer months. But on January 29, 1966, John William Francis Harrison was murdered in his home on a day when Lucas was visiting his mother below the mountain. There were

Figure 11.4. Frank emerging from the plant house built along the side of his new house. Rancho del Cielo, Tamaulipas, 1953. Photo by J. Heck.

two men. They used a knife and clubs. He was found early on Sunday morning by a young boy to whom he gave a bucket of milk every day. A year earlier, in 1965, Frank had deeded his ranch to Texas Southmost College in Brownsville, and had thereby established a small biological station open to students of all nations. He is buried at his Sky Ranch. He was sixty-five years old.

Today the Rancho del Cielo is a famous destination for students and birders from all over the world. Frank would be proud, and he would like that very much.

12

Bird Specimens Collected at Lake Olomega, El Salvador

JOE T. MARSHALL, JR.

After completing his Ph.D. under Alden Miller at the University of California–Berkeley, Joe Marshall embarked on a long career of ornithological and mammalian research, including fieldwork in southeast Asia and Middle America. The fieldwork related here resulted in the publication of Marshall (1943); he is perhaps best known for his work on Asian rodents (Marshall 1977) and long-term bird studies (Marshall 1988).

I have been reproached for some disemboweled bird skins collected at Lake Olomega—those from which the carefully placed cotton stuffing was untimely ripped. The study skins were soaked in a boat accident. To save them I removed the body stuffing and tried to dry them, afraid they would rot in the tropical heat. An example is the Royal Flycatcher (*Onychorhyhchus mexicanus*) skin, serviceable for study but empty of stuffing.

The circumstances are thus. The Vertebrate Paleontology Museum and the Museum of Vertebrate Zoology together mounted an expedition to El Salvador in 1941–42. It was led by Dr. R. A. Stirton from Paleo, who had accompanied Adrian van Rossem on an earlier expedition throughout El Salvador for the Dickey Collection in Pasadena. By January or early February of 1942 we arrived at the Olomega Rail Station for six weeks of collecting in the tropical deciduous forest on the far (south and west) side of the lake. "Stirt" arranged with the local fishermen to take us across the lake to a farmhouse, part of which was rented from a hospitable farmer, including the shaded porch. In six or perhaps nine or a dozen huge dugout canoes we crossed the lake with our gear. At the farmhouse, Stirt paid off the boatmen and arranged for them to paddle us back in six weeks. As an afterthought, he called them back and paid them for that future return trip—apparently so that he would not have to interrupt his geology work by returning to make the arrangements. Stirt and Bill Gealey (geology) then trekked down the river to the coast, returned in a couple of weeks, and then went to another part of the country.

On the appointed day of return, only one canoe showed up. The rest of the boatmen had long since spent their money and lost interest in us. The lone boatman took the personnel across to the station and then went back, presumably to make numerous trips to take our gear and specimens, packed carefully into the prefab pine boxes Paleo used. But no! Just at sunset the canoe hove into view with *all* the boxes piled on. At the edge of the lake it tipped over, and as the load was carted to the station we could see water sluicing out of some of the boxes. One was a bird box, which I immediately opened so as to start taking cotton out of the few skins that were already soaked.

The six weeks at Lake Olomega were most interesting zoologically. The personnel I remember being there were Milton Hildebrand (mammals), John Davis (herps), Joe Marshall (birds, with emphasis on complete skeletons), John Tucker (botany), and Nate Geer (cook). Old Nate was Stirt's uncle. We scraped aside our skinning tools, formalin, sawdust, and arsenic from the porch table when Nate brought out the meals. Milt Hildebrand kept a photographic history, especially of habitats, from start to finish of the expedition.

Lake Olomega, the stream, deciduous forest, swamp forest, and lovely spring at the base of the nearby mountains teemed with wildlife. There were spider monkeys (*Ateles geoffroyi*), Jabirus (*Jabiru mycteria*), and King Vultures (*Sarcoramphus papa*). The lake was full of birds, mostly big ones. Wild Muscovy Duck (*Cairina moschata*) males came into the farmyard to mate with the domestic Muscovy females. On my birthday, February 15, I hired a boatman to paddle me on the lake, and I shot a wretched excess of specimens. Davis and Hildebrand pitched in and helped me save them.

We wore greasemonkey coveralls as protection from ticks and their larvae. The seed ticks started as a spot on the pant leg if you brushed against vegetation, and this pod quickly grew as the thousands looked for a way to get at the skin, where they would burrow in and die. We carried twig whips to beat them off our clothes. Iguanas had the strange habit, when startled by our walking the trail beneath them, of doing a loud belly-flop onto the trail—like a gun shot—then running off. The day Stirt and Gealey returned from the coast, I had shot a crested forest eagle [probably an Ornate Hawk-Eagle, *Spizaetus ornatus*—ed.] above the spring and I could not find it. Stirt went with me, and I pointed in the exact direction it had flown. Stirt plunged into the dense woods, ticks and all, and came back with the gorgeous specimen, smelling of skunk—their favorite food. It turned out later that day that Hildebrand had a skunk in a trap at the spring.

By late May 1942 we were all back in Berkeley, where Dr. Alden H. Miller generously arranged a curatorial assistantship for me to fill until I got drafted. Why did I not restuff the specimens at the time? Search me. Perhaps they had not yet arrived, as they had to be shipped overland on account of war danger at sea. I did, however, write up the Salvadoran bird novelties (Marshall 1943) for *The Condor*, which means they must have arrived before I was drafted in November 1942.

Or perhaps I was just distracted. Things happened fast for me in that period after returning from El Salvador. Introduced to Elsie Rader by Paul Illg on a blind date, I married her on August 19, 1942, at the San Francisco Courthouse after a whirlwind three-week courtship. Illg was best man; Dr. E. Raymond Hall thought I shouldn't be in such a rush. Mrs. Hilda Wood Grinnell had Don Hoffmeister take her car with me and our suitcases over to the Shaw Hotel in San Francisco. Elsie and I rented a little apartment on Eddy Street overlooking a park; she continued work at the Civil Service Commission and I commuted daily to the museum on the Big Red Train into November.

13

Green Mansions of Tamaulipas

PAUL S. MARTIN

Paul S. Martin is professor emeritus of geosciences and former director of the Desert Laboratory at the University of Arizona. The experiences related here began a long career in biology. Publications resulting from this fieldwork included Martin (1951), Robins et al. (1951), Martin et al. (1953), Edwards and Martin (1955), and were the prelude to further important work in northeastern Mexico (Martin 1956, Martin and Harrell 1957).

What was it like to collect birds and to conduct fieldwork in Mexico in the early days? For me it all began at Cornell University in Ithaca, New York, half a century ago, when I lost a ping-pong game to Ernest P. (Buck) Edwards and won a trip to the tropics—to tropical Mexico—a dream come true.

South from Ithaca

I entered Cornell in the fall of 1946, an eighteen-year-old freshman, ready and eager to study zoology in general and tropical birds in particular. I pestered the ornithology faculty, both Arthur A. Allen and Peter Paul Kellogg, for their ideas on how to get to the tropics. I wrote to William Beebe of the New York Zoological Society, offering to wash dishes at his tropical field station in Venezuela, never dreaming that it might be easy enough for him to recruit domestic help locally. Not surprisingly, Beebe did not reply.

In the late 1940s the Cornell campus saw many World War II veterans resuming or beginning classes. I envied those who had tropical experience. Bill Dilger had been stationed in India. Ed Reilly had been in Panama. Dwain Warner had been to New Caledonia and collected the island's famous endemic, the Kagu (*Rhynochetos jubatus*).[1] Before the war he and Bob Lea had collected birds in tropical parts of Mexico with George Miksch (Doc) Sutton and Olin Sewall Pettingill. Serving as an officer in the army, Sutton had taught arctic and jungle survival to the troops.

At the northeast edge of the Cornell campus, with hemlock woods bordering its north side, Fernow Hall was the home base of ornithology, mammalogy, ichthyology, herpetology, and conservation faculty, students, and collections at Cornell University. All these fields offered separate courses. Although we did not know it, we were living in the heyday of whole-organism natural history, untroubled by too many "test implications of new models" and other scholarly pretensions yet to come. If we did not anticipate the degree to which we would witness the conversion of the natural vegetation of our favorite haunts into farmland or suburbs, we were well aware of the historic extinction of the Great Auk (*Pinguinus impennis*), Passenger Pigeon (*Ectopistes migratorius*), and Ivory-billed Woodpecker (*Campephilus principalis*), and the perilous status of the Whooping Crane (*Grus americana*). Because of their diversity, the tropics in particular invited attention.

On the top floor of Fernow, dormer windows housed desks for ornithology grad students. Some, such as Bill Dilger, emulated Cornell's famous former bird artists, Louis Agassiz Fuertes and George Sutton, and drew birds at easels. Another feature of the top floor was a refrigerator and gas range in a small kitchen. Kitchen privileges were not limited to grad students. Undergrads showing promise as ornithologists were welcome too, providing they helped at KP, contributed road-killed rabbits, squirrels, or pheasants to the larder (otherwise heavy on starch), "liberated" apples from the Cornell University orchards, or toted surplus food over from the Home Economics cafeteria. I doubt the facility would have passed current sanitary or safety codes. On the other hand, as an educational resource it was an inspiration for my subsequent attempts as a faculty member seeking to enhance habitat for students at the Desert Laboratory of the University of Arizona, surrounded by saguaros and thorn scrub species on the west side of Tucson.

One night in the fall of 1947 the ping-pong table near the kitchen cubicle was, as usual, the center of a vortex of activity. The student cooks, Brina Kessel and Bob Dickerman, were ready to convert it into a dinner table as soon as grad student Buck Edwards, who had collected Mexican birds for Doc Sutton, finished a game with me.

Afterward Buck asked if I might consider joining his spring field trip to Mexico. I don't think my losing at ping-pong had anything to do with the offer. Beyond a strangled "Yes!" I was speechless. I knew that Buck was completing a dissertation on the birds of Lake Pátzcuaro, wherever that was (in the state of Michoacán, in central Mexico). I knew that Mexico was tropical, and I assumed (wrongly) that Pátzcuaro was too. I would drop out of school for a semester to help Buck collect birds and put up specimens. What a lucky break!

In fact, the entire Lake Pátzcuaro basin lies above 1,800 meters in elevation, too high for most tropical species of animals or plants. Uncultivated parts of the mountains above the lake support oak and pine woods and fir forest. While there are Blue Mockingbirds (*Melanotis caerulescens*), White-striped Woodcreepers (*Lepidocolaptes leucogaster*), and Brown-backed Solitaires (*Myadestes occidentalis*), the majority of the resident birds are temperate species that range north into the western United States.

I was not the only winner of a ticket to Mexico. Roger Hurd, who kept an apple orchard outside Millerton, Pennsylvania, volunteered his services. Although not a Cornell ornithology student, he was keen for adventure, he could cook, and he proved to be a great "people person." In addition, Roger had wheels, the chassis of a new International one-ton truck sporting a home-made metal shell fitted out with bunks. The corrugated aluminum roof of the shell extended out over the back door, reminiscent of the overhang of a gypsy wagon. It was the prototype of a camper. In early February we started south. I was too excited to sleep at night.

In 1948 cross-country driving was poky. The best highways were two lanes or suicidal three lanes, the middle lane for vehicles passing in either direction, a design that increased the speed of travel at the cost of more head-on collisions. The Pennsylvania Turnpike, the only four-lane, divided-median, high-speed highway of its kind, ran at right angles to our southbound route and offered no help. In the absence of interstates or bypasses, we could not escape strings of traffic lights stopping vehicles on the main streets of every burg along the route. The more towns we could drag late at night when traffic was minimal, the better.

East of the Mississippi River we found that thirty-five miles per hour was a good average speed, not including stops for food and gas. Driving in unbroken shifts, we might make seven hundred to eight hundred miles in twenty-four hours. Texas was flat, with better roads and fewer towns. Near Corpus Christi, Attwater's Prairie-Chickens (*Tympanuchus cupido attwateri*) showed up in grassland where they were supposed to be. Roger and I could add a new species to our life lists. We would soon add many more.

At McAllen, Texas, we left the United States and entered Reynosa in the state of Tamaulipas, Mexico. At Mexican immigration we presented birth certificates and received our tourist cards, and at customs Roger got his permit for the truck. One more bureaucratic detail remained. A leftover from World War II, Mexico retained designated military districts along the border. All weapons in the hands of foreigners required permits that had to be registered with the local *comandante*. We found the military barracks, and Buck presented our shotguns along with .410 and .22 auxiliary barrel inserts, especially designed for bagging small birds with minimal damage to their skin and feathers. The burly officer in charge inspected Buck's bird-collecting permit issued by the Departamento de Caza y Forestal in Mexico City, as well as Buck's gun permit, and then he asked to see our weapons and ammunition. The .22 caliber shell casings loaded with pellets (miniature shot shells) caught his eye.

"*¡Cartuchos de munición!*" the officer exclaimed. Their tiny size broke him up. He waved us out the door roaring with laughter.

Beyond the border cities and irrigated fields near the Rio Grande we entered the vast gray-green thorn scrub of northern Tamaulipas, sometimes called "chaparral," although it lacks the scrub oaks and manzanita of interior chaparral in the mountains of the West. I was not thrilled. The bleak landscape was open, hot, dry, barren, and desolate. The compact desert shrubs with small leaves, stout twigs, and harsh-textured or thorn-protected foliage looked like a poor habitat for birds. Exploring the waist-high scrub I felt totally exposed and kept looking over my shoulder for trouble, not that there was anything to worry about. This was a far cry from my dream of a dense tall tropical jungle filled with parrots, monkeys, and toucans. Ironically, I would happily spend most of my life based at the Desert Laboratory of the University of Arizona at the edge of Tucson, surrounded by 869 acres of Sonoran thorn scrub in a climate more arid than this. But meeting the desert was not love at first sight.

We camped in the brush near a town of continuous adobe walls and with the intriguing name of General Bravo. Who was the General? Was his family name in fact Bravo, or was that a descriptive adjective, earned by valiant conduct in a military operation?

Early the next day as we neared Monterrey, magnificent mountains loomed up through scattered clouds behind the city. This was more like it. Outside Monterrey a few peaks of the breathtaking escarpment of the Sierra Madre Oriental reach 3,600 meters. The Rocky Mountain crest west of Denver is higher than the top of the Sierra Madre outside Monterrey, but not relatively higher, because the lowlands around Monterrey are much lower in elevation than Colorado east of the Rockies. What a change from the vast flatness of southeastern Texas and northern Tamaulipas. We had arrived at the backbone of the continent.

Near Monterrey we stopped for brunch at a roadside restaurant and had a chance to devour fresh, locally grown papaya. The weather was delightful, and we congratulated ourselves at such an easy escape from the icy blasts of a Finger Lakes winter in central New York State. As we settled down at an outside table I had the distinct feeling that we were being watched. Then I noticed Black Vultures roosting on the back wall of the patio, sharing the al fresco ambiance. They appeared to be waiting for our leftovers.

Like all Mexican roads in those days, the Pan-American Highway was wide open. Livestock—cows, donkeys, horses, pigs, and poultry—ranged freely, grazing the green strip on one side of the road before crossing at leisure to sample the other side. Inevitably, speeding traffic took its toll. Until the government fenced the federal highways, it was a good time for scavengers. As we sped past a stinking, bloated carcass of a *burro* or a *vaca*, scattering its funereal retinue of vultures along with an occasional Mexican Eagle (Crested Caracara; *Caracara cheriway*), we might spot more vultures circling ahead, portending the next road kill. Given such severe mortality, we wondered how the subsistence farmers and villagers with their smallholdings along the highway could expect to reap much benefit from their animals.

At Montemorelos the heady scent of citrus blossoms and bags of fresh tangerines in roadside stands advertised at bargain prices brought us to a stop. A gallery forest of tall, statuesque Montezuma bald cypress (*Taxodium mucronatum*) lined the rivers and provided riparian habitat for parrots and Bare-throated Tiger-Herons (*Tigrisoma mexicanum*).

Forty kilometers south of the main plaza in Ciudad Victoria, the capital of Tamaulipas, a road sign informed us that we had crossed the Tropic of Cancer. Within another 25 to 30 km the highway swung west toward the foot of the Sierra de Guatemala (the local name for a segment of the Sierra Madre Oriental) and we found ourselves in truly impressive tropical vegetation— at last! Here was the real stuff, a tall dense tropical deciduous forest, complete with *chaca* (*Bursera*), strangler figs (*Ficus*), *guasima* (*Guazuma*), *huapilla* (*Bromelia*), palms, bamboo, elephant ear, and, around small mud-and-wattle houses, dooryard patches of cultivated papaya, guavas, bananas, pineapples, limes, and other tropical fruits. From a distance we could spot important ranch houses or tractor sheds (which also served as sleeping quarters) by their emergent massive *orejón* or monkey ear trees (*Enterolobium cyclocarpum*). Here, some 330 km south of the border, many plants of the tropical lowlands of Central or South America found their northern limits.

That night we camped under a tall spreading cypress by a mule-powered sugar mill on the bank of the Río Sabinas within the small Spartan ranch of Everts Storms, an expatriate Texan. Two years earlier, while searching for Sutton's former field camp at Rancho Rinconada, Buck had discovered and befriended Everts. We were at the edge of the tropics that Sutton and Pettingill wrote about in "Birds of the Gómez Farías Region" in *The Auk* in 1942, to be followed thirty years later by Sutton's book *At a Bend in a Mexican River*. The contact with Everts would prove to be our key to the cloud forest and other ecological treasures of the region. Meanwhile, we indulged in an afternoon skinny dip in the sparkling waters of the Río Sabinas below Everts's ranch.

Mountains of Mystery

A few miles to the north, between forested ridges at the foot of the Sierra Madre Oriental, the Río Sabinas emerges from its *nacimiento* or birth place, a magnificent big spring, full of large gobioid fish, turtles, and freshwater prawns, which are crustaceans much larger and more attenuate than the crayfish we knew from eastern rivers and streams. Not surprisingly, because they percolated through cavernous limestone, the powder-blue waters were charged with calcium carbonate. Surrounding mountains support tropical semi-evergreen forest and, at higher elevations, cloud forest and pine-oak forest. Everts Storms assured us that those who bathe in the buff in the *nacimiento* of the Río Sabinas will always return. My first bath there was on this 1948 trip, and my last bath there, with a troop of University of Arizona students, was in 1978. While I have not been back since, just writing about the place now is a form of returning.

In Tamaulipas most of the Sierra Madre is cavernous limestone. No matter how hard it rains, even in hurricane season, most drainage in the mountains soon vanishes underground, to emerge at the foot of the mountains in great springs or *nacimientos*. These are the sources of the Río Sabinas, the Río Frio, and adjacent rivers flowing east to the Gulf of Mexico. After they leave the mountains, the rivers are diverted to irrigate agricultural crops, especially sugar cane.

With his ranch close to the foot of the mountains, Everts did not need irrigation to grow sugar cane, maize, tomatoes, and a variety of tropical fruits. He told us to help ourselves. When we shook Everts's tree, we had to be quick to beat the pigs to the fall of ripe avocados. A wild species of avocado grows in the mountain forests. Although the much-praised mangoes were not yet ripe, we dined on papaya and on unfamiliar varieties of locally grown bananas, sold in local markets, another exotic experience. In the 1940s papaya, mangoes, and more than one kind of banana were unknown in most grocery stores in the eastern United States.

Storms had come to Tamaulipas early in the century to work in the oil fields of Tampico. For a while he and other Americans escaped the Mexican Revolution by hiding out in uninhabited parts of the rugged Sierra de Guatemala. He named his Río Sabinas ranch Pano Ayuctle, Huastecan for *calabasas*, or pumpkin ford. The 1:50,000 scale CETENAL map of the Gómez Farías region lists it as Rancho Calabasas. He was known and loved throughout the Gómez Farías region. Once his valise fell off the baggage rack on top of the local bus, a loss he discovered only after he reached his destination. From El Encino to El Limón word spread along the Pan-American Highway, and within a few days some passerby walking the roadside discovered and returned his luggage, unopened.

As happened to many others after the Mexican Revolution, a large part of Storms's ranch was expropriated. Ejido La Azteca, a small settlement across the River, was one result. If there was any bad blood in the aftermath of his loss of land, it was not obvious to us. The *ejidatarios* at La Azteca were on good terms with Everts, and like all other people in the region, they treated us kindly and in later years guarded a hygrothermograph station I set up in a small patch of tropical evergreen forest that hugged the base of the mountain between the *ejido* and Gómez Farías.

Everts and his ranch hands made sugar in the traditional way, feeding a few cane stalks at a time into a small mill powered by a mule. The cane juice trickled into a bathtub-sized wooden trough, its bottom sheathed in metal. The cane juice was boiled down until the concentrate could be poured into molds to make brown cones of raw sugar (*piloncillo*) wrapped in the leaves of the sugar cane. When dry, it took a hammer or a hatchet to break a *piloncillo* into smaller pieces. Although many small-scale ranchers, including Everts, used oxen for plowing and for other heavy work, including pulling stuck vehicles out of the mud in the rainy season, some of the farmers cultivating the rich, black soils cleared from former palm forests around Chamal, El Limón, and Ciudad Mante had small tractors. The big mechanized industry in the region was sugar cane grown in fields irrigated by the Río Guayalejo and its tributaries, with large commercial mills producing refined sugar at Ciudad Mante and at Xicotencatl.

With alternating patches of deciduous forest, semi-evergreen forest, and cleared land bordered by living fences of guasima, *huapilla*, and other fast-growing trees and shrubs, the country teemed with wildlife. Everts's cane fields harbored boa constrictors. At night huge toads (*Bufo horribilis*), big enough to fill the bottom of a bucket, lumbered into our camp to feed on the bugs attracted by the intense light of our Coleman pressure lamp. Large black iguanas (*Ctenosaura*) lived in trees near Chamal and Gómez Farías. The strangler figs harbored a large fence lizard (*Sceloporus serrifer*), which I later described as a new subspecies. The most exotic of all the lizards was the spindly-legged, bright green cacique iguana in the genus *Laemanctus*, a new record for Tamaulipas (Peters 1948). The tropical viper or fer-de-lance (*Bothrops atrox*), locally known and feared as *cuatro narices* (four nostrils) or *cola blanca* (white tail), occasionally appeared swimming with us in the Río Sabinas. Herpetologists at the University of Michigan showed interest in our specimens of *Bothrops* and the tropical rattlesnake (*Crotalus horridus*). Apparently both were new records for Tamaulipas.

In 1949, in woods near the river, Roger Hurd killed a tayra (*Eira barbara*; locally *tepe-chichi*, 4–5 kg), a fierce tropical carnivore that dropped to the ground and attacked him after he shot and wounded it in a tree. He managed to club it to death, smashing the stock of Doc Sutton's shotgun in the process. He returned to camp with bad news (he had destroyed their only collecting weapon) and good news (they now had a specimen of a rare tropical mustelid). Sutton considered Roger's experience "one of the most amazing reports I had ever listened to concerning an encounter between man and beast" (Sutton 1972: 88–91).

Cow trails through the dry forest were infested with ectoparasites: full-sized ticks, tiny "seed" ticks, and minute chiggers. An allergic reaction to their bites kept me up itching half the night. I noticed that Everts and the local people could walk the same trails apparently with no ill effects.

However, they could not avoid malaria, a chronic health problem for Everts and many others throughout the lowlands. We took our anti-malarial pills faithfully. To Everts's dismay we boiled our drinking water, or chlorinated it with Halazone tablets. He teased us about "doctored" water and served river water at his table. Nevertheless, that summer another bird collector in southern Tamaulipas came down with typhoid. We had reason to be cautious.

We stalked trails through the brush and along the Río Sabinas hunting Blue-crowned Motmots (*Momotus momota*), cotingas (*Pachyramphus*), and ant tanagers (*Habia*). In spring we found a variety of warblers and other migrants from North America. These we could identify with the help of Roger Tory Peterson's *Field Guide to the Birds of Western North America*. To learn the native birds we had little to go on beyond occasional descriptions of calls or behavior in Sutton and Pettingill's annotated list. The first field guide, *Birds of Mexico* by Emmet R. Blake, did not appear until 1953.

Although the local people had Spanish or Huastecan common names for many of the native plants, especially the trees and shrubs, there seemed to be few local names for the birds other than game birds. The only secure identification was a bird in hand, destined to become a specimen suitable for taxonomic study. We followed the classic procedure: when in doubt, shoot first and ask questions afterward. We selected our ammunition depending on the size and distance of our prey. We hunted herons, ducks, and large hawks with a 12-gauge shotgun loaded with large shot. For starling-sized species we inserted a foot-long, .410 gauge auxiliary barrel (aux) into the 12-gauge. Sparrows or smaller birds at close range fell to .22 shot shells from a stubby aux the size of a 12-gauge shotgun shell and sometimes used by skeet shooters. This was the miniature armament that had amused the *comandante* in Reynosa. The trick was to anticipate the size of the next bird to be collected. It was pretty much guesswork. Many intended victims flew away while the would-be collector struggled to add or subtract the aux.

Then there was the matter of recovery. If not killed but only winged, the targeted trophy might flutter to the ground to escape in a thicket, or hide under cover. Proper procedure meant rushing up to the place where one thought the bird had fallen, marking the spot with a hat, and then hunting the vicinity in circles of increasing size. Following Sutton's protocol we refused to give up the hunt without making a thorough search. Once in a great while the victim, given up for lost, appeared under the hat.

In the afternoon, when birds were less active, and sometimes long into the night by the intense light of a hot, hissing Coleman lantern, its delicate mantles burning white gasoline and requiring periodic pumping to restore pressure to the tank, we worked at specimen preparation. Beginning with a midventral incision, we carefully separated skin from body, scraped away any layers of fat with a scalpel, cleaned the feathers of grease, dusted the skin with borax as a preservative, tied wing bones together, stuffed the eye sockets, filled the body cavity with cotton spun around a short stick, and sewed up the abdomen. In dry air we moistened the thread as well as the skin on either side of the incision before sewing the skin shut, arranging the feather tracts and pinning out the specimen on cardboard. The task was not complete until labels and catalogue entries had been written up in India ink, including locality, elevation, distance from nearest town, habitat, name of collector, date of collection, field number, sex, gonad size and condition, and anything else of note, such as stomach contents or behavior. Some field parties carried scales and weighed their freshly killed specimens. Breast meat of larger birds often found its way into the next day's soup or stew.

Occupied with such arcane operations, our camp soon attracted the attention of locals, initially small fry, then older siblings, and finally heads of households, including various members of the Osorio family as well as Everts's cook, Doña Petra. The word spread quickly. Everybody around Rancho Pano Ayuctle knew about us or had seen us wandering along the trails looking at *pájaros* (birds) with our binoculars and shooting the ones we wanted for specimens. Now they knew about the strange things we did with them.

Until his generosity began to deplete our stock and Buck asked him to quit, Roger Hurd won friends among the mothers with small gifts of needles and thread. Later, Roger's boundless enthusiasm for befriending anyone at any time pulled us through some heart-stopping encounters after dark when strangers happened upon us in some bootlegged campsite we hoped was remote enough not to attract the attention of potential *bandidos* (bandits).

Everts promised that when we returned from Michoacán in April he would help us outfit a collecting trip up into the mountains, where he said there were monkeys, a lost mission, and a lake at a place called La Joya de Salas. From down below, when not enveloped in the clouds, the montane forests west of the Río Sabinas looked dense, unbroken, and mysterious. To the best of our knowledge no other biologists had explored the place. I looked forward to being in the first party to do that.

Sutton Skins and Sibley Skins at Lake Pátzcuaro

South of Tamaulipas in San Luis Potosí we stopped at El Salto, following a river and travertine-rimmed pools of blue water to a majestic waterfall encrusted with travertine draperies. I'm told the site has been lost to a small generating station. Military Macaws (*Ara militaris*) haunted tall *sabinos* (cypresses). Buck attempted to capture some of the macaws on film with his new movie camera.

After a few days we broke camp and returned to the Pan-American Highway, driving out of the tropical lowlands above Tamazunchale, around hairpin turns, into cool fog, and through mossy forest. Farther above, the highway left the pines and oaks of the mountains and entered a sun-blasted plateau of thorn scrub with rope cactus (*Opuntia imbricata*), yuccas, and other spiny, spiky, or oily shrubs. Goat herders lived in low, scattered stone huts behind stone walls that extended to the far horizon. In Mexico City we braved city traffic to return some Sutton specimens to the Departamento Forestal y de Caza y Pesca, the source of our permits.

From Chihuahua to the Isthmus of Tehuantepec the higher parts of the Mexican Plateau support forest or woodland with dozens of species of pines and hundreds of species of oaks. The vast majority are endemic to Mexico. Above the Lake Pátzcuaro basin in Michoacán we found a variety of pine, oak, and pine-oak communities, less disturbed in *pedregal* (lava boulder fields) than elsewhere. Until we were invited to stay in Pátzcuaro at the Estación Limnológica we camped out in the pine woods or on the southeastern shore of the lake near a large marsh, where we studied the marsh birds.

Then another field team, Charles Sibley with his student assistant, both from the University of California at Berkeley, showed up at the Estación Limnológica. Few specimens existed of the water birds that wintered on Lake Pátzcuaro. While Roger took off on his own to visit the erupting volcano at Paricutín, the rest of us joined forces for a day of duck shooting from a motor launch. Sibley occupied in the bow, Buck and the boatman the stern, and Sibley's assistant sat across from me, both of us amidships.

Approaching our first target, a Bufflehead (*Bucephala albeola*), Sibley raised his gun when, to his horror, out of the corners of his eyes, he detected double-barreled shotguns aimed forward on each side of his head close to his ears. The Nimrods behind him were ready to shoot too! Profanity erupted from the bow and, somewhat crestfallen, we lowered our weapons. That was not enough. We were instructed to empty the chambers and point our guns away from the boat. We were led to understand that shooting at birds from the front of the boat was the exclusive prerogative of whoever sat in front. Then Sibley bagged his duck. I began to appreciate Buck's wisdom in his seat selection. We motored on after our next target.

That night Buck and I eyed a major problem, the large number of water birds to skin and stuff. Sibley scoffed at our concern.

"You do Sutton skins? Don't waste your time. All you need is enough of the specimen to measure the beak and the tarsi, with the skin supported by a stick jammed into the base of the skull. No need to try to build back the body with cotton or sew up the midventral incision. Don't you know the importance of sample size? Have you looked at Ernst Mayr's *Systematics and the Origin of Species*? We deal with populations and intraspecific variation. That requires a series of specimens to make a definitive quantitative sample from each region within the range of a species. Are you evolutionary biologists or amateurs?"

While we set to work, Sibley cooked dinner for us, offered to share his gallon of wine (no takers), and helped with some of the skinning. After writing up their field notes for the day he and his field assistant climbed into their sleeping bags and soon began snoring, long before Buck and I called it quits with our Sutton skins.

A few years later Cornell's much loved professor of ornithology, Arthur A. Allen, retired, and a search committee was appointed to seek his replacement. Some committee members felt the Cornell tradition was lacking in academic rigor. The solution would be new blood and the hiring of a new systematist, one conversant with evolutionary theory. The search committee selected Charles Sibley. On his initial inspection of Fernow Hall, Sibley arrived at the grad student bull pen on the top floor, where he found Bill Dilger, his pipe in his mouth, at work behind an easel. At times Dilger supported himself drawing parakeets or canaries for the French's Bird Seed Company. I suspect that both men had anticipated this moment. According to legend Sibley stared at Dilger and asked who he was and what he was doing, which was quite obvious.

"Pleased to meet you, sir. I'm Bill Dilger, painting these parakeets."

Sibley bristled. "Mr. Dilger, don't you know you are wasting your time? Are you a student of ours? Name me one eminent scientist that has drawn birds." Aimed at Sutton, Fuertes, and the heart of the Cornell tradition of illustrating bird books, the question was loaded. Bird artists were lightweights, not scholars.

"Why, that's easy," Bill replied, "Leonardo Da Vinci, sir."

At Pátzcuaro I was dismayed, in part because I felt that Sibley might be right in speeding up the preparation of skins if they were not crucial in evolutionary interpretations of bird speciation. To detect significant variations in morphology, the evolutionary biologist needed large samples, at least a dozen individuals each, from each of many different localities.

At the same time Doc Sutton was our sponsor, at his own expense. He had a deep interest in our discoveries. Buck talked of writing and illustrating a Mexican field guide, which would require stuffed specimens of high quality. His *Field Guide to the Birds of Mexico* (Edwards 1972; see also Edwards 1955, 1998) was the result. The best Sutton paintings were rich ecological vignettes. With identifiable plants in the backdrop, Doc Sutton's birds came with their habitats. They communicated artistic, educational, emotional, and scientific value all rolled into one. Had the academic critics gone too far?

Still, the Sibley pronouncement resonated. Some zoology students at Cornell, such as Max Hecht, Danny Marien, and Ken Parkes, expounded the virtues of the New Systematics. Evolution, a new course at Cornell taught by a geneticist, attracted lots of students. I was interested in biogeography, which also required large samples for analysis. In fact, if one wanted to collect large numbers of specimens in minimum time for the study of population variation, the future seemed to lie in reptiles and amphibians, which did not need to be skinned but could simply be injected, tagged, and preserved in formaldehyde. Or in small mammals, which could be trapped and did not have feather tracts to complicate the skinning process. Plants were the best of all. They defined habitats. Except for succulents like cacti and agaves, a mass collection that yielded ample material for study of population variation could be pressed quickly. Admittedly, in wet weather and especially in the wet tropics, the drying process could be tedious. Some plants, such as *Sedum*, were so durable that they resisted any amount of air drying in the press, retaining enough green leaves to propagate, months later, in the greenhouse. I was beginning to think of going AWOL from ornithology. Nevertheless, birds were the reason I was in Mexico. Birds were the real grabber. And shooting and examining birds in the hand (I didn't care to admit this) was such a rush!

After a month in the Lake Pátzcuaro basin we hit the road for the pine-oak forests of the Sierra Madre Occidental in western Durango, where we searched without success for one of Mexico's rarest birds, which Buck had hoped to photograph: the Imperial Woodpecker or *pito real* (*Campephilus imperialis*). In early April we left the pines and drove east across the grasslands of Durango through Torreón and into the uninhabited creosote bush plains of Coahuila, to Monterrey and south, retracing our route back to the tropics of Tamaulipas for that trip Everts had promised into the mountains with the monkeys, the lost mission, and the lake. Everts greeted us with mail. Besides news from my parents in West Chester, Pennsylvania, there was a letter for me from Ann Arbor, from Doc Sutton. He had heard of our plans to explore the mountains above the Río Sabinas and that I would spend a month up there. He sent reprints I had requested, most notably his seminal "Birds of the Gómez Farías Region." He offered guidance:

> I call to your special attention that at the Pano Ayuctle you are practically at the type locality of *Chaetura vauxi tamaulipensis* and of *Coccothraustes abeillei saturata*, so either of these birds would be especially desirable as specimens. I assure you you'll not shoot too many of the swifts. They come too close to sitting in the lap of the gods for that. As for the grosbeak, the last specimen I shot fell into a deep fissure among rocks on one of those slopes to the west of the River [Río Sabinas] and I never even saw it after it fell. Perhaps it had only been crippled.

The swifts and grosbeaks immediately became high priority items to collect. Doc continued:

> Paul. Be sure to take full notes on breeding activities. More information on the wren *Nannorchilus* would be welcome. Do those birds build those fine nests, or does some other species of bird build them? Any information on the breeding of the Ant Tanagers would be good to get. I suspect that they nest semi-colonially. But the differences in the nesting of the two species should be looked for.

I did what I could regarding observations on breeding birds. The wren *Nannorchilus* (White-bellied Wren, now *Uropsila leucogastra*) was not up in the cloud forest, and the ant tanagers (*Habia*) did not breed there.

Heaven's Ranch in the Clouds

Like many dry season days in the coastal lowlands of eastern Mexico, the early morning of April 10, 1948 was clear and warm and heating up rapidly. Buck, Roger, and I were hard at work repacking our gear once again, the inevitable task of travelers. Faced with four days in the mountains for all of us, and at least a month for me, the operation involved some fine-tuning. What guns, ammo, specimen panniers, grub, and personal gear could we pack up on our backs or on those of two mules? Until Buck returned, the rest would go home in Roger's truck or remain in storage at Everts's house. Like most Huastecan dwellings his was a simple affair, made of poles set vertically, partly sealed with mud, and open for ventilation beneath an overhanging palm thatch roof that shed most of the rain. The thatch provided suitable habitat for mice, lizards, scorpions, and snakes. Everts enjoyed one luxury, a cement floor. His cook shack and small dining table were in a separate *jacal*.

Already we were dripping perspiration and we had not seen the mules yet. Everts had recommended an early start, not because the trip would take all day—it would not—but because that way we would be far enough up into the mountains to escape the heat load of the lowlands. By 9 a.m. hope of an early start faded. In their large woodland pasture the *bestias* eluded discovery and capture. By 10 a.m. I was beyond impatience. By 11 a.m. three mules finally appeared. Recovering from a bout of malaria, Cruz, our intended guide, did not want to go. With promise of a riding mule and extra wages, Everts persuaded Cruz to change his mind. By noon the mules were packed, we topped off our canteens, splashed across the pumpkin ford of the Río Sabinas, and strode past the village huts at Ejido La Azteca, where kids and their mothers peeped at us through cracks in the walls of their homes.

We cut around boulders and entered the forest to begin climbing, first up to a bench at 300 meters, then steeply to switchbacks along a *malacate* (the ruins of a rusted winch and cable from earlier logging days), then up a steady ascent, dripping sweat. The mountains ahead looked just as formidable as they had at the start. Stopping for breath, I drained my canteen. An hour later, thoroughly dehydrated, I was happy to see Cruz holding the mules back from a *charco* (small water hole). The odorous, tea-colored water was barely potable. Cruz said there was a better water source ahead. The mules did not hesitate when their time came.

Later in the afternoon we left the old lumber road to find ourselves on a narrow trail enveloped by cool air and the blessed shade of dense, tall forest, inhaling the refreshing scent of rotten wood, and treading a deep, rich, leaf mulch. In response to Roger's question, Cruz assured us that Rancho del Cielo was *muy cerca* (close by).

"*¿Que distancia?*" (how far?) Roger persisted.

"*Una legua,*" came the reply. In my dictionary a league is about three English miles.

Along with oppressive heat, we had left behind the Great Kiskadees (*Pitangus sulphuratus*), Red-billed Pigeons (*Patagioenas flavirostris*; which before lumbering were not collected from or known to breed in the cloud forest), and low-flying Red-crowned Parrots (*Amazona viridiginalis*) screaming a deafening *heelo, heelo, cra, cra, cra*! We had left the tropical lowland plants

Figure 13.1. At the corral on the north side of Rancho del Cielo. *Left to right:* George M. Sutton, Frank Harrison, Paul S. Martin, Demetrio Osorio, Roger Hurd, Everts Storms, and his riding mule, March 1949. Photo by P. Martin.

that I was just getting to know, such as strangler figs, *palo de rosa* (*Tabebuia*), *chaca* with its thin papery bark (*Bursera simaruba*), and the conspicuous blue-flowered vine known locally as *bougainvillea de la montaña* (*Petra*).

More to the point, and guaranteed to stir the blood of bird hunters no matter how trail weary, we heard bird calls completely new to us. On the forest floor Buck collected a gamebird with a melodious whistle ending in *pitch-wheeler, pitch-wheeler, pitch-wheeler*. It proved to be a long-clawed or Singing Quail (*Dactylortyx thoracicus*). We recognized some calls as belonging to birds of the montane and not the lowland forest, such as Spot-crowned Woodcreepers (*Lepidocolaptes affinis*) and Mountain Trogons (*Trogon mexicanus*). Here the trogons found plenty of rotten snags to excavate for their nests. Most memorable of all the bird songs was the heart-stopping, cascading chant of the Brown-backed Solitaire (*Myadestes occidentalis*), composed, it would seem, to add value to the magnificent mountain forest and *barranca* (ravine) scenery found in Mexico.

Roger rushed up to report a dead coral snake on the trail. With red, black, and yellow rings it indeed looked like a coral snake. We saved the specimen, which turned out to be a harmless colubrid, the coral snake mimic *Pliocercus elapoides*, known to feed on small salamanders. One distinction, the number of scale rows being seventeen instead of fifteen, is not a feature likely to be appreciated by ophidiophobes hoping to distinguish the mimic from the real thing in the field. Who wants to pick up what looks exactly like a live coral snake to determine its identity by counting its scale rows? In the cloud forest I found only mimics. The venomous coral snakes (*Micrurus*) lived at lower elevations (Martin 1956).

Following Cruz, we picked our way through the trees and around lichen- and moss-covered, rough-edged boulders. In the deep shade Cruz had trouble following the twisting, narrow trail. Buck recognized sweetgum (*Liquidambar*), tall, slender trees more than thirty meters high, their trunks clear of branches beneath a surprisingly small leafy crown in a tight canopy. In place of the woody vines that drape tropical trees of the lowlands, especially around clearings, we found epiphytic orchids, ferns, mosses, and abundant tank bromeliads (*Tillandsia*), the latter topped by pink flowering spikes resembling budding gladiolas. Their clasping leaves might hold at least a pint of water, which was attractive to a variety of small animals including salamanders and many invertebrates. We threaded our way between limestone pillars or spires blanketed by clumps of succulent-leaved agaves (*Agave celsi*).

Besides sweetgum, Buck noticed hickory, walnut, redbud, and other trees found in the eastern United States. The forest was taller, denser, and much richer in epiphytes than any I had seen before. Occasional small palms (*Chamaedorea*) added an exotic touch, as did blue millipedes on the forest floor. Although the place only lacked Rima the Bird Girl to qualify as Hudson's *Green Mansions*, I did not envy naturalist W. H. Hudson, who wrote his novel about an imaginary Venezuelan forest that he never actually saw. Here in the mountains of southern Tamaulipas we were not just imagining green mansions, we were in them.

As dusk descended, Cruz gave his riding mule free rein to help find the trail, obscured by fresh leaf fall from the evergreen oaks. Unlike the oaks of the eastern United States and Canada, most oaks in Mexico defoliate in spring, the dry season, rather than in the fall.

We hoped to reach our destination before dark. Cruz warned that on a foggy night without a flashlight or moonlight it was impossible to find the way "*sin ayuda de las bestias*" (without help from the mules). Finally, in the gathering gloom, the forest opened into a clearing bordered by a rough, worn fence connecting rock piles. A short, wiry man in his mid-forties with dark, curly hair and bushy eyebrows, dressed in blue jeans and *huaraches* (stout leather sandals soled with old automobile tire tread) sounded a gruff word of greeting. Instantly I felt at home.

News of our coming had preceded us, and Frank Harrison (Don Pancho) had supper waiting. Cruz and Frank saw to it that the mules would get theirs as soon as they were unloaded. Wasting no time with introductions, we headed for Frank's water bucket. Even here, in all this moss-draped dampness, surface water and springs were surprisingly scarce. Frank caught runoff in a rain barrel beneath his roof and carried drinking water in buckets from a small spring. Ducking under the low sweep of the eaves, we assembled in Frank's small log cabin to be served his specialty, thick buttermilk pancakes drenched in honey from Gómez Farías, with fresh butter from milk from his cows and peach preserves from his orchard.

To our protestations of a supper worthy of kings, Frank demurred: "'Tain't nothing, boys, just hunger's sweet sauce."

After supper Frank fielded questions about this magical place. He had been there since April 1933 (letter to the author, October 9, 1954).

"Are there jaguar?"

"Yeah, I've hunted *tigres* into the caves and shot them. The tigres and occasionally the bears come after my *becerros* [calves] and *novillas* [heifers]."

"Army ants?"

"Every year or two they clean out my cabin, all the rats, mice, scorpions, centipedes, and vinegaroons [whip scorpions]. When the ants come in I move out with the grub. In a day or two I can move back."

"What's that flapping around inside the cabin?"

"Probably vampires. They attack my cows, and screw worms infest the wounds. They don't bother people. And don't worry about taking your quinine." We took Atabrine. "The mosquitoes up here don't carry malaria."

"Out in the woods off the trail, watch out for balanced rocks over trap-door sinks. If you fall in and break a leg, or even if you don't, you may not be able to climb out. You're done for unless someone happens along." Frank shared our biological interests and briefed us with little prompting.

"Yes, the swifts nest here in hollow trees, and also in caves, along with motmots, hummingbirds, and owls. No, this is not the season for *faisán real* [royal pheasants, alias Great Curassow, *Crax rubra*]. They come up in late fall when the acorn crop is ripe. Keep an eye out for *ajoles*." The *ajole* is the Crested Guan (*Penelope purpurascens*); both it and *Crax* are game birds larger than the chachalaca, in the same family, and all are excellent fare.

"So that big leaf stung you? Don't touch it! It's *mala mujer*." Attracted by tiny Bumblebee Hummingbirds (*Atthis heloisa*), at the edge of a clearing I had brushed a tall spreading shrub with big, deeply dissected leaves and white flowers: *mala mujer* (bad woman), genus *Cnidoscolus*, in the spurge family. My arm still smarted.

"Down in Veracruz they have one even worse, *mal hombre*," Frank advised: *mal hombre* (bad man), genus *Urera*, in the nettle family; after lumbering it apparently increased in the cloud forest. Frank may have been mistaken. Marie Webster of Austin says the stinging hairs of *mal hombre* are not as painful as those of *mala mujer*.

"It's true, when he comes up into the mountains Don Everisto spends most of his time at La Joya. He's a Texan, and he likes the wide open country, with good places to hunt deer. Here we have the *verenda*. We'll go out some night with your flashlights and hunt them." Only Buck had heard of the *verenda* or tropical brocket, *Mazama americana*, a diminutive tropical deer even smaller than the dwarf white-tailed deer (*Odocoileus virginianus*) in the lower Florida Keys.

"I don't know where Everts gets his idea of monkeys up here, but Felix Burgos says there are flying squirrels over at Casa de Piedras." Everts Storms may have been right nevertheless; the spider monkey, *Ateles geoffroyi*, is listed from Tamaulipas in Leopold (1959). Later, among the small mammal bones from owl castings littering a cave floor near Casa de Piedras, I found jaws of flying squirrels, (*Glaucomys volans*; Koopman and Martin 1959).

"No, there is no more lumbering than what you saw from before the war along the trail above the *malacate*," said Frank. Lumbering had ceased ten years earlier. Most of the cloud forest remained uncut. That situation soon changed. Within two years, four-wheel-drive World War II surplus lend-lease trucks hauled logs to mills in the mountains, or, loaded with boards, lurched down incredibly rough, narrow, bouldery tracks from Rancho del Cielo, San Pablo, Casa de Piedras, and eventually from many other parts of the mountains to drying yards east of Gómez Farías and elsewhere in the lowlands. In the 1950s botanist Jack Sharp of the University of Tennessee narrowly escaped severe injury or worse when the lumber on the truck he was riding down the mountain broke loose on a pitching turn and spilled him off. Felix Burgos, who later became mayor of Gómez Farías, lost a son in a lumber truck accident.

We were thoroughly impressed with Frank's knowledge of the mountain forests and their natural history. He told us of two other ranches in the cloud forest. One nearby belonged to a neighbor, Paul Gehrlich (or Gellrich), a German national. In World War II Mexican soldiers arrested Paul at his ranch on some dubious spy charges. For the duration he was held at the cold, damp prison on Cofre de Perote in Veracruz. At the other ranch lived Felix Burgos and his family from Gómez Farías, according to Frank a half-day's walk to the southwest at a place called Rancho Viejo near Casa de Piedras. If our experience that day was an example, we had considerable respect for what a "half-day's walk" in this rough country might be like.

We did not ask the obvious question: what was Frank doing living a hermit's life up in the cloud forest? Later, Everts told us that Frank had been a school teacher at Chamal (now López Mateos), a small gringo colony in the lowlands. *Chamal* is the local common name for *Dioon edule*, a native cycad found on sunny limestone cliffs. In the 1930s, after he came out second best in an affair of the heart, Frank left for the mountains. Or perhaps it was to escape malaria. I prefer to share the view of many who befriended Frank over the years—that he was wise enough to appreciate the incredible beauty of Rancho del Cielo and did not waste his time in a vain search for something better (see Webster and Webster 2002).

Frank was a horticulturist. He had an orchard of peach, plum, and crabapple trees and an English walnut. He raised flowers for various lowland markets, especially gladiolas, and also amaryllis, gloxinias, and Easter lilies. In a small plant house, the walls of which could be opened on clear days to admit some sun, he grew potted plants, including begonias native to the region. He received copies of the American Begonia Society's journal, *Begonian*. Around holidays, especially Easter, local buyers would come to Rancho del Cielo for lilies and other cut flowers, which they would transport down the mountain by burro to Gómez Farías and then by bus to churches in Ciudad Victoria. In other seasons the burros would pack out loads of fruit. When I was back at Cornell making plans for a trip in the spring of 1949 Frank wrote asking for a backpack, pressure spray tank, and chemical spray to control lichens infesting his trees, for Cellotex roofing for his greenhouse, and for 32-20 rifle cartridges to hunt *tigres* and *verenda*. In 1951 in his jeep Byron Harrell hauled up a wood stove for Frank, the gift of Leland Blalock, a neighbor of Everts Storms. In 1957, when there was plenty of scrap lumber around sawmills, Frank built a new frame house to replace his drafty old log cabin. In those years his sister Ethyl (Mrs. Fred Williamson) came from Romeo, Michigan, to visit Frank at El Cielo.

As more biologists learned of the cloud forest and the Río Sabinas, both Rancho del Cielo and Rancho Pano Ayuctle became de facto biological field stations. Whether they intended it or not, both Frank Harrison and Everts Storms found themselves cast in the role of field station managers. Scientists, professionals, or students in training whom we knew or who are mentioned in documents and publications as visiting these places in the ten years after Buck Edwards, Roger Hurd, and I walked to Rancho del Cielo in 1948 included Dean Amadon, curator of ornithology, American Museum of Natural History; Jean T. DeBell, University of Minnesota; Robert T. Clausen, professor of botany, Cornell University; Howard Crum, botanist, Michigan State University; Rezneat Darnell, ichthyologist, University of Minnesota; Irby Davis, ornithologist, Harlingen; Robert Dressler, botanist and orchid specialist,

Harvard University; William Fox, botanist, University of North Carolina; and Byron Harrell, ornithologist, University of Minnesota. Byron was the first to undertake many months of research at all seasons at Rancho del Cielo.

In addition, Frank Harrison hosted Bruce Hayward, mammalogist, University of Michigan; William B. Heed, zoologist, Penn State University; Efraím Hernández, ecologist, and students from Monterrey; Joyce Heckenlaible (now Heck), ornithologist, University of Minnesota; Pauline James, biologist, Pan American College; Marshall Johnston, botanist, University of Texas; Edgar Kincaid, ornithologist, Austin; Eugene Lefebvre, ornithologist, University of Minnesota; John Maciewicz, zoologist, Cornell University; Richard MacNeish, archaeologist, National Museum of Canada, Ottawa; Marian Martin, zoologist, University of Michigan; Ted Miller, ornithologist, University of Michigan; James E. Mosiman, zoologist, University of Michigan; Jim Poppy, ornithologist, University of Michigan; C. Richard Robins, zoologist, Cornell University; Royal Shanks, ecologist, University of Tennessee; William Schaldach, zoologist, University of Kansas; George M. Sutton, ornithologist, University of Oklahoma; Thomas Uzzell, herpetologist, University of Michigan; Charles F. Walker, herpetologist, University of Michigan; and John Wolfe, botanist, Ohio State University. Undoubtedly there were others.

I'm sure between 1948 and 1957 there were many more visitors than I have indicated. Obviously the visitor stream and all this activity ended Frank's life as a hermit. He took it in stride. Everts Storms considered the increasing number of students to complete a thesis on their fieldwork in the Gómez Farías region to be graduates of U.P.A., the self-styled Universidad de Pano Ayuctle. "U.P.A. is proud of her graduates," He wrote to me with avuncular pride in a letter of August 7, 1955.

In 1953 Frank Blesse built a cabin next to Frank Harrison's, which he later sold to John Hunter, also from Brownsville. Both had discovered Rancho del Cielo through Harrison's articles in trade journals about his hybrid gloxinias and begonias. John Hunter's interest led Frank to will his land to Texas Southmost College (now the University of Texas at Brownsville); Hunter was a member of its Board of Trustees.

As part of the First International Palynological Congress held at the University of Arizona in Tucson, Bill Byers, Jim Mosiman, Ike Russell, and Carlos Seravia of Córdova, Argentina, helped me plan and lead a field trip to El Cielo. By commercial flights or in vans, two dozen paleobotanists and palynologists arrived in Brownsville, Texas, in March 1962; drove to Xicotencatl to inspect a recently excavated fossil mammoth; then drove back to the Río Sabinas, where Frank had arranged for two lumber trucks to take us up to El Cielo and on over the mountain to La Joya de Salas.

Returning to April of 1948: well fed and comfortable in the fresh mountain air, we were delighted to find ourselves at the Ranch of Heaven—my translation. The alternative, Sky Ranch, seems less appropriate. We traced an overpowering sweet scent to large, bell-shaped crepuscular white blossoms on Frank's *reina de noche* (queen of the night, *Datura suaveolens*), a cultivated shrub that is a magnet for pollinating hawk moths, as are its sweet-scented herbaceous relatives. We dug out our sleeping bags. Frank said it did not look like rain, and the dense short carpet grass outside his cabin provided a natural mattress.

My last question to Buck concerned the low hoots coming from the edge of the forest. He thought we might be hearing a Mottled Owl (*Ciccaba virgata*), not found in the United States. Just before dawn the owls were still hooting, while the Blue-Crowned Motmots tuned up with owlish *poots* of their own. Among the birds I found owls to be especially fascinating. For one thing, their regurgitated pellets provide an excellent record of small mammals found in the region. I yearned to collect that owl, whatever it was.

The next day Cruz returned to Pano Ayuctle, and Paul Gehrlich appeared to guide us northwest over the top of the Sierra to the mountain village of La Joya de Salas. A few miles north of Rancho del Cielo, back on the main trail between La Joya and the lowlands, we stepped aside for a string of six burros loaded with grain sacks. With them, alone and on foot, came their young wrangler Antonio, quite at home in these lonely woods, a twelve-year-old in a straw hat with a *morral* (sisal string bag) containing tortillas for his lunch. He was one of the boys from the Osorio family who would host us at La Joya. Following custom, Antonio solemnly bid us *adios* four times as he shook hands with each of us in turn before he continued on his way down to Rancho Pano Ayuctle to deliver shelled corn. Obviously he was considerably more trailwise than we were. The scene was deceptively peaceful.

A few years later I learned that Antonio Osorio was bushwhacked and killed at a narrow pass on a trail outside La Joya, victim of a mountain feud that involved his older brothers and some rival clan. In the country, blood feuds and killings are not unusual. Southern Tamaulipas may not be as lethal as rural Oaxaca, where a man has better than a 30 percent chance of being killed before he turns fifty (Greenberg 1989). Even before the days of the drug lords the *campo* knew deadly feuds.

The owner of the new sawmill at San Pablo, Sr. Luis Ubando, had a reputation for missing payrolls until in desperation his destitute employees left the mountains to seek work elsewhere. When least expected Ubando would appear at his mill, pay back wages to the few remaining workers, hire replacements for those who had left, and start over. He was widely despised. In a confrontation he gunned down an unarmed employee. Frank Harrison himself was murdered outside his cabin in 1966. His assailants, thought to include some of the agrarian newcomers to the cloud forest from Michoacán, expected to rob Frank of money he did not have. In particular they wanted his ranch (see Webster and Webster 2002).

As soon as we left the cloud forest to enter the pines, noisy Mexican Jays (*Aphelocoma ultramarina*) announced their presence with distinctive squawks. At around 1,400 meters they replaced the Green Jays (*Cyanocorax yncas*), while *pino triste* (drooping-needled pines, *Pinus patula*) replaced *Podocarpus*, the cloud forest gymnosperm widespread in the southern hemisphere. After more climbing we reached a partly eroded sinkhole, Agua Zarco, where a small spring was one of the few sources of semi-potable water to be found on the route—and uncertain at that. A few tall evergreens known as *cedro* (*Cupressus*) grew here, relatives of the cypress trees found in the Desierto de los Leones outside Mexico City. Other trees and shrubs included basswood (*Tilia*), magnolias (*Magnolia*), small yew trees (*Taxus*), two species of dogwood (*Cornus*), bay (*Myrica*), and an attractive evergreen shrub in the tea family (*Ternstroemia*). Later we learned that the rock rattlesnake we collected would be described as a new subspecies of *Crotalus lepidus*. On big boulders Buck collected a handful of *Sedum* (stone crop, a succulent) of a species that a year later would bring down for a visit Cornell's plant taxonomist who studied the evolution of *Sedum*, the late Robert T. Clausen.

Thanks to the lack of surface water, the pine-oak forest at the top of the mountain at 1,800–2,300 meters in elevation was free of livestock and uninhabited except for travelers like ourselves on the La Joya de Salas trail. Along with other wilderness attributes, it supported black bears (*Ursus americanus*), Maroon-fronted Parrots (*Rhynchopsitta terrisi*), and three species of lungless salamanders. Nevertheless, it was hardly remote. By listening closely from a ridge top on a damp day when the air was still, I could detect a familiar rumble: the faint sound of unmuffled truck traffic beyond the foot of the mountains on the Pan-American Highway, some 13 km due east and 2 km below us.

From the relatively wet pine-oak forest on the east side we hiked into drier forest on the west side, with many similarities to the pine-oak communities we had visited in Michoacán and Durango. Temperate forests of pines and oaks in the Sierra Madre Oriental and Sierra Madre Occidental crown the Mexican Plateau. In addition, we found handsome spreading *madroño* (*Arbutus xalapensis*), the smooth red trunks of which brighten pine-oak forests here and elsewhere. The pine-oak communities find their northern limit north of the Mexican border in the sky islands of southern Arizona, southern New Mexico, and west Texas (Marshall 1957).

Northwest of La Joya, trails descended into the arid Jaumave valley, dominated by creosote bush (*Larrea*), candelabra cactus (*Myrtillocactus*), arborescent yucca, and other xerophytes representative of southern parts of the Chihuahuan Desert. The linear distance from the cloud forest near Rancho del Cielo to desert scrub with creosote bush around Jaumave is less than 40 km, a remarkable biogeographic juxtaposition.

Like opposing folds in an accordion, the wet and dry sides of Mexico's sierras feature a rich mix of highly diverse wet and dry biotas in close proximity by virtue of steep climatic gradients. The transect we had experienced in the last few days reflected the basic change in forest composition and structure to be expected as one ascends in elevation from the lowlands or *tierra caliente* into the cool *tierra templada* of the mountains. Almost two hundred years ago in his exploration of the route from the tropical lowlands of Veracruz up into the Sierra Madre Oriental to glaciers on the high volcanoes outside Mexico City, the geographer Alexander von Humboldt described the fascinating tropical montane gradient. Some of the plants we were seeing (if not yet recognizing) belonged to species first described from Mexico by Humboldt and his team, which included Bonpland and Kunth.

At La Joya, a settlement of perhaps forty-five *jefes de familias* (heads of households), we found Everts's friends Doña Geronima and Don Cayetano Osorio, who introduced us to their sizable family. Displacing some of their older *niños*, they offered us their *casa de cocina* (cook house) for sleeping quarters and specimen preparation. The cook house had one drawback to which we could hardly object. At first light when the roosters began to crow and flap their wings, Doña Geronima and her daughters María and Chucha would enter chatting softly. In the traditional way they ground *masa* (corn kernels soaked in lye) with a *mano* (stone roller) on a stone *metate*, soon accompanied by the gentle pat-patting of hands shaping corn tortillas, a crucial part of our breakfast. Gradually, the delightful scent of hot tortillas on a small grill perfumed the tiny room. Sun splashes glinted through cracks in the walls. I heard a distant gunshot and looked around to find that my companions were already up and about, not slugabed under the feet of the breakfast cooks.

The small fields and dooryard gardens of the tiny houses around the lake of La Joya are surrounded by low stone walls topped by large clumps of prickly pear cactus or the sharp, stout, bayonetlike leaves of agave, a much larger species than the flaccid, easily crushed agaves growing on limestone spires in the cloud forest. In season, the living fence provides food and fiber for the villagers. In addition, it is habitat for packrats (*Neotoma*) and other small mammals, towhees (*Pipilo*), wrens, fence lizards, and snakes. Believing it must be another tropical specialty of Mexico, I admired the bell-shaped, intensely red flowers of a dooryard shrub. Later I discovered it was not a native. It was *granada* (pomegranate, genus *Punica*), introduced from the Mediterranean and widespread in gardens in highland Mexico and the southern United States.

Although we missed Everts up here in his favorite haunts, we remembered his stories. He once told us how the lake at La Joya originated. The local people sealed a sinkhole in the middle of the valley by sewing together four cow skins. Briefly they held water, until the cow skins rotted and the water again drained down into the sinkhole. The villagers repeated the process with rocks. This time the seal held. My doubts about Everts's story did not alter the fact that the mountains were cavernous, with one tremendous *sotano* (sinkhole) on a bench to the east of La Joya de Salas featuring a straight drop of over six hundred feet to a platform and with no bottom in sight.

Everts had told us of the time he had landed at La Joya in a light plane. He and a pilot friend from Chamal, said to have been General Eisenhower's personal pilot in World War II, had their eye on the sizable crop of epiphytic orchids flowering in trees near La Joya. In the dry season orchid pseudobulbs, the size of a cigar, supported beautiful lavender blossoms that festooned the limbs of *encinos* (oaks). Everts had determined that the orchid market in south Texas would be lucrative, and he and his pilot friend intended to transport live orchids from La Joya directly to a wholesale florist in the Rio Grande Valley.

Don Cayetano and other men and boys at La Joya moved rocks and graded a short *pista de aterrizaje* (airstrip). After landing, Everts and his friends denuded some oaks of epiphytic orchids, filling all available spaces in the plane with boxes of live plants. Eager to get the orchids out of the midday heat and off to market, the pilot gunned for takeoff. That was a mistake. There was no wind; the air was hot; and the pilot was not operating in the lowlands, as was his custom, but at a higher elevation in decidedly thinner air. Near the end of the pista the plane's wheels began to leave the ground—unfortunately not quite soon enough for the undercarriage to clear a stone fence beyond the end of the runway. Although the plane was totaled, no one was killed. On one of his trips to La Joya, Byron Harrell was bemused to see children in the village playing with a wheel of the airplane. When roads finally came to La Joya, Fred Webster reports that the oaks were stripped and all the epiphytic orchids were hauled out by truck.

Everts would live many more years, to die of a heart attack during his favorite moment of the day, while taking his accustomed late afternoon dip in the cool, refreshing waters of the Río Sabinas. He is buried in a small *campo santo* on the bank of the river.

After three days of good collecting around La Joya, Buck, Roger, and I returned to Rancho del Cielo. There they left me with plenty of cotton, the drying rack for bird skins, the pannier for storing them, a shotgun and aux, and some extra pesos. Until Buck's return from Ithaca, I would be able to explore the cloud forest as a guest of Frank, the best of all possible mentors.

The first day I followed Frank's suggestion that we investigate "Crystal Cave" and other sinkholes near his clearing. There must be many thousands of caves and sinkholes in the tropical evergreen forest, cloud forest, and pine-oak forest above Gómez Farías. New genera and species of cave invertebrates, including a blind scorpion, would be collected in the region by international cave research teams. I was interested in the vertebrates, and beyond nesting birds such as Vaux's Swifts (*Chaetura vauxi*), Mottled Owls, and motmots, the caves yielded amphibians, including a supposedly rare species of barking frog (*Eleutherodactylus hidalgoensis*); we found many individuals in the caves.

The prize was a new species of lungless salamander, described by Michigan's amphibian specialist, Charles Walker, as *Pseudoeurycea scandens*. The specific name *scandens* alluded to the animal's climbing habit. It was one of several species of local salamanders that scaled trees to find its way into tank bromeliads. We also collected them underground on the vertical walls of caves.

On the second day I decided to explore the forest on my own. Beyond Frank's fence at the south edge of his field, I discovered a mixed flock of Green Jays, Blue Mockingbirds, Mountain Trogons, and a Squirrel Cuckoo (*Piaya cayana*), all screaming their alarm calls and mobbing something. In my experience, in their breeding season birds are especially prone to mob predators. A medium-sized owl, slightly smaller than a Barred Owl (*Strix varia*), flew out of a tree and on into the forest. Not noticing the fog drifting in among the trees, I rushed after the avian mob. Harried at each stop by screaming birds, the owl kept trying to escape by flying deeper into the forest. Finally I got close enough to bag my prey; it proved to be a Mottled Owl.

While Mottled Owls are fairly common in the cloud forest, I did not know that at the time. Stalking, shooting, and capturing a trophy triggers an adrenaline rush familiar to all hunters, including bird collectors. Some say the rush is genetically rooted in hominid behaviors accompanying the evolution of our species. At the time I was innocent of such sociobiological theorizing. While wrapping my trophy in a cone of butcher paper to protect its feathers, I noticed that the woods were full of hungry mosquitoes. Then I began to realize that while chasing the mob of birds chasing the owl, I had paid no attention to where I was going. Where was Rancho del Cielo? To the north perhaps. Which way was that? Fog streamers and the bouldery roughness of the forest floor prevented line-of-sight travel.

Before the invention of global positioning instruments, the classic boy scout solution to being lost in mountains without a compass was simply to head downhill until you came to water, and then to follow the water. Sooner or later you can be sure to come to a road or a house or at least a path. In this case the boy scout rule of thumb would not help. According to Frank, between his ranch and the Río Sabinas at the foot of the mountain there was no surface water. I was on an extensive bench with no more idea which way was down than which way was north! Instead of searching for a way down, perhaps the solution was to climb a hill and hope to get a view of some landmark from above the mists.

Frank said there were only two clearings in the forest besides his own: the corn field of his neighbor, Paul Gehrlich, and Rancho Viejo, inhabited by Felix Burgos and his family, miles away. I had to find a clearing or wait for the fog to lift and search for a trail. The main north-south trail, the way we had come in, was not well marked and could easily be obscured by fresh leaf fall, as we discovered when Cruz had his troubles while guiding us to Rancho del Cielo. Would I notice if I crossed it? Later I realized that in fact I had crossed it, unknowingly.

After walking aimlessly through the fog for a time, I came to the foot of a hill beneath a small patch of blue sky. The climb up would be a simple matter, and at first it was, until the trees gave way to dense, tangled agaves, blackberry vines, and my nemesis, *mala mujer*. The stinging shrubs guarded loosely jumbled, sharp-edged karst limestone boulders famous for their "tear pants" weathering. The habitat is favored by orchids; Dressler (1962) reported eighteen species on North Hill north of Frank's. At the time I was oblivious to orchids. Eventually, peering down from a perch on a boulder through the swirling mists, I caught a glimpse of a distant clearing. Although it did not look like Frank's, faint sounds of chopping meant it was inhabited.

I found Paul Gehrlich repairing the fence around his corn field. He could not believe that I had managed to get lost, had had to climb South Hill to find my way, and in fact had crossed the trail to Gómez Farías before I came to Paul's place. He led me to the path back to Frank's.

Two years later Paul's health deteriorated (Frank had mentioned that Paul had syphilis), and in 1950 Frank's neighbor hanged himself from a beam of his house. Within another year Paul's clearing provided the site of a new lumber mill. Paul's great ambition had been to make his fortune or at least to earn a good living when lumber mills came to the forest. Although he missed his chance, the name of a mill on his property, now immortalized on the 1:50,000 scale topographic map of the Gómez Farías region, is San Pablo.

The weeks at Rancho del Cielo passed quickly. Mid-May arrived all too soon. I assembled field notes on nesting behavior and prepared a representative collection of the breeding birds along with some of the transients or visitors from the tropical lowlands below, the pine-oak forest above, or North American species in their spring migration.[2] While the resident species included many that were new to me, few were new to museum collections from northeastern Mexico. After the severe *norte* of February 1–3, 1951, when temperatures descended to minus 6° C at Rancho del Cielo, Frank Harrison collected a new bird record for the state of Tamaulipas, the Black Thrush (*Turdus infuscatus*). The freeze killed vast numbers of tank bromeliads growing on the trunks of trees in the cloud forest (Martin 1951).

If biogeographic novelty were the objective, I was looking at the wrong part of the biota. In fact, I was so focused on the birds that I failed to appreciate the trees. Within a year, botanists and plant geographers would begin to set that right when the next collector, well trained in ecology, sent them herbarium specimens. His name was Byron E. Harrell. He wrote a superb master's thesis (Harrell 1951) on the birds of Rancho del Cielo, and he censused both the breeding birds and the trees, the latter including both eastern temperate and montane tropical elements in a remarkable association (Sharp et al. 1950; Hernandez et al. 1951).

In mid-May Buck arrived with his jeep and trailer. We drove to El Salto in San Luis Potosí to search for macaw nests, and then we returned to Lake Pátzcuaro for more collecting and field observations in the critical season for breeding birds. We collected 238 specimens of 104 species, 8 of them new for Michoacán (Edwards and Martin 1955). Nevertheless, for me the Tamaulipas experience overshadowed everything else. I had already begun to dream of a return.

Letters from Doc

In Ithaca in the fall of 1948 I learned that Buck did not plan his next trip to Mexico until spring. I couldn't wait. Fortunately, two close friends were ready to go. Bill Heed, a neighbor and West Chester Bird Club member, would take a semester break from Penn State University to join a Mexican trip. So would C. Richard (Dick) Robins, a classmate at Cornell who had spent the summer of 1948 collecting birds in the West with Bill Dilger. His family knew Doc Sutton from Sutton's days as state ornithologist of Pennsylvania.

Meanwhile, mail arrived from Sutton at the Museum of Zoology in Ann Arbor, the majority of them full-page, single-spaced letters rich in content about what birds to look for and how to prepare specimens; his rebuttal of my tilt toward "Sibley skins"; and a succinct comparison of the goals of a professional (bread-and-butter) collector, oriented toward sale of specimens, and those of the researcher or field naturalist, oriented toward learning more about birds and their taxonomy and distribution. Sutton wrote of his own professional life at the time, in transition from freelancing to a more secure faculty position at the University of Oklahoma; of his plans for contributions to the *Arctic Encyclopedia*; of his problems with publishers in not getting promised advances for his paintings; and of his plans to come down in 1949 with Roger Hurd. He wrote all this in the spirit of a long-term friend and mentor. Here are samples:

> November 9, 1948: By this time you may have written to Van Tyne [Josselyn Van Tyne, curator of ornithology at the Museum of Zoology, University of Michigan, was not interested in northern Mexico]. I'd like to have you know, however, that I *am* deeply interested in good Tamaulipas material of all sorts, and especially in material from Soto la Marina and Alta Mira. And the important fact is that between now and your departure time you can be doing something by way of turning out a perfect skin. By this I mean *perfect*. You'll be down there at a season when the birds are in fine plumage. By this time there's no reason why your specimens should not average better than good. This is where I may be of real help. How can we work it out? . . . It isn't clear to me how everything is going to get done in the next few weeks [Sutton was working on plates], but I'm a great believer in charging ahead, so keep right at the skins and let me help in any possible way. The important thing is for you to be ready to do a bang-up job.
>
> November 16, 1948: Because your letter seems important to me I am dropping everything to answer it. I enjoyed the talk I had with you [in Ann Arbor with Buck in June] and I believe in you. I therefore want your friendship—to put the matter bluntly. I hope that there will be no misunderstandings between us. First of all, I suspect I have neglected to acknowledge the Rancho del Cielo notes. They probably are the *major basis* for a forthcoming paper which will get written when Roger and I return. *They are just that important.* My plan may change, of course, but I'm sure such a paper is in order and I want to write it.[3]
>
> There are two sorts of collecting. Worthington used to charge a flat rate, and he'd go after enough catbirds and the like to get his day's wages and then dig for the rare things as the remainder of his time allowed. *That is not good ornithology.* It is good business, but not good ornithology. See the difference?
>
> December 13, 1948: In that whole area [the Gómez Farías region and southern Tamaulipas] we must constantly be on the lookout for wholly unexpected tropical things. The best proof of this to date (to my way of

thinking) is that lizard *Laemanctus*. No slow-moving creature of that sort could have made its way to the Río Sabinas without finding tropical conditions contiguous from Tabasco to Gómez Farías. I'm especially interested, too, in the northernmost tip of this tropical finger. I think it must be west or southwest of Linares. Leopold [A. Starker Leopold of the University of California–Berkeley] wouldn't have found Motmots there without good reason. Keep working at the birdskins.

I never took his courses. Except in Michigan in the summer of 1949 and on a few other occasions, our paths never crossed. He left Ithaca for Ann Arbor before I entered Cornell, and he left Ann Arbor to become a faculty member at the University of Oklahoma before I entered the University of Michigan as a grad student in the Museum of Zoology.

To work up our collections at Ann Arbor in the summer of 1949, he found accommodations for Dick Robins, Bill Heed, and me, along with zoologist Shirley Windnagle of Cornell. At the Museum of Zoology we crowded into Doc's office and plowed through his extensive reprint and correspondence files between forays into the bird range for specimens to compare with our own. I found the process of identifying our Mexican specimens almost as fascinating as collecting them in the first place. It was a very happy time, with song fests in the evening, Doc playing a small pump organ for accompaniment. Over a three-year interval he helped us through the publication of various manuscripts, our first attempts at scientific writing (Martin 1951; Martin et al. 1953; Robins and Heed 1951; Robins et al. 1951).

Return to Tamaulipas

Thanks to a thorough introduction to Mexican fieldwork assisting Buck Edwards in 1948 and with strong encouragement from Doc, I yearned to return. In early February 1949, Bill Heed, Dick Robins, and I, all college juniors raised in eastern Pennsylvania, escaped winter by somehow wedging ourselves into a Willys four-wheel-drive jeep my parents helped to finance, pulling our gear in a Sears and Roebuck trailer modeled after the type of rig favored by Buck Edwards. Heading south we made a few stops en route. In Baton Rouge we visited Dr. George Lowery, a sponsor of tropical research and curator of the tropical bird collection at Louisiana State University. In Harlingen, Texas, we visited Mr. and Mrs. L. Irby Davis. Irby Davis was using the Cornell technique, bird song recording, to help identify tropical birds. His recordings revealed that different populations within a species might vary not only in their feather color, as one could see in traditional museum collections, but also in their songs. On a return trip to Brownsville, Mrs. Davis invited us to bring our specimens to her high school biology class and to explain our interest in Mexico's fauna. We had two magnificent six-foot yellow and black tiger rat snakes (*Spilotes pullatus*) from west of the Río Sabinas. They stole the show.

Lowery and his associates assembled field collections from around Xilitla in San Luis Potosí, just south of Tamaulipas. How we longed to find Tamaulipan populations of toucans, King Vultures (*Sarcoramphus papa*), and, in the case of plants, tree ferns or the other tropical species that the LSU collectors found in eastern San Luis Potosí. The ratio of tropical to temperate birds (and other plants and animals as well) increased steadily on a gradient through eastern Mexico from south Texas south to Tabasco. We wanted to enrich what was known of southern Tamaulipas.

Like so much in biogeography, it all turned on knowing both where a species lived and where it didn't. Establishing a record is straightforward. Classically it meant specimens in museum collections. Establishing absence, a negative record, is another matter entirely. Absence is intangible. It cannot be shot, skinned, stuffed, and labeled. The most to hope for is some sort of consensus or opinion of field workers. For example, while no one to our knowledge had found toucans in Tamaulipas, that did not mean they were not there. Perhaps toucans lurked in tropical habitats in Tamaulipas that no collectors or qualified observers had visited.

At the start of our 1949 trip Dick Robins, Bill Heed, and I decided to test the idea that some tropical birds reached their northern limit near the coast, rather than at the foot of the Sierra Madre. Sutton had encouraged us to try both Soto la Marina east of Victoria and tropical lowlands near Altamira, north of Tampico. We decided to explore the thorn forest of the coastal plain northeast of the Sierra de Tamaulipas, a region I understand has since been extensively cleared and cultivated. We left the new Matamoros-Victoria highway at the entrance of a small dirt road where a very small sign pointed to Soto la Marina.

I stopped to consult a young woman standing alone at the junction and nursing an infant. She verified that this was our road, and asked if she could she ride along with us.

"*¡Como no!*" I replied gallantly from the driver's seat.

"*¿Con mi familia?*" she added, as six or seven people of all ages, and mostly male, emerged on cue from behind bushes or scrambled up out of a ditch where we had not spotted them. It was a classic case of bait and switch.

We thought our jeep and trailer were already pretty heavily loaded with field equipment, food, and duffel in addition to the three of us, not to mention Cellotex roofing for Frank's plant house and spraying equipment for his orchard at Rancho del Cielo. Interpreting any response short of an outraged "No!" as affirmative, the multitude somehow managed to attach themselves to the jeep and trailer and we were off, with Bill and Dick clinging to the small side steps of the jeep, having yielded their part of the front seat to the mother and her infant. The jeep tires bellied out ominously with the load. I drove slowly, trying with scant success to avoid raising clouds of dust out of deep, dust-filled ruts. But there was a bright side. Our passengers proved to be a guarantee of a friendly reception in Soto la Marina, where the whole town turned out to inspect us when we arrived, hours later.

At a suitable camp in the thorn scrub (*monte*) outside town, local *muchachos* brought us slider turtles and an armadillo (*Dasypus novemcinctus*) from pools in an arroyo. The field catalogue indicates that in our first two days in the thorn forest we collected a Red-billed Pigeon, a Brown Jay (*Cyanocorax morio*), a Plain Chachalaca (*Ortalis vetula*), and a Crimson-collared Grosbeak (*Rhodothraupis celaeno*), all birds one might find as far north as the Rio Grande valley (the grosbeak is accidental there). We decided to explore the country closer to the coast. Instead, sooner than planned, circumstances led us to return the way we had come.

On our third day at our field camp on the Río Soto la Marina, Dick lost his appetite, and that night he slept fitfully. Never one to complain, in the morning Dick did admit to a severe backache. He was also running a high temperature. Bill and I consulted our book on tropical medicine with little to show for our efforts. We decided not to tempt the fates, loaded up, made as soft a bed as we could for Dick in the middle of the jeep with his head next to the gear shift and his feet in the extension box, and drove back to the highway, unencumbered this time by hitchhikers. Since Brownsville was much farther away, we decided to seek medical aid in Ciudad Victoria.

Dick suffered in silence through a painful ride. He was very sick. By midafternoon he had been admitted to the hospital in Victoria. Bill and I could camp in Dick's room and help him translate if necessary. We received our share of attention from the nurses—"¡*Vienen tres gringos, jovenes, guapos, en el cuarto 102!*" (Three attractive young gringos have come to room 102!). A young doctor who spoke good English examined Dick and took X-rays. Spots on Dick's lungs were diagnosed as pneumonia. Not to worry, he would begin treatment (penicillin shots), and the prognosis was good.

In a day or two Dick's temperature was down, his back pains had disappeared, and X-rays verified that the spots were gone. Could Dick's illness have been triggered by exposure to dust and spores on the road to Soto la Marina? Our hospital expenses were modest, no more than a stay at a local motel. We left for the Río Sabinas then trekked up to the cloud forest, where I collected salamanders and snakes while Bill and Dick continued to La Joya to start a project on the oak-pine birds. In the middle of March, Doc Sutton and Roger Hurd came up for a few days, and we spent them together up in the pines scrambling through very rough karst country, hunting without success for high-flying, noisy but elusive Maroon-fronted Parrots, which I had stalked unsuccessfully the year before. To the best of my knowledge no one has obtained specimens of this species in the Gómez Farías region.

In early April we left the mountains to launch an expedition east into the Sierra de Tamaulipas. Down at Rancho Pano Ayuctle we discovered a venerable 1929 Model A Ford, a panel truck with Minnesota plates parked under one of Everts's monkey ear trees. He emerged from his siesta and greeted us warmly.

"Why hullo, boys; how's La Joya and Don Pancho?"

"People up there are fine; Frank says the peach crop should be good this year. Who is your Minnesota visitor?"

"I think he said 'Brian Harold.' He's out in the *huapilla* hunting *perdiz* [tinamou]; it's for his thesis."

Bill, Dick, and I exchanged glances.

"Hmm. Lots of luck! That's a hell of a project," I muttered.

While Everts and his *vaqueros* did not seem to mind the ticks and chiggers on the trails through dense *huapilla*, the main tinamou habitat, the ectoparasites raised hell with gringos new to the country, especially those whose immune systems overreacted to the unfamiliar bites. To make matters worse, the margins of the swordlike leaves of the ground bromeliad locally known as *huapilla* (*Bromelia pinguin*) were armed with recurved hooks. Our attempts to leave the cow trails for deeper parts of the thicket resulted in painful lacerations. It paid to cut a new trail, a slow job requiring skilled machete work. The birds were ventriloquists. Who knew where their low whistles came from? Possibly one could study them from above, in a blind on stilts. In the breeding season, males could be lured into view by an imitation of their whistle. This was not yet the breeding season though, and the birds stuck to their haunts in the *huapilla* thickets like rails in a cattail marsh.

Streaked with sweat through his hunting jacket and wiping his glasses, Byron Harrell (alias Brian Harold) emerged from the *huapilla*. No, he had not seen any tinamou, although we could plainly hear them from where we stood. "When do they nest?" Byron asked as we shook hands.

"They are easier to see up at Rancho del Cielo in the cloud forest," Bill volunteered. "It's cooler up there; the forest is free of ticks, chiggers, and malaria. And besides, there is no *huapilla*."

Byron scratched himself absent-mindedly, a serious sign, I thought, of chigger trouble ahead. We could see that he was considering his options.

"Here, have a look at some trophies." We showed Byron some of our cloud forest specimens, including nightingale-thrushes and euphonias. Then to our amazement he offered to check their ranges in Ridgway's *Birds of North and Middle America*. It came in many volumes and was out of print (Ridgway and Friedmann 1901–46). What was he talking about?

We followed Byron to his truck. Inside on a rack on one wall he had not only a complete set of Ridgway but also a set of Hellmayr and various other crucial reference works on tropical birds, or on Mexico, all checked out of the University of Minnesota's library for the spring semester.

"The few people at Minnesota interested in Mexican birds," Byron claimed, "promised not to recall any of these 'til I'm back."

On the opposite side of the truck on another set of shelves were tin cans of various sizes, shining in silver and gold with large numbers printed in grease pencil on the sides of the cans where labels had been removed.

"What's with the numbers on these cans?" Dick asked.

"Before I left Minneapolis my major professor and other friends held a shower. They knew I was traveling on a shoe string. They gave me their extra canned goods for the trip." His professor was Doc Sutton's former field assistant Dwain Warner.

"And what about the numbers?"

"Well, they claim I don't ever write home, and now they think I'll have to. When I write they will reply with a key to the numbers, indicating the contents of some of the cans."

"Yeah. So you just open anything and take your chances?"

"Actually it's not hard to guess contents by can size and shape. It's a break from eating beans, *fideo* [pasta], and tortillas down here. Want some sweet pickles?"

While Byron arranged with Everts for a mule and guide to Rancho del Cielo, we loaded the trailer for our trip to the Sierra de Tamaulipas. Just before we left, Everts gave us another letter from Doc. It could not have come at a better time.

> Ann Arbor, April 3, 1949. I believe I should undertake to underwrite your entire Sierra de Tamaulipas enterprise *even if I can't promise to take all the rest of the birds*. The point is that that region needs to be better known. I have no desire to monopolize the field, so will take the collection and even allow you publication rights, the understanding being, of

course, that I will be consulted concerning selection of possible types, etc. I am really keen to help you fellows get going—and am possibly just as much interested in that as I am in the birds themselves. So hop to it; get big birds and small; and put them up the best you can. I'd say the average of those at hand is very good. Fortunately there has been no destruction by insects and no molding. That is good. . . . Don't let up on that ten dollar owl. Soon may he die.

Sutton especially wanted screech owls from southern Tamaulipas. We collected one. And, with his blessing, we did hop to it in the Sierra de Tamaulipas and north of Tampico, getting big birds and small.

We squeezed into the jeep and started east across the coastal plain from Ciudad Mante toward Tampico. Near Bernal de Horcasitas a distinctive volcanic plug rises abruptly above a gentle fan. From a distance it looks like the crown of a mighty sombrero. Here we found a road through dry tropical thorn forest heading north toward the distant blue dome of the Sierra de Tamaulipas. We drove on a surprisingly good dirt road, a mystery since we found no settlements and few clearings. We passed no other traffic. Suddenly we came upon a big clearing sporting a well-graded airstrip, long enough to accommodate a commercial passenger plane like a DC-3. What did this mean? A major oil exploration, perhaps? What was going on?

As the road climbed up out of the tropical lowlands we came to another surprise. In front of us was a *brecha*, a narrow gap in the scrub forest cleared for a brand new barbed-wire fence. To top it off we arrived at a large gate complete with a guardhouse! We had not seen its like before in rural Mexico. The gate was not locked, and no one was around; we drove on through. We climbed up past huisache and mesquite grassland into spreading oaks draped with Spanish moss, habitat for the Tropical Parula (*Parula pitiayumi*) and other warblers. Distant ridges supported pines. The oaks and pines looked like the dry pine-oak country around La Joya de Salas at 1,500 meters, above and to the west of the cloud forest. Nevertheless, here we were at only 900 meters.

In the Sierra Madre Oriental at this elevation between Rancho del Cielo and Gómez Farías, cloud forest gives way to tropical semi-evergreen forest. Here the mountains were much drier, there were no mists, and none of the local oaks, hickories, or pines resembled the species to be found below Rancho del Cielo. Nevertheless, we were high enough to feel some relief from the bakeoven temperatures experienced in the dry tropical thorn forest near the airstrip. It was another lesson in Humboldtian life zones, this time on a drier gradient.

What was the meaning of the big air strip, why was this road so good, and who owned the gated land on which we trespassed? Where was everybody? We topped a rise and gasped. Down below us was the answer. Within a spacious valley and enclosed by a new stone wall behind a massive gate, we viewed a luxurious new stone hacienda with tiled roof, at least a six-bedroom spread, in final stages of construction. There were modern outbuildings, a large corral, new pickups and cattle trucks, a grader (hence the good road), breed Brahma steers, and horses and mules of a size not often seen in rural Mexico. Nowadays one would suspect that such opulence reflected the investment of a mighty mafioso, a successful drug lord.

This was a far cry from the impoverished rural villages we had visited, like Soto la Marina, Gómez Farías, or La Joya de Salas. Wherever we had been in rural Mexico we had not been turned away; but we had not encountered a place like this. We were collecting birds for George M. Sutton. In at least a few circles that name meant something. Perhaps the owners shared our enthusiasm for ornithology. We drove up to the main gate and proceeded to make ourselves known.

We had bungled into the hacienda of Clint Murchison at siesta time. In the late 1940s, according to *Time* magazine, he was one of the ten wealthiest Texans. Besides half of the top of the Sierra de Tamaulipas, his Mexican holdings included Isla de Lobos off the coast of Veracruz. We were received by his ranch manager, Howard Reed, another Texan, who welcomed us to Hacienda Acuña, answered our questions, and invited us to spend the night at the Hacienda itself.

The next day we asked for and received help in locating a field camp. We were relieved that no one suggested we base ourselves out of one of the spare rooms inside the hacienda. Switching from a field camp routine to plush indoor accommodations is not as easy as it would seem. And collecting birds around the hacienda might spoil our welcome. This was not Frank Harrison's Rancho del Cielo.

Howard Reed took us three miles northwest of the hacienda to a camp site under spreading oaks just above a deep ravine in tropical dry forest. He promised to supply riding mules and a guide so that we could expand our operation. Close to our camp there were *tinajas* (rock cisterns), one of the few sources of permanent water. Brahma steers from the hacienda polluted some of the *tinajas* but not all of them. We filled our five-gallon can from one that was clear. We discovered larval newts (*Diemictylis*) in another *tinaja*, an added bonus because we knew of them only in the eastern United States. Howard invited us for dinner in a few days, when he said Mr. Murchison would be present to receive us.

When the day came, we cleaned our boots, dressed in clean khakis, combed our hair, and shaved. We selected two of our bird skins, an Elegant Trogon and an Acorn Woodpecker, to serve as house gifts. Accompanied by a much younger woman—bedecked with jewels, overdressed, and overexposed, I thought—Murchison received us as though we were old family friends from Dallas. We learned that the duke and duchess of Windsor, no less, had flown in recently for a visit (we knew the airstrip). We learned that the famous herpetologist Raymond Ditmars had collected the tropical rattlesnake at Murchison's island, Los Lobos, on the Veracruz coast. We expressed a keen interest in visiting the island ourselves, and eventually Howard Reed mentioned a motel and a date when he would meet us outside Tampico to take us there.

When the time came, we drove to Tampico and spent two nights in the designated motel with no sign of Howard Reed. Giving up on him, we left Tampico driving north to Zamorina and east along newly blazed truck roads laid out for seismic prospecting by rigs from the oil fields. The tracks led us into sparsely inhabited, undisturbed tropical deciduous forest behind the coast. The tracks ended when mangroves appeared in salt water at the edge of a coastal lagoon. Fresh water was hard to find. I discovered that boiled sea water is too salty to substitute for fresh in cooking breakfast oatmeal. With the exception of some new records of shorebirds for the Tamaulipas coast (Robins et al. 1951), we found no novelties.

In June we returned to the Sierra de Tamaulipas to discover nesting Black-headed Nightingale-Thrushes (*Catharus mexicanus*), a species we knew only from the cloud forest above Gómez Farías. We did not expect to find them in dry open pine-oak woodland. Another surprise was the presence of Red Crossbills (*Loxia curvirostra*). The small size of their gonads, examined in birds we collected, did not indicate breeding activity.

A year later, through our encouragement, herpetologists Karl Patterson Schmidt and Hyman Marx of the Field Museum in Chicago wrote to Murchison for permission to visit the Sierra de Tamaulipas. From his reply they understood that they would be welcome. But when they arrived the guardhouse was occupied, the gate was locked, and nothing they could say or do would induce the guard to let them through. Had we poisoned the well, so to speak? Nowhere else in Mexico in those days did we or any other field collectors, to our knowledge, find themselves shut out from interesting habitat. It portended things to come on both sides of the border, when the discovery of rare or endangered species clashed with property rights, at least in the minds of some land owners.

Fast Forward Fifty Years

In mid-June Dick and I left Bill at Rancho del Cielo. He returned north with Byron Harrell, helping nurse Byron's ancient Ford out of Mexico, a major adventure in itself. On our way north Dick and I visited George Williams at Rice University in Houston and George Lowery and his field team, Robert and Marcy Newman, at Louisiana State University in Baton Rouge. At the time, Williams and Lowery were embroiled in a hot argument about trans-Gulf versus circum-Gulf migration of songbirds. Evidently both routes were important. We envied the rich tropical element, including toucans, that the Newmans had found in San Luis Potosí just south of southern Tamaulipas.

By the end of 1949 my interests shifted from birds to herpetology and biogeography. In the 1950s, with help from other field parties and from local residents, I assembled a collection of twenty-five hundred reptiles and amphibians representing a hundred species from the Gómez Farías region (Martin 1956). Byron and I reviewed the biogeography of the Mexican cloud forest and concluded that interconnections with temperate forests in the eastern United States predated the Pleistocene (Martin and Harrell 1957).

After Ed Deevey published *Biogeography of the Pleistocene* (1949), it was clear that to probe the dynamic world of the last ice age and its mysteries would require a historical approach such as fossil pollen analysis or other techniques of Quaternary paleoecology. Armed with advanced degrees, including two years as a post-doc plus a National Science Foundation grant, I managed to land a job at the University of Arizona. Using radiocarbon dates and the mummified contents of caves in arid parts of Arizona and adjacent states, University of Arizona students helped me pursue the last ground sloths and other extinct ice age megafauna. We searched for the cause or causes of their extinction, "not finding game large enough in this or any vegetable wilderness," to steal a few words from Thoreau's *Walden*.

Dick Robins and Bill Heed followed career shifts of their own. Dick became an ichthyologist and marine biologist at the University of Miami and is now emeritus curator of ichthyology at the Museum of Natural History of the University of Kansas (Courtenay and Robins 1997).

Bill fell under the influence of Dobzhansky's *Genetics and the Origin of Species*, studied evolution of wild *Drosophila* (fruit flies), took his Ph.D. at the University of Texas, and joined me at the University of Arizona, where he taught genetics and evolution. He discovered the secrets of wild species of *Drosophila* inhabiting yeasty cactus rot of columnar cacti found in the thorn scrub and thorn forest of the arid tropics (Fogleman 1990).

Through all this, Doc Sutton kept us on a mailing list that included queries for guidance about what to do with his Mexican bird collections, because he felt we were a part of them. He and Dick Robins kept close contact, and Dick tells me that our specimens are now in Wilmington, Delaware, at the Delaware Museum of Natural History.

In the Sierra Madre above the Río Sabinas, on land he purchased and gave to Texas Southmost College in Brownsville, Doc Sutton financed habitat preservation for birds such as Crested Guans and for mammals such as jaguars (*Panthera onca*). The "Sutton Reserve" is a part of the field station at Rancho del Cielo.

In the 1950s, in recognition of the unique ecological features of the region, including the cloud forest, Byron Harrell and I began an abortive campaign for habitat protection, supported by scientists on both sides of the border, including Enrique Beltrán, Irby Davis, Efraím Hernández, Karl Koopman, Jack Sharp, and others. We raised more than eight hundred dollars, a trivial sum but enough in those days to purchase (if not to secure) a sizable tract of uncut forest. We left it with Everts Storms, who offered to act as our agent in any transaction. Our hopes died with Everts in the early 1960s, and we failed to recover our assets in the settlement of his tangled estate.

I suspect it was just as well. Land acquisition by foreigners, especially in parts of Mexico close to the international boundary, can be a legal challenge. Only the genius of John Hunter and his friends in Tamaulipas and Texas, not to mention the interest and influence of Mexico's leading conservationist at the time, Enrique Beltrán in Ciudad México (Simonian 1995), and especially the enthusiastic collaboration of Frank Harrison, could have succeeded in turning El Cielo into a field station and reserve maintained by Texas Southmost College. Much of the incredible effort is laid out in *The Road to El Cielo* by Fred and Marie Webster (2002).

Although we failed in our attempts at purchasing a tract of uncut cloud forest, I feel that our research efforts and publications helped to support Mexican conservationists in their establishment in 1985 of the El Cielo Biosphere Reserve, embracing 144,530 ha in the Gómez Farías region and administered though the Universidad de Tamaulipas.

In July 1988, thanks to an invitation extended by Humberto Sosa, who collaborated with ethnobotanist Gary Nabhan to protect threatened cacti and succulent species in the dry parts of the Gómez Farías region, I participated in the first *Simposio de Investigacion en La Reserva de la Biosfera "El Cielo,"* held in Ciudad Victoria. It was an opportunity to meet Gonzalo Halffter, the scarab beetle specialist who founded Mexico's Institute of Ecology and succeeded Enrique Beltrán as a leader of Mexico's conservation movement (Simonian

1995). Along with faculty and students from Mexico's Universidad Autónoma de Tamaulipas (UAT), Universidad Nacional Autónoma de México, Programa Hombre y Biosfera, and France's Université Pierre et Marie Curie, Paris, and participants from seventeen other institutions, I attended a three-day session held at the UAT in Victoria.

The program covered many aspects of ecology, basic and applied, a stimulating and moving experience that showed the value of the Gómez Farías region as a tropical study site for university students from Mexico City, Tamaulipas, Texas, and elsewhere. There were heated verbal exchanges among the Mexican ecologists regarding the effectiveness of their country's national parks, in which protection of biota runs up against hard-won rights of land use by rural people. The value of the research in guiding conservation, management, and sustainable use of El Cielo, as well as other reserves, was obvious. It was my first exposure to the concept of community-based management (CBM) of reserves, in which local people who derive some economic benefit from a reserve become stakeholders, with a personal interest in the fate of the reserve (Western and Wright 1994).

There have been awesome changes. From Barbara Warburton at Texas Southmost College I learned of a terrible fire in 1971, following lumbering of the decade of the 1960s, a hurricane, and an unusually severe drought. The fire raged for months. Hollow trees turned into virtual blast furnaces as flaming gasses roared upward (Webster and Webster 2002). I never imagined a firestorm could burn through the cloud forest where the mean annual precipitation for Rancho del Cielo is 100 inches (2.54 meters), based on twenty-two years of data supplied by Larry Lof, director of the Rancho del Cielo Station. Normally wildfire would be out of the question.

Recent findings in historical ecology and the earth sciences reveal that the natural environment has been and is exposed to more destructive changes over time than we once thought. Archaeological remains around Rancho del Cielo indicate prehistoric human activity and presumably prehistoric disturbance, perhaps at a scale even beyond what happened in the second half of the twentieth century. Fire, drought, freeze, and hurricanes are among the historic hazards, while extinction of mammoths, giant edentates, and other megafauna at the end of the ice ages reflects more ancient ones. The failure of the Gómez Farías region to support more tropical species like toucans and monkeys may bespeak a more turbulent history than we imagined during our trips in the late 1940s and 1950s. "Pristine wilderness" is in the eye of the beholder.

I understand from Fred Webster that the reserve initiated by George Miksch Sutton, John Hunter, Barbara Warburton, and other faculty of Texas Southmost College still harbors Crested Guans. If the Great Curassow survives in the region it would be there. Jaguar persist and have been seen in the streets of Gómez Farías. There has been a seismic shift in consciousness regarding natural area management since the 1940s. Still, there are major problems in sustainability, as the conference of 1988 on El Cielo indicated. The República de México has a variety of splendid biosphere reserves (Simonian 1995). Mexico and the Estado de Tamaulipas can take particular pride in the one in the Gómez Farías region that includes El Cielo.

In recent years the Green Mansions of Tamaulipas have become a training ground for students and their mentors from both sides of the border and from other lands. While the bird collecting days are long past, there is much to learn, not least about sustainability and its handmaiden, community-based conservation management. George Sutton would have urged us on. He would have admonished us to "hop to it!"

Acknowledgments

I thank Ernest P. Edwards, Byron Harrell, William B. Heed, Larry Lof, Mary Ellen Morbeck, Ken Parkes, C. Richard Robins, Steve Russell, Jennifer Shopland, Fred and Marie Webster, and Kevin Winker for various kinds of editorial help; residual errors are mine.

Notes

1. Editor's note: In his dissertation, Warner (1947) recorded only purchasing a captive male Kagu for four dollars. He also recorded that the peak of trapping this species for export had occurred before WW II and that, fortunately for its preservation, export had recently been outlawed.

2. Among the non-passerines at Rancho del Cielo I put up specimens of a Thicket Tinamou, Sharp-shinned Hawk, Great Black-Hawk, Ornate Hawk-Eagle, Bat Falcon, Singing Quail, White-tipped Dove, White-crowned Parrot, Squirrel Cuckoo, Tamaulipas Pygmy-Owl, Mottled Owl, two Vaux's Swifts, an Azure-crowned Hummingbird, two Amethyst-throated Hummingbirds, a Bumblebee Hummingbird, Blue-crowned Motmot, Golden-olive Woodpecker, Acorn Woodpecker, Yellow-bellied Sapsucker, two Smoky-brown Woodpeckers, and a Pale-billed Woodpecker (which Sutton preferred to call the "Flint-billed Woodpecker"). Among the passerines I shot and stuffed two Olivaceous Woodcreepers, three Ivory-billed Woodcreepers, two Spot-crowned Woodcreepers, three Gray-collared Becards, a Dusky-capped Flycatcher, Olive-sided Flycatcher, Wood-Pewee, Tufted Flycatcher (*Mitrephanes phaeocercus*), Green Jay, Spot-breasted Wren, Blue Mockingbird, and a Northern Mockingbird, the latter feeding on mulberries. Frank's mulberry tree was a great spot for novelties. Although

mockingbirds are common in the drier parts of Tamaulipas, they were rare in the cloud forest. In addition, I collected three White-throated Robins, two Clay-colored Robins, an adult male and an adult female Brown-backed Solitaire, three Black-headed Nightingale-Thrushes (*Catharus mexicanus mexicanus*), a Rufous-browed Peppershrike, Solitary Vireo, Warbling Vireo, Crescent-chested Warbler, MacGillivray's Warbler, Hooded Warbler, three Wilson's Warblers, a Canada Warbler, a Hepatic Tanager, a pair of White-winged Tanagers, two Flame-colored Tanagers, a Red-crowned Ant-Tanager, five Hooded Grosbeaks (*Coccothraustes abeillei*), three Rufous-capped Brush-Finches, an Eastern Towhee, two Grasshopper Sparrows, a Chipping Sparrow, and a Lincoln's Sparrow.

3. Sutton's plan did change. The obvious person to write about the birds of Rancho del Cielo turned out to be Byron Harrell, who spent much more time studying birds in the cloud forest than did any of the rest of us. To my knowledge, George Sutton made only one brief visit. If his field collectors showed serious interest of their own in a new area they would be encouraged to publish their findings. Such was the quality of the man.

14

A Kekchi Odyssey

DON OWEN-LEWIS

> Don Owen-Lewis went to British Honduras in the early 1950s as a Maya Indian liaison officer to the Kekchi people. He purchased and developed Missouri Farms when Belize gained its independence, and he became an important liaison to and supporter of science in Toledo District, hosting field camps of archaeologists, ornithologists, and other researchers for decades. He has retired from a career as a farmer in Toledo District, Belize.

After four years in the army toward the end of World War II, mostly spent in Burma, I decided to go into agriculture. I could not get into a university without studying up on chemistry, so I went to the Royal Agricultural College instead. It was not until I graduated that I realized my mistake: it was almost impossible to get a decent job. No one much cared about the piece of paper verifying my educational achievements. If you came from a farming background and had plenty of practical experience, you had a better chance. I did get a job managing a dairy farm in Shropshire, but it was hard work: milking twice a day seven days a week. The pay was not too bad, but the future looked rather bleak. It was about this time that I read *The Ancient Maya* by Sylvanus Morley (1946), an account of the ancient civilization that flourished in Central America over a thousand years ago. I was fascinated by these people, their history, and their way of life. When I found on one of the maps in the book that British Honduras was right in the middle of the Maya area, I began to find out as much as I could about this forgotten quarter of the world. In the process I came across Aldous Huxley's famous remark: "If the world had any ends, British Honduras would certainly be one of them."

I started devising ways and means of getting a job in the area, writing letters to anyone even remotely connected with the country to ask about job prospects. Finally, in desperation, I wrote to the colonial secretary of British Honduras, asking for his help and advice. He wrote to tell me that a soil survey team had just completed a survey of the remoter parts of southern British Honduras and that they had come across a number of villages peopled by

Figure 14.1. Don Owen-Lewis feeding his chickens at Missouri Farms, Big Falls, Toledo District, Belize, January 1998. Photo by K. Winker.

Kekchi—highland Maya from Guatemala. These people had only one small school and no medical facilities. Infant mortality was horrendous. Some villages could only be reached by paddling up rivers and others by walking barely discernible trails. The government was looking for someone to live among these people to gain their confidence and, in brief, to be their guide-philosopher and friend. Was I interested?

After an interview and a medical, I was on my way to Jamaica on a banana boat, and within three weeks I was in Belize City—a ramshackle wooden town a few inches above sea level. Just two days later, after a whirlwind tour of government departments, I went down the coast in the government launch *Patricia* to Punta Gorda, where I met District Commissioner Alec Frankson. The following day I went down the coast a few more miles by sea and then up the winding Temash River as far as we could go. From there we continued by rowboat to Crique Sarco village, where I was deposited with my bags just as dusk was falling. As I stood there, I was viewed with curiosity and suspicion by a semicircle of Kekchi in tattered clothing. The new Maya Indian liaison officer had arrived.

I lodged in a one-room shack that had been built for the Catholic priest, though he had never used it. In fact, he had never been to the village. None of the Indian houses had any internal partitions. Privacy was something that just never occurred to these people. One of my earlier recollections is waking one morning to hear a baby crying, and there, sitting on a bench inside my little shack, was a family group. They had pushed my pile of clothes to the end of the bench and were patiently waiting for me to wake. I got out of bed, and as nonchalantly as possible I walked across to my clothes and pulled on my shorts. The little girl had a heavy fever, and they wanted medicine for her. The only language spoken was Kekchi. Although there were a several young men who had learned a few words of English from their visits to Punta Gorda, there was no one to interpret for me. However, there was another village about four hours' walk away, Otoxha, that had a small school and a Carib school teacher.

I had myself paddled down to Barranco on the coast and engaged three carpenters to build me a house in Otoxha. Once we had decided where the house should be, they felled some trees nearby (one was a mahogany), then squared them up and proceeded to cut them into planks with a one-man rip saw. I remember that they charged me nine cents per square foot. As soon as they had put up the house and the Indians had thatched it for me, I moved in. No one in Otoxha village had a radio. These people rarely had any visitors, and most of them had never seen anyone like me before. At my first meeting with the men of the village the Carib school teacher, Mr. F. B. (Dondon) Cayetano, offered to interpret. About fifty men turned up, but none would enter the building; instead they peered at me through the chinks in the walling. They were afraid of me, I think, because I represented authority, and they were recent immigrants from Guatemala, where for hundreds of years their people had been mistreated and exploited.

Wherever I went and whatever I did, I always seemed to have a retinue of boys and young men watching. It was a little unnerving, but after a few days I got used to it, and they gradually got used to me. My wristwatch fascinated them. I regularly had to take it off and it was passed around so that everyone could hear it ticking. At that time I smoked a pipe, and quite a lot of the men and women in the village did too. It was their custom to pass their pipes around, and I was expected to do the same. It never tasted quite the same by the time it came back to me. I decided to smoke cigarettes instead.

I started a serious attempt to learn the language. I wrote down everything that was said to me (in my own phonetics), and every evening Dondon would come across to tell me what it meant in English and at the same time give me Kekchi phrases for things I wanted to say. Thus I learned sentences as well as words, and the learning was easy because no one except Dondon and some of the children could speak anything other than Kekchi; my notebook was in constant use. After about two or three weeks I was able to start constructing my own phrases, and the Indians were delighted to help me as much as possible, although there were some wicked young fellows who deliberately led me astray.

Looking back on this, it was a pleasant existence for me and very satisfying. The government supplied me with a lot of very basic medicines, and I was able to try to do something about the appalling health problems. People had their own bush doctors, but they had no remedies for hookworm or malaria, which were a killing combination. One woman told me she had had eleven children, but only two had survived.

On a visit to Aguacate village I found an emaciated old woman lying in a ragged hammock in an old broken-down house. She had been abandoned by her husband, who had gotten himself another wife. Apparently she had been sick for a year, and there was nothing the bush doctor could do to help her. I suggested constructing a litter and having her carried down to the government hospital in Punta Gorda, but she flatly refused to go. She said she was going to die and that she wanted to be buried in her own village. When I next went to Punta Gorda I described her symptoms to the government doctor, and he gave me several different sorts of medicine for her. I duly gave these to the bush doctor, who promised to see that she took them. I facetiously told the old lady that she would be dancing before I next saw her. She was not amused.

However, when I saw her about a month later, she had in fact been dancing, and I was amazed to find that she was probably in her mid-thirties. The doctor had been nearly sure that she had a hookworm problem that had led to acute anemia.

On a tour of some villages with an army doctor we saw a young woman who had a baby a few months old. She was lying in a hammock with one foot propped on a stool. Her foot was badly swollen and seeping pus. The smell was dreadful, and a small boy with a fan was trying to keep the blowflies from settling. We did our best to persuade the woman to go to the hospital, but she said they would chop off her foot, and asked what good was a Kekchi woman with only one leg? The doctor left her some ointment but said amputation was the only way to save her life. The local bush doctor, however, was poulticing the foot with leaves from the jungle and giving her some dreadful concoction to drink. He cured her completely, although she did complain that one foot was a lot longer than the other. Occasionally there were remarkable cures like this.

The village headman was called the *alcalde*, and he was paid by the government to keep order. By and large, the system worked very well. He sometimes served for many years, but it was more usual for him to serve just one year. Sometimes he nominated his successor, and sometimes he would nominate the man who had given him the most trouble during his year of office. Serious offenders were sent down to Punta Gorda for the district commissioner to deal with, but this rarely happened. Drunkenness was a problem, particularly on the Catholic feast days of Easter and Christmas. There was a social stigma attaching to anyone who did not get drunk on these days—man or woman.

The Maya people, particularly the Kekchi, were some of the most pleasant people I had ever met. They were considerate to one another and kind to their children, although men did treat their wives badly on occasion. But the customs of the village were quite strict, and anyone who transgressed would eventually earn the censure of the *alcalde* and village elders.

I soon managed to get a dugout canoe of my own (made of mahogany), and with an outboard engine I would make the trip to Punta Gorda every six or eight weeks to buy a few supplies. There were no shops in the villages. Apart from a few basics like machetes, kerosene, soap, and shotgun shells, the jungle and the corn fields supplied all the Indians' needs. I found myself following their example and shooting birds and animals whenever necessary.

One day a little girl named Rosa accidentally drank a bottle of kerosene that she thought was water. Her distraught parents asked me to take her down to the Punta Gorda hospital in my boat, so we set out—her parents, a small brother and sister, an old man named Antonio who came along for the ride, me, and my dog. At the mouth of the river the current was strong, and the sea was exceptionally rough. Because of the great amount of sediment carried by the river you have to go out to sea for about a mile before you can turn to go up the coast. We had nearly reached the turning point when I saw three extra-large waves coming. I knew our little boat was in trouble, so I turned around and went back the way we had come as fast as I could. But the waves caught us and swamped us when we were still about half a mile from shore. The boat turned over, and we were pitched into the sea. Luckily, we could touch bottom between the waves, and we were able to struggle against the current toward the shore. I was carrying the little boy and herding my erstwhile passengers ahead of me (including the dog), when a Roseate Spoonbill (*Platalea ajaja*) flew low over our heads. I will never forget it. I had never seen one before, nor have I since.

I left my passengers sitting on the shore and swam across the mouth of the river to the nearby village of Barranco. When the people there heard that I had swum across the mouth of the river they were appalled. Apparently, due to the debris and muddy water, it was a favorite place for barracuda and sharks. Sometimes ignorance is bliss. The village policeman had a much larger boat than mine, and he went and picked up my passengers, who were none the worse for their experience. In fact, the little girl Rosa had drunk so much sea water that the kerosene was quite forgotten. I wanted the villagers to go and look for my boat. They said they would be unable to find it because it would have gone out to sea—but that it would come ashore the following day and that they knew exactly where it would be. They were right. I told them I was ashamed of myself for not judging things better. But they said it also happened to them from time to time, even though they were born on the coast. I had journeyed up the coast many times and had never had any trouble before, because there is a string of offshore islands joined together to form a barrier reef. The capsizing was an experience I'll never forget. Maxie, the small boy whom I had carried ashore, is now a grandfather (people sometimes marry at fourteen), and he still vividly remembers the mishap too.

My partiality for the Crested Guan (*Penelope purpurascens*) once nearly landed me in bad trouble. I was walking from Crique Sarco to Santa Teresa, a distance of about twenty-five miles, with just my dog for company. When we were about halfway there, some guan flew across the trail, which was about three feet wide. I took off my pack, dropped it on the trail, and took off after the birds. I followed them for some distance until they flew off. Because I had been looking up in the air I had not noticed where I was going, and I could not find the trail again. After about an hour I was completely lost, and I had no idea in which direction to go. My food, compass, blanket, etc. were all in my pack. All I had was a rifle, a machete, and a dog. Though the temperature was in the high eighties, I was in a cold sweat. The whole area was covered in virgin forest, with the nearest house in the village I was going to, which was perhaps four hours' fast walking away.

There was a large *Ceiba* tree that I made my base. I propped my gun against it and started cutting trails in a straight line in all directions. I knew I was within two miles of the trail, but in what direction I had no idea. I even got annoyed with my dog (a boxer). He knew where the trail was, but he wouldn't tell me. It started to get dark, and I tried to see where the sun went down, but it was impossible. Though it was a clear night this was no help to me, because in this country Polaris is only 16° above the horizon. I had no matches, so could not light a fire; we just sat at the base of the tree and waited for dawn. We had nothing to eat. Even Indians when lost would probably die of starvation in a few weeks. The following day I extended my lines, and at about midday I came out on the trail exactly where I had left my bag. I reached Santa Teresa that night without any guan. It was a very frightening experience. No one would have come looking for me.

The Indians often kept birds as pets. The partridge (Great Tinamou, *Tinamus major*) was a favorite, as was the Great Curassow (*Crax rubra*). The former laid eggs on the ground, often at the base of a tree, while the latter made its nest about twenty feet from the ground in a small tree. The tinamou eggs were laid in a clutch of about seven and were a little smaller than a domestic hen's egg but of a beautiful blue-green color. Hunters would find the nests and take the eggs home to hatch under a domestic hen. The birds made good pets, though they often roosted on the roof beams of the thatch-roofed kitchen, and it was hazardous to pass below them. The Great Tinamou has a very loud, plaintive whistle, usually given at dawn or dusk but often given at midday as well. The bird I wanted for a pet was the Scarlet Macaw (*Ara macao*), but nests were hard to find. I once deliberately winged one and tied it to the top of my pack, hoping to get it home, but it made a fearful noise and the rest of the flock followed me from tree to tree for about an hour, until my captive died. It is wonderful to see them feeding in a big tree, particularly in the evening, but they are fearless and easy to shoot.

This leads me to an episode of which I am not proud. I was paddling down the Rio Grande toward evening when we heard macaws making a great deal of noise around the next bend. They flew off when they saw us, and we then saw the cause of the disturbance. It was a gigantic bird, and one of the Indians with me said, "Shoot it! Shoot it! It's good to eat!"

I did, and when I went to pick it up I realized that it was a Harpy Eagle (*Harpia harpyja*). That evening I gave the bird to a friend, Carol Young, who took it into Punta Gorda the following morning. He told everyone he had shot it in his pasture and that it was carrying a deer it had killed. It was a huge bird. Its ankles were thicker than my wrists.

I once found a Plain Chachalaca (*Ortalis vetula*) nest with two eggs, which I took home and placed under a hen. A few days later the eggs hatched. Even though they were just a few minutes old I had trouble catching them. The only way I could get them to eat was to chew the food myself and put it in their mouths. When they got bigger they would eat only what I gave them and what was growing in my garden. They would not go into the forest. Several times I took them a few miles from home and released them, but they invariably got home before me. I eventually gave them to an Indian, who I suppose ate them—I did not enquire too closely.

In 1962 British Honduras became Belize and got self-government, and I found I was out of a job. But we had come a long way in the nine years I had been there. Crique Sarco now had a school, a resident nurse, an agricultural assistant (my friend Dondon), and a police station that was in contact with Punta Gorda via shortwave radio. We also had an airstrip, of which we were very proud. In addition, the trails linking the various villages were much improved. All the villages now had schools, and in some instances proper roads as well, passable in the dry season. We had even gotten ourselves a motorized barge that made a trip every two weeks to Punta Gorda loaded with produce, pigs, and people. It was very impressive, and it all made a great difference to the standard of living. The people were now able to buy themselves boots and shotguns and even the occasional radio.

There was really no longer a need for a Maya Indian liaison officer. But having been in the country ten years, I found it difficult to contemplate returning to England. So I bought some land on the Rio Grande and became a farmer. The land had originally belonged to a southerner who had left Missouri after the Civil War. It was in the middle of over a thousand square miles of jungle. Four families living a few miles upriver were the only other people in the whole area. But in the future the government intended to put in a road to link the area with the rest of the country.

There were four of us: an orphaned god-daughter four years old, a Kekchi woman and her little boy of the same age, and myself. Initially, we could get to the land only by paddling a dugout canoe up the river. Later I invited three families from Crique Sarco to join us in clearing some land. We cut and burned and then built ourselves a small settlement beside a little spring. I had a small tractor that I brought in as soon as the river was low enough to cross, and I started to stump and plow and plant corn and beans and rice. I was convinced that with the help of machinery and modern know-how I would be able to show the people how some of these crops should be grown. Luckily I did not tell them so, because I soon found out that the Indian method of planting with a sharp stick was much more efficient. Initially we grew only crops for subsistence, because there was no road and no market for our produce. But gradually things changed. Most of Crique Sarco followed us and settled nearby, and then the Southern Highway was put in, passing within a mile of us.

Originally the fishing in the river was wonderful, and the bush was teeming with wild game of all sorts. Macaw, guan, and curassow were to be seen or heard on most days. As soon as a bridge was built across the Rio Grande I was able to drive the tractor out to a little store about seven miles away and stock up with groceries from time to time. We cleared and fenced a pasture and built up our herd of Brahma cattle, and we started keeping bees. It was a wonderful place for bees. They loved the flowering trees and vines, which gave the honey some wonderful flavors.[1] We also planted as many different kinds of fruit trees as possible.

At about this time I met Jacky Vasquez, a local hunter with a somewhat murky past. He showed me his jaguar caller. It was made of a gourd that had a large hole at each end. Over one end was pinned a piece of dry deer skin about five inches in diameter. Through a small hole in the center of the piece of skin some plaited horse hairs were threaded. These were knotted at one end so that they would not pull through the hole. The horse hair was smeared with wax. To operate the caller you put the gourd under your arm, inserted your hand into the opening, lightly grasped the horse hair at its base, and pulled gently, letting your fingers and thumb slide down the hair. This produced a sort of cough that was amplified by the gourd to sound remarkably like the cough of a jaguar. I had no sooner seen his gourd than I wanted one of my own, but Jacky was not interested in making one for me. He was reluctant even to show how to make the various calls, but he did tell me some remarkably tall stories of his hunting successes. It did not take me long to locate a suitable gourd and piece of deer skin, and with the cooperation of an obliging horse and a piece of beeswax I was in business. Together with Santiago Rash, a neighboring Kekchi, I walked to an open space about half a mile from my house, and we started calling just as dusk was coming on. We called every few minutes for about half an hour with no results. Discouraged, we gave up and started for home. But we had not gone fifty yards when we heard a series of coughs behind us. My immediate thought was that it was Jacky playing us for fools, but when we shone our lights we saw a large jaguar (*Panthera onca*), sitting up like a dog exactly where we had been standing. When we went closer he slipped back into the bush and we could no longer see him, but we heard him from time to time.

Figure 14.2. A captured calf-killing jaguar (*Panthera onca*), Big Falls, Toledo District, Belize, January 1998. Photo by K. Winker.

One year we established a new village, Laguna, and I decided to open a new direct trail to neighboring Santa Teresa, about seven miles away. I thought we would easily be able to do this in one day, so four of us set out: a visitor I had staying with me, Vicente Ack, my driver, my dog, and myself. In parts the bush was thick, and progress was rather slow. We couldn't understand why we hadn't reached our destination, so we went on cutting the trail with our machetes until it was too dark to see. As it got dark, rain came. We could not light a fire, so we just propped up some palm leaves against the base of a large tree and tried to get comfortable, eating some food we had brought. After a time I heard a humming noise—for all the world like a truck double de-clutching to go up a hill. We were at least ten miles from a highway, and there was no hill. I asked Vicente what the noise was. He said it was a jaguar, and that it wanted my dog. For some time past I had noticed that the dog was behaving strangely and trying to get under my blanket with me. Hearing this, I redoubled my efforts to keep him out. Still, the humming went on, and it was impossible to tell where it was coming from. It seemed to be all around us. But I had a rifle, and I fired several shots into the air. When we awoke in the morning there were some large jaguar footprints very close to our little shelter. We were so near our destination that we could hear the roosters crowing in the distance—a lovely sound.

Over the years things have changed a good deal. We had difficulty finding a market for our beef, and our bees were killed out by the killer bees from Brazil when they reached Belize. Then came the 1980s Florida freeze, and all of a sudden there was a good market for our oranges. We plowed the pasture and planted oranges. There are probably between five and ten thousand people living where only five families lived before. Spear fishing, netting, and poisoning with bush vines in the old Indian way have made the fish in the river dwindle alarmingly. Hunting for subsistence and for sale has made great areas of the jungle almost empty of game. Large areas have been designated as forest reserves, but it is difficult to keep the animals in or the hunters out. Thus although the jungle is often intact, there are few game animals left. The first to go are the Scarlet Macaws. There are probably only two or three small flocks left in the whole country. Curassow, guan, and wild turkey are scarce, and the jaguar, tracks of which were to be seen on a daily basis, will soon reach the stage where the population is too small to be viable. It is a sad state of affairs, but it seems inevitable.

Myself, I never hunt now and can't remember when last I used my rifle, except to shoot my cat. She seemed to live on a diet of birds and lizards. The final straw was when she robbed the nest of a Southern House Wren (*Troglodytes musculus*) of young. Removing that predator was well worthwhile. In March 1998 I had eight species nesting either on the house itself or within just a few feet of it: the Great Kiskadee (*Pitangus sulphuratus*), Brown-crested Flycatcher (*Myiarchus tyrannulus*), Bananaquit (*Coereba flaveola*), Southern House Wren, Ruddy Ground-Dove (*Columbina talpacoti*), Crimson-collared Tanager (*Ramphocelus sanguinolentus*), Blue-gray Tanager (*Thraupis episcopus*), and Rufous-tailed Hummingbird (*Amazilia tzacatl*). One of the Ruddy Ground Dove nests was built on the cross member of my satellite TV dish, and one year alone the birds hatched and raised five clutches of two eggs. The nest, normally about one inch high, grew to about five inches thick.

This is a wonderful location for birds. I used to plant my garden with flowers that I liked, such as roses, zinnias, and lilies. But now I plant only for my birds: *Bauhinia* for the hummingbirds, a sort of bush spinach called callalloo with seeds the Painted Buntings (*Passerina ciris*) love, Suriname cherries for the tanagers and trogons, papayas for the toucans and ornithologists, and ylang ylang for the robins (Clay-colored Thrush, *Turdus grayi*). I wonder who Mr. Gray was and why he should be immortalized in this bird's name.[2] The robin is a wonderful singer, reminiscent of the English Blackbird (*Turdus merula*), but it sings only in the spring and summer when nesting.

Some of the changes that have occurred in the region are good and some are not so good. The Indians were once all nominally Roman Catholic, and there was a great deal of drunkenness. As earlier noted, the big Catholic feast days were days on which there was social pressure to get drunk, and some of the fiestas went on for several days. However, an influx of the Evangelical religions, some of which forbade alcohol, has countered this. Many of the Kekchi were delighted and became converts, whereupon they could decline drink because it was against their religion. The effect was amazing. Almost overnight, drunkenness ceased to be a problem among the Kekchi. Now if they see a drunken man they laugh and pity his family. I used to think drunkenness among native people could not be helped, that perhaps something in their genes made these people extra susceptible to the effects of alcohol, but my view has changed with this switch.

The flip side to this religious invasion, however, is that even small villages with populations of no more than three hundred may have up to six churches. The different churches usually get help from their American sponsors, and all seem to despise and be jealous of one another, producing strife that has led to the burning of homes and even murder. Some people are finding they can return to Catholicism without returning to drinking.

The Kekchi have come a long way since those early days in Otoxha and Crique Sarco. Children and grandchildren of the people who were so frightened of strangers now drive and own pickup trucks and buses. Many are schoolteachers and civil servants. Some have graduated from universities in England and the United States. The high school in Punta Gorda, which admitted the first Kekchi student in 1965, is now predominantly Kekchi.

Notes

1. Editor's note: This was indeed some of the most exotic and best-flavored honey I have ever had. Don was kind enough to share some of his last stock with a wayward ornithologist in the avian nonbreeding season of 1997–98.

2. Editor's note: The Clay-colored Thrush, *Turdus grayi*, was named in honor of George R. Gray (1808–72), an English ornithologist who worked at the British Museum and studied avian genera (Jobling 1991).

15

Civil War and Rain Forests in the Chimalapas

A. TOWNSEND PETERSON

A. Townsend Peterson, Ph.D., is curator and professor at the University of Kansas Natural History Museum and Biodiversity Research Center. The fieldwork related here was the beginning of an intensive multiyear survey effort, the results of which were reported by Peterson et al. (2003).

In 1991 three companions and I, partly by accident and without really knowing what we were getting into, decided to explore the eastern arm of Oaxaca. Binford, in *A Distributional Survey of the Birds of the Mexican State of Oaxaca* (1989), had called the region the "Sierra Madre de Chiapas," unfortunately, as you will see, since it is known in Mexico as the Chimalapas because it is made up of two *municipios*, Santa María Chimalapa and San Miguel Chimalapa. The Chimalapas have always been something of a mystery in Mexico, partly because of the inaccessible and inimical terrain and partly because of poor relations with the local residents. The region was among the very last parts of Mexico to be mapped carefully; reasonably accurate large-scale topographic maps were not produced until the mid-1980s. The Chimalapas region, according to the Atlas Nacional de México, is the largest one south of San Luis Potosí with zero economic assimilation, and to this day substantial parts of the Chimalapas remain unvisited and untouched by humans.

We entered the Chimalapas late one night in May 1991, driving north from Matías Romero and then east along the Uxpanapa Road. One of our group had worked previously at a small town called Chalchijapa, lost at the northwestern base of a low mountain range called the Sierra de Tres Picos; he said there was decent rain forest nearby, so we decided to work there. We wove our way along rough dirt roads, including several crossings of the Río Chalchijapa, and finally stopped before an especially intimidating crossing, set camp at the side of the road, and slept the night.

We woke up before dawn, crawled out of our tents rubbing eyes, and stretched backs sore from too many hours of driving the previous day and a night spent on uneven beds. As the day dawned, we realized that we were in the middle of a small clearing in otherwise continuous virgin lowland rain forest. I had seen forest as pristine and endless years before in Amazonian Brazil but never expected to see anything so extensive and well preserved in Mexico.

Quickly we assembled binoculars, tape recorders, and other equipment for a day's work and took off walking into the forest. We soon met up with most of the birds characteristic of lowland rain forest in Mexico: Keel-billed Toucans (*Ramphastos sulfuratus*), Rufous Piha (*Lipaugus unirufus*), and even the rare and secretive Scaly-throated Leaftosser (*Sclerurus guatemalensis*). We found an immature Black Hawk-Eagle (*Spizaetus tyrannus*) perched just a few meters above the trail, which was the first record for Oaxaca, and I collected a Black-faced Grosbeak (*Caryothraustes poliogaster*), the tissue and genetic material of which would make a fascinating comparison with its sister species, which I and other companions had collected in Brazil years before. Because of time constraints and other complications, our work at Chalchijapa had to remain incomplete, but we were fascinated by the pristine forest and the abundant birds.

Two years later our research team returned to Chalchijapa in a more organized fashion. They established a camp halfway up the slopes of the Sierra de Tres Picos. They were the first scientists to explore the upper parts of that mountain range and were amply rewarded for their efforts. They discovered new populations of the Resplendent Quetzal (*Pharomachrus mocinno*): finding an isolated population in such well-preserved forest is like money in the bank for the long-term preservation of wild populations of this species. Also present were populations of the Highland Guan (*Penelopina nigra*), another endangered species found only in cloud forests in southern Mexico and northern Central America. The team documented populations of several bird species not previously known for Oaxaca, and together with records and specimens accumulated nearby twenty-five years previously in the vicinity of Sarabia by William Schaldach and his colleagues, the rain forests in the northwestern Chimalapas are now known to hold some 323 species of birds, more than any other site in Mexico. Other members of the team made even more exciting discoveries. The botanists encountered many rare and little-known plants, and the herpetologists discovered a species of lizard of the genus *Xenosaurus* ("strange lizard") and another of the genus *Anolis*, both of which proved to be new to science.

Our stay at Chalchijapa in 1991, however, was brief, and we hurried on east through what is called the Uxpanapa region of southern Veracruz to our next destination—the junction of Oaxaca, Chiapas, and Veracruz—where we hoped to be the first scientists to explore the Sierra Espinazo del Diablo. Our arrival was far from easy or convenient. Our vehicle, called a Combi—much like a VW bus—was not up to fording the Río Uxpanapa beyond Poblado Once, and so there we left it, and we hired a more able vehicle to carry us to Poblado Catorce. In Catorce, none of the local people wanted even so much as to discuss our hiring burros to take our equipment to the tiny pueblo called San Isidro La Gringa at the base of the mountain range. Apparently conflicts between La Gringa and another pueblo, San Francisco, made the passage quite dangerous. Finally, a widow who had lived in La Gringa prevailed upon a man who had some horses, and he consented to take us there.

The walk to La Gringa took more than five hours, all through a long clearing in the forest along the banks of the river. We were completely exposed to the hot tropical sun. We arrived in the pueblo exhausted, but we were warmly welcomed in the mayor's house and were served cool lemonade and invited to rest in hammocks. We were offered the local schoolhouse as accommodation—it was not in use because that year no teachers had been sent to La Gringa. We spent about an hour making the last arrangements for the ascent of the mountain range the next morning. Then we bought the last four beers in the town and retired to the river in a desperate attempt to cool off from the day's long walk and the tropical heat.

Once it became dark, we emerged from the river, ate a meal in the home of one of the families living in La Gringa, and were on our way to the schoolhouse to go to bed when a young man aged about twenty stopped us along the trail. He looked agitated, perhaps worried and upset at the same time. He told us he was a police officer for the pueblo, and asked if we were the people who had been bathing in the river. When we answered affirmatively, he told us not to do it again, and to take care not to approach the river bank for any reason.

What we had not understood was that La Gringa and San Francisco, the pueblo on the opposite bank of the river, were at war, and had been so off and on for many years. The week before, a youth from La Gringa had been killed, and two days later the people of La Gringa had burned several houses in San Francisco, and thus the situation had degenerated into violence and misunderstandings. La Gringa was a settlement from Chiapas, and San Francisco was from Oaxaca—we were definitely *in* Oaxaca, but the Chiapanecos had been living there for some time, and this was the root of the problem.

Regardless of human conflicts, we left early the next morning on the long, slow climb up the Sierra Espinazo del Diablo. Initially we followed a tributary of the big river, but then the trail turned abruptly up the mountainside and left all water behind. The climb was too steep to ride comfortably, so most of us walked alongside and guided the animals. Finally, at an elevation of about

700 m, we stopped and set up a crude camp beside the trail, a miserable hour's trudge up from the nearest source of water.

Setting out immediately to explore, we found the trail full of jaguar tracks, probably representing the mate of a male that had been killed above El Catorce the night prior to our arrival there. The birds near our camp were for the most part those typical of rain forest: Great Tinamou (*Tinamus major*), Short-billed Pigeon (*Patagioenas nigrirostris*), Violet Sabrewing (*Campylopterus hemileucurus*), and White-collared Manakin (*Manacus candei*). We were hoping to ascend high enough to find cloud forest, a habitat that has a completely different set of dominant bird species. The first suggestion that our wishes would be fulfilled was the appearance of an individual of the rare Stripe-tailed Hummingbird (*Eupherusa eximia*) in a mist net we had placed near camp—the scant information about this species suggests that it lives along the border between rain forest and cloud forest. Dinner that night was rich fare of *asadura*—Joaquín, a young man from La Gringa whom we had hired as a guide, had shot a collared peccary (*Tayassu tajacu*), and we feasted on garlic-broiled liver, kidneys, lungs, and heart, while the rest of the beast smoked slowly over the open fire.

The next morning, four of us set out with but a liter of water (all we had left!) to explore the highest parts of the Sierra Espinazo del Diablo. We climbed for several hours, until the forest began to change—trees were shorter and held more epiphytes on their branches, fewer lianas hung from the canopy, and we even found a few tree ferns, so we knew we were entering cloud forest. The birds also changed, and we soon found Spotted Woodcreepers (*Xiphorhynchus erythropygius*), Scaly-throated Foliage-gleaners (*Anabacerthia variegaticeps*), Emerald Toucanets (*Aulacorhynchus prasinus*), Slate-colored Solitaires (*Myadestes unicolor*), and many other birds typical of cloud forest. We even heard the characteristic calls of quetzals from far away along the mountain ridge. Elated at being the first scientists to reach this isolated island of cloud forest, we quickly set about business, collecting examples of plants, specimens of each bird species (except the quetzal), and a few amphibians that we found along the trail.

Unfortunately, by afternoon we had no more water, and after reaching the summit of the range (about 1,200 m), we had to begin our descent to camp. We had found and excavated a small mudhole on our way up, and descending, found it now full of water, mud, and snails. To our surprise, the jaguar (normally nocturnal) had visited the water in our absence and had left many tracks in the mud; it was probably just as thirsty as we were. We drank the hole dry, using straws made from hollow plant stems to get the last few drops, and continued on our way back to camp. Although exhausted, all were awake far into the night preparing and preserving the specimens collected.

The return trip to La Gringa was uneventful, and we soon set out once again for El Catorce. When two of us arrived, after having drunk several bottles of soda and juice, it became apparent that the other two were not coming. To our horror, we realized they had taken a wrong turn and were on their way to San Francisco. We spent a frantic hour of waiting and searching, but they finally appeared, hot, tired, and thirsty, but otherwise okay.

Now fascinated with the Chimalapas, we set out to enter the region via the southeastern corner, which is the route most familiar to biologists. We returned to Matías Romero, turned south to La Ventosa on the Pacific coastal plain, and then went east to the pueblo General Pascual Fuentes, locally known as El Jícaro. There, after asking advice from local residents, we went north on a dirt road that took us into the pine forests high on the slopes of Cerro Baúl, and then down into the dry valley that holds Colonia Rodolfo Figueroa, Rancho Cerro Baúl, Díaz Ordaz, and Benito Juárez, among others.

It was not until late at night that we arrived in Díaz Ordaz, and we looked for someone who could direct us to the road to our destination, the next pueblo, Benito Juárez. To our confusion, and in stark contrast to the kind greeting awaiting travelers in most of Mexico, we were met by blank stares and stony expressions. No one offered help of any sort. We took the road that appeared to be the continuation of that by which we had entered, found it to be in terrible shape, and in order to avoid an accident had to have one of our group running in front of the vehicle. The going was painfully slow, and we ended up spending the night halfway to Benito Juárez camped by the side of the road.

The next morning, after driving the remainder of the distance into the pueblo and talking with the mayor, we came to understand why our reception in Díaz Ordaz had been so cool. Díaz Ordaz is another Chiapaneco settlement, and it is in conflict with Benito Juárez, a Oaxacan pueblo, just as with La Gringa and San Francisco. In this part of the Chimalapas, the confrontations seemed to be on a larger scale than in the Uxpanapa pueblos—just four months previously, the Chiapanecos had invaded Benito Juárez with twenty-six truckloads of armed men. The Oaxacans fled into the hills and circled around to attack from behind and capture prisoners, and the matter had to be resolved by negotiators from the two state governments. The tension and occasional conflicts continued, however.

We, on the other hand, were soon in very good hands. On the recommendation of other scientists, we contacted Don Salomón, a patriarch and founder of the pueblo, who had worked for years as a guide and field collector for a botanist from Mexico City. (It turned out that as a young man he had actually been employed to carry food up to the camp at El Carrizal that the renowned ornithologist J. Stuart Rowley had set up when he was collecting birds in the area!). Don Salomón and his wife Doña María quickly welcomed us into their home, which was the most beautiful that I have seen in Mexico—cement foundation and floors, and decorated all over with live wildflowers that Don Salomón had collected. There, after a short spell watching birds in the hills behind town, we packed for the next day's ascent into the mountains, dined, and spent the night in an extra room.

In the morning we drove back to Díaz Ordaz accompanied by Don Salomón. He had a friend there to whom we entrusted the Combi, and we set off walking into the mountains. The ascent was nearly vertical, over trails that were rarely used and full of brambles. Much of the hike was through still-smoldering wildfires. We had to take special care in several traverses not to fall into the pits full of hot coals left after trees (roots and all) had burned. When, about seven hours of hard struggle later, we reached the ridgetop and were still in severely degraded forest, I confess I was more than a bit angry, and was close to telling Don Salomón what I though of him.

Luckily I managed to hold my tongue, and after about two kilometers' easy walk along the ridge, we entered truly beautiful virgin cloud forest. We set up camp at the widest point on the ridgetop—about four meters wide—as evening set in, and the magic began almost immediately. From several sides, we heard the wild ascending calls and crazy wing noises of the rare and endangered Highland Guan, which lives in cloud forests from southern Mexico to Nicaragua and is quickly extinguished by human hunters in more populated sites because its meat is so tasty. We counted as many as twenty-three singing males audible from camp alone.

I ran off in pursuit of a hollow, tremulous song that sounded like that of a tinamou. Tinamous rarely fly, and so I was very surprised when my crude imitations were answered by a dive-bombing, medium-sized brown bird that I could not identify. It was not until the following day that I collected one and figured out that it was a Pheasant Cuckoo (*Dromococcyx phasianellus*), so named because of its 20 cm long tail. The species ranges from southern Mexico south to Bolivia, but it is everywhere rare and poorly known.

The true prizes, of course, were the quetzals. Each day we saw two or three pairs—the spectacular male with his streamer tail and the shyer female nearby. Such density of quetzals as we documented almost certainly exists nowhere else in Mexico. We also found many other interesting, if less spectacular, birds of cloud forests: Tawny-throated Leaftossers (*Sclerurus mexicanus*), White-faced Quail-Doves (*Geotrygon albifacies*), and Azure-hooded Jays (*Cyanolyca cucullata*), among others. The terrain was extremely difficult to work in, both because it was so steep and because it was so easy to lose oneself on the slopes. We returned to Benito Juárez after five days of work. Baths in the river and Doña María's excellent venison stew were most welcome.

Over the ensuing eight years we have come to regard the Chimalapas as one of the biologically richest regions of Mexico. The rain forest trees in the region are unique, with several endemic genera and others that have their closest relatives in Africa, leading one botanist to suggest that the Chimalapas have been a refuge of rain forest habitats since the Cenozoic, more than 100 million years ago! New species of reptiles and amphibians are described from the region each year—more than eight species are known only from the Chimalapas, not counting the *Xenosaurus* and *Anolis* lizards discovered by our team's herpetologists, which are only now in the process of being described scientifically. The rain forests of the Chimalapas hold the richest single-site avifaunas known in Mexico; other habitats in the region, such as cloud forest and pine-oak forest, hold additional species not found in the lowlands.

The region comprises about 367,000 hectares. Of that immense area, only about one-sixth has been disturbed, and the rest remains essentially untouched by humans. Much work remains to be done on the biological diversity of the region—several mountain ranges have not been explored biologically; the upper reaches of the rivers Corte and Uxpanapa have not been penetrated; and all of the sites that we visited in those first trips need more careful study. Perhaps most intriguing is a patch of elfin forest—a kind of dwarf cloud forest found at high elevations—that the adventurer and explorer T. MacDougall found in the 1940s near the peak of the Sierra Atravesada in the southern part of the region. This habitat type is essentially unknown elsewhere in Mexico, and scientists have not investigated this patch since MacDougall's visit. In fact, elfin forest has never seen scientific study north of Honduras. Enough work remains in the Chimalapas alone to keep a team of biodiversity scientists busy for several years.

I need to back up and provide some background as to how the Chimalapas got to be such a mess, yet at the same time remain so blessed with pristine natural habitats. In 1580, in the *Relaciones Geográficas* for Oaxaca, Juan de Torres de Lagunas and two other respected men of Tehuantepec described the Isthmus region, including the Chimalapas, to the Spanish colonial government (see Acuña 1984). In response to a question about the region's economic possibilities, they responded as follows (my translation):

> Only in one pueblo subject to this Villa de Tehuantepec called Chimalapa [is there any potential for logging], which would be at twenty

leagues from [Tehuantepec] amidst some mountains. It is hot and humid land, although somewhat temperate. There are many trees: cedar, pine, and Spanish oaks. And they say that there are balsam trees and also the trees from which they extract the oil of liquidambar, and there are some trees which they say hold a pepper of the size of a garbanzo. They drink this pepper in cocoa and others even eat it: it is not as good, nor as healthy, as that which is brought from Spain. And the wood of these trees has very little possibility of use because it is in mountains so bitter and removed from populated areas, and because it is so difficult to extract. (Juan de Torres de Lagunas, 1580)

Four hundred years ago, the Chimalapas were too remote and difficult to permit easy access and exploration. What I have been able to piece together of the early history of the region is that the main settlements, Santa María Chimalapa and San Miguel Chimalapa, were originally populated by the Zoque, a people of Mayan roots. The area was relatively prosperous, though isolated, until the first visits by Spaniards. I have not found estimates of the population of the pueblos in the Chimalapas proper, but the Tehuantepec region as a whole held some 20,000 people around 1550. By 1580, however, the human population was reduced 84 percent to only 3,200 inhabitants. The loss of life was due to plague after plague introduced by the foreigners, almost extinguishing the Zoques; thinking that the location of Santa María Chimalapa might be cursed, they moved the pueblo several kilometers down the road. The remains of the old pueblo can still be seen on an afternoon's walk from the present pueblo.

After that time, the Chimalapas were all but depopulated, its towns almost empty. The Chimalapas today are the largest region of Mexico south of Coahuila and Baja California Sur with the lowest population density ranking: 0–0.6 inhabitants per square kilometer. From the 1960s through the 1980s, however, the Mexican government was creating large reservoirs for flood control elsewhere in Oaxaca, displacing perhaps 20,000 members of the Chinanteco ethnic group. Those people were resettled in the Uxpanapa region (the northern portion of the Chimalapas in the drainage of the Río Uxpanapa), then unpopulated and pristine. The settlement of the Uxpanapa was so hasty that the pueblos were not even named but just numbered: Poblado Uno, Poblado Dos, and so forth up to Poblado Dieciseis! Thus the Chimalapas now have people again. Unfortunately, with the huge influx of new inhabitants—people from elsewhere who do not have the same intimate connection with the natural environment of the Chimalapas—the rain forests of the lower Uxpanapa have been all but destroyed.

For the past forty years, another sort of conflict has plagued the Chimalapas, that of illegal entry by external commercial interests from the east. Extremely powerful influences from Chiapas, on the pretext of caring for the well-being of Chiapaneco indigenous peoples being settled illegally in the region, invaded the eastern Chimalapas, cutting valuable rain forest trees for sale of wood, ranching thousands of head of cattle, and apparently cultivating several types of illegal drugs. Conflicts arose, of course, between Oaxaqueños and Chiapanecos, and as we observed in San Isidro La Gringa and Benito Juárez, many lives were lost.

In 1977 the people of the Chimalapas mounted an effort to remove the invaders, removing some twenty sawmills and five thousand head of cattle, but in the grand scheme of things, their efforts were to no avail. In 1986, to the embarrassment of the government of Chiapas, the brother of the state's governor was arrested in the Chimalapas, where he had been coordinating the illegal extraction of wood and growing of coffee. He was detained in an isolated settlement in the southeastern Chimalapas, and to avoid Chiapanecos was tied to a wooden frame and carried overland to the Oaxacan authorities, where he was eventually turned over to the Chiapan government. Armed conflicts in the zone under dispute continued at least until 1991, especially between the pueblos of Benito Juárez and Díaz Ordaz.

In recent decades the Chimalapas have fascinated the Mexican government as a grand economic opportunity. One plan was to install a huge dam on the Río Corte to water the agricultural lands of the Isthmus and make it the breadbasket of Mexico. Another proposal would have made the Chimalapas into a huge national park, and others would have crossed the region with railroads or highways. Ten kilometers of a highway were constructed in extreme southwestern Chiapas, but the project foundered in the difficult terrain in the foothills of the mountains where we worked, and the highway lies abandoned. All these invasions, plans, promises, and projects served only to alienate the people of the Chimalapas—the owners of the land. Finally, in the past two decades, they have taken matters more into their own hands.

In 1991 and the beginning of 1992, the people of the Chimalapas began negotiating with the *campesinos* who came from Chiapas, and on December 20, 1993, the parties achieved an agreement to cease hostilities. This is not to say that all is now smooth going, but at least a dialogue has begun. Even more pleasantly surprising is that the people of the Chimalapas have decided to set up their own ecological reserve, creating the first Reserva Ecológica Campesinal in Mexico, where they will be able both to use and to preserve their natural resources.

In July 1994 a meeting was held near La Gringa in which many different scientists, politicians, and conservationists were invited to participate in the planning of a "pilot area" for management and conservation in the Chimalapas. That area is the land near La Gringa, including 40,945 hectares of forested land, including the entire Sierra Espinazo del Diablo. The reserved area does not cover the whole Chimalapas zone yet, but people have taken a huge step in that direction, and the Reserva Ecológica is off the ground.

16

Lost in the Tuxtlas

JOHN H. RAPPOLE

After completing his Ph.D. at the University of Minnesota (1976), John H. Rappole went on to a faculty position at the University of Georgia and then to Texas A&I University to be better positioned for studies of avian migration in Texas and Mexico. He is now a researcher at the Smithsonian Institution's Conservation and Research Center, Front Royal, Virginia. The field experiences related here were part of the effort behind Rappole and Warner (1980), Ramos and Warner (1980), and much future work in Los Tuxtlas (e.g., Rappole and Morton 1985; Rappole et al. 1989; Winker et al. 1990a, 1990b, 1992; Ramos and Rappole 1994; Rappole 1995).

During a trip home to western New York, I had an opportunity to reflect on the nature of field research, ornithological or otherwise. The impetus for this reflection was a broken alternator, which occasioned a series of unplanned nocturnal pauses along various Pennsylvania highways. My young son-in-law, Dave Stewart, noted that this was the first time in his twenty-eight years that he had ever broken down on the road. This assertion was so startling to me that it forced me to begin thinking about the nature of field research, where a broken vehicle is generally the least of one's problems. On my last trip to the Tuxtla mountains in January of 1994, we were broken down, stuck, or otherwise detained by vehicle problems about ten times (though only twice did we actually have to hike out for parts). In fact, when I began to add up in my head the difficulties encountered during twenty-five years of fieldwork, it seemed to me that perhaps as much as a third of my time had been spent dealing with various logistical problems.

I thought of the time in Costa Rica with George Powell and Rafa Flores, when we learned that Suzuki jeeps float. Or the time in the Tuxtlas when the battery fell through the floor of Jorge Vega's Volkswagen. Or the time with Kevin Winker in Catemaco, Veracruz, when I had to use my pants to put out a fire in the right rear wheel well of our (appropriately named) Blazer. That same Blazer actually burned up completely during fieldwork in Belize some years later.

Figure 16.1. John Rappole during heavy rain and flooding in Los Tuxtlas, Santa Marta range, Sierra de Los Tuxtlas, Veracruz, November 12, 1986. Photo by K. Winker.

Some people think of these difficulties as adventures. Most field biologists view them merely as distractions, or more to the point, a pain in the ass. So what is the difference between the field biologists of the world and the Indiana Joneses? I think it is a matter of style and attitude. While many of us share the same experiences as old Indy, and certainly some of my colleagues show as much resourcefulness in meeting these crises, we just don't have the dash that goes with the legend. Also, you have to look the part. While I admire the intellectual contributions of many of my peers, I have to admit that I can't think of any who could double for Harrison Ford. I have met a few tall, handsome, leading-man-type field biologists over the years, but most of these desert the field shortly after completing their doctorates to work for government agencies or other conservation organizations, where their appearance and style are an asset.

Consider, for example, Dr. Mercedes Foster, a fine field biologist who has worked at the National Museum of Natural History for a number of years and has as much field experience as any other tropical biologist I know. Dr. Foster does not look like Indiana Jones, and she does not pontificate on the swollen rivers crossed, poisonous snakes encountered, guerilla groups escaped, etc. However, after a quarter century of conducting research in the remotest parts of Peru, Paraguay, Costa Rica, and Mexico, she probably has as much actual experience with these kinds of impediments to success as your average Cuban mercenary. Yet Dr. Foster is recognized for her excellent research on manakin social behavior and her crusade to bolster the ornithological literature holdings of libraries in the Neotropics.

Early in my career I received a memorable lesson in the proper attitude of a field biologist toward "adventures" from my advisor, Dr. Dwain Warner. My first trip to Mexico was in 1973. In February of that year Dwain took Dick Oehlenschlager, Paul Haemig, and me on a whirlwind tour of eastern Mexico in a search for study sites for my Ph.D. work, which was to begin in the fall (Paul's account of the trip appears in chapter 10). We logged a lot of miles in Veracruz and neighboring states looking for the right place to study the biology of migratory birds wintering in tropical evergreen forest. We were not having much luck until Dr. Arturo Gómez-Pompa invited us to visit the field station of the National Autonomous University of Mexico (UNAM) in the Tuxtla Mountains of southern Veracruz.

Though located only 90 km or so south of the great port city of Veracruz, the Tuxtlas are remote. The reason for this is that they have some very difficult terrain of steep mountain crags, deep gorges, and cataracts, along with rainfall levels that in some places exceed four meters per year. In those days, to get to UNAM's Tuxtlas field station you had to drive right through the heart of the

Tuxtlas to the lovely lakeside town of Catemaco, and then follow a winding, muddy track 30 km northward, past the Coyame turnoff, over the Dos Amates pass, and down through the lowland villages of Sontecomapan and La Palma, crossing the usual split log bridges, until you came finally to two guard huts and a rusted sign that constituted the sole evidence of the university's presence at the site. And forest. Much of the forest was gone in the Tuxtlas, even by 1973. But not at the Estación de Biología Tropical Los Tuxtlas field station. There towering ancient rain forest giants still loomed over the temporary water course that passed for a road. When we saw the forest, we knew we had found the site for our work. Our only problem then was to work out the logistics, beginning with where my wife Bonnie, our two children, and I could stay. The guard said that should be no problem. Go back south three kilometers and we would see a sign for the cabanas of Hotel Playa Escondida. Simply follow that turnoff to the end, he said, and we would come to the promised hotel.

When we first saw the cabanas at Playa Escondida it was not raining. But it had been, and it would later. It is hard for me to think of the Tuxtlas without thinking of rain. It rains there all the time—except in April and May. On driving into the hotel compound, located on a spectacular bluff fifty meters above the ocean, we met the proprietor and his wife, Raúl and Julieta García, and the only two paying customers, a rather sad-looking young Harvard professor who was studying wasp ecology and his undergraduate assistant. The Harvard group had had abysmal luck. Since their arrival a week earlier it had rained continuously, and they had found only one wasp nest of the proper species.

Despite their gloomy warnings regarding weather and work conditions, we were ecstatic. The forest was great. The birds were great. And there was even a place for us to stay while we were doing the fieldwork. What more could we ask for? The only thing that bothered me was the long drive from the cabanas to the biology station. I could picture driving the four kilometers on the (slightly) improved cattle path that led from the main road to the cabanas, plus the three kilometers along the main road to the station—a half-hour drive when it wasn't raining—day after day, back and forth. It seemed like a waste of time and effort, particularly since from the topographic map, the distance as the White Hawk (*Leucopternis albicollis*) flies was no more than a kilometer. I was sure I could walk it in less time than the truck could drive it.

We had arrived in early afternoon, and once settled in our concrete block rooms we set up our mist nets nearby that day and the next. We next moved netting operations over to the station, working there until about six or seven nets were up, and then we started back for the cabanas at about 4:30 in the afternoon. I had been expounding to my companions on how easy it should be to walk from the station to the cabanas because of the steep isosceles triangle formed by the main road and Raúl's road to the cabanas. I finally demanded to be let out along the main road so that I could prove it to them. I cut straight down a steep slope and across a field of dense second growth, and in fact met the truck as it was slowly negotiating its way along the last kilometer to the cabanas. This demonstration however, was not sufficient. I explained that there must be a path used by the local people, and that I would start at the cabanas, find it, proceed to the station, and then return. It was about 5:00 by this time.

I set out heading straight west toward where I knew the station was located, following my compass. I went up, and up, and up through beautiful rain forest until I reached the top of the little reason for the detour followed by Raúl's road—Cerro Balzapote. Cerro Balzapote is 211 m in elevation, according to the surveyor's marker at its peak, and it lies exactly in between the biology station and the cabanas. There were no paths except those followed by the mazama or brocket deer (*Mazama americana*), peccaries (*Tayassu*), and an occasional hunter.

By the time I reached the top, light levels had gone well past the murky stage. Starting out half an hour before in the brightly sunlit pasture, I thought that I had until at least 6:00 before it got really dark, but night comes early in the forest in February. By 5:30 the light was nearly gone, and I knew I was not even halfway to the station. Most smart folks would have turned around at this point, but I kept thinking I would soon hit the road. Besides, it was mostly downhill.

As I set off down the western slope, night noises were beginning to build to their evening crescendo: katydids, frogs, bats—wonderful, unknown stuff. An owl hooted—*whew whew whew whew*. I was thrilled. Everything was so new and different, and as the light disappeared completely I felt as though I were inside the forest, like Jonah inside the whale. By the time I was halfway down, I heard another owl species. At least I suspected it to be an owl; it had a muffled, descending *bu bu bu bu bu bu bu* call. Soon it was completely dark, so dark that the only things I could see were twigs and branches covered with brilliant green phosphorescent fungi and the glowing "eyes" of elater beetles.

Since I had no light, my compass was no use. Nevertheless, I still thought I would soon hit the road and kept stumbling along downhill. Instead, I came to a boulder-clogged arroyo, a very disconcerting discovery. The creek did not fit with the lie of the land in my head. It forced me to doubt my sense of direction, and I finally had to accept that I probably could not find the road in the dark. Now a second worry began to weigh on me. My companions would surely be concerned. They were probably already busy trying to get Raúl to form a search party from the nearby fishing village of Jicacal. What an embarrassment. So I decided to hurry along as best I could, hoping that they would wait at least a little before rousing the countryside.

I reasoned that a stream could end at only one place in this part of the country, namely the ocean, and that once at the ocean I could follow the beach to Raúl's cabanas. The stream also had the advantage that one did not need a flashlight to follow it. The logic may have been impeccable, but the giant boulders along the arroyo made for tough going in the wooly dark.

After a half hour or so of groping, falling, and crawling over rocks and logs, I came out into the open. The trees were gone, replaced by a brilliant, starlit sky. I could now see enough to know I had reached the edge of a pasture delimited by a barbed-wire fence. I climbed through the fence and up out of the arroyo. Off to my left at a distance of five or six hundred meters, I saw what seemed to be car lights. Figures were moving in the lights, and I could hear a horn honking. I was quite sure this was the search party. Thoroughly chagrined, I set off across the pasture toward the lights.

After proceeding just a few meters on this route, I heard a heavy, galumphing sound and glimpsed a large white form heading rapidly in my direction, causing me to increase my pace sharply. Just moments earlier, fatigue and the bumps and bruises sustained in various tumbles had made me feel hard-pressed to move at all, but with the rapid approach of that form, which I now took to be a Brahma bull, I found myself fairly flying over the grass. The bull was faster. Fortunately, I had a head start. I reached and dove through the fence on the far side of the pasture a few meters ahead of my pursuer, leaving only a few layers of skin on the barbs in the process.

I picked myself up and realized I was in a stubble corn field. The vehicle lights had disappeared. Depression—my rescuers were already heading off, I supposed, spreading out in all likely directions to find me; best keep moving toward what must be a road. A few minutes later I saw a tiny light come bobbing up over a rise and move along diagonally away from me only thirty or forty meters ahead. I ran up and found a little girl, seven or eight years old, walking through the stubble carrying an oil can with a lighted wick. I was conscious I must appear as some sort of terrifying apparition, looming up out of the dark, but I didn't know what else to do.

"*Hola*," I said.

"*¿Hola, señor, de donde viene usted?*" she said, sensibly enough. Unfortunately all I understood was the "*hola*." I took French in high school. My training in Spanish began on the first day of our trip, when Warner made me go and arrange for rooms for the night.

So in response to her polite question, I said ungrammatically, "*No hablar español.*"

"*Veng,*" she said, and since I did not respond to her request, she reached out and took my hand and began leading me along like the helpless idiot I was. We walked a hundred meters or so and then, to my great surprise, entered a lane bordered by huts. We were in a village, but there was practically no light whatsoever, only occasional flickers of firelight seen through cracks and spaces in the stick walls of the huts. I had not even seen the village until we entered it. We walked together a bit farther, and then rounded a corner into a pool of light from the only light bulb in the place—over the front of a hut that served as the village store and bar. By this time, we had attracted a crowd of twenty-five or thirty people of all ages and sexes.

At this stage in my career, I knew the words *cerveza, quarto, baño, hablar, camino, cabanas,* and *biólogo,* and I have to say that the prospect of trying to convey my predicament and learn the way back to the hotel using this vocabulary in my fatigued state seemed daunting. My audience, however, was undeterred. They thought I was great fun. They offered me food and drink while asking me a hundred questions, to most of which I could only smile foolishly repeat my ungrammatical, *"No hablar español."* Nevertheless, I eventually understood that I was in the *ejido* Balzapote. They offered perfectly logical solutions to my problem. First, they told me I was quite welcome to stay the night—a bed would be found with no difficulty whatsoever. They made me understand that if I chose that option, there would be a truck coming by in the morning that could take me right to Playa Escondida. When they understood that I really wanted to get back (still worrying about the search party), they said well then, take a horse. I told them I did not think that was a good idea. I just wanted to be put on the *camino* to the cabanas. That turned out to be easy enough. Like Dorothy in Munchkin Land, I was standing on it. Just keep walking along this road until you come to Raúl's sign, then walk on in—about an eight-kilometer stroll, but no rocks, logs, or Brahma bulls. Piece of cake.

Before leaving, I made one request. Could they please sell me a lantern like my little guide's? They tried to present it to me as a gift, but I gave them ten pesos for it, about $1.50 at the time. I still have that lantern.

We said our good-byes, shaking hands all around, and I headed off down the road. This was my first experience with poor country folk, but I have found it to be typical in many other places visited since. They tend to accept people as they are, and unless you provide any reason for them to behave differently, and they are the warmest, best people in the world.

The walk back was long but completely uneventful. I arrived at the cabanas at about nine that night. As I limped up the road, I could see my companions seated around a table on the patio, drinking, laughing, and joking. There was certainly no evidence of imminent organization of a search party or any other sign of distress.

As I stepped into the light, Dwain said without the slightest indication of surprise at my bedraggled appearance or tardiness, "Hello, John. Find anything interesting?"

"Sorry I'm late."

"No problem. Unfortunately, we couldn't hold dinner, but there's plenty of beer."

"I was in a panic. I thought you would all be worried—maybe down at Jicacal organizing a search party or something."

"Well, no. Actually we hadn't thought much about it. Figured you'd probably got turned around a bit at night in the woods, and would show up by morning. I suppose if you hadn't appeared by tomorrow night, we would've started to think about where to look for you, although that's a mighty big place out there. Probably wouldn't have made much sense."

They were more interested in the two owls I had heard. One was the Mottled Owl (*Ciccaba virgata*), a common species in the region, but the other they thought might be a Spectacled Owl (*Pulsatrix perspicillata*), for which there were no records at the time in the Tuxtlas; it has since been found to be fairly common where lowland forest remains. After that, the talk drifted to other subjects and plans for the next day's work.

I had learned a few lessons. First, a good field biologist does not go out looking for problems. Second, if he is so foolish as to do so, it is his own affair, and he should not expect others to waste their time on his stupid mistakes, regardless of the amount of style or dash. Third, it is the quality of the information one brings back that is of primary importance, not the incidental occurrences along the way. I took those lessons to heart, though I cannot claim to have acted on them always. And I still think my companions at Playa Escondida might at least have *pretended* to be a little worried.

17

Six Trips to Mexico, 1939–1950

CHARLES G. SIBLEY

Charles G. Sibley (1917–1998) received his Ph.D. from the University of California–Berkeley in 1948 following 1941–45 military service. His dissertation research focused on hybridization between species pairs, a program he carried on for decades. Publications developed following the trips related here included Sibley and Davis (1946), Sibley (1950, 1954), Sibley and West (1958), and Sibley and Sibley (1964). He was among the founders of molecular systematics and was widely known for his formative role in using molecular data in avian systematics. He was elected to the U.S. National Academy of Sciences in 1986. For more details, see Corbin and Brush (1999) and Ahlquist (1999).

In 1938 I was a third-year undergraduate majoring in zoology at the University of California in Berkeley. I had spent the summer of 1938 as an ornithological field assistant to Jean M. Linsdale at the Hastings Natural History Reservation and had been collecting specimens of birds and small mammals since 1937. In the fall of 1938, Seth Benson invited me to accompany him as a field assistant during a collecting expedition to Sonora, Mexico, in the spring of 1939. This meant taking academic leave for the spring semester, when I would be in my last undergraduate semester, and it would delay graduation to January 1940.

In 1939 Seth Benson was thirty-four years old and looked about eighteen. He had done a brilliant study of the small mammals of the white gypsum sands region of New Mexico for his Ph.D. under Joseph Grinnell and had then been hired by the University of Michigan. However, Annie M. Alexander, the philanthropic angel of the Museum of Vertebrate Zoology (MVZ) at Berkeley, thought so highly of Seth that she urged Grinnell to bring him back as assistant curator of mammals, and she provided support for his work in Mexico. Seth's goal at the time was to assemble a collection representing the populations and species of pocket mice (*Perognathus*) and their relatives and to write a monograph on their taxonomy and distribution. He had begun his fieldwork in Mexico in 1936, accompanied by William B. Richardson. In Nogales, Sonora, Seth had found Margarito Delgadillo, a Mexican laborer, and had trained him to collect and prepare specimens. Margarito had gone with Seth on annual expeditions since 1936.

I had taken four years of Spanish in high school, was familiar with the grammar, and had a reasonably large vocabulary. Seth had no formal training in Spanish but had studied on his own and was able to converse and understand spoken Spanish. Margarito spoke no English, so we spoke Spanish when the three of us were together, including several hours almost every day while we were preparing specimens. My vocabulary and fluency improved each day, and I learned many words and phrases never encountered in a classroom. This daily seminar was to be useful during subsequent trips to Mexico, Central America, South America, and Spain.

Sonora, 1939

From January to March 1939, I helped Seth with preparations for the trip, studied publications on Mexican birds and mammals, and continued to collect near Berkeley. Annie Alexander had made a gift of a half-ton panel truck for Seth's use, and our equipment filled this small space, which was slightly larger than a modern station wagon. We left Berkeley on March 27. The next day as we drove east from Los Angeles, we passed through the small town of Glendora, where Seth ran a stop sign without seeing it. I had seen it, and I also saw a highway patrol officer sitting on his motorcycle on the side street. I told Seth, and he looked in the rear view mirror and saw the officer coming after us. Seth pulled over and stopped. The officer had noticed that the license plate of the truck carried the letter "E" in a diamond-shaped outline, indicating that it was a California state vehicle. He asked Seth why we had a state-licensed vehicle, and Seth explained that he was a University of California professor and we were en route to Mexico. The officer was not inclined to give us a ticket, but his curiosity was piqued; he asked what we planned to do in Mexico. Seth gave a brief description of our intentions, including trapping small mammals and preparing specimens. The cop listened with amazement as Seth tried in vain to make it sound like Big Science. When Seth finished, the cop exclaimed with undisguised scorn: "Well now, ain't that a helluva hard job!"

But he let us go on our way. That phrase became our theme when we were coping with heat, dust, bad water, getting stuck in the sand, and other misadventures—one would say: "Well now, ain't this a helluva hard job?" We had many opportunities to recall the cop in Glendora. At some point Seth and I disagreed about the town in which the incident occurred. I claimed it was Glendora, but he was certain that it was Monrovia. We bet a dollar, with the winner to be decided on the return trip. When we returned on May 18, Seth approached the same intersection, went by, made a U-turn, drove back (stopping at the stop sign this time), went on through, made another U-turn, drove on west a half mile, stopped, and took out a dollar bill and handed it to me. We spoke not a word.

As we were driving through Arizona we stopped for refreshments and Seth ordered a beer—his youthful appearance prompting the bartender to demand proof that he was over eighteen! On March 29 we stopped in Tucson to visit with Dr. Charles Vorhies at the University of Arizona; we also saw Lee Arnold. Vorhies told us that Major Allan Brooks, the bird artist, was staying in a nearby motel and collecting birds in the vicinity. We went to the motel and Mrs. Brooks answered our knock. Seth explained who we were and our wish to meet the major. "Oh, so you are bird persons too," said Mrs. Brooks in a British accent. We talked with Brooks for a short time, then continued to Nogales, Arizona, for the night.

On March 30 we passed through customs and picked up Margarito Delgadillo in Nogales, Sonora. The collecting began on March 31 and continued until May 16, when we began the return trip. My field notes and Seth's are on deposit at the MVZ, but some items were not recorded therein.

At the first meal in our first camp Seth established the "pecking order"—he was No. 1 and his aluminum cup had *two* bands of wire around the handle, Margarito was No. 2 and his cup had *one* band of wire. I was No. 3 and my cup had no band of wire on the handle. The scarcity of water made it imperative to avoid using any more than necessary, hence we seldom washed the cups, and each had to identify his own. Thus the wire bands served two functions—status and sanitation.

In the field our daily routine, other than travel, consisted of setting traps in the late afternoon—at least a hundred "Museum Specials," plus a few rat traps if there was evidence of wood rats (*Neotoma*). Margarito often set several steel traps for larger mammals. At dawn we picked up the traps and the "catch," and after breakfast Seth would examine the specimens and allot them to each of us. We would prepare study skins and skulls until mid-afternoon, then often break camp and drive to a new location. At times we would stay at a locality for more than one day. We collected birds when possible or when something of special interest appeared, but pocket mice, kangaroo rats (*Dipodomys*), and other small rodents were the primary goals.

On March 31, 33.4 miles south of Santa Ana, Sonora, Margarito saw a Gila monster (*Heloderma suspectum*) and shot it with a light load. The wounded lizard crawled beneath a large boulder, and Margarito came back to camp to get a shovel and our help. Seth and I went with him, and after some excavation

Seth was able to reach in and pull the animal out by the tail. As he did so he saw a second Gila monster lying motionless just inside the opening with its nose about two inches from his bare arm. After the wounded lizard was extracted, Seth grabbed the second one without incident. The wounded individual was pickled in formalin and the other one was placed in a box. Seth wanted to send it to the Mexican Department of Fish and Game (Caza y Pesca) in Mexico City as a gift to the officials who had issued collecting permits and had indicated an interest in having a live Gila monster. On April 1 in Hermosillo, he tried to mail the Gila monster to Mexico City—the postal authorities were reluctant but finally agreed.

We arrived in Guaymas on April 5 and had lunch with the American consul and his family. From the consul's Mexican secretary we obtained directions to Bahía San Carlos, ten miles northwest of Guaymas. This was a beautiful site on the shore of a shallow mangrove-lined lagoon that was an arm of the larger Bahía San Carlos. We picked oysters from the roots of the mangroves, and Seth speared a small shark using a large scalpel tied to a stick. We ate the oysters, part of the shark, and sampled a rattlesnake and the hind legs of kangaroo rats. The surroundings were spectacular—cliffs, the bay, and across the bay the conical peaks of a small range called Las Tetas de Cabra (Teats of the Goat). I have been told that by 1998 this area had become a tourist resort with large hotels accessible on a paved highway.

On April 12 we camped next to the ruins of Fort Guásima, a relic of the wars between the Yaqui indians and the Mexican government. We picked up cartridge cases from the last battle (ca. 1932). Seth shot a deer on April 15. The inside surface of the skin was thickly stippled with short, dark streaks that we determined to be the broken tips of cactus spines that had penetrated the hide and lodged in the dermal tissues.

The pressure was always on to obtain as many specimens as possible in the least amount of time and get them prepared before they spoiled in the hot weather. Seth set fifteen specimens per person per day as the optimum, and when I began the trip I had "put up" a few small mammal specimens. He made it a competition, always noting the number each of us had prepared when we had to break camp and move on. The day arrived when I reached fifteen specimens, and I announced the fact.

Seth replied, "Good. Now do it every day!"

However, from then on I noted a change in his attitude—I had been promoted to a useful member of the trio.

We spent April 19–22 in Camoa on the Río Mayo. Camoa is the type locality for several species of mammals first collected by Nelson and Goldman, including a hog-nosed skunk (*Conepatus* sp.) and a tree-dwelling woodrat

(*Teanopus phenax* = *Neotoma phenax*). The vegetation was arid-tropical, and there were many waterbirds on and along the river, including Wood Ibis (now Wood Stork, *Mycteria americana*) and ducks. Several of the locals helped us with the collecting. One brought in a live hog-nosed skunk with its mouth wired shut and its tail tied forward under the body. He told us he had grabbed it by hand, and that by pulling the tail forward under the abdomen and over the anal region he had prevented it from spraying—we were impressed!

On April 23 we arrived in Alamos, a charming colonial town in the foothills of the Sierra Madre Occidental. With the change in altitude there was a change in the vegetation and the birds; Black-throated Magpie-Jays (*Calocitta colliei*) were common. We continued on April 25 to Guirocoba, a Mexican village with the McCarty Ranch nearby. The McCartys were U.S. citizens who had been there for many years, and the older family members were in their sixties. We camped near the ranch house and collected in the area until May 4, including a side trip to an arroyo two miles east of Guirocoba. We collected a pair of Aplomado Falcons (*Falco femoralis*) as well as other birds of the arid tropics.

Figure 17.1. Charles Sibley and Margarito Delgadillo preparing specimens under a *guanuchil* tree, one mile west of Alamos, Sonora, April 23, 1939. Photo by S. B. Benson, MVZ Archives, University of California–Berkeley.

Figure 17.2. Camp under a *huisache* tree at Potrero Santa Ana, 7.6 miles south of Matehuala, San Luis Potosí, May 23, 1940. The International panel truck was purchased by the museum in 1936 and used for many expeditions to Mexico into the 1940s. From this locality other camps were reached by burro. Photo by S. B. Benson, MVZ Archives, University of California–Berkeley.

A radio had been installed in the truck, and in the evenings we often tuned in to a local station for news and music. Most of the people at Guirocoba had never heard a radio and each evening would cluster around to listen to the music. All had seen airplanes, but few had been to the coast or seen a train. We also had an audience when we were preparing specimens at our camp in the shade of streamside cypresses near the McCarty ranch house. Guirocoba was our southernmost camp, and we began the return north on May 4.

After several more camps near Guaymas and Obregón, we arrived at Estero Tastiota on the Gulf of California on May 13. As we approached an area that looked good for a camp, the left rear axle broke! We would have been in serious trouble, but nearby was a beach house owned by a man who had a business in Hermosillo and who was expecting a mechanic to repair an outboard motor. The mechanic arrived, examined the axle, and brought out a new one two days later. In the meantime we collected, fished, and went swimming. One day we saw hundreds of Brown Pelicans (*Pelecanus occidentalis*), Brown Boobies (*Sula leucogaster*), and Brandt's Cormorants (*Phalacrocorax penicillatus*) plunging and diving into the surf close to shore. As the waves rose we could see thousands of small fish. We stripped and went into the water among the fish and the diving birds—when we swam underwater the fish were all around us, with the pelicans and boobies plunging nearby and the cormorants swimming next to us. We left Estero Tastiota on May 16 and arrived in Berkeley on May 19, 1939.

Soon after our return I unpacked the birds we had collected and was laying them out in the main gallery of MVZ, preparing to catalogue and install them in the collection. Grinnell emerged from his office and walked toward me—his first words were stimulated by the sight of some specimens exposed to the sunlight streaming in through the western windows—"Oh, oh, never leave specimens in the sun, it fades the melanins, you know—did you have a good trip to Mexico?"

I moved the skins and we discussed the specimens. To close the bill of a specimen of the White-crowned Parrot (*Pionus senilis*), I had inserted a pin up through the mandible into the maxilla.

Grinnell picked up the bird and asked, "What do you call this, the Pin-chin Parrot?"

It was a wonderful moment and the last time I saw Joseph Grinnell. On May 27 I went on a trip with some friends to Mendocino County. When I returned on May 30 I learned that Grinnell had died of a heart attack on May 29. He was sixty-two years old (1877–1939). There are several biographies of Grinnell, including one by his wife, Hilda Wood Grinnell (1940), and another by Jean Linsdale (1942).

Eastern United States and Mexico, 1941

On May 10, 1941, John Davis and I left Berkeley in a new General Motors panel truck purchased with a gift from John's mother. We had installed interior cabinets for books and specimens and a twenty-gallon water tank. We drove to Fallon, Nevada, where we visited Ray Alcorn, who had collected for E. R. Hall in Nevada. We knew Ray from his visits to Berkeley. By May 12 we were near Medicine Bow, Wyoming, collecting along the way on what was then Route 30, a two-lane road with little traffic. We often shot birds from the road and picked up road kills. We could camp at many places by driving a short distance from the road. On May 12 we collected birds near Medicine Bow; fifteen miles southeast of Laramie; and at twenty miles east of Cheyenne.

We camped on May 13 at Sutherland Reservoir, near Sutherland, Nebraska, and on May 14 we were in Iowa. We had developed a method for skinning specimens as we drove—on his knees the passenger held a dishpan containing some sawdust and skinned out the birds and mammals we obtained en route. In the evening we would complete the preparation. On May 14, as we were driving along at about 40 mph in Carroll County, Iowa, two flickers (*Colaptes*) flew across the road just in front. The second one hit the windshield, bounced off, and was propelled by the airstream through the open window and into my lap! I picked it up and tossed it to John, who had the dishpan in his lap.

We made camp beside the Des Plaines River in Dupage County, Illinois, twenty miles southwest of Chicago, on May 15 and the next day we were in Ann Arbor, Michigan, where we visited Josselyn Van Tyne at the University of Michigan Museum of Zoology. I had brought some specimens of Oak Titmouse (*Baeolophus inornatus*) for comparison with the types of some races in the Michigan collection. Van Tyne showed me the case containing the types, which I opened. But when I pulled out a tray it was a short tray, and I dumped the contents—type specimens—on the floor! Van exhibited remarkable restraint. By May 20 we had arrived at the home of John's elder brother, George Davis, near Harriman in Orange County, New York. We collected in the vicinity until June 1, during which we included a trip to Moriches Inlet and Montauk Point and a visit to the American Museum of Natural History, where we met Ernst Mayr, Frank Chapman, John T. Zimmer, James Chapin, and the mammalogists.

On June 3 we drove to Cambridge, Massachusetts, and on June 4 we visited the Harvard Museum of Comparative Zoology and met James L. Peters. I was looking at the titmouse specimens in each museum. Peters suggested that we could camp in his yard for the night and he directed us to his home near Ayer in Worcester County, Massachusetts. En route, I went through a flashing yellow light and was stopped by a policeman who gave me a warning, though no ticket. Peters sat quietly between John and me during the episode. As we had approached the flashing light, Peters had said, "Watch the flashah," in his Harvard accent, but I had missed his meaning. From then on, John would say, "Watch the flashah" whenever we encountered one. Peters had an apple farm of several acres. We parked the truck outside his back door and set up our cots and sleeping bags. We had dinner with Jim and his wife. At about 2 a.m. the horn of the truck suddenly began to sound. I jumped out of my sleeping bag and as I got the hood open, Jim Peters appeared on the back porch in nightshirt and with a nightcap on his head! I ripped the wires from the horn, and we all went back to bed.

The following day we returned to George Davis's house in Harriman, New York. The door was locked, so we rang the bell—and *Babe Ruth* opened the door. We were stunned, but we introduced ourselves, and he stuck out a huge hand. It turned out that Ruth had become a friend of the Davises and often visited them. He was past his prime but still impressive.

We picked up Robert W. (Bob) Storer at his parents' home in East Orange, New Jersey, to accompany us for the remainder of the trip. Our next destination was Washington, D.C., where we contacted Alexander Wetmore, then the assistant secretary of the Smithsonian Institution. I had brought the fossil tarsus of an Oligocene hawk to compare with the type specimens of species described by Wetmore. This was the fossil that Alden Miller and I described in a joint paper in 1942 as *Buteo fluviaticus*. Wetmore knew we were coming and was most cordial. He took me to the fossil collection, and we compared the tarsus with all of the available material—the joint decision was that it differed from all described species based on tarsi. Wetmore took the three of us to the National Zoo for lunch and to see the Emperor Penguins (*Aptenodytes forsteri*), recently brought from Antarctica by Admiral Richard E. Byrd. We went into the refrigerated room with the penguins and watched them being fed fish by one of the staff. I recall standing next to one of the big birds—tempted to reach out and pet it but warned by Wetmore that it might not welcome the gesture. It was a memorable day, and Alex Wetmore and I remained friends until his death in 1978. I saw him many times over the years, at meetings of the American Ornithologists' Union (AOU), at his home on one occasion, and at International Ornithological Congresses and other gatherings. He was always kindly, courteous, and a dear friend.

About Alex Wetmore. At one AOU meeting in the 1950s or 1960s, we were discussing the classification of birds. With reference to his classification he said, "Well, I think it just needs a bit more tinkering and we'll have it about right." He gave me a copy of the fifth edition of the AOU *Check-list* (AOU 1957) with the following written on the flyleaf: "Inscribed to Charles G. Sibley, with the regards and admiration of Alexander Wetmore. Cape May, New Jersey, September 13, 1957." I treasure the volume but have to wonder how he would feel today about the Sibley, Monroe, and Ahlquist (Sibley and Ahlquist 1990; Sibley and Monroe 1990) classification.

John, Bob, and I continued south along the Atlantic coast, collecting and picking up road kills as we went. We were in Prince Georges County, Maryland, on June 17; near Kitty Hawk, North Carolina, on June 18; and at Alligator Lake, North Carolina, on June 19. By June 22 we were in Daytona Beach, Florida, where we stayed at the home of John's mother. From there we collected at various nearby localities including on Merritt Island, now the site of the Kennedy Space Center. At that time it was a mosquito-infested area of salt marshes and tidal channels. To collect and also to avoid the mosquitoes, Bob drove the truck slowly along the dirt roads. I sat on the right fender with a shotgun, and when we saw a desirable specimen Bob stopped, I shot, John dashed to grab the bird, and we moved on. On one occasion as I walked out into a tidal marsh to try to collect Seaside Sparrows (*Ammodramus maritimus*), the mosquitoes rose like a cloud, getting into my mouth, eyes, nose—I ran for the truck.

On June 29 our shotguns and other items were stolen from the truck during the night. I had no money to buy a new gun, but Mrs. Davis said she would collect for the guns on her insurance "floater," and she gave John the money to buy a new gun. We went to Jacksonville and found a hardware store that had one 16-gauge L.C. Smith Field Grade left in stock. John insisted that I should have it—it cost fifty-five dollars, and I still have it in 1998. The L.C. Smith Field Grade was the favorite gun of Joseph Grinnell. It was said that he never cleaned it—he just bought a new one as necessary. The Field Grade was not made during World War II, and it was discontinued soon thereafter. I carried this shotgun to many countries on all subsequent field trips and to the Southwest Pacific during World War II.

We left Daytona Beach on July 3 and made camp twenty miles southwest of Orlando in Orange County, Florida. I took the new shotgun and walked out from camp across a clearing in the pine woods. A Pileated Woodpecker (*Dryocopus pileatus*) called from across the clearing, then took off and flew toward me—I took it on the wing with the first shot fired from the gun. The next three birds were also woodpeckers, a Red-bellied (*Melanerpes carolinus*), a Red-cockaded (*Picoides borealis*), and a Downy (*Picoides pubescens*).

We continued via Lake Okeechobee to the Florida Keys and collected on Lower Matecumbe, Sugar Loaf, No Name, and Big Pine Keys. One night, we were plagued by mosquitoes and placed our cots almost at the water's edge on the windward side of a small island, with a large tarpaulin rigged over the top of the truck and over our cots alongside. During the night a thunderstorm hit, and we were soon soaked as the violent wind drove the heavy rain in under the tarp. We climbed into the truck, and when the storm abated we rolled up the tarp and our wet sleeping bags and drove to Key West, where we spent the rest of the night sitting on the seawall at the end of the road.

Between July 8 and 12 we drove up the west coast of Florida and along the Gulf Coast of Florida, Alabama, Mississippi, Louisiana, and Texas to Brownsville, Texas, where we contacted L. Irby Davis. We collected near Brownsville for a few days, then left the shotgun, ammunition, and other items in Irby's garage. We crossed the border into Mexico on July 17 and drove to Mexico City, where I obtained collecting permits. John bought a beautiful Spanish-made 16-gauge double-barreled shotgun, and we obtained ammunition, including having special loads prepared. On July 23 we were collecting birds near Cuernavaca and then near Chilpancingo, Guerrero, by July 26. In Chilpancingo we

Figure 17.3. Charles Sibley preparing specimens under a *palofierro* tree, five miles west of Hermosillo, Sonora, October 28, 1941. Photo by S. B. Benson, MVZ Archives, University of California–Berkeley.

found Wilmot W. Brown, a well-known collector of birds for museums. Brown and his wife, both elderly, were living in a couple of rooms on a street in the town. He could no longer collect in the field, but he bought specimens from young men who brought them to his window on the street. He made beautiful skins and let us watch him. He had metal troughs of various sizes in which the completed specimen was laid, then wrapped with thread. This produced the round-backed specimens for which he was known.

On July 27 we were in Pie de La Cuesta, eight miles northwest of Acapulco, which was then a small town on the coast. On the beach at Pie de La Cuesta we rented a room in a small hotel with geckos on the ceiling. We returned north to Puebla by July 29 and to Jalapa, Veracruz, on July 31. On August 1 we were at Boca del Río, five miles southeast of Veracruz on the Caribbean coast. We returned to Mexico City, and on August 5–7 we were at Tamazunchale and near Xilitla, San Luis Potosí. We returned to Brownsville, then drove almost nonstop from southeastern Texas to the California border, where we made an all-night stop in the desert, then to Berkeley the next day.

Tiburón Island, Sonora, 1941

During the fall semester of 1941, Seth Benson again invited me to accompany him on a collecting trip, this time to Tiburón Island, the largest island in the Gulf of California, or Sea of Cortez. We left Berkeley on October 24 and arrived in Nogales, Arizona, on the 26th, where we visited Fred Dille, a well-known professional collector. On October 27 we passed through Mexican Customs, picked up Margarito Delgadillo in Nogales, Sonora, and drove south toward Hermosillo. I collected a Mearns' Quail (*Cyrtonyx montezumae mearnsi*) 31.4 miles south of Nogales. In Hermosillo we bought supplies and drove five miles west, where we made camp and set out traps. On October 29 we drove to Kino Bay on the Gulf, obtained a small boat, and went out to a nearby small island called Pelican Island, where we set traps. Magnificent Frigatebirds (*Fregata magnificens*), Brown Pelicans (*Pelecanus occidentalis*), and other waterbirds were abundant, but we caught no mammals on Pelican Island. Until November 3 we collected near Puerto Kino while waiting for a boat to take us to Tiburón Island. We left Puerto Kino on a fishing boat on November 3 and arrived at Ensenada del Perro, a locality at the south end of Tiburón Island, at 4:30 p.m. Our equipment was landed on the beach, and we set up camp.

We had noticed many flies in the area, and they soon became a nuisance. The source was shark carcasses piled up like cordwood a few hundred yards down the beach. The shark fishermen took only the livers for extraction of vitamin D and left the carcasses, which were moving with the fly larvae developing in them. Hatching flies covered the nearby creosote bushes, and the area was saturated with adults. To avoid the pests we ate breakfast before sunup and dinner after sundown and prepared specimens under mosquito netting. Most of the preparation of the small mammal specimens was my responsibility. I would weigh and measure the specimens, put on my hat, sit down at the camp table, and arrange the mosquito netting to cover myself and the table. The temperature inside the tent was in the nineties, and the flies would almost cover the netting while I was working underneath. We tried to burn the shark carcasses, but there were at least a thousand of them, and our supply of gasoline was limited. We thought again of the policeman in Glendora in

Figure 17.4. Charles Sibley and Margarito Delgadillo holding *lisas* (mullet), Tiburón Island, Sonora, November 7, 1941. The fish had been dynamited at Ensenada del Perro near the south end of the island and then left by fishermen; note the many flies in the air. Photo by S. B. Benson, MVZ Archives, University of California–Berkeley.

1939–"Well now, ain't that a helluva hard job." We had a small boat and used it several times to fish near the shore and escape the flies for a while.

Seth wanted to obtain specimens of the Tiburón Island deer—a different subspecies from the mainland form. He got one on November 9, which we skinned and butchered, saving the skin and skull. The next day Seth again went deer hunting. He did not return at sundown and had not taken a flashlight. Margarito and I were worried, so we lighted the Coleman lantern as a beacon and with flashlights and guns went out to find Seth. We walked along the ridge at the head of the series of canyons that led down to the water, stopping at intervals to shout, flash the lights, and fire a gun. Then, from far down the same canyon where he had killed the deer the day before, we heard Seth shout. Margarito stayed on the ridge, and I worked my way down through dense brush, cactus, and rocks. As I got to within about fifty yards of Seth he shouted to me to circle around and come up behind him—"There's a rattlesnake buzzing a few feet in front of me!"

I circled around, came up to him, and with the flashlight saw the coiled rattler, which I shot. Seth had been standing there for more than an hour in the darkness, waiting for the moon to rise so he could see to work his way up the canyon without running into cactus spines, falling over rocks, or stepping on rattlesnakes.

The boat returned on November 11 and took us back to Puerto Kino. We collected in the vicinity of Puerto Kino until the 17th. A boy brought us a living porcupine (*Erethizon dorsatum*), which was captured when he had set fire to its nest in a clump of brush and cactus. The animal was in good condition, although it had been singed by the fire and had lost some spines and hair in the process. We made a cage of a wooden box, and Seth decided to take the porcupine back alive and keep it until its hair and quills grew back. Desert-dwelling porcupines are not common, and this was the first specimen he had obtained. We left Puerto Kino on November 18 and drove east and north through Hermosillo, stopping near the road for the night. The porcupine in its box was locked inside the truck. In the morning we found it clinging to the steering wheel, which it had gnawed in several places, perhaps attracted by the salt from sweaty hands. It took some maneuvering to get the animal back into its box, but we improved the latch and continued to Nogales and across

Figure 17.5. Charles Sibley getting equipment ready to load, Ensenada del Perro, Tiburón Island, Sonora, November 11, 1941. The boat would take the party to Kino. Again, note the flies. Photo by S. B. Benson, MVZ Archives, University of California–Berkeley.

Arizona. We arrived at the California border around 2 a.m. the following night and stopped for the agricultural inspection. The inspector came out and asked that the back of the truck be opened—which was done. The inspector shined his flashlight into the truck and there, sitting on top of its box, was the porcupine.

"What the hell is that?" asked the inspector.

"A porcupine," Seth replied.

"Well," said the inspector, "you can't bring that into California."

"Oh, yes, we can," said Seth.

"How do you know?"

"Because I helped to write the regulations, and porcupines are native to California."

The porcupine died before it had time to grow new hair, so there is a singed *Erethizon dorsatum* specimen in the MVZ collection.

California and Mexico, 1946

In October 1941 I was employed by the U.S. Public Health Service to survey mammalian populations in the Great Plains for bubonic plague. The field season was from early in 1942 through October. I joined the U.S. Navy in November 1942 and was commissioned in early 1943. In 1944–45, for nineteen months, I was a communications officer on shore bases in the southwest Pacific and the Philippines. During this time I collected about seven hundred specimens of birds and a few mammals, which are in the Museum of Vertebrate Zoology. I was discharged in December 1945.

I registered as a Ph.D. candidate in zoology for the spring semester of 1946. For a thesis project I had decided to study geographic variation in the Spotted Towhee (*Pipilo maculatus*) of the western United States and began to assemble the literature and to examine the specimens in the MVZ collection. During the spring, a shipment of specimens arrived from Helmuth Wagner, a German zoologist who was living and collecting in Mexico. Frank Pitelka, who was curating the collection, unpacked Wagner's skins and called my attention to some towhee specimens from the Mexican highlands. Frank had tried to identify the specimens from the literature and found that they did not match any of the descriptions, so he suggested I look at them. The specimens were puzzling, because the literature on the Mexican towhees and the specimens from Wagner suggested that there were either several species, or possibly hybrids, involved. The mystery was so compelling that I decided to go to Mexico to investigate the situation. John Davis had decided to study the Canyon Towhees (*Pipilo fuscus*), so we planned a joint trip for the summer of 1946.

We left Berkeley on June 22 in Davis's panel truck—the same one we had used in the summer of 1941. We passed through Laredo, Texas, and into Mexico and arrived late on June 28 in Mexico City, where we stayed the night in a motel. During the night a door handle of the truck was broken off in an attempt at burglary. On June 30 we drove north to Pachuca and Real del Monte, six miles east of Pachuca. This is the type locality of *Pipilo maculata*, described by William Swainson in 1827, so it was a logical place to begin. We found a camp site in a small clearing in the fir forest at 9,600 feet. By July 3 I had obtained sixteen specimens of "Spotted Towhees," and it was apparent that the mystery was deepening. Two species had been recorded from this area, *Pipilo maculatus* and *Pipilo macronyx*, but my specimens from this one locality bridged the morphological gap between them. This was the beginning of the study of the effects of hybridization between the Spotted Towhee (*Pipilo maculatus*) and the Collared Towhee (*Pipilo ocai*); the Spotted Towhee was treated as a subspecies of *P. erythrophthalmus* at that time. The field study was to continue at intervals until 1958 and is recorded in four publications (Sibley 1950, 1954; Sibley and West 1958; Sibley and Sibley 1964).

One day Davis had gone to an area where Canyon Towhees were present, and I hunted in the area where I obtained the specimens noted. I returned to camp at noon and began to prepare lunch. I heard a shot from John's gun and expected him to walk into camp in a few minutes—but he did not appear until late in the afternoon. He had become disoriented and had passed close to the camp without recognizing the area. He continued until he encountered a man and managed to communicate the problem. Fortunately the fellow knew who we were and the location of our camp, and he brought John to the site. It was a sobering experience, and we took extra precautions to stay oriented thereafter.

We left the camp near Pachuca on July 4 for Mexico City, and on the 6th drove east toward Puebla and the volcanic peak of the Cofre de Perote. We made camp in the pines at 8,700 feet on the north slope and began collecting on July 8. No *P. ocai* were found. We moved on the next day and searched until July 11 for a way to ascend the slopes of Mt. Orizaba in the vicinity of Chalchicomula, Puebla. We arrived in Chalchicomula on the 11th and ascended a track up the mountain to a point eight miles northeast of Chalchicomula at 10,350 feet. This was as far as we could go, and our camp was in a sparse stand of pines and firs with a potato field on one side and a wheat field on the other. The snow-capped peak of Orizaba loomed above us, and towhees were present.

The following morning we found that we had been robbed of our cooking utensils, tableware, an axe, and some food— everything we had left outside the tent or the truck was gone. I hunted for two hours and got eight towhees that showed evidence of hybridization between *ocai* and *maculatus*. We then drove down to Chalchicomula and reported the theft to the mayor and the police. We suspected a certain individual who had visited our camp the previous afternoon, and we provided his description. At the time I never expected to hear more of this episode, but there would be a sequel in 1948.

Late on July 12 we drove back to Mexico City, where we bought new utensils, before driving south to Oaxaca and to Mitla on the 15th to see the Zapotec ruins. We collected Canyon Towhees in this area, then drove back to Oaxaca and took the road to Ixtlán, which ascends the east side of the Cerro San Felipe. We made camp in oak woodland at 7,400 feet, about fifteen airline miles northeast of Oaxaca, where we found typical *P. maculatus*. We moved higher to 8,900 feet and found *P. ocai*. In subsequent years I found them together in this area without any evidence of hybridization.

On July 18 we returned to Mexico City and visited Helmuth Wagner, who had collected the specimens that had caused me to decide to study the Mexican populations. Wagner had also collected towhees near Pachuca and believed *macronyx* and *maculatus* to be conspecific. During our discussion about the towhees we debated the status of the populations at Pachuca and elsewhere. Wagner, a tall man, lived in a small apartment with low ceilings, and he walked about as he discoursed on the problem of "subspacements" (subspecies). At one point he exclaimed in his German accent: "Can you tell me what it is a subspacement? No you can't tell me what it is a subspacement! Erwin Stresemann couldn't tell me what it is a subspacement!" John and I treasured the moment and often used Wagner's "subspacement" in our conversations.

On July 19 we drove up into the saddle between Mt. Popocatepetl and Mt. Iztaccihuatl at about 12,000 feet, then back down to camp at 9,700 feet, where we collected greenish-plumaged *macronyx*-type towhees the next morning. We then drove south via Cuernavaca and Taxco to Chilpancingo, where we again visited Mr. and Mrs. Wilmot W. Brown at the Hotel Mexico, as we had in 1941. They had been there for nine years, and Brown remembered our previous visit, but Mrs. Brown was ill and did not recognize us.

On July 21 we drove to Omilteme, a tiny sawmill town at 7,400 feet in the mountains west of Chilpancingo. Omilteme is the type locality for several birds first collected by Mrs. H. H. Smith in the 1880s, including a subspecies (*guerrerensis*) of *P. ocai*, named by A. J. van Rossem in 1938. The type is one of Mrs. Smith's specimens in the British Museum. The towhees were scarce, and we got only two specimens, but Brown told me that he had obtained a good series from Omilteme for Milton S. Ray, a private collector in San Francisco whose collection was to go to the MVZ. I obtained the information I wanted on voice, habitat, etc., and we returned to Mexico City on July 24.

The next day we collected Canyon Towhees near Mexico City and visited the Pyramid of the Sun at Teotihuacán. On July 26 we collected Canyon and Spotted towhees near Salazar, west of Mexico City. We moved to Temascaltepec on the 27th and obtained permission to camp in a vacant house at 5,500 feet near the town. We collected several birds, but no towhees, although *P. macronyx* had been recorded from Temascaltepec in the past century. This area is a famous type locality under the name of Real de Arriba, where Deppe collected. John and I published a note about the locality (Sibley and Davis 1946).

We left Temascaltepec on July 30 and drove west across the "trans-plateau" highlands on Highway CN #4 through Morelia and Quiroga to Zacapu, and on July 31 to Pátzcuaro, where we collected Canyon and Collared towhees until August 1; the next day we drove to Guadalajara. On August 3 we returned south along CN #4 and took a side road that led us to a camp in the Sierra de Tapalpa, fifteen miles west of Sayula at 7,450 feet. *P. ocai* were common, and we collected here until August 6, when we returned to Guadalajara. On the 7th we began the return trip via San Luis Potosí, collecting Canyon Towhees along the way. I had collected ninety-nine specimens, and they showed that the Mexican towhees presented a complex pattern of variation due to hybridization between *maculatus* and *ocai* in some places, gradients between them in others, and apparent sympatry without interbreeding in Oaxaca.

Spring in Mexico, 1948

The material collected on the 1946 trip and examination of specimens borrowed from other museums revealed some of the complicated pattern of variation in the Mexican red-eyed towhees and identified the areas that had to be sampled to provide a complete picture. To avoid the summer rains and to take advantage of the greater amount of song in the spring, I planned a trip beginning in February. On February 16 I left Berkeley with James Basil Bowers and Henry E. Childs, Jr. John Davis generously let me use his panel truck, and we drove to Laredo by the 19th and into Mexico the following day.

We camped on the Mesa de Chipinque at 4,000 feet, ten miles southwest of Monterrey, Nuevo León, the night of February 21, then continued south. On the 23rd, near El Limón, I shot an Aplomado Falcon (*Falco femoralis*) that was hit but flew off and dropped into the arid scrub. I retrieved the bird, but when I returned to the truck discovered that I had become the host of an enormous number of *pinolillos,* tiny red ticks. I brushed off all I could see on my clothing, but some had already penetrated deeper and were an irritant for several days.

By chance, we met a Louisiana State University field party consisting of George Lowery, Bob Newman, his wife, and two students. We had stopped on a ridge crest between Antigua Morelos and Nuevo Morelos to look at the view, and the LSU group saw my binoculars as they drove by.

From February 24 to 26 we collected eighteen Spotted Towhees at 5,000 feet near Ciudad del Maíz, San Luis Potosí. We arrived in Mexico City on the 27th and drove west on CN #4 the next day to a locality fifteen miles east of Zitácuaro, Michoacán, at 9,500 feet. Towhees were abundant and proved to be near the midpoint of the trans-plateau cline between *maculatus* to the east and *ocai* to the west. From March 2 to 4 we collected at around 9,000 feet on the Cerro de San Andrés, twenty miles south-southeast of Morelia, Michoacán. The towhees occurred from about 8,500 feet to the top of the mountain at 11,200 feet, and most had the rufous crowns of *ocai*, although showing the influence of introgression from *maculatus*. This general area is called Mil Cumbres, and it proved to be closest to the midpoint on the trans-plateau cline between the two species.

On March 5 we made camp fifteen miles east southeast of Morelia at 7,300 feet in pine-oak woods, about twenty-eight airline miles from Cerro de San Andrés. Towhees were scarce and wary, and we got few specimens. We drove to Pátzcuaro on March 8 and located a party from Cornell University at the Limnological Station on the lakeshore. Ernest P. (Buck) Edwards, Paul Martin, and Roger Hurd were collecting in the area. On March 9 all six of us went hunting on Lake Pátzcuaro in an outboard motorboat (described in chapter 13).

On March 10 we went to Guadalajara for supplies and to obtain information about what we knew as the Sierra de Cuyutlán, a mountain on the north shore of Lake Chapala. Three hybrid specimens in the American Museum of Natural History, collected by A. C. Buller in 1892, suggested that the towhees on this mountain should be interesting. After several false starts, and discovering that the local name for the mountain was Cerro Viejo, we met Sr. Agustín Pérez Gómez, who provided hospitality (lunch and beer) at his house in Cuyutlán, arranged for pack burros, and safeguarded the truck in his courtyard. We left Cuyutlán at 7 a.m. on March 12, ascended Cerro Viejo, and camped at 8,500 feet near a spring in oak woods with dense undergrowth. Towhees were abundant, and we collected three on the way up. We collected on Cerro Viejo until the morning of March 16 and obtained seventy-four specimens. The teeming population of towhees on Cerro Viejo proved to be a "hybrid swarm"—no two specimens were identical. They ranged widely in color and pattern, but there were no "pure" individuals of either species. Cerro Viejo was like an island in a sea of mesquite-grassland, with *ocai* populations in the highlands to the south and *maculatus* populations in the Sierra Madre Occidental to the north. Apparently juveniles of both species had dispersed across the inhospitable lowlands and found suitable habitat on the summit of Cerro Viejo, where they interbred.

We returned to Guadalajara late on March 16. On the 17th and 18th we drove to the coast at San Blas to see the lowland tropical avifauna. We planned to camp on the beach, but the biting "sand flies" caused us to seek a room in town. We found a room to rent in a private house facing the main square and moved in after the room had been cleaned and whitewashed. In the evening we were sitting in our room with the door open, skinning birds and writing notes when a middle-aged man walked up to the door, looked at us for a moment, and said: "Hello there California—you look like you're from Berkeley," and introduced himself as Chester Lamb.

It was a great moment—to meet the well-known collector under such circumstances was delightful. Chester had dinner with us, and we spent the evening talking about MVZ, birds, and people. The following day he came with us in the field. Lamb was collecting for Robert T. Moore and living in a hotel in San Blas. His collecting method was amusing and sensible, since he was getting the bare minimum for his specimens. He would station himself under a tree and shoot the first ten or so birds that came within range, return to his room, and prepare the specimens.

On March 19 we rented a *canoa* and paddled up an *estero* in the mangroves northwest of San Blas. Birds were abundant, and we took several specimens, including a Rufous-necked Wood-Rail (*Aramides axillaris*). Chester Lamb again joined us for dinner. He also hunted and had dinner with us on March 20 and 21. Chester agreed to let me look through his catalogues for towhee records, so we planned to go to his home in Irapuato, where he lived with his wife and family. He gave me a letter to his wife to let her know that he had given his permission for me to inspect the catalogues.

We left San Blas on March 22 and spent the night in Guadalajara. The next day we drove to Irapuato, Guanajuato, and I obtained the catalogues from Mrs. Lamb. We put up at a hotel, and I inspected the six-inch-thick catalogues. He had used an idiosyncratic numbering sequence, with numbers from 1 to 11,758 used twice; 11,759–30,143 were used just once, and no specimens were numbered 30,144–41,900. Number 41,901 was used on April 17, 1945, and the catalogue ended with No. 45,608 on April 8, 1947. Thus, Lamb had collected 45,608 specimens up to April 8, 1947.

On March 24 we drove from Irapuato to thirty miles east of Morelia,

Michoacán, where we camped at 8,500 feet in a stand of pines, firs, and oaks. We collected there until March 27, when we moved east on CN #4 to a side road that led to Lago Sabaneta and camped at 8,000 feet at Sabaneta, six miles south-southwest of Ciudad Hidalgo, Michoacán. We got a few towhees and four Whiskered Screech-Owls (*Otus trichopsis*).

We then went to Mexico City and Oaxaca, and by the same route Davis and I had taken in 1946 to the area east of Cerro San Felipe, where we made camp at the highest point on the road at the village of La Cumbre, five miles north-northeast of Cerro San Felipe, Oaxaca, at 9000 feet. We collected here until April 5, obtained a good series of both species, often under the same bush, and found no evidence of hybridization. Thus in Oaxaca we had found sympatry, on Cerro Viejo a hybrid swarm, and across the trans-plateau mountains a gradient from one species to the other. More was yet to come.

Leaving La Cumbre, we drove southeast on the Pan-American Highway to Tehuantepec City, where we spent a miserable, noisy, hot, mosquito-plagued night at the misnamed Hotel Oasis. On April 6 we continued across the Isthmus of Tehuantepec through Juchitán, Zanatepec, and Tapanatepec to Tuxtla Gutiérrez. Much of the road was unpaved, and it took us eight hours to go 186 miles. The ascent to the Chiapas highlands began as a series of switchbacks that rose 4,750 feet in the first twenty miles and to 7,800 feet after thirty-five miles. We arrived at San Cristóbal de Las Casas in the late afternoon, 239 road miles from Tehuantepec. We bought some souvenirs, including inexpensive colorful hand-woven fabrics from Guatemala. We returned along the road to a point five miles northwest of San Cristóbal to a side road, where we spent the night. The next day we found a camp site nearby. The area was in pine-oak woodland about four airline miles northwest of San Cristóbal. I had developed a painful infection in my left thigh and stayed in camp to apply hot compresses to it.

Spotted Towhees (subspecies *chiapensis*) were abundant, and there are no *ocai* south of the Isthmus of Tehuantepec. On April 8 I collected near the camp and encountered a local landowner who introduced himself as Rudolfo. I asked about the local animals, and he told me that wolves were common, as were coyotes, deer, and other mammals. I asked about bats, and he offered to guide me to a bat cave. As we walked he told me that in 1914, during the Revolution, a family of wealthy landowners (*hacendados*) had hidden in the cave and that all had died of hunger. I doubted the story until he showed me human bones in the cave, including an unmistakable human tibia. He said the skulls were buried in a pile of rocks on the cave floor. Later in the day, with Rudolfo as guide, Bowers and I went to San Cristóbal and bought more of the hand-woven textiles from Guatemala.

We collected until April 9. My infected leg had become more painful and had developed into a boil. I decided to return to Oaxaca or Mexico City for medical help. We broke camp late in the afternoon so as to cross the hot Isthmus during the night. One tire had a slow leak that had to be pumped up every thirty miles, so progress was slow. I had fixed a bed in the back of the truck so that I could lie down and reduce the pressure on my leg. About ten miles east of Tapanatepec, at about 2 a.m., we came upon a Baird's tapir (*Tapirus bairdii*) in the middle of the road. It made no attempt to flee but moved back and forth across the road as it ambled along in the headlights. Several times it turned and came toward the truck, once coming close alongside when we stopped. We could see that it was a male with white-tipped ears, a white spot at the base of each ear, three hind toes, and a brownish iris. The movements of his proboscis as he sniffed the air were fascinating. We followed the tapir for about ten minutes before temptation overtook me, in spite of my painful leg. I got out of the truck, ran up behind the tapir, and slapped him on the rump. Off he went down the road at full speed, then up the hill into the brush, and we could hear him crashing through the vegetation. Later we saw two coatimundis (*Nasua nasua*) run across the road.

We arrived in Oaxaca at 2 p.m. on April 10. While Basil and Hank got the tube repaired, I found a doctor and had my boil lanced. He extracted a long core and gave me some penicillin ointment; the pain subsided, and the deep hole in my thigh soon healed. We left Oaxaca the next day and drove to Mexico City, where we spent April 12 replenishing supplies. The next day we drove via Pachuca, Tulancingo, and Villa Juárez to Tuxpam on the shore of the Caribbean to survey the cross section of the mountains and see the eastern tropical lowlands.

On April 14 we returned to the highlands in heavy rain, which impeded our work for the next two days, and on the 16th we went to the town of Chalchicomula on the west slope of Mt. Orizaba, near where Davis and I had camped and been robbed in 1946. In Chalchicomula I went to the police station, explained to the officer on duty about the 1946 robbery, and asked for some guarantee of security this time. He promised that he would see to our safety, if need be even taking an armed guard with us up the mountain. However, we had to wait until the next day to talk to the mayor and the chief of police. The next morning the mayor's secretary arrived, and after hearing my story and examining permits and passports, he wrote a letter to the *juez de paz* (justice of the peace) of the Ojo de Agua area, charging him with our security.

We ascended to the village of Ojo de Agua via the same road Davis and I had used in 1946 and located Sr. Juliano Serrano, *juez de paz*. He read the letter and looked puzzled; I explained that we wanted some guarantee of security from another theft in the night. He assured me there was no danger, and I repeated that we had been robbed. After various delays and false starts we decided to camp near where Davis and I had camped in 1946. We ground our way in low gear up the slope to 10,500 feet and camped about four hundred yards from the 1946 site. Our position was at a turn in the footpath used by woodcutters and snow gatherers to ascend to higher elevations. Word of our contact with the police and Sr. Serrano had spread, for the foot traffic avoided us by cutting across a field well away from our camp. One day three men visited us, and we talked for a couple of hours. They were cordial, so I told them of the 1946 robbery, which they knew about, and they told me that the man we had described had been sent to jail but was now free. They also said they did not think he was guilty but thought he had been used as a scapegoat. I asked where he was now and was told that he was in the neighborhood, which made us wonder whether we might be confronted by an angry but innocent man who had served time because of our charges.

On the slope of Mt. Orizaba, *ocai* tends to occur in the undergrowth of the fir forest between 10,000 and 11,000 feet, and *erythrophthalmus* is most abundant in brushy thickets below about 10,000 feet. At our location at 10,350 feet towhees were abundant, with both "pure" species and occasional hybrids. We collected eighty-six specimens, and I studied a transect in which both species seemed to be distributed throughout an area of 850 × 1,100 feet, in which I found five pairs of *maculatus* and four pairs of *ocai*. Both species often occurred in the same patch of brush. From both trips, plus specimens in other museums, I assembled 109 specimens from the west slope of Mt. Orizaba. Of these, thirteen showed evidence of hybridization, six were most like *maculatus*, and seven tended toward *ocai*. The "pure" adults from the overlap zone were about evenly divided between the two species.

This camp was unpleasant because the nights were below freezing, the days were cold, and a constant wind blew dust from the plowed fields into our tent and equipment. We left the area on the evening of April 20 to head for Mexico City, then Valles, Linares, and west toward Galeana, Nuevo León. Some eight miles southeast of Galeana, at 6,000 feet, we collected twenty-two *maculatus* on the 22nd and 23rd, including the type specimen of *P. m. orientalis*, which I described as a new subspecies in 1950. We had the twenty-two towhee specimens prepared by noon on April 23, so we broke camp and drove to Laredo, Texas, passed through U.S. Customs, and spent the night in a motel. From there we drove nonstop to Berkeley, taking turns napping on a bed fixed up on top of the load. During the summer and early fall of 1948 I wrote my doctoral thesis: "Species formation in the red-eyed towhees of Mexico" (Sibley 1950).

In 1949 Alden Miller contacted me and asked if I had a copy of the thesis manuscript. Fortunately, I did. It turned out that in February the 118 Ph.D. theses submitted in the fall of 1948 had been destroyed and would have to be retyped by the graduate school. The *San Francisco Chronicle* published the following on August 7, 1949 (my 32nd birthday):

BERKELEY

Tch Tch

A tragic loss was revealed to the world last week: "Bionomics of Tomato and Tobacco Hornworms" and "Drainage of Mexico City During the Colonial Period" and "Species Formation in Mexican Red-eyed Towhees" and 115 other University of California post-graduate theses. En route, last February, from the campus storehouse to the University Library for cataloguing and use as general reference material, the weighty tomes ended up at the city dump. There they were burned. No one could understand how it happened. The loss became known last week but university spokesmen were reluctant to comment. An anonymous official wailed: "It was a terrible mistake."

Summer in Mexico, 1950

In 1950 I was an assistant professor of Zoology at San Jose State College in San Jose, California. The Mexican towhee problem still had loose ends, so I decided to go again to Mexico in the summer of 1950. I obtained a grant of $1,050 from the American Philosophical Society and used $500 of it to buy a war-surplus army ambulance, which was a four-wheel-drive Dodge Power Wagon. The vehicle was in fair condition, except for the huge tires—and they were to become a major problem. Three San Jose State College students, Andrew C. Browne, Eugene A. "Olie" Olson, and Raymond E. Williams were enlisted as unpaid assistants. For the trip to Guadalajara they drove the Dodge Power Wagon, and my wife Frances, our two-year-old daughter Barbara, and I used our Pontiac sedan. The $550 remaining from the American Philosophical Society grant covered most of the expenses for the truck and fieldwork—the remainder, and our personal costs, came from our savings.

We arrived in Guadalajara on July 3 and rented a small suburban house for Fran and Barbara and to use as our headquarters. The boys and I left Guadalajara in the Dodge on July 5 and drove south twenty-two miles to a road leading to Autlán, then via various roads to the vicinity of Cocula and up a rough road on the west slope of Cerro Tecolote, 6,800 feet, five miles southwest of Cocula, Jalisco. No towhees were found, so we returned to Guadalajara and, among other things, got a tire recapped—the first of many tire problems. On

July 8 we drove west on the road to Tequila and to Las Norias, where we left the road and proceeded through gates and fences to the village of Sandovale, 3.3 miles from Las Norias. I obtained four burros and a packer; we climbed Cerro Tequila in the afternoon and camped in pine-oak-madrone woods at 6,600 feet, seven miles south of Tequila, Jalisco. We collected on Cerro Tequila until July 15 and obtained sixty-nine towhees. The plumages of the population on Cerro Tequila showed the effects of hybridization, with an average hybrid index score of 18 on a scale of 0 = pure *ocai* to 24 = pure *erythrophthalmus*; a score of 12 indicated specimens with averaged plumage characters at the midpoint between the two species.

On July 18 we went to Ameca, fifty miles west of Guadalajara, then via La Vega and Ahualulco de Mercado to the north base of the Sierra de Ameca. With three pack mules and a packer, we ascended into the Sierra de Ameca on the 19th and camped at 5,650 feet, six miles north of Ameca, Jalisco. We collected there until July 24 and obtained eighteen towhees, which averaged 12.0 on the hybrid index.

We spent July 26 on the road to Tepic, Nayarit, looking for a way to ascend into the mountains at the southern end of the Sierra Madre Occidental. We were unsuccessful, although we tried at various places. We made a brief visit to San Blas on the coast, so the boys could see some of the lowland tropical birds, before returning to Guadalajara.

Ray Williams was a reservist in the marines, and on July 29 he received orders to return to the United States and report for active duty with his unit; later he spent some time in Korea, but he returned safely and I saw him again in 1953. I took Ray to the airport early on the 30th, then Olson, Browne, and I drove south from Guadalajara to San Luis Soyatlán, a village on the southwest shore of Lake Chapala at the base of Cerro García. I hired a man and his four burros to take us up Cerro García. We left San Luis at 3 p.m. and climbed steeply to a ridge east of the summit, where we camped in oak-madrone woods at 8,500 feet, thirty-two miles south of Guadalajara. Towhees proved abundant, and we collected fifty-eight by August 2. The average hybrid index was 8.0, thus on the *ocai* side of the midpoint, as we expected from the location of Cerro García relative to other known populations. By this time we had begun to predict the average hybrid index of the next locality before we collected there, and we bet a bottle of rum on the predictions. Rum and Coca-Cola was our only libation, and my experience proved useful in winning most of the bets.

A remarkable event occurred at this camp. One morning while hunting towhees I gave imitations of a Ferruginous Pygmy-Owl (*Glaucidium brasilianum*), which often excites interest in other birds. I heard a reply from a real Pygmy-Owl and moved toward the sound, calling at intervals. I saw the bird, fired, and it fell—and Olson shouted from the other side of the hill, "I got it!" He had been approaching the bird from the opposite direction, and we had fired simultaneously! When the bird was skinned we found both #10 and #12 pellets in the specimen—we had used different sized shot and had both hit the bird. We returned to Guadalajara on August 3.

While on Cerro García I had developed a severe backache, so I went to a doctor in Guadalajara, who diagnosed it as *reumatismo*—I didn't believe it; I was only thirty-three. I found a second doctor, who also said *reumatismo*, so I believed it. Too much rain and cold weather. He prescribed some pills and Baume Bengue, and the pain subsided.

On August 5 we drove south and southeast from Guadalajara to Jiquilpan and thirty miles south of Jiquilpan to Mazamitla, Jalisco. We made camp in pine-oak woods four miles west of Mazamitla at 6,800 feet. Towhees were not common but we got twenty-nine, which had an average hybrid index of 2.3, thus close to pure *ocai*.

On August 8 we left Guadalajara and drove northeast forty-seven miles to Tepatitlán, where a mountain called Cerro Gordo is situated thirteen miles east-southeast of Tepatitlán. We found a rocky road up Cerro Gordo and were able to drive to a camp site at 8,000 feet in oak woodland. Towhees were abundant, and we obtained forty-two specimens with an average hybrid index of 22.8, close to pure *erythrophthalmus*. From the 9200–foot summit of Cerro Gordo I could see Cerro Viejo, Cerro García, and the mountains of the Sierra del Tigre at the south end of the Sierra Madre Occidental. The mountains of central Michoacán were visible to the southeast. Other oak-covered hills and ridges were visible, providing dispersal pathways and breeding habitat for towhees between the higher mountains.

We drove northwest via Yahualica on August 10 and made camp on the Mesa de los Puercos, at 8,000 feet, twelve miles west of Yahualica, Jalisco, in pine-oak-madrone woodland. We could see Cerro Viejo and Cerro García to the south and Cerro Tequila, Sierra de Ameca, and Cerro Gordo. We collected fourteen towhees with an average hybrid index of 23.5 = nearly pure *erythrophthalmus*. *Ocai* influence was indicated by chestnut shaft streaks and/or a greenish cast in the dorsal plumage of some specimens.

We returned to Guadalajara on August 12 and on the 14th drove east to Zapotlanejo and, via various roads, to La Paz, a village at the base of Cerro Grande. Here we obtained horses and burros, and on the 15th we ascended Cerro Grande to camp at 7,600 feet, eighteen miles east-southeast of Guadalajara in oaks and thorn scrub. Towhees were abundant, and we collected thirty-six specimens, of which the average hybrid index was 22.6. We could see more than a hundred miles from the summit, including all the mountains we had visited.

On August 19 we investigated an area southwest of Guadalajara but found no towhees. On the 20th we drove east on the Mexico City road to Zamora, then northeast via muddy, poor roads searching for a way to ascend a small range of hills. We had to return to Zamora, got bogged in deep mud for four hours, and had a flat tire. On the 21st, after the fifth patch was applied to the bad tire, we drove southeast on the main highway and turned north near Carapán to Purépero and on to Changuitiro, an agrarian community at the base of a mountain called El Fraile. I arranged for saddle horses and burros, and on the 22nd we ascended El Fraile with an entourage of about ten people. More had intended to come because they did not believe my story about collecting birds; they thought we must be prospecting for gold! I showed them my collecting permit shortly before departure, and many lost interest. We got the tent up just before a rainstorm hit, and all the men and boys crowded inside. I skinned two towhees we had collected on the way up to show them what we were doing. The locality was Cerro El Fraile, 8,200 feet, fourteen miles northeast of Zamora, Michoacán. Towhees were common in the brushy understory of the oak-madrone woods, and we obtained sixteen, with an average hybrid index of 21.7. Some were nearly pure *maculatus*.

We left El Fraile on August 24 and proceeded to a camp at Las Joyas, 7,700 feet, twelve miles west of Zacapu, Michoacán. This was twenty-one airline miles southeast of El Fraile, but the average hybrid index of our twelve specimens was 8.8. This proved to be the most rapid character gradient in the entire study. The abrupt change was correlated with the change in vegetation and a change in rainfall pattern. El Fraile is a comparatively arid locality of oak-madrone woods, and nopal cactus occurred at the summit; at Las Joyas pines were dominant with few oaks and madrones, but with alder thickets and no cactus. Near El Fraile the corn crop was stunted from lack of rain; at Las Joyas the corn was high and the grass was green. This pattern reflects the topography and prevailing wind direction. The rains come from the south and are intercepted by the mountains in which Las Joyas is located; El Fraile is in the rain shadow of these southern mountains. Thus, the character gradient seems to be due to the combination of distance and ecology; *maculatus* occurs mainly in relatively dry oak woodland and chaparral; *ocai* in moist coniferous forest.

On August 28 we left Guadalajara with Ray Alcorn and his two Mexican assistants. We had contacted Ray in Guadalajara, where he was living while collecting mammals for E. Raymond Hall at the University of Kansas. We had arranged to make a joint trip to a mountain range south of Ixtlán del Río, northwest of Guadalajara. We arranged for pack burros and saddle horses, and on the 29th we left Ixtlán and began the ascent of a mountain called El Faro. I had made it clear to the packer that we wanted to go to the summit, or close to it, but at about 6,000 feet he stopped and began to unload the burros. I reminded him of our agreement, and a vigorous argument developed in Spanish. The packer was sullen, arguing that it was too late and he had to return home. I offered more money and threatened to report him to the authorities—though I had little idea of what they might do. Finally he agreed to proceed, and we went on up the mountain. Ray had understood little of the argument, but he could see and hear that it was heated. Afterward, Ray told me that the packer, who had been facing me, had had his hands behind him on a large knife in his belt. Ray had a .38 revolver and he told me he had been prepared to shoot if the packer had drawn the knife! This frightened me more than the argument, which was mainly bluff on both sides.

We made camp near the summit of El Faro at 6,800 feet, six miles south of Ixtlán del Río, Nayarit. We collected there until September 2 and got thirty-one towhees with an average index of 15.8. Ray had a permit for two deer and urged us to help him. On August 30 I shot a doe that seemed attracted to my "squeaking" for towhees. The venison was appreciated, and the skin and skull are in the Kansas University Museum of Natural History.

I had wanted to investigate the Teziutlán area north of the Cofre de Perote on the eastern edge of the plateau, which Bowers, Childs, and I had traversed in 1948. I decided to go to Teziutlán in our Pontiac with Fran and Barbara, while Browne and Olson would go with Ray Alcorn to some localities west of Guadalajara.

We set out on September 5 for Mexico City, with a tourist stop in Pátzcuaro, and arrived in Teziutlán on the 7th, obtaining a room at the Hotel Virreynal. For the next two days I collected towhees three miles west of Teziutlán, Puebla, at 7,300 feet, and got eleven specimens. All were hybrids, with an average index of 13.0. We drove south to Tehuacán to examine the topography and vegetation, then northeast to Puerto Morelos, the high point on the highway between Tehuacán, Puebla, and Orizaba, Veracruz. From September 9 to 11, I collected in the region near Puerto Morelos near the Puebla-Veracruz border and obtained twenty specimens, of which thirteen were pure or nearly pure *maculatus*, with an average index of 23.4, and six were pure or nearly pure *ocai*, with an index of 0.14. Thus, there was evidence of occasional hybridization.

Returning to Mexico City, we visited the Museo Nacional de Historia Natural, where a hybrid from Zoquitlán, Puebla, and a pure Spotted Towhee were mounted on the same perch and labeled as male and female! I visited Rafael Martín del Campo at the Instituto de Biología and met other biologists. From Mexico City on September 13 we drove north through Toluca, then via Querétaro and Celaya to Irapuato, where we visited Chester Lamb, then on to Guadalajara.

September 14 was spent packing and getting the Dodge tires repaired, including having one recapped. The following morning we found that the tire was unsatisfactory and had to have it redone. When we began the return trip I drove ahead in the Pontiac, and a few miles from Guadalajara I realized that the truck was not in sight behind. We waited for a while, then backtracked, and a few miles back there was the Dodge, with the ten-foot-long recap draped across the hood. It had peeled off, and the boys did not dare drive on the bare surface of the tire. We returned to Guadalajara and again a recap was done. This lasted to Laredo, where we had to buy a new tire to get home.

18

Fifteen Years of Studying Birds in El Salvador, 1966–1980

WALTER A. THURBER

Walter A. Thurber (1908–2008) was a teacher, scientist, and science text author. He went to El Salvador in the mid-1960s with the U.S. State Department to foster science education. This assignment resulted in his meeting his future wife, Amanda, and together they undertook a fifteen-year effort in bird and natural history study that profoundly affected the cultural appreciation in El Salvador for the natural world and the scientific understanding of the country's avifauna. Scientific reports of their work appeared in Thurber and Villeda (1976, 1980) and Thurber (1980, 1981).

I entered the study of El Salvador's avifauna by the back door. The U.S. State Department, operating through some of its agencies, instituted a program to provide textbooks for children of the public elementary schools of Central America and Panama, where there were few or no textbooks. Individual countries provided experienced teachers to do the writing; the State Department provided funds for the administration and hire of *asesores* (specialists) in curriculum planning and preparation.

An *asesor* for the science curriculum was needed. I had produced elementary science textbooks and could say, *¿Dónde hay un buen hotel?* in impeccable Spanish, as a result of studying language records in anticipation of mountain climbing in Mexico. Also, I was available—having discovered that my income tax on royalties and salary combined was more than my salary, I had retired. My contract with the State Department extended over three years, and I stayed on call an additional year while we got the manuscripts ready for publishing.

For me El Salvador was a fascinating place. On my first morning I was out before breakfast, enchanted by the flowers, butterflies, and especially the birds—all new to me. From then on I was out whenever duties permitted. I soon became acquainted with Amanda Villeda, the *asesora* in language arts. She had been born in a small town in Guatemala, attended the Guatemalan Normal School, taught for several years, then attended Indiana University, where she obtained B.S. and M.S. degrees, followed by a year at Hull University in England. Obviously, she was fluent in English.

Amanda, with her delightfully accented English and a rich lore of local plants and animals, and I with my fractured Spanish and a more academic science background, made an interesting and compatible team. We soon added a third member: a taxi driver who owned his own car became intrigued with our investigations and took us wherever we suggested. He always carried his *pistola* in case we met up with *malandrines* (bad guys).

Well before my contract with the State Department expired, I was sure I wanted to remain in El Salvador to make a serious study of the avifauna, especially the effect of the burgeoning human population on bird life since studies made twenty-five and fifty years before. Amanda had left the Central American project for a similar position in Bolivia, but found the situation less challenging and returned after three months. I had a partner again!

Preliminaries

Such a serious investigation demanded long-term studies rather than short, disconnected visits. I wanted to concentrate on species distribution and life history studies. Little did I know that many distractions would interrupt me, but these would add immeasurably to the richness of my life and, to some extent, to the lives of others.

We would need nets and a banding permit. The Cornell Laboratory of Ornithology appointed me a "field collaborator," which gave me status with bureaucracies in both the United States and El Salvador. The U.S. Fish and Wildlife Service qualified me as a "master bander" so that we could obtain nets and bands for migrants to and/or through El Salvador. Later I would buy bands with my own numbers for use in El Salvador, the numbers recorded in the Bird Banding Laboratory of the U.S. Fish and Wildlife Service.

With a battery of cameras and lenses and flash equipment I considered myself properly equipped, but Lucy Engelhard, bioacoustician of the Cornell laboratory, and Andrea Priori, her assistant, persuaded me to take a tape recorder as well. Their advice was to change my life.

As I look back, the cooperation provided by so many agencies in El Salvador seems unbelievable; it was as though everyone was anxious to have me proceed. Through my service with the Agency for International Development–Regional Office for Central America and Panama (AID-ROCAP), I became acquainted with many helpful people. The Organización de Estados Centro-Americanos (ODECA), with which I was affiliated in the textbook program, appointed me *asesor de ciencias naturales* after the textbook program terminated, and they provided me with an official carnet and license plate for the truck-camper I was to buy; this was helpful when entering and leaving the country and in moving about the country with the truck-camper.

The National University of El Salvador appointed me *profesor visitante*, thus obtaining for me the cooperation of the university faculty. J. Francisco Serrano, head of the Division of National Parks in the Ministry of Agriculture, whom I had met while lecturing to biology classes in the National University, recommended my appointment as *asesor* in that ministry, where I served under him and the chief of the Forestry Division.

Carlos DeSola, *director general de cultura y deportes* of the Ministry of Education, was very interested in our studies and had me appointed an *asesor* to the Natural History Museum and *asesor* in science education. Soon after, when he was appointed to the Instituto de Turismo, he had me appointed *asesor* for the parks under the jurisdiction of the instituto.

Reviewing the credentials, it seemed that every branch of the government seemed willing to help me except the Ministry of Defense; then I remembered that I had been given a letter explaining my presence and signed by a colonel—and fortunately, too. One day on the road to Volcán San Salvador I had my camera mounted on a gunstock mount. A military jeep roared past— *rrrrumph*—stop. Then—*rrrrumph*—in reverse. Two officers got out with pistols drawn. I realized then how much my camera and mount resembled some strange and deadly weapon. But as soon as the officers noted the signature on my letter they were all respect and departed peacefully after I let them look through the camera lens.

The letter proved handy in another instance, just after the "Hundred-hour War" with Honduras. Amanda and I had walked to the center of a bridge and were looking down into the water when two soldiers rushed up waving their rifles. Again the letter brought immediate respect. And again, after letting them look through our binoculars, we departed in peace.

Home Away from Home

Obviously, serious bird study demanded lengthy stays at definite locations where we needed accommodation. I had no objections to roughing it for short periods, but I had no desire to make a career of living in thatched *chozas* with mosquitoes and other vermin. Some type of movable living quarters would be desirable.

After much discussion and advice I bought a heavy-duty eight-cylinder four-wheel-drive truck with oversized tires that had mud-gripping treads. In place of the standard truck body, I adapted the type of body once used by telephone repairmen, a body with steel lockers along the sides. On this body I bolted a small camper, which slept two comfortably and four by doubling up. It had a two-burner propane stove, a gas furnace (it gets cold in El Salvador's mountains), and a gas-electric refrigerator. I modified the water supply tank to more than double the previous capacity, thus providing enough potable water for a two-week stay.

The camper was wired for both 12-volt and 110-volt electricity. The 12-volt system was rarely used, because it put a severe drain on batteries and would have required frequent recharging. In a few places we had access to 110-volt lines, courtesy of the owners, and we used these for lights and the refrigerator, thus conserving propane and extending our stays.

The camper had two closets, in one of which I installed shelves for storage of such items as cameras, binoculars, and tape recorders, all properly padded to reduce jouncing on rough roads. I also built in a bookcase with sliding doors for our field library of fifty or so volumes. This was also properly secured to protect the books.

To expand upon the very limited work and living space inside the camper, I mounted an awning along one side of the rig with curtains of rain-repellent material and of mosquito netting. This provided a snug working and lounging space when furnished with a folding table and chairs. Two folding cots provided accommodation for additional guests; on occasions when visiting groups were large—students or Peace Corps volunteers—some slept on a waterproof ground cloth.

A luggage carrier bolted to the top of the camper carried a twenty-foot extension ladder for the inspection of nests. When nests were too high to be examined from the ladder, it might give access to limbs from which one could clamber farther up. But the ladder did not solve all problems. I found an incubating Roadside Hawk (*Buteo magnirostris*) 15.5 m up in a *mongollano* tree, a prickery tree with spines on the upper trunk. After I had shinnied up the upper trunk several times to measure the eggs, to weigh and measure the nestlings, and to take photographs, the trunk was no longer prickery—but my legs were.

Amanda's vote for the most unforgettable experiences with the truck-camper was our first trip up to the suitably named Finca El Imposible. This was an abandoned coffee plantation in the western highlands, interesting to us because it contained the last large expanse of virgin forest in El Salvador. Our route led across a knife-edge ridge between two chasms. On the way in the weather was dry and there seemed no special danger, but on the way out, after torrential rains, the edges were crumbling as water poured down the roadway. Amanda recalls walking backward along the knife-edge, knees shaking, directing me to keep the wheels away from the crumbling edges. The rains had left the road surface like grease. Going down the steepest portions I kept the truck in four-wheel-drive and double low, with fingers crossed. I dared not touch the brakes lest we slide over the edge into a chasm below.

My most vivid memory associated with the camper was the drive to Los Esesmiles, a site on the highest ridge in El Salvador. The route up which A. J. Van Rossem and later Joe Marshall had ascended on horseback with pack mules had been bulldozed to provide a narrow track. I was suspicious of the outer shoulder, which did not seem well consolidated. Consequently, I hugged the inner side. On rounding a curve I saw to my horror a full-sized bus descending. The driver and I got out for a conference. I checked the outer shoulder, and as I suspected, it was crumbling in many places. We both walked up and down the road until we found a somewhat wider excavation where the outer shoulder seemed firmer. The bus driver backed up to that spot, pressing the right side of the bus against the bank. I loosened my left mirror to give me a few more inches of clearance, then gingerly crawled forward, almost scraping the paint, guided by Amanda and a passenger from the bus. When our truck finally crept to the firmer center of the road my relief was audible. And no small part of my relief was the knowledge that we would not meet another bus, and that during our return we would be on the inner side of the track.

Amanda and I were in another situation that, though not presenting physical danger, could have been a serious setback. We went to the lowland Hacienda Los Pinos repeatedly because of the richness of the avifauna. The hacienda could be reached by motor vehicles only in the dry season. But one year the rains came early. We were already preparing to leave when the first afternoon downpour struck. We knew we had to get out before the next afternoon's rain. We were up at dawn, throwing the remaining unpacked items into the camper. I made no effort to examine the route—a narrow lane that crossed a trickle of water by a temporary causeway of brush. We could hear the torrent in that former trickle and knew the causeway was already dissolving.

Between us and higher ground was now a large pool with water several inches deep, which I knew was turning the firmer ground beneath into liquid mud. I put the truck into four-wheel-drive (which in those primitive days had to be done with a wrench) and dashed across that pool at full speed. We made it, and without stopping we headed for the higher pastures of the adjoining hacienda. There were no gates, but I dropped wires from the posts and drove over them (replacing them, of course) until we reached the barnyard of the other hacienda, which had an access road to the highway. Looking back, we could see enormous cumulus clouds soon to deluge the Hacienda Los Pinos again. Had we not left when we did, we might not have used the truck-camper before the next dry season. No tractors could have entered. A double team of oxen would have been belly deep in mud without budging the truck.

Migration Spectaculars

There was a time when I regularly visited Hawk Mountain in Pennsylvania. Although I was never there on a record-breaking day, I saw some impressive flights. One day there was not a single hawk, but thousands of monarch butterflies (*Danaus plexippus*) were winging steadily southward—a day I shall never forget. There were days of thousands of Broad-winged Hawks (*Buteo platypterus*), great "kettles" made up of hundreds.

But these hawk flights were insignificant compared with the *azacuanes*—enormous flights of great streams of birds at mountaintop height in El Salvador. Although most Salvadorans think of the *azacuanes* as involving a single kind of bird, they are actually an amalgam of several species—Turkey Vultures (*Cathartes aura*), Swainson's Hawks (*Buteo swainsonii*), Broad-winged Hawks, and a few other species tagging along. The flights of *azacuanes* are fairly predictable. For generations, rural Salvadorans governed their activities by the *azacuanes*; northbound *azacuanes* heralded the onset of rains and the time to plant, while southbound *azacuanes* meant that the dry season and harvest time were at hand.

Autumn flights of *azacuanes* are spectacular. For hour after hour, day after day, flocks of these birds pass along the peaks and ridges of El Salvador. My field notes show that in 1971 I saw *azacuanes* daily at Cerro Verde (2,000 m) between October 10 and 24; I had to leave on October 25. They came in flocks of 100–1,000 birds, with stragglers from one group almost overtaken by the next. Between 8 a.m. and 4 p.m. there was almost never a moment when at least one flock was not visible.

Between October 12 and November 4, 1925, A. J. Van Rossem saw flocks of 200 to 1,000 birds at Divisadero (500 feet elevation). He identified Turkey Vultures, Broad-winged Hawks, Swainson's Hawks, and some Red-tailed and a few Marsh hawks (*Buteo jamaicensis* and *Circus cyaneus*). "The hawk migration reached its peak on October 21 in an enormous flight, or rather series of flights, which occupied the greater part of the day. It was not possible to make any estimate of the number that passed, but it must have been in the tens of thousands," he wrote (Dickey and Van Rossem 1938: 116).

Spring migration was never as spectacular as that in fall, being more dispersed, but I saw flocks of up to five hundred Turkey Vultures and smaller flocks of Swainson's Hawks. Van Rossem reported seeing spring migration one day only.

Azacuanes probably travel only in daytime; we have few records. In 1974 I occasionally saw Broad-winged Hawks after sunrise in woodlands south of the migration route, suggesting that some had dropped there for the night. Incidentally, a few of these seemed to have full crops, as though they had hunted after daybreak. Van Rossem found a few Broad-winged Hawks wintering at Mt. Cacaguatique; apparently some of this species abandon the migrant stream. Van Rossem also reported that during spring migration in 1927 numerous Swainson's Hawks spent the night of April 27 on an old lava field.

I had no time to follow up my numerous questions about *azacuanes*. Once I saw a huge wave of Broad-winged Hawks in southeast Texas but noted no Turkey Vultures or Swainson's Hawks. In Panama I once saw a massive flow of Turkey Vultures and Broad-winged and Swainson's hawks. Where did these species join together? Did Turkey Vultures of Mexico rise to join the flow? I noted no change in numbers of Turkey Vultures of El Salvador before and after the *azacuanes* passed and doubt that local birds joined the migrants.[1]

An invitation to spend a night at a beach house on the Pacific gave me a once-in-a-lifetime experience on May 1, 1969. I ambled down to the beach early, expecting to see only a few shorebirds and a pelican or so. But I found the sky full of birds—thousands—determinedly winging their way northward: a few over the beach, many just offshore, and thousands farther out for as far as eye could see. Generally they flew low, mostly below fifty feet. The majority were small white terns; I do not pretend an ability to distinguish Arctic Terns (*Sterna paradisaea*) from Common Terns (*S. hirundo*) in flight, but I believe these were the latter. Most exciting to me were Sabine's Gulls (*Xema sabini*), a species I had seen only once before. Between 8 a.m. and 6 p.m. some fifty-five Sabine's Gulls were near enough—some over the beach itself—for positive identification. Most were singles, but there were a few flocks of five to eight birds.

Jehl (1974), studying the near-shore avifauna, sailed along the coast of El Salvador from April 15 to 17, 1973. He registered gulls and terns well dispersed, with most 8–32 km offshore and several as close as 2 km. Apparently in 1969 some freak of the winds pushed this normally offshore band of migrants landward, squeezing them into the narrow ribbon almost over my head.

Strangely, although I remember my excitement as I counted and scribbled notes, my most vivid lasting image was of the incredibly blue sky, flecked with moving white dots that flickered, the flicker changing as the sun climbed, and changing again as the sun dropped toward the west. I sat glued to the beach all day, my host sending me breakfast and lunch but otherwise leaving me alone. I would have stayed until after nightfall, but my host had to return to the city in the evening, and dragged me reluctant from this marvelous show.

El Salvador has a resident population of Northern Rough-winged Swallows (*Stelgidopteryx serripennis*), many of which nest in drainage tubes inserted into embankments along streets and around buildings. Swallows entering these tubes do not pause at the entrances, as might a woodpecker, but approach with folded wings and dart in like arrows. I wasted a lot of time expecting (though not hoping) to see a swallow misjudge. This manner of entrance is appropriate, of course, for entrance into burrows in sand banks, where an attempt to land at the entrance would crumble the friable soil, but it appeared startling when applied to ceramic tile.

El Salvador also hosts countless thousands of migrant Rough-winged Swallows through the dry season. Many of these spend their nights in cane fields. Hilda Lovo of the science writers group in the textbook program, who often accompanied Amanda and me, learned of a site where morning flights of these swallows was impressive. She and I drove there one morning but were too late; all was silent. The next morning I went alone, arriving well before dawn.

All was dark except for the stars. A rooster at the nearby *choza* tried to push along the dawn but retired after a few crows. A local dog yapped nervously at some imagined disturbance, stimulating neighbors into brief, half-hearted responses. The first sign of approaching dawn was a burst of Mexican music from the *choza*; the *señora de la casa*, according to local custom, had switched on her portable radio as soon as she left her blanket. Chopping sounds followed; she was about to prepare breakfast for her as-yet inactive *señor*.

Even as I noted the first yellowing of the eastern sky, I realized that I had been hearing a faint sound for some seconds. The sound was too uniform to be called twittering, but too structured to be called a murmur. I call it a "twittering murmur," or a "murmuring twitter." At first the sound seemed to come from nowhere, but as it intensified it could be localized as coming from the cane field. The sound swelled, first here, then there; the effect was dizzying.

Just before the sun appeared, several birds popped up from the canes. Then, as though communicating by some electronic means, birds poured upward in a column perhaps a hundred feet high, which mushroomed out at the top. (Anyone who has seen a flock of chimney swifts dive into a chimney has seen the same effect in reverse and on a smaller scale—a swirling mass of birds that all of one mind funnel down into the chimney.) The swallows swirled about for a few moments at the top of the column until all had gathered, then as of the same mind departed together. Suddenly all was quiet. The show was over.

Net Surprises

Amanda and I had a good assortment of nets in various lengths and mesh sizes. We usually used those of standard lengths and of meshes suitable for warblers and sparrows. With nets of small mesh we occasionally lost a larger bird that fell into a pocket, worked its way along to an end without becoming enmeshed, and escaped; but if one of us arrived in time it was easy to close the pocket around the bird and retrieve it. In nets of small mesh we captured birds as large as Sharp-shinned Hawks (*Accipiter striatus*), a Lineated Woodpecker (*Dryocopus lineatus*), and a Green Heron (*Butorides virescens*).

For net supports we used aluminum tubes cut into four-foot lengths to fit into one of the steel lockers of the truck body. These were threaded at the ends to screw into steel unions. Thus we could have nets at eight or twelve feet or even higher, but higher nets had to be lowered to extract birds and thus were not very efficient. The poles were guyed with nylon twine (softer materials soon deteriorated in damp weather) and metal tent stakes.

I also rigged a system of pulleys so that nets could be hung well up between two trees, but these too had to be lowered to extract a bird, a two-man job. I hoped to get some woodpeckers, but our most interesting capture was a little Green Kingfisher (*Chloroceryle americana*), which chanced to choose a route through a woodland at Sabanetas.

As we extracted birds from the nets, we placed each in a separate bag made of lightweight nylon mosquito netting. We made up these bags in assorted sizes, some suitable for hummingbirds, others large enough for hawks and owls.

One rule that Amanda and I followed was to inflict as little suffering on our netted birds as possible. We were always especially anxious to take them from the nets quickly. To avoid delays we each wore an apron of our own design. Each apron had three pockets. Two were for the bags in which we put the birds—small bags in one pocket, larger bags in the other—thus reducing the time spent searching for the appropriate bag. The center pocket contained a pair of thin leather gloves. On the breast of the apron were small pockets in which were kept crochet hooks, forceps, and scissors to speed up extraction of the birds as needed.

Some birds have powerful bills and give painful nips; even some of the larger sparrows were a problem. Rufous-browed Peppershrikes (*Cyclarhis gujanensis*) could draw blood. Two workmen at Cerro Verde, desirous of helping us (but contrary to our requests) tried to take a peppershrike from a net; one declared ruefully, "*Es un pájaro muy bravo*" (That's a very angry bird). For this reason we carried leather gloves in our aprons. One day Amanda left out the gloves, and that was the day a Lineated Woodpecker fell in a net. She got the woodpecker out, but it immediately attacked her bare arm. She screamed for help but did not drop it. Fortunately, I was close enough to rush to her aid and bag it. We have a nice framed photo of that bird to remind Amanda of the event.

During our early years of netting, Amanda and I could expect a wave of Ruby-throated Hummingbirds (*Archilochus colubris*) at Cerro Verde in September; a few might remain through the dry season (northern winter), but most passed on. During our last years relatively few Ruby-throated Hummingbirds arrived at Cerro Verde. According to many authorities, these tiny birds, weighing less than four grams, had crossed the Gulf of Mexico on their way to El Salvador. At one time there were those who claimed this impossible—that the birds did not possess sufficient fat reserves for such a journey; then it was hypothesized that favorable winds could waft these little migrants onward with minimum expenditure of energy. No matter what the explanation, the Ruby-throats were there, on the peak of Cerro Verde.

Holding a netted Ruby-throat in one's hand, and thinking beyond its mere physical appearance, one must marvel at its presence there, and shudder at the dangers escaped, and feel pity for the hundreds or thousands that may have perished if the wind shifted a few degrees, holding them back or forcing them away from land until their energy reserves were totally exhausted. I do not suppose we were gentler with Ruby-throats than with any other birds, but they did seem especially precious, and we grieved if one was injured or killed; certainly we did not want to be the cause.

No phenomenon of migration ever affected me as deeply as the first time I held in my hand a Townsend's Warbler (*Dendroica townsendi*) that I had banded the year before. One may note on a range map that this warbler nests from Alaska to Oregon and winters south to Nicaragua, but this stirs no emotions. Now, however, I was holding *my* warbler—a part of *me*. It had first come to me by some unknown workings of nature, had received my band, flown back north to breed, and then had returned to me in the very same place we had first met. This could not be mere coincidence. This emotion, which I cannot describe, is more than wonder, more than amazement. It never wore thin. It doubled and tripled when I recovered a bird banded two or three years previously. Try to imagine how I felt when I recovered a Tennessee Warbler (*Vermivora peregrina*) six years after banding it. It was banded in 1971 as a juvenile, recovered in 1972, and again in 1977, and was thus in its seventh year. This palpitating bit of flesh and feathers had made fifteen trips from and to some place in or near Canada.

I have never accepted fully the idea that migrants are hatched with a map already in place in their chromosomes; this suggests that the genes that determine the map are inherited, and this would involve both parents. I prefer the suggestion of Paul Schwartz, who netted and banded Northern Waterthrushes (*Seiurus noveboracensis*) at one site in Venezuela and transported them some hundreds of kilometers away to another site in Venezuela before releasing them. All the birds recovered the next year were taken at the site of release, not at the site of original capture. Schwartz believed that the waterthrushes learned a route during their return north and followed it thereafter.

Schwartz's hypothesis explains some of my observations following Hurricanes Fifi and Carmen in 1974. After the hurricanes, I netted several species never before reported for El Salvador, and some of these returned in later years. Two Hermit Thrushes (*Catharus guttatus*) were netted and others were seen at Cerro Verde the winter following the hurricanes; another was netted a year later, and a fourth was netted two years later. The winter following the hurricanes we netted thirteen Nashville Warblers (*Vermivora ruficapilla*) and saw many others at Los Planes de Montecristo, and we netted three at Cerro Verde; during the winter of 1975–76 we netted and saw others at Montecristo and Cerro Verde. One of these was retaken at Cerro Verde in 1978, and El Salvador's Museum of Natural History has a specimen taken in 1978 near San Salvador. Seemingly, these birds were pushed south into El Salvador by the 1974 hurricanes and learned the route during their return north; the wintering range of the species was at least temporarily extended (Thurber 1980; Thurber and Villeda 1976, 1980).

Occasionally there were days when birds fell into our nets faster than we could remove and process them. We were especially concerned about migrants arriving early in the day, knowing that they had traveled all night and were exhausted and hungry. We wanted to release them as soon as possible. Sometimes we cut short the processing, only weighing, measuring, and banding. On a few occasions we closed the nets rather than take more.

One morning at Cerro Verde I had gone out as usual at daybreak to open the nets while Amanda prepared tea and *pan dulce* (sweet pastry) for whenever I found free moments. I was opening a line of about six nets and was working on the fourth net when I looked back. The nets already opened seemed full of little birds—Wilson's Warblers (*Wilsonia pusilla*)—and more were coming. Even as I looked, two fell into the half-opened net beside me. I jumped to extract the tiny creatures, fortunately so recently arrived as not to be seriously entangled, and closed the nets as I proceeded. I ran out of bags, according to my notes, with the sixteenth bird, and Amanda had not yet arrived. So I let the remaining little creatures go, not too regretfully. The time recorded for the captures was 6:15 a.m., and I limited my processing to weight, length, tail, wing, sex, cap, and age.

A similar overflow occurred at Hacienda Los Pinos in the lowlands, where we had set up a line of some ten nets. I had opened the nets and, after Amanda arrived, returned to the camper with a few early arrivals. Soon a little boy whom we had taught to carry the bags carefully brought me some more bags of netted birds before I had finished processing the first. Then he came with more, and then some more. There were bags of birds hanging all around the canopy. Amanda sent word that she needed help. She wanted to close the nets; birds were arriving faster than she could take them out. I hustled to her aid and we closed the nets, releasing all but some of the more interesting species. Then I could return to the camper and take care of the poor creatures hanging under the canopy. All this by 8:30 a.m.! My notes do not reflect our near panic that caused us to release so many birds, mostly Inca Doves (*Columbina inca*), but that was a hectic hour or so. Probably I did not finish my *pan dulce* and tea until almost noon.

It was not unusual for us to net and process more than fifty birds in a morning, but the captures were usually spread out, and we did not have to leave the birds in the bags for long periods. It always pained me to release a bird without banding it, because that might be the bird I would capture in some succeeding year, or better yet, the bird that someone else might capture on the breeding grounds.[2]

After a bird (and I) had suffered the process of capture and extraction from a net, I wanted to obtain all possible information from it. Thus processing became complex. I had printed forms for data on which each bird was given a number denoting the year, month, day, and order of capture, so that reference to notes was simplified. Place, time, temperature, and any special habitat were recorded, and standard measurements (e.g., length, tail, wing chord, bill) were recorded, together with colors of soft parts (i.e., iris, eye lids, cere, legs, feet, gape, mouth, and other bare parts). Age and sex as shown by plumage were noted. If a bird was molting, the stage was indicated together with sketches of rectrices and remiges. Each bird was checked for incubation patch, worn primaries, abnormalities, etc. After I learned to "skull" a bird, this was added to the processing routine; this technique of closely inspecting skull development through the skin can provide an age assessment in most passerines. Parasites were sought and collected, and these were keyed to the bird's number. Finally the disposition of the bird was recorded: band number if banded, photograph if taken, results of dissection if made, and museum collection if it was prepared as a research specimen.

Obviously, on some days pressures were great, and rather than subject birds to a lengthy holding time, we skipped some of the lengthier procedures, such as skulling, and did not record all colors unless some seemed abnormal. There were even days when processing was limited to weighing and banding; on those days I did not get even a sip of tea or a bite of *pan dulce*.

Not everything that came to our nets was welcome. For example, the burro that blundered into a line of nets at Hacienda Montecristo, panicked, and dragged five nets through the brush did not do those nets a bit of good.

Amanda has a deeply imbedded horror of snakes. She recalls with a shudder the scarlet-banded kingsnake that for some reason climbed a slanting tree trunk at Cerro Verde and landed up in a net that brushed the trunk. The snake fought back, grabbing mouthful after mouthful of threads, which immediately got hooked in its teeth. Amanda objected strenuously to my proposal to extract the snake and free it, threatening never to set foot there again if I did so. She was unmoved by a field guide illustration showing that this was not a coral snake, and the assurance that coral snakes would not be present at a cold 2,000 m elevation. Nor did my efforts to impress her with the beauty of this harmless animal make any difference. I did begin to unhook the snake's teeth, but as soon as I made a little progress, it slithered in my hands and grabbed another mouthful. Reluctantly, as a person who hates to see death come to any living thing (except mosquitoes, ticks, and Communist terrorists), I gave up and sacrificed the snake. Only when Amanda saw the carcass did she relax. One promise she gave was not to mention to the local people that I had killed a snake; I did not want my reputation as a protector of wildlife to be stained.

Worse than the snake were bats. For a reason I do not remember, I left a net open one night; in the morning I had a fine but unwanted catch. All but four bats were freed with minimum trouble, but those four were in a mess. A snake has only a mouth full of teeth and no legs. A bat has a mouth full of teeth, a tail, two legs with clawed toes, and two wings with a claw on each; it can tangle itself in a dozen ways, and those four bats seemed to have involved themselves in all ways possible. I freed two bats by cutting several threads on each. For the other two I could see that I would have to sacrifice completely either the net or the bats. I killed the bats; one had bitten Amanda, and I did not feel much pity.

At Hacienda Los Pinos we had an unsolved who-dunnit. A net stretched along a roadway in a dense, dark section of woodland captured many large-winged moths, but in a short time only the wings remained; the bodies were neatly snipped out and presumably eaten. This suggested some large bird that could hover without being trapped, as I have seen large hummingbirds take insects from spider webs. One day I saw a Squirrel Cuckoo (*Piaya cayana*) leave the net area, but I could not imagine that this bird could maneuver so skillfully. Then another day we found a Tennessee Warbler in a net, its skull opened and brain extracted; the mystery was increased because the net had been attended only a few minutes before.[3]

Name that Song

When Lucy Engelhard and Andrea Priori of the Cornell Laboratory of Ornithology suggested that I take a tape recorder to El Salvador to record bird songs, they could not have imagined what I was letting myself in for. El Salvador was no paradise for recorders of bird songs. It is one of the most densely populated countries in the western hemisphere, exceeded at that time only by Haiti. When Amanda and I went there in 1966 the population was about 2.5 million; when we left in 1980 it was almost 5 million. This meant that there were hundreds of thousands of babies crying, children chattering, young males playing soccer with the shouting this game demands, women calling for children and one another, and carpenters sawing and hammering to build new dwellings in which to raise more children.

As a country advancing technologically, El Salvador had most available means of transportation: autos and light trucks with bleating horns; diesel-powered trucks and buses belching visual and aural contamination; and *motos* with mufflers bypassed according to directions given by manufacturers to produce maximum noise. And, of course, airplanes—only a few judged by world standards, but concentrating the noise of arrival and departure because passenger aircraft served one central airport. Crop dusters wove across cotton fields for hours at a time, spewing noise while spewing venom without prejudice on boll weevils, harmless insects, soil organisms, aquatic life, lizards, birds, and babies. And—at the low end of the technological scale—ox carts, the iron-shod wheels of which crunched pebbles of dirt roads at the pace of two kilometers per hour.

As a rural-based community just moving into urban life, Salvadorans clung to their domestic animals—cows, horses, a few burros, and dogs. I believe that Salvadoran dogs were selected for their tendency to go into hysterics. Let one dog lift its voice when stimulated by some real or fancied disturbance, perhaps a dream, and its canine neighbors take up the cry, followed by others farther away, and then even more still farther away, like waves spreading from a pebble dropped in a pool, until at last all are exhausted and fall silent with nothing accomplished.

Roosters were omnipresent, not only in rural areas but even in the centers of cities, including at the homes of the wealthy, where some families had a flock of hens, each dominated by a vociferous rooster. It was rare to make a tape recording that did not feature a rooster crowing in the background. My constant request to the Cornell Lab was for a rooster filter; until such was developed I had to depend on a razor blade to snip out those unwanted vocalizations.

High on the technological scale were portable radios. Every true Salvadoran wanted one—heaven may be for tomorrow but a radio was for today if played at full volume. The only check was the price of batteries in this poor country. Otherwise, the atmosphere would have pulsated from midnight to midnight with synthetic Mexican music, which for some reason unclear to me the Salvadorans adored.

I soon discovered the problem of people-noise in El Salvador. At the Hacienda Los Pinos I located a site where each evening a *cenzontle* (Clay-colored Thrush; *Turdus grayi*) gave its evening call—actually a call uttered at times of low light: before sunrise, at sunset, and when an advancing storm darkens the sky. The situation seemed excellent for adding components of the species' broad repertoire to my and Cornell's collection.

I went to the site in late afternoon while the afternoon breeze was still rattling the palms. The breeze died just before sunset, and just as the young men on the hacienda were freed from work and could engage in a brief *futbol* scrimmage with necessary vocal accompaniment. As the sun neared the horizon I began to fret, but the game stopped shortly after sunset. The thrush uttered a few tentative calls. But now was the time for the evening Pan American flight, which roared overhead, its thunder echoing and re-echoing. The evening Sahsa flight followed. After that came a small single-engine plane, flying low and not as noisy but taking forever to go by.

Quiet at last; time to press the record button. But, no—two women returning from market were heard from far off, talking and laughing. They had trouble crossing a trickle of water on some slender poles; one fell in with a scream. They had to stop and discuss the event, loudly and with much giggling. Then, perhaps stimulated by the trickle they had just crossed, they put down their baskets and urinated. Finally, they proceeded, their voices receding slowly into the distance. At last, silence! But the *cenzontle* had called it a day. And so did I.

Recording was not always frustrating. I needed only a few minutes to obtain a good recording of the display vocalizations of a male Blue-black Grassquit (*Volatinia jacarina*), the generic name of which means "acrobat," most appropriate. This delightful little creature perches on the tip of the tallest grass stalk or forb in its territory, leaps straight up, vocalizes *bree-zreep*, and drops back again to the same perch. I drove up to a field where a dozen or so grassquits were displaying, directed my microphone at the nearest one, and pressed the record button. *Voilà*. That's all there was to it.

On playback I was pleased with the quality of the sound, and also with the ambiance—other grassquits displaying in the background; no dogs or roosters. But I was puzzled by some odd clicks before each vocalization. As I eventually discovered, these were the wing-flapping sounds as the bird accelerated upward. Thereafter, whenever I was watching and listening to displaying Blue-black Grassquits, I gave attention to these wing noises, and I became more conscious of the wide variety of wing sounds made by other species.

Amanda's election of the number one frustration was our effort to tape the evening song of the Ruddy-capped Nightingale-Thrush (*Catharus frantzii*), known in El Salvador as *pata seca*. This does not translate as "dry foot," as might be assumed from the dictionary, but rather as "thin leg" in the indigenous vocabulary. The bird is one of El Salvador's two most beautiful songsters, the other being the Slate-colored Solitaire (*Myadestes unicolor*). Both inhabit the cloud forest of the Northern Cordillera, where their songs echo through the trees and crags with a beauty that made my throat tighten.

Of course I had to obtain a recording that would do justice to this bird. Almost all the remaining cloud forest in El Salvador is at or near the Hacienda Montecristo, and I tried again and again to find a location there with both a superb songster and an ambiance that would provide a favorable background. Some of my recordings were fair, but I wanted the best possible. At last, I found what I wanted—at the end of a long, tortuous foot trail by the brink of a yawning *barranca* that provided both suitable echoes and a faint sound of rushing water. I also determined the hour at which this bird began its evening song.

Amanda and I set up the recording equipment the following afternoon and settled back to wait. The afternoon darkened and reached the stage when the Nightingale-Thrush would begin to sing. My finger was on the record button. The bird uttered its first glorious phrase. I pressed the button. But at that very instant a *campesino* began to chop his firewood. It soon became obvious that he was cutting enough wood for the coming season. We picked up our equipment and plodded back through the darkness to the camper, Amanda fuming. The story does have a happy ending, however. We went back the next afternoon. The campesino had cut all needed firewood. No dogs or roosters had anything to say. The Nightingale-Thrush cooperated, and we made a fine recording.

The National Audubon Society and the Cornell Laboratory of Ornithology planned to produce an album entitled "Beautiful Bird Songs of the World," and I was asked to contribute my choices. I provided recordings of the Ruddy-capped Nightingale-Thrush and the Slate-colored Solitaire as well as a few others of lesser beauty. When the album appeared I was saddened, and a bit annoyed, to find that the Nightingale-Thrush recording had been replaced by my recording of the Brown-backed Solitaire (*Myadestes occidentalis*), an interesting but by no means beautiful songster. So my recording of the Ruddy-capped Nightingale-Thrush languishes in the Cornell Library of Natural Sounds, recognized by no one but myself as one of the world's most beautiful songs.

We had a briefly frustrating moment when I was recording the song of a Rufous-and-white Wren (*Thryothorus rufalbus*). This species is especially talented. To quote from *Cien Aves de El Salvador* (One Hundred Birds of El Salvador, Thurber 1978):

> Other species of the [Wren] family in El Salvador are not especially accomplished singers but this wren deserves to be ranked among the best of all singers. Heard at a distance the song is flute-like. Heard closely, one may be startled, sometimes amused, at odd opening and closing notes. The repertory is amazing; one bird sang twelve different songs within ninety minutes. The bird is also attractive to see but is adept at slipping away before being more than glimpsed.

One day at Cerro Verde when people-noise was at a minimum, I began to record the song of one of the most accomplished of this species, one I had been trying for some time to obtain. Amanda was sitting beside me. During the recording a park worker stopped directly in front of us. *"¿Está grabando?"* (Are you recording?), he asked in a loud voice. With a variety of grimaces and hand signals, Amanda persuaded him to move on.

This kind of incident was not uncommon, but neither was it a true problem. Wherever we went people were interested and anxious to cooperate. Once they understood that we did not want them to touch the birds in the nets, or disturb nests, or be noisy when we were recording, they did all they could to help and to educate others as to what we were doing.

Probably everyone who has recorded bird songs has experimented with playback to stimulate the same or another bird. I used the technique to call out a Gray-breasted Wood-Wren (*Henicorhina leucophrys*) I had heard but not seen; it became so excited that it flew into a net, and I made a positive identification. I would like to caution those who record the song of such an excited bird that this may not be natural song, but probably differs from normal vocalization in rhythm and phrasing; the recording should be thus annotated.

I sometimes amused the workers on the Hacienda Los Pinos by recording and playing back the crowing of one of the local roosters. The rooster's antics were hilarious. Not only was this a diversion for the workers, but it showed them what we were doing and encouraged their cooperation. For example, when I planned to record the vocalizations of nestling Golden-fronted Woodpeckers (*Melanerpes aurifrons*), two workers eagerly cut poles and constructed a tall tripod on which to mount the microphone; they were as excited as I when we obtained a good recording that included not only the cries of the hungry nestlings but also sounds made by an arriving parent—wing noise, scraping of claws on bark, and faint vocalizations.

Among the rewards of our fifteen years in El Salvador is the memory of our experience with a cock *gualchoco* (Buffy-crowned Wood-Partridge; *Dendrortyx leucophrys*). Several *gualchoco*s moved into abandoned gardens in Parque Cerro Verde and enlivened our mornings with their vocalizations. I obtained some good recordings. Just for fun, Amanda and I took our equipment to a section where we had been hearing a single *gualchoco* somewhat isolated from the others. We seated ourselves in a small open space beside a craterlike depression near the summit of the mountain. The *gualchoco* responded vigorously from the other side of the depression to the first playback. We enticed him closer, hearing him advance through the second growth beside the crater. At about two hundred feet we could also hear his excited clucks and frantic scurrying among the dead leaves; occasionally he emerged into a roadway but quickly popped back under cover. The closer he came to the recorder, the more excited and less timorous he became.

At some twenty feet from us he left cover and began to run around in the small clearing where we sat. We froze. He peered into the adjoining brush on every side, at one time coming within six feet of us. He just could not find that other bird. Because we did not want to frighten him by moving a hand toward the recorder, the stimulation wore off and he slipped back into the brush, still clucking nervously.

One morning I intended to carry out a plan for a composition of *gualchoco* vocalizations, with one bird in the foreground and a chorus of others in the abandoned gardens below. However, the day before I must have eaten something with potent gas-forming qualities. My intestines were like those of the duchess in the famous limerick:

Her rumblings abdominal
Were simply abominable.

I could not restrain the roaring. Thus the *gualchoco* chorus had another participant. My basso-profundo was the star; the *gualchoco*s provided solos, duets, choral responses, and antiphonal effects. The tape, when submitted to the

Cornell Library of Natural Sounds, was a sensation! Lucy and Andrea insisted that it was a valuable contribution. Unfortunately for posterity, I had an attack of self-consciousness and refused to donate the tape to the Cornell archives.

Most of my recordings were of bird vocalizations, but some were nonvocal—drumming of woodpeckers, tapping of woodcreepers on decaying logs, ground-doves foraging in leaf litter. Once I even recorded a flock of Black Vultures (*Coragyps atratus*) jostling about a cow carcass—wing flapping, scuffling, grunting, hissing—with a background of buzzing carrion flies.

Black Vultures provided me with a once-in-a-lifetime experience at Cerro Verde. I was in the park during a strong, dry *norte* (a steady wind out of the north that may persist for days). I heard without special interest what I assumed was a child tootling a three-toned whistle. Yet inwardly I was bothered. I had seen no children. Finally, I looked about and realized that only gardeners and I were in the park; there were no children. I dropped everything to investigate.

The sounds were coming from a most unlikely source—half a dozen Black Vultures. They were diving with folded wings from some 200–300 feet above the summit, flattening out at about my level, then circling about to the north side of the peak, where the upslope wind carried them aloft again. They repeated this maneuver over and over. The sound was produced when a vulture braked to check its dive, spreading its wings and fanning wide its tail. I believe the sound was caused by wind whistling between the rectrices, similar to that occurring during the display flight of Wilson's Snipe (*Gallinago delicata*).

My sense of excitement and satisfaction was interrupted by the thought to record this, so I rushed to my car and assembled my recorder. Unfortunately, by this time the thrill of diving seemed to have palled for the vultures, and my recordings lack the verve of the earlier display. Still, they verify my tale. I wrote a short article titled "Aerial play of Black Vultures" (Thurber 1981), which may have invoked sneering on the part of some.

But I am not to be intimidated. Ever since I watched the antics of an American Crow (*Corvus brachyrhynchos*) above half-frozen Fall Creek on the Cornell campus a long time ago, I have questioned the explanation of animal behavior being totally programmed. This crow had some object that it dropped, recovered by dives, half-rolls, or half-somersaults, and then dropped again. Overcome by curiosity, I clapped my hands to startle the crow into dropping the object, then, at the risk of health and limb, crossed the stream to obtain it. It was an ice-cream cup of the waxed paper variety, without any trace of food, odor, or color. Nonetheless, the crow seemed to be having a good time, and I always regretted my interference.

The Compleat Photographer

I planned to use cameras for record-keeping: photos of habitats, nest sites, nests, eggs, nestlings, and, with netted birds, identification, plumage stages, molt, development of incubation patches, abnormalities, etc. I took two versatile cameras, another of the between-the-lens variety, and a Polaroid.[4] The first two could use interchangeable lenses; I intended to use one of these with color film and the other with black-and-white. The third camera was to be used for habitat photos. As it turned out, I did not use either black-and-white film or the Polaroid camera; instead I kept the first two cameras loaded with color film of different speeds. The between-the-lens camera turned out to be especially useful for photos of nests, eggs, nestlings, hand-held birds, and habitats.

For a couple of years I went along happily, shooting roll after roll and building up a library of photographs. If any of my photos had artistic merit I was pleased but not excited. I had no intention of producing photos of exposition quality.

Then John Dunning's *Portraits of Tropical Birds* (1970) came into my life. I was stunned. How did he get those secretive little birds of the brush to pose so delightfully? How did he get up into the treetops close enough to photograph those active treetop birds? Dunning's book may seem dated today, but one must consider the rapid advances in photographic equipment and four-color printing since 1970. Also, present tastes have been set by the hundreds of nature photographers who devote their lives to bird photography, submitting only their best to editors, who in turn select from these only the very best for publication, truly the cream of the cream.

Dunning generously described his procedures. He photographed netted birds in a cage, and he provided a diagram with details of construction of the cage. I wasted no time in making a modified version. My cage was one meter by one meter by three meters. The framework was of one-meter aluminum strips held together with bolts and wing nuts for rapid assembly. The frame was encased with white muslin to provide a well-lighted interior. At one end a zippered opening admitted a camera lens; at the other end a square of blue cloth simulated the sky if such was desired.

Depending upon the species to be photographed, an appropriate habitat was simulated in front of the "sky." If the bird was of the perching type, a twig or other perch was clamped to a standard; a length of tree trunk was added for a woodpecker, or moss-covered rocks, decayed wood, and ground-litter for terrestrial species. Flash units were clamped to standards at the front of the cage. Zippered openings along the sides allowed access to the interior for arranging the props and equipment.

At last a bird was admitted to the cage, and I sat back to await developments. Surprisingly, I rarely waited long before the bird was in position to be photographed effectively, although there were exceptions. Some birds flew about wildly for a time, often landing on and clinging to the cloth of the cage; it was Amanda's task to loosen the bird's claws without harming it. Some birds persisted in concealing themselves behind the habitat setting. Again, it was Amanda's responsibility to stir up the bird until it posed properly.

The resulting photographs roused much excitement. They correlated beautifully with our tape recordings. Amanda and I prepared scripts using combined visual and audio effects. I had been asked to speak at the Centro Cultural El Salvador-Estados Unidos and used one of our scripts for a presentation. We were a bit nervous, but we were assured that attendance was usually sparse and the audience forgiving; probably only a dozen or so people would occupy the forty chairs provided.

At 7 p.m. the prediction seemed accurate, but a call from Television Educativa asked us to hold up a bit because some of its personnel were on their way. At 8 we were asked to wait yet a little longer so that additional chairs could be brought. At 9 we had literally a full house. Not another chair could be squeezed in. People were standing against the walls. Many who could not enter were crowded in the corridors. There were even some who had climbed up to the windows. Amanda and I would have been crushed if the equipment or procedures had failed. But all went smoothly. We realized that in the future we would need larger facilities for public presentations.

We learned then and in coming years how eager Salvadorans were for ties to their natural heritage. Their society, once primarily rural, was rapidly losing its roots, and people felt the loss. Our photos and recorded bird songs invoked memories, and audiences responded eagerly. We repeated the first program a few weeks later, this time in the commodious Sala de Exposiciones in the Parque Cuscutlán. Amanda and I do not always agree on details—she remembers that there may have been four hundred chairs; I remember only that there were many people standing in the rear of the hall.

During the following years we presented programs on many occasions—at the university, at private and public schools, a social club, a teachers' conference, and in the auditoriums of two banks. Our largest audience was in one of the latter, Las Cajas de Crédito, which seated some fifteen hundred people and was crowded. We varied the programs, using new slides and new recordings. Some people attended again and again.

I had 8×10 prints made from the best photographs. Ken Kingston, head of the Special Projects Division of Eastman Kodak, took a special interest in these enlargements and personally supervised the process, thus setting standards for later work. I mounted the prints on large boards. We organized two displays for the Sala de Exposiciones already mentioned, each of about seventy-five prints. The first was scheduled for one week, but attendance was so high that it was held over for another week. I was given a record of daily attendance; it was certainly impressive and far outdrew the usual art exhibits.

One program was entitled *"Las Bellezas de Cerro Verde"* and introduced an exhibit of prints of birds, flowers, sunsets, and landscapes photographed in the park. The Instituto de Turismo, which administers the park, sent out invitations embellished with a four-color reproduction of one of my photos and provided programs similarly embellished.

Amanda and I could not be present for another exhibition of prints, and we missed a special feature. Children from the public schools and many parents were brought to the Sala de Exposiciones to view the exhibit. But first the children were grouped on the steps of the building to sing songs about birds to their parents seated in front. One song was *"El Clarinero"* (the male Great-tailed Grackle, *Quiscalus mexicanus*), written by a well-known Salvadoran composer.

I was always generous with the prints. A set showing the birds of the university campus was placed on permanent display in the library of the School of Natural Sciences. Relevant prints were displayed in the Hotel de Cerro Verde and in the headquarters of the Instituto de Turismo. Some were given to the Museo de Ciencias Naturales. The Ministry of Education framed about eighty prints under glass and had shipping crates made for them; these were sent on a rotating basis for exhibits in the Casas de Cultura in cities throughout the country.

Our photographs were also used in a number of other ways. In its bimonthly journal the School of Natural Sciences at the university published articles based on the photos. The national government's annual included several pages in full color. An agricultural journal printed birds on its cover in full color and included an insert showing birds of the country. The magazine of the automobile club published several articles (bylined WAT) illustrated by our photos. A bank used a photo on one of its calendars.

From time to time the local newspapers included articles about our work using black-and-white photos, but after two of them obtained four-color presses for Sunday supplements, the newspapers blossomed with spectacular full-page reproductions of our most appealing photos. The Ministry of Education, as part of its conservation education propaganda, printed a large poster proclaiming *"Protejamos a Los Pájaros"* (Let's Protect Our Birds), which featured our photo of the *torovoz* (Turquoise-browed Motmot; *Eumomota superciliosa*). This poster was distributed widely to schools and government agencies, and for some years it was difficult to enter or leave the country without seeing one of these posters in an office of Migración (Immigration).

I encouraged the Salvadoran Congress to declare the *torovoz* the national bird, even as Guatemala's national bird is the Resplendent Quetzal (*Pharomachrus mocinno*). The *torovoz* is a distinctive and attractive bird and is familiar to Salvadorans, whereas the quetzal is rarely seen by Guatemalans. I was pleased when some deputies to the Congress prepared an appropriate bill. A group of designers even began work on applications of a stylized rendition for use on fabrics, lamp shades, pottery, and the like. However, I heard nothing more about the fate of the bill.

The use of our photos in the book *Cien Aves de El Salvador* gave us much satisfaction. The Ministry of Education had acquired a modern four-color printing press and wanted to do something spectacular. We were approached with the suggestion of publishing a book based on our best photos, with text in both Spanish and English. We settled on a hundred birds with a major photo on each right-hand page and a supplementary photo on facing pages. I insisted on double authorship with Amanda but got nowhere.

Otherwise, the book turned out to be almost all I could desire—excellent colors, crisp typefaces, high-quality paper, excellent binding. My chief complaint was its organization. I had planned to put the four-color section at the beginning, followed by general material. I tried to explain how to set up the folding mechanism to allow this, accomplished easily with their excellent equipment, but what does a gringo ornithologist know about book production? A reader opening the book is faced first with several pages of type and gets to the photographs only if persistent.

The Ministry of Education and other officials in the government were proud of *Cien Aves*. Copies were bound in leather and stamped with gold for the *duque* of Cadiz, cousin of King Juan Carlos of Spain, when he visited El Salvador. The president, vice president, and other dignitaries signed the presentation copies. But not the author. Nor was I ever given a deluxe copy bound in leather and stamped in gold. I have not been bitter—I know the official mind. This was not a deliberate slight; it was just that no one thought of it. But somewhere in the Royal Library in Madrid rests my book with my name on the cover and on the accession card. Who could ask for more? Amanda tells me a deluxe copy was also presented to the emperor of Japan by the Salvadoran Minister of Education.

El Amigo de los Pájaros

Raúl Monzón, director of programming for Radio Station YSU, came to see us one day. "Would you be interested in preparing a program for my station?" he asked.

"Of course," we told him, always delighted to spread the message to a new audience. "What do you think would most interest your listeners?"

"Anything on birds, and especially your recordings of songs."

We inquired whether we should limit ourselves to the birds of the capital, San Salvador, or if his audience was broader.

"Could you do two programs," Raúl jumped on me, "one on the birds of the city and one on the birds of the countryside?"

"Should the second program be on upland birds or lowland birds?" I asked mischievously.

The result was a long discussion, with new ideas surfacing and a final decision to produce a series of fifteen programs of forty-five minutes each, the series to be titled *El Amigo de los Pájaros* (The Friend of the Birds).

Amanda and I set ourselves to working out details, occasionally joined by Raúl, who helped especially with the format. I had considerable experience with this type of radio presentation. Back in the days when frequency modulation first entered the airwaves, New York State was allotted a channel for the *FM School of the Air*, to be broadcast to participating schools. I had taken on a series of some thirty elementary science programs, using children and teachers of the (then) Cortland State Teachers College Training School. I had learned a great deal about how to keep the action flowing and how to help listeners identify with participants.

We had no problem with distinctive voices. My own is somewhat dry, with a Yankee tinge and professorial delivery. Amanda has a low, warm voice, sympathetic and easy to identify with. Raúl had a rich, well-trained voice, confident and appealing. Raúl announced all the programs, and when he participated he served as moderator—asking questions, clearing up the unclear, and summarizing. Amanda was the eager observer, full of questions, happy to add her own knowledge. I was the general authority but ever willing to admit ignorance. We made a good team.

Each program had a different emphasis. The first, which dealt with urban birds, explained how to attract birds to home patios with feeders, baths, and plants that provide food, including nectar for hummingbirds, and was designed to awaken sympathy for birds and, incidentally, for all life.

Some programs dealt specifically with the plight of birdlife. One, titled *"Los*

Pericos Pasan" (The parakeets are passing), used the title of a poem written by Alfredo Espino, a popular Salvadoran poet. These parakeets were familiar to all of San Salvador: every evening large, noisy bands flew over the city to spend the night in a nearby coffee plantation (since cut down), then left in the morning. The program began with the sound of a band of parakeets in the distance, gradually becoming louder as Raúl read the poem. We discussed the nests in holes in soft volcanic rock, described how and what the adults fed the nestlings, and played recordings of the adults coming and going to their nests, with the cries of hungry nestlings. We told how people came with ladders to take out the nestlings for sale as "pets," the high mortality involved, and the diminishing population during the past fifty years. We explained the double significance of the title of the program—that the parakeets were not only passing over the city each day but were slowly passing from the avifauna. We told the story of the Scarlet Macaw (*Ara macao*), once common in the lowlands but by then extirpated because of nest robbing for the pet trade, hunting for food, and elimination of nesting sites. We also described the plight of other parrots and parakeets on the verge of extirpation.

The radio programs were an undeniable success. Raúl, who wanted to broaden the offerings of YSU beyond *novelas* (we call them soap operas), mounted an intensive campaign to develop an audience. Through the cooperation of Director-General de Cultura Carlos DeSola, who provided three hundred of the previously mentioned posters showing the *torovoz* (Turquoise-browed Motmot), Raúl began playing as "spots" each day a different bird song with an announcement of the coming program and an offer of a poster to all who wrote in giving the name of the bird and the date of the program. The response was immediate, and the supply of posters disappeared rapidly. Carlos gave all that remained in stock and set the presses to printing thousands more.

Station YSU employed an extra operator to handle telephone calls and telegrams. Station director Héctor Amaya told me that they received more than ten thousand calls, possibly an exaggeration, but indicating a substantial number nonetheless. Raúl told us that each morning there were people lined up before the offices opened for posters. Amanda recalls the letter from a lady in the far east of the country, too poor to come to San Salvador but who wanted a poster so much that she sent a *colón* (then forty cents) and an address to which to mail the poster; we sent the poster and sent back the *colón* as well.

Many people wrote personally to *"El Amigo de Los Pájaros."* We still have those letters—546 of them, according to Amanda's count. The letters ranged from scrawls on scraps of paper to beautifully written paragraphs on letter paper elegantly ornamented with colored pencils. All were grateful for our work in El Salvador; complaints that foreigners, *extranjeros* or gringos, had to tell Salvadorans about Salvadoran birds were the only sour note.

Many of the letters were truly touching. One lady recalled that many long years before, when she was a girl, an owl like the one we recorded had called in a tree in the patio of her home on moonlit nights, and that our program had made her cry at the memory. Another woman invited friends who had no radios to listen to her radio so that they could share in memories. A teenage boy, sorrowful because his friends enjoyed killing birds, invited them to his home to hear the program, hoping their attitudes might be changed. A laborer who worked at some distance from his home stopped work early each day, practically running home so that he could arrive by 5 p.m. for the program. Two convicts wrote letters of appreciation. One added, "Tell people not to put birds in cages. I know how it feels." Very touching was a letter from two women hospitalized for a long period with no distractions and few visitors; each afternoon they waited eagerly for the program, discussing the previous programs and their memories, and after the program talked long about what they had heard. Every letter received was answered with a note of thanks, signed by Raúl Monzón, Amanda, and myself.

Flight from Paradise

Why did Amanda and I leave a place we loved so much and in which we seemed to be so much loved? The answer is summed in one word—*Communists*. I use only this one word without modifiers because in my lexicon the word embodies a whole thesaurus of malignant words—vile, pitiless, deceitful, evil, inhumane, treacherous, thieving, assassins, cheaters, liars, murderers, merciless, vicious, vermin, thugs. U.S. policy was reprehensible, and the American news media made no effort to obtain unbiased news.

Many of our friends and acquaintances were murdered by the Communist scum. One was the young man who served as watchman at the Centro de Televisión Educativa, with whom Amanda frequently chatted while I was inside working on programs. His lowly status did not save him one night when a carload of assassins gunned him down—this was just part of "the campaign to sow terror," as it was explained to us. Higher on the socioeconomic scale was Carlos Hidalgo, a promising young artist whom Carlos DeSola and I had twice sent to workshops in Trinidad given by renowned bird artist Don Eckelberry. Don told me Carlos had a talent that needed only experience to develop. But Carlos never had a chance. As director of the tiny National Zoo he was eliminated as part of the Communist reign of terror; one night his car was forced off the road and he was killed. Shortly before his murder, Carlos gave me one of his best paintings, a Black-and-white Owl (*Ciccaba nigrolineata*), which I value highly but view with bitterness.

Roberto Coma, vice president of the Instituto de Turismo, with whom I worked on plans for preservation in the Parque Cerro Verde, was abducted for ransom. During the fracas he was shot in the belly and developed peritonitis. Instead of placing him on the steps of a hospital, those vile creatures let him die and buried him on the patio of the house where he had been imprisoned. A newly appointed Minister of Education spent all of one evening talking with me about ways to give conservation education more emphasis in public schools. He had refused to accept a bodyguard because he was *del pueblos* (one of the people) and would not be touched; he believed that the terrorism was purely a local movement having no connection with events elsewhere. Shortly after our conference he was gunned down as he left home for work.

My heart still aches for the ambassador from South Africa and his wife. Elderly, a true gentleman, and interested in our work, he occasionally came to Cerro Verde to watch us net and process birds. He was abducted, and because his government refused to accede to the terrorists' demands, he was allowed to starve. From time to time those vermin provided to the press photos of the poor man, each time thinner and thinner. In the meantime, his wife was grieving hopelessly in the ambassadorial residence. We never knew when he died or what the vermin did with his body.

By 1978 the Communists were in nearly complete control of the National University. The dean of the School of Science and Humanities, René Vaquerano, who offered me a full professorship in 1970, was terrified into resigning, and the Communists took control of that division of the university as well, except for the Department of Natural Sciences; the chairman, José Salvador Flores, resisted, even though he was under constant threat. Shortly before I left he told me with tears in his eyes how telephone calls constantly terrified his wife and children, and although he changed his number again and again, the scum had ways of quickly finding his new number. I served under Flores as visiting professor until 1980. In 1978, he advised me not to appear on campus but rather to meet with students and faculty in my apartment. I did go onto the campus once in 1979, when the Department of Biology honored me for my work in conservation. Amanda and I were nervous about attending, but all went quietly. I was gratified to see the main auditorium completely filled with students and faculty for the event.

Nonetheless, I was shocked at what the Communists were doing to the campus. Graffiti covered every wall, indoors and out: "*Viva Fidel*"; "*Viva La Revolución*"; the Communist symbol of hammer and sickle with the sickle replaced by the Latin American *corvo* (a curved knife); names of Communist "martyrs"; and the photo of a girl killed in a deliberately provoked confrontation with police. Overhead, a loudspeaker spewed out hate-hate-hate.

During the last years of the 1970s there were increasing rumors that the threatened "final push" was near. At the U.S. Embassy I asked the attaché to the ambassador, who had been on one of our Christmas Bird Counts, if I could store my archives in the embassy until the situation became stable. He told me that would be impossible, adding: "Walter, if I were you I would leave El Salvador without delay."

His advice agreed with that of friends both in and out of the government. We considered moving to Guatemala, where Dr. Mario Dary, rector (president) of Guatemala's national university, the Universidad San Carlos, knew me well and had invited us to work in Guatemala. Moreover, Amanda's family lived there and had many contacts who would help us become established. However, it was a painful decision. We had several hundred migrants banded and could hope that some were back to be recaptured. We had enough data on the hummingbird called the Green Violetear (*Colibri thalassinus*) for a monograph on the life history and habits of this species, but we wanted to tie up a few loose ends. We also had unfinished studies of a number of other species. And I was on the thesis committees of three promising students and hated to walk away from them.

But to stay even if conditions did not worsen would have been impractical. The Communists had almost complete control of the eastern third of the country and made frequent incursions into the midsection. Thus the newly established reserve at Lagunita El Jocotal was out of bounds for us, and the Hacienda Los Pinos was of doubtful safety. During our last visit to the Hacienda El Imposible in the west, a large band of men with heavy packs passed through the hacienda one night. Presumably they were Communists, and we no longer felt comfortable about remaining there. We decided to move to Guatemala.

Now we had the problem of taking across the frontier the belongings we had accumulated through the years, avoiding confiscation and excessive customs duties. We were lucky, compared with the experiences of some of our acquaintances at the hands of the Latin American bureaucracy. Several Salvadorans trying to move real property from the country had it confiscated before they could cross the border, and the Guatemalan customs agents charged heavy duties on property that was not confiscated.

Amanda was a close acquaintance of the Guatemalan consul to El Salvador, who had diplomatic freedom to cross the border without question; he took in his car our cameras, tape recorders, binoculars, and record players, except for the large speakers of the latter. Luis Fiallos, who had spent much time with us at Cerro Verde, solved this problem by removing the speakers from his minivan-camper radio and carrying ours, assuring the customs agent that our speakers were those registered for his vehicle.

We knew the truck-camper would be a problem but did not want to suffer the delay to obtain proper papers. It bore New York state license plates because my residency status in El Salvador permitted this. (It also bore ODECA plates, long invalid.) We decided that Luis Fiallos would be better able to cope with customs agents than a gringo could, and that he would drive the truck-camper with Amanda as passenger. I would follow with our little Ford packed with clothing and personal items.

The Ford and I had no problems; I think I still had a valid Visa de Cortesía from the Guatemalan embassy from my days with ODECA. I was treated with all deference and courtesy. But Luis and Amanda encountered the expected problems. The truck-camper and papers were carefully inspected. No one could make a decision about what to do. Amanda can be very insistent, though, and probably mentioned the names of several acquaintances in the government. Perhaps telephone calls were made. After some hours an agent appeared with the news that we could enter but would have to appear shortly at the proper office to obtain permission to remain in the country. Thus we avoided inspection at the border and were able to unload all our equipment before official inspection.

Amanda and Luis took the Ford back to El Salvador twice for additional belongings, once passing by a different route, where she thought inspection might be more lax. And so we got out all of our extensive library. Later, a friend of Amanda's sent a truck with a Guatemalan license and a driver to San Salvador to pick up all that remained.

As he had promised, Dr. Dary had set in motion procedures that would allow me to live and work in Guatemala. Amanda, as a Guatemalan citizen, had no problem. I immediately had interviews with officials that would lead to residency status. Amanda rented a five-room apartment in a secure place where we could live and work when not in the field, and where our belongings would be safe when we were away. I met with the then president's brother in the Ministry of Agriculture to obtain permission to drive the truck-camper around the country. Dr. Dary was also making arrangements for us to work in a biological reserve called Biotop El Quetzal, which included a large expanse of virgin forest. The officials in charge wanted us to concentrate on the Resplendent Quetzal, but they were persuaded that broader studies might be desirable.

It appeared that Amanda and I would be able to take up almost where we had left off in El Salvador. We had a close relationship with Jorge Ibarra, director of the National Museum, and could expect to work with him. We had spoken with Director-General de Turismo Alvaro Arzu (who would be president of Guatemala from 1996 to 2000), about preparing a cassette of bird songs in cooperation with Cornell, and we had his enthusiastic endorsement. And as for conservation education, Amanda had been a teacher in both public and private schools, and then *asesor*a in teacher training. She knew almost everyone of importance in the field of education and would be welcomed in whatever we might be able to do.

But then Mario Dary was assassinated by Communists. Apparently history was repeating itself. Communists were entering eastern Guatemala by boat from Cuba. They were infiltrating from the north from Mexico, and the violence in El Salvador was spilling over the frontier. After El Salvador fell, which seemed likely at the time, Communists would invade Guatemala from the south. We were persuaded to abandon our study of Central American birds.

It seemed a pity to break up such a compatible couple as Amanda and myself. Better that I should ask her to marry me and move to the United States. I did, and she did.

Notes

1. Editor's note: From observations in south Texas and southern Veracruz I surmise that individuals of all of these species are migrants from the United States and Canada occurring separately or together, depending on vagaries of weather and migration timing. Thurber's suspicion that the Turkey Vultures of El Salvador are resident matches my own for those of eastern Mexico.

2. Editor's note: Recapturing a bird at or near the same place that it was originally banded on its breeding or wintering grounds occurs regularly. However, in nongame birds it is vanishingly rare to obtain a recapture that links an individual bird to both its breeding and wintering areas. This is the result of bird dispersal and the scale of human effort in relation to the sizes of bird populations and ranges.

3. Editor's note: *Piaya cayana*, generally too large to be captured in nets for small songbirds, seems a likely culprit for the moth predation. The warbler predation has the signs of an *Accipiter* or *Micrastur*.

4. Editor's note: Between-the-lens cameras had a shutter inserted between the lenses; they were largely phased out in the 1960s when reflex cameras with interchangeable lenses and focal plane shutters became more popular.

19

Recollections of Mexico: People and Places

DWAIN W. WARNER

Dwain W. Warner, Ph.D. (1917–2005) began a long career studying birds in Mexico in 1941 as an assistant to George Miksch Sutton and Olin Sewall Pettingill on a joint expedition with Cornell University and Carleton College. His doctoral studies at Cornell (1939–47) were interrupted by World War II service in the army (1943–46), spent mostly in the South Pacific. He went on to a forty-year career as a professor and curator of birds at the University of Minnesota and the Minnesota (later J. F. Bell) Museum of Natural History in Minneapolis. For more details, see Winker (2006) and Winker et al. (2006). The field experiences related here resulted in publications varying from biodiversity surveys and natural history observations (e.g., Warner and Mengel 1951; Warner and Beer 1957; Warner 1959) to a taxonomic revision of the Singing Quail (*Dactylortyx thoracicus*; Warner and Harrell 1957) and later work on migrant ecology (e.g., Ramos and Warner 1980; Rappole and Warner 1980).

With all the things that came up and engaged my academic interest over the years, I felt I had never settled on one avenue to pursue seriously. I was always working with a student who wanted to do this, or a colleague who wanted to do that, and there was a world of work to do. But the scattershot approach gradually coalesced into a degree of order, and working in Mexico proved a keystone. By the time we finally settled in for long-term research in Los Tuxtlas, we had good objectives in mind and learned a great deal. But it took us a while to reach that stage.

Byron Harrell

When Byron Harrell started out in the graduate program at the University of Minnesota, all he wanted was to work in Mexico. He went there, and nobody heard a word from him. We had zero communication. Sometimes even his family would not hear from him for months; his father would call me all the time. The year was 1949. Nuevo Morelos and Antigua Morelos have some of the most fascinating plant communities I had ever seen. I wanted to get into

Figure 19.1. Dwain Warner in front of his hotel room at the Motel Playa Escondida, Sierra de Los Tuxtlas, Veracruz, January 25, 1983. Photo by K. Winker.

Tamaulipas that way for a look, so I spent time there, staying in a little hotel owned by a family named McCall. I didn't do much collecting; I was just driving and looking. I found out that Byron had gone up to the cloud forests, which were rapidly being cut. On that trip I realized that Mexico was being scalped. The forests from Jalapa to Veracruz were being cut so fast you couldn't believe it. I had collected with George Miksch Sutton in some of those forests.

I never did find Byron on the 1949 trip. All I found was a trace: I stopped at the Río Sabinas, and people remembered him being there. On the next trip, with Jim Beer, Tex Wells, and Steve Pospichal, we did find Byron, although we could easily have missed him. Toward the end of our trip, around Christmas or New Year's, we were already en route homeward. We decided to go to Tampico and then inland—there was no road up the coast then; we had to go to Ciudad Mante then north to Victoria. We were on an oil road, where the only vehicles normally to be seen were giant trucks. It was a lonely road, and we were hungry. We had been driving the whole day in the rain and had not eaten much.

All of a sudden at two or three in the morning we came to a jeep, parked at a tilt on the side of the road. I looked and saw Minnesota license plates—Byron Harrell's jeep! The canvas doors were flapping in the breeze. We shone our flashlights in the ditch—no body. One of us was smart enough to open the gas tank and shake the jeep. No gas. Empty. That was Byron's habit. He never checked his fuel gauge.

Assuming Byron had set out to get some gas, we drove on through the darkness. About eight miles farther down the road, the rain had stopped, and here came a long-legged guy walking along, gas can under one arm. Walking back to his jeep, all the way from Tampico or some suburb south of the big river. Walking along a Mexican oil road in the middle of the night. What did he say?

"Hi! I didn't expect to see you guys." Nothing spectacular from Byron.

Byron worked down there for a long time. When he made it to Los Tuxtlas, he walked all the way from San Andrés Tuxtla to the coast, and he wrote a letter telling us he had found some fantastic cliffs that just plunged into the sea: the old lava flows. He also said he had left his camera on a fallen log—it may still be there.

On the Pacific Coast

In the spring of 1954 Allan Phillips and I were out on the west coast of Mexico. Partly we went for quail. Someone had looked up the notes of the famous field biologists E. W. Nelson and E. A. Goldman from their collecting in humid mountain habitats on the west coast (see Goldman 1951). Such habitats are rare, and one was Putla, south of where Allan and Anita Downs lived in Tlaxiaco.[1] Nelson and Goldman had described a new form of bobwhite quail (*Colinus* sp.) from there. Also, up in the Jalisco and Colima area they had found patches of humid forest that were not necessarily on the volcanoes. Allan had been looking at some of these on a map and suggested we should go there, or as near as we could get.

Picture an oceangoing dugout canoe carved out of a single gigantic log and propelled by a dinky little outboard motor way down on the side. We took one of these from Puerto Vallarta down the coast of the Bay of Banderas to a tiny village called Chimo, where we arrived on a Sunday. Allan was already seasick, but we had to climb out of that boat and into a smaller one to get ashore. In this town every man seemed to be carrying a cock around under his arm for the cock fights. We wanted to reach a place called El Refugio Suchitlán and were looking to hire horses to take us up the mountains. Right in Chimo that Sunday afternoon Allan collected a Prothonotary Warbler (*Protonotaria citrea*) and another small bird. But he made the mistake of putting them on a windowsill of our quarters, and a cat ate them!

It was clear that these people had never seen anything like us before. Here were some strangers behaving very strangely indeed, wandering around town with guns under our arms. The next day we went up the mountains on pack horses. Various other people were going up too, some carrying fish. To us it was a hell of a steep and rugged trip, though no more than normal procedure for the others on the trail. When we got to El Refugio, we rented a little room in one of the houses, where we were introduced on the first night to every bug you could imagine. But the food was delicious, and the townspeople had the schoolteacher attend to us. They decided we were educated and that they should treat us to associating with the finest and most educated person in the village.

There were about ninety families. They had almost nothing, yet they were the most amazingly hospitable people you could ever meet. Water was in short supply at that time of year. All the fresh water they had was from a little sump; enough to drink but not much more. Asked what we liked to eat, I said, "Oh, beans and meat." Late that night I woke up and looked out—I'd heard something. There in the moonlight was the *patrón*, a fairly young man, saddling a horse and putting a rifle in the rifle scabbard on the saddle. In the moonlight he looked like Pancho Villa himself. I was thrilled by that vision, and I'll never forget it. At dawn, when I woke again and discovered all the bed bugs, body lice, fleas, and ticks all eating on me, the fellow was back with the horse heavily lathered. Across the back of the saddle was a goat, shot. I'll never forget that, either—he had gone out and gotten us a goat. How do you go out at three in the morning and come back at dawn with a dead goat? Perhaps he snaggled it from someone else, or maybe there were some wild ones, who knows. But we got little slivers of goat meat over the next couple of days. That goat was split up I think ninety-four ways; the whole town ate that goat.

We had packed two Cambridge cans up there on horseback, and we worked to fill them with specimens. We went night-collecting for owls and whip-poorwills, and everywhere we went, we had an entourage. Almost everyone had a slingshot, and the birds took a beating.

Bob Dickerman

Dickerman showed up at our house in Mexico City in 1953 or 1954. I was on sabbatical, and my family and I were living in Mexico for a year. Bob and an assistant named Jesús were collecting for E. Raymond Hall of the University of Kansas. Hall had his secretary write to Dickerman and request that he not refer to his field assistant as "Jesus" any more. Dickerman had to send all his field notes to Kansas, and the notes were replete with such details as "Jesus went into town and got drunk and got laid again last night" and "Jesus is working out fine, but he can't cook very well."

Chuy was that man's nickname, and he and Dickerman both had big, round festering sores on their legs. We got them to a doctor, who asked what they were eating. They had a vitamin B deficiency—not enough tomatoes, the doctor decided. They had been up in the northern desert, where there weren't any tomatoes. He was a sharp young doctor; he gave them vitamin B supplements, and those sores cleared right up. Field biologists are not known for their diversity of foods.

Nobody knows Mexico like Dickerman, not even Allan Phillips. Dickerman really got around. Don't underestimate Allan, though; he would take buses and travel with friends. But Bob always had a vehicle. And if you have wheels in Mexico and can afford the gas you can see a lot of Mexico. I don't know anybody who traveled in Mexico as much.

Off to Mexico—Again

For my first ten years at the University of Minnesota I always had classes; sometimes even in the summer, when I taught at Itasca. After ten years I did not have classes in the fall. By the 1960s I used to go to Mexico just to get away from the university. With a wife and five children, I was never personally in a position to take on a big, long-term project that would require a lot of field time. But the Mexicans always made it easy; I had permits to collect specimens in all the parks if I thought I needed them for documentation.

I had enjoyed quail ever since I began hunting them while growing up around Northfield, Minnesota, so at one point I suggested a survey of the fifteen or so quail species that were hunted in Mexico. I wanted to focus not on the common ones, like *Odontophorus guttatus*, but on the rest, species like the Bearded Wood-Partridge (*Dendrortyx barbatus*), which were all either endangered or about to be. I looked at a lot of quail, and it was hard work. Dickerman is good at that, with a mountain climber's long legs. Somebody still ought to study the quail of Mexico thoroughly. They are likely to be pursued by hunters until there are none left, even though it is a resource that could be managed.

Near Tulancingo there was an old hacienda that had been taken over by a hunting club. I was invited there several times, and I went to hunt ducks. The outfit served scotch and eggs for breakfast and would set you up with two men in a boat, one to run the boat and the other to reload your gun. Just as fast as you could shoot and empty the gun, he would reload it. The place was owned by two brothers associated with the ancient silver mines of Pachuca, and they loved to talk about quail. Before starting work at the University of Minnesota I had turned down a job at Texas A&M, where I had been invited to work with W. B. Davis. I never met him in my life, although we corresponded, and he spoke with me on the telephone. I met lots of his students in Mexico, but whenever I met his students in the field, Davis wasn't there. He was always in Mexico City, they said, while groups of students went out collecting birds, mammals, and herps for him. They used to bring all their food with them and their own cook, whom they sent out to shoot birds; Bob Mengel and I met him up on a ridge one day.

Another person I met in Mexico was Rollin Baker, one of Kansas's fair-haired boys working under E. Raymond Hall. He would go on to produce a major work on the birds of Micronesia (Baker 1951). Baker had been in the Pacific in World War II and was good company. Hall once came up to us and put one arm around me and the other around Rollin and said, "Here are two of my finer boys."

I said, "What? You consider me one of your boys, Dr. Hall?"

And he answered, "Well, yes. I don't really know much about you, but I consider you one of my boys."

He said he had heard good things about me, but I reckon this was really more of a comment on my judgment: I had succeeded in stealing Bob Dickerman away from him.

Welder and Los Tuxtlas

The refuge of the Rob and Bessie Welder Wildlife Foundation in San Patricio County, Texas, was established in the 1950s and formally dedicated in 1961. We got hooked up with the Welder refuge through Clarence Cottam, whom I knew from years before, and I went down for its inauguration. Lee Jacques had also been invited down when the Welders wanted to build this fabulous place. At the inauguration were a bunch of herpetologists from the American

Museum of Natural History. We went out at night with flashlights and caught water moccasins and unfamiliar toads. I had known Cottam from meetings and such over the years, but it was on this trip that I really got to know him. He had remembered that I worked with migrants, and he called me in Minnesota to ask whether I was still working in Mexico. He suggested I visit because the refuge was right in the path of the big migrations. Remember Mrs. Connie Hagar of Rockport, credited with the discovery of large-scale hummingbird migration on the Gulf of Mexico? He was impressed by that, and he thought an inland perspective was needed. Out of that developed a lot of support from Welder for migration studies—work by John Rappole, Dick Oehlenschlager, Mario Ramos, and Bruce Fall.

Allan Phillips in Mexico picked out Mario and sent him up to Minnesota by bus to meet me for some work at our Lake Itasca field station. I drove in to Park Rapids to meet him at the bus station. There he was in the dark at about 11:30 at night, all alone in a new country. When Mario came he used to show us little pictures of two girls; one was named Isabel, and she helped him and eventually won out in his affections.

John Rappole came to the University of Minnesota in 1968, recently back from Vietnam. Clarence Cottam of the Welder Refuge believed in me—we put in good proposals and he liked my choice of people. That was how we got Rappole started with a Welder fellowship.

Mexico was changing fast. To get more systematic about work there and to establish long-term studies, we needed a more predictable site, and we planned to set out and see if we could fine one. We had almost reached the border when I learned from my sister in Phoenix that my mother had died, and I was confronted with the stark choice of proceeding into Mexico or going to my mother's funeral; I decided on Mexico. In February 1973 we looked hard for remnant forest. We eventually went to Mexico City and talked with Bernardo Villa and people at the Instituto de Biología at UNAM, and they told us about their new field station in Los Tuxtlas, with six square kilometers of forest. My first visit to Los Tuxtlas during our 1973 reconnaissance was what you might call a pilot run. We had brought along just enough equipment to see whether this was what the students involved wanted to do. We did a lot of pilot-running up and down those muddy slopes, but it was clear that Los Tuxtlas had what we needed to do some really interesting research.[2]

The Stone Room

For some reason I don't recall, one night I wound up all alone in a hotel down in Coatzacoalcos, having gone down from Los Tuxtlas to pick up some supplies. It was a big stone hotel with great thick walls and just shutters on the windows, no screens, no glass. The weather was cold and damp. The room featured a little iron bed with a suspicious-looking mattress, a single light with its switch on a hanging central cord, and a dinky little rickety stand by the bed, where I deposited my pistol and flashlight; there was nothing else in the room. The door did not reach down to the floor, and there was also a lot of space above it, and it had just a crude lock.

Pooped, I took off my clothes and I lay down on that sack. It was so damp that it felt as if I could practically squeeze water out of the mattress. When things finally quieted down in the halls, I dozed off. But I woke up feeling something on my chest. What in the world was there? Without thinking I grabbed my pistol, though it would not have been much protection—I had been shooting lizards, and it was loaded with birdshot. I flicked on the flashlight, and found two of the biggest cockroaches in the world standing right on my chest and looking me in the face. Their antennae were up there waving over me. I swept them off me with the flashlight. They hit the wall, and I shone the light down and saw them running for the door. *You bastards*, I thought, and *boom*, I touched off the gun. What a mistake! That stone room! I was just about deaf. And all that blue smoke was hanging there in the room.

I shut off the flashlight because people soon began dashing up and down the hall yelling in the kind of language I'd never heard in my life. Their commotion continued for about an hour, during which I never turned the light on. I just lay there, worrying that they would see the smoke coming from out of my room. But no one pounded on my door.

In the morning I could not even find a piece of those cockroaches; I must have blown them right under the door into the hall. I couldn't hear for three days. Never shoot a gun in a stone room.

Notes

1. Editor's note: Nelson and Goldman worked with the U.S. Biological Survey in Mexico from 1892 to 1906. The late Allan Downs was a professor of art at the University of Minnesota until he retired to Mexico; Anita still has a home in Tlaxiaco, and their daughter Lila is a renowned singer.

2. Editor's note: See Paul Haemig's and John Rappole's chapters for more on this important trip, which began a long-term research effort still going over three decades later.

20

Studying the Birds of Los Tuxtlas

KEVIN WINKER

Kevin Winker, Ph.D., is curator of birds and professor at the University of Alaska Fairbanks. The field experiences included in this narrative were undertaken as part of his master of science thesis at the University of Minnesota, the scientific reports of which were included in Winker et al. (1990a, 1990b, 1992, 1995).

The Coxcoapan

The Sierra de Los Tuxtlas, an isolated volcanic mountain range in southern Veracruz, was where I did my master's thesis research on the Wood Thrush (*Hylocichla mustelina*) with John Rappole and Mario Ramos. The Coxcoapan River in Los Tuxtlas was a major part of daily life during the Wood Thrush years. A rocky, fast-moving mountain river, its level changed rapidly with each rainfall. At times it was a pleasant, easily crossed stream, bringing cool, good-tasting water from the mountains. But at other times it was the quintessential raging torrent—a roaring, murky, turbulent maelstrom. The river was very dangerous in the latter stage; we would marvel at the deep base notes of large, grinding boulders being pushed and rolled along the rocky bed. During lower water levels the river bed served as a boulder trail, and one quickly became adept at using the uneven footing when it was available. Like the steep, muddy slopes, though, it took a few days before one's walking abilities adjusted. Slow progress and heavy arm-waving for balance were two signs of the novice. When I was back in that habitat again a few years ago and feeling clumsy, I remembered Steve Stucker and I racing at a full run down one of the boulder beds with full packs on our backs. That spontaneous sprint followed months of familiarization; what is surprising now is that it did not seem out of the ordinary then.

I first arrived at the Coxcoapan on February 1, 1983, with Dick Vogt and John Gerwin. We were walking in to meet John Rappole at the nascent Wood

Figure 20.1. View of the Coxcoapan River valley from above La Península de Morenos, Sierra de Los Tuxtlas, Veracruz. January 8, 1984. Photo by K. Winker.

Thrush study site. Vogt, fully accustomed to the situation, waded straight in to cross over to La Península, the village on the other side. John Gerwin and I tried to keep our feet dry, but we wound up wasting time; there were too many rivulets to cross on the way to the study site, and taking off our boots at each crossing was not feasible. Rappole and his group used chest waders for their commute. At the end of a long day of walking in wet boots, I wished I had waders too.

I returned to the Coxcoapan with John Rappole and Jacinto Hernandez that fall (September 1983). John and I had driven straight through from Kingsville, Texas, leaving in the afternoon of the day before and stopping in Xalapa that morning for Jacinto. After we had been jouncing down the uneven Mexican highways in the Blazer for the better part of twenty-four hours, the calmly flowing river looked very good. We had just jounced for a long final hour on what was essentially a horse track back into the Ejido de La Península de Morenos, a small village lying across the river. John Rappole and Mario Ramos had established a base here the year before: they had pulled in a small trailer that was to be a home for a number of young biologists for many months over the next three years.

Upon our arrival we went straight to the river and splashed cold water over our heads before beginning to get our small home on the riverside in order. When our junk was put away, we went up to the study site to clean trails and net lanes. This site was in primary rain forest understory, with forty-eight nets set fifty meters apart on a grid of 6 × 8 nets that John and Mario had set up the previous November. I was not accustomed to working in lowland montane rain forest, and I found it all very strange. The slopes were slippery, the plant spines sharp, and the bird sounds exotic. Next day we began opening nets to get the kinks out of the daily routine before John had to head back up to Texas. The first bird I caught was a Blue-crowned Motmot (*Momotus momota*)—quite a bird for my first Neotropical resident in the hand. As seems to happen frequently when in the field, we kept on happily working until it was suddenly surprisingly dark, then we stubbed our toes on the rocks during the long hike back to the trailer with the single flashlight we'd had the foresight to bring along.

A Rope Bridge

When I knew where all forty-eight nets were located, we next worked on a method of crossing the river. With rain, it often became uncrossable. Living on one side of it and working on the other required some means of crossing. John and Mario had put up a rope bridge the year before, but an eight-day rainy spell before we arrived had taken that bridge out as the river rose to unprecedented heights. Putting it back again was not overly difficult. The apparatus was simple: two ropes were strung tightly between two strong trees on either bank, each rope with a high and a low end, and the two ropes forming an "X" over the river. On each rope hung a pulley. Use of the bridge involved climbing a crude ladder we had made on each tree, pulling the pulley back up to your side with a light rope attached to it for that purpose, putting on a harness, clipping the harness to the pulley, and stepping off for a quick, wild ride over the raging torrent. When it worked, which was most of the time, it was rather fun. We used it only when the river presented a problem in crossing because of its depth, but that was fairly often that year.

When we had gotten the ropes strung and tightened, John took a slow ride across and almost bounced on some of the rocks on the far bank. Jacinto laughed uproariously, and shouted over the roar of the river, "*¡Viva la biología!*" We oiled up the pulleys and tightened the ropes; subsequent rides were faster and safer.

The harness was a crude, crotch-crimping affair that we carried with us to have it available when needed. When hanging in that thing with a full pack on your back you were glad that the ride was short. Later that season, when the river had again risen to roaring heights, I had to take the bridge one morning after having been able to walk each day for a couple of weeks. As I hooked up

Figure 20.2. John Rappole crossing the Coxcoapan River using the harness and pulley on the rope bridge, La Península de Morenos, Sierra de Los Tuxtlas, Veracruz, late 1983. Photo by K. Winker.

to the pulley I vaguely noticed that some kids had tied a stick to it to use it, probably in play. It was rigged so that you could sit on it. I just let it dangle and went about my business. But two-thirds of the way across I came to a dead stop with a dull twang and an extra-good harness crimping. And I learned that to fasten their stick they had used more than ten feet of the light pullback rope on the pulley, leaving me an adequately helpless distance from my longed-for destination. My pack was full and made me top heavy, so I had to hold myself up with both hands to remain upright. As gravity kept relentlessly trying to hang me upside down from my tightly crimped crotch and the river roared thunderously a few feet below me, I gave some thought to how I might get out of this mess. My pocket knife was a difficult stretch behind me in a pocket of my pack, preventing its being regularly soaked in my pocket—but in this instance not very useful. And my arms were getting tired trying to ease the crimp and keep me right-side up. What an odd predicament. Fortunately for me, gravity caused the stick and its strange, looping knots to give up before I did, and its slipping gave me enough additional distance to get my feet on a springy root sticking far out from the bank. This little additional help enabled me to unclip from the pulley and hand-over-hand it the short remaining distance to the far bank. The rope bridge washed away again before the next season.

The River Bites Back

On December 17, 1983, it rained buckets. We had several things that needed doing, and netting was not likely to be possible, so I went into town for supplies and John Rappole, back down in Los Tuxtlas again, went up to the study site to check bird locations and open nets if the rain stopped. I disliked going into town (still do!), but I was also getting a little tired of having tuna every night for dinner.

In San Andrés Tuxtla I picked up supplies and got the rear window of the Blazer repaired. It was rolled up and down by an electric motor, and as seemed inevitable with such gadgets in their early incarnations, it had ceased functioning in the down position. That repair wound up taking the better part of the day, and it was getting dark when I returned. The "road" back in to the Coxcoapan crosses several small rivers, and they had become rather high with the day's incessant rain: it was the only time that I recall the headlights being doused by the raging, muddy water. I was amazed that the engine did not die and can only imagine that I accidentally kept a steady bow wave going in each of the crossings. The river itself was also very high, and when I got back to the trailer and darkness was upon us, I was surprised that John was not back yet.

He showed up at the door shortly thereafter, looking very wet. He had been tumbled by the river—twice. He was very lucky to have returned uninjured. At that stage the river is a roaring, boulder-grinding bastard.

And it kept on raining, giving us serious trouble in getting up to the study site to check on transmitter-bearing birds on the following days. The only way across the Coxcoapan was our rope bridge, but even after crossing, the water was so high on December 19 that we had difficulty reaching the study site without sustaining bodily damage in the usually small tributaries. Ordinarily, we were able to cross these small streams with waders, but now the streams were ferociously raging little rivers. I used a seven-foot citrus-wood staff for balance (very effective in steep, muddy country), and it was particularly useful in these rocky, rushing streams. Under these conditions our waders were dangerous. They could rapidly fill with water, and I remember taking them off to cut the drag, crossing in my underwear.

When we made it back to the *casita* in the village where we kept our gear, it was still pouring rain, so we gathered up some rope and brought it back up the trail to string across the worst of these tributaries. With the water levels still rising, we did not want to be completely cut off from the study site—or worse, to be dragged down into the grinding maelstrom of the main river in an attempt to cross. And in the pouring rain in the middle of a muddy, raging, grinding torrent this seemed highly likely. Once the ropes were up, the danger of being swept away was much lower, and the downpour continued unabated. We knew we would be using those ropes for some time to come. We were finished and heading back to the trailer for some hot food when a man and his son showed up on the opposite bank looking very skeptical about trying to cross. From their gear it was clear that they had been out checking and retrieving their *camarone* (prawn) traps, but it was also clear that the boy could not make it across this stretch of water. He was simply too small. The fear in his face was plain to see, and his father wisely decided not to push it; I have no idea how else they would have gotten home.

There is an advantage to being large, and hand-over-handing it across this wild water using the rope was not very difficult for me, particularly when I did not fight it in the channel, letting the bottom go and just keeping a hold on the rope. So, stripping down to my underwear again, I went back across and, shouting to be heard and understood over the noise of the water, got the kid to climb on my back. My return was more rapid, because young Pedro was practically strangling me with his arms locked around my neck.

The river reached out again a few years later: my turn came on November 11, 1986. John Rappole, Ben Robles, John Klicka, and I were down setting up a new site at the Estación de Biología Tropical of the Instituto de Biología, Universidad Nacional Autónoma de México (UNAM). The idea was that it would be easier to track nonterritorial Wood Thrushes on the flatter terrain of the Volcán San Martin than it was in the rough Sierra de Santa Marta (it was). The season before had driven us ragged running up and down the steep, craggy slopes of the Coxcoapan valley. But we had to go back into La Península to see our old friends, drop off some things for them, and pick up net poles. Unfortunately, we had to do this in a pouring rain (why would we ever think it could be otherwise?). And it had been raining for some time.

Just past Coyame we found that the road was simply gone. We decided to angle in along the little road remaining to the nearby Ejido de López Mateo. We parked the Blazer by a new river that came roaring over a cliff in a thirty-foot chocolate-brown waterfall and cut off the road. Then we began walking in, carrying bundles of clothes and other gear in plastic trash bags. When we thought it was time to cut off the road and head across-country to La Península, we did so. Without a machete, with bags in each arm, and with the afternoon advancing, it was in retrospect something that might better have been done the next day.

The bags were awkward to carry, and getting snagged on vegetation and tearing, they gradually got heavier and heavier as the contents became soaked. Darkness found us in a mixed patch of *selva* (forest) and second growth, struggling under these awkward loads toward the Coxcoapan along the bank of one of its tributaries. And we just kept on going, stumbling among boulders, dropping bags into the water, inadvertently leaving a new pair of Leitz binoculars at one of our rest stops—all in jet-black darkness and rain.

Although Ben got rolled by the river and carried downstream about thirty meters before extracting himself, we got ourselves and our miserable cargo across the swollen river and were greeted enthusiastically by our friends at La Península. Apparently we were the first people foolish enough to cross in at least four days. We enjoyed hot glasses of La Península coffee while catching up on events of the past year. But all too soon we had to pack up and go. We tied our net poles (ten-foot lengths of metal electrical conduit) into bundles of fifteen and began making repeated crossings to ferry them back. The clouds had thinned somewhat, and a strong moon provided some light between rain bouts, which was a welcome change. But the poles were heavy and the river was still raging. After going down in a minor way a couple of times I fell in a fast, deep area and the poles came under with me, dragging me down and downriver. I fought to hang onto the poles, get my head above water and keep it there, get out from under the bundle, and grab rocks to stop myself before I hit the rapids below, but I was not having any luck. Just before I hit the real serious stuff I shoved the poles off and stopped myself. I was only a little banged

Figure 20.3. The rainforest field laboratory at the Wood Thrush (*Hylocichla mustelina*) study site, La Península de Morenos, Sierra de Los Tuxtlas, Veracruz, 1984. Photo by K. Winker.

up, but the poles were gone. We were all soaked and exhausted, but we had hours more fun that night marching back out to the truck and then making the long drive back to the Hotel Playa Escondida, where we eventually arrived at 2:00 a.m.

Ants and Other Biting Creatures

The insects of Los Tuxtlas provided me with no end of education and entertainment—good and bad. Watching gorgeous animals like tarantula hawk wasps and morpho butterflies was fascinating, and occasionally we would have to pick incredible beetles and other flying insects out of the mist nets. But too many insects would come aboard and take samples of us without being invited. I remember thinking at one time that I could probably identify most common species of ants with my eyes closed—by their bites. The soldiers of leaf-cutting ants were particularly remarkable. Their heads and mandibles are huge, and when they bite you there is no mistaking their seriousness: They bite hard and don't let go. You can bat or brush at them, but it does no good. You can pull them off, but the body comes away from the head and the mandibles remain painfully buried in your flesh. Then you pull at the head and it comes away from the mandibles, which you have to ease out individually, like sharp, curved slivers. You quickly learn how to avoid these animals. There is a brilliant, metallic-green flying insect in Los Tuxtlas that would often come and hover just in front of us with its wings beating in a blurred buzz. It moved so fast, though, that I could never tell for sure what it was. I was pretty sure it was a fly—it was the right size and of a color that I knew flies could possess. One day I reached out very fast and grabbed one. *Yow*! I let it go again just as quickly when it instantly gave me a terrific sting. As I scraped the stinger out of my throbbing and rapidly swelling hand, I realized that there are some weird bees.

The little black biting flies that we called no-see-ums were new to me. When first exposed to them I could barely feel them as they bit. My body quickly adapted with this exposure, though; after a while I could feel them quite well, their bites far out of proportion to their minute size. The mosquitoes were easily managed. They were always around in low numbers, but they were the slowest, most elegant-looking mosquitoes I have encountered. Most were a bright metallic blue and had what looked like two "decorative legs" with powdery white tips that arched up over their backs and forward to hover above their heads. Their approach is demure and ladylike, and you needed repellent only if you just flat out didn't want to be disturbed. These were pretty remarkable animals compared with their relatives from the north.

Another new insect phenomenon for me at La Península was the army ant. I first experienced these on our study site after being drawn to a concentrated area of bird activity on and near the forest floor. As these armies move through the forest, every other animal that can move does so to get out of the ants' way. The insects that they put up draw many species of birds, which feed on the escaping horde at the leading edges of the ant army. These ants are ruthless, and their bites are painful (or deadly, if you're small). Occasionally you have to go into the middle of a *marabunta* (army) to get a bird out of a net before they can get to it. Because this takes a little time, you are invariably bitten repeatedly, no matter how hard you stomp your feet. But early on, before becoming attuned to these armies and the bird sounds that mark their presence and movements, I saw what they can do to a bird in a net—they kill it and begin to take it to pieces. These are serious little carnivores.

One night in late November 1983, Jacinto and I were peacefully sleeping in the trailer when I was jolted awake just before 4:00 a.m. by hundreds of ants crawling over me and biting the hell out of me. I was asleep one moment and only vaguely aware of something odd, and it seemed that the next moment a hundred bites were delivered simultaneously. I felt as if I came fully awake in midair two feet above my bunk with arms flailing, beating the little biters off in pitch darkness. When I thought I had gotten most of them off, I found my flashlight and shone it on my bunk, where I saw *hundreds* of ants.

As I waved the light around, I realized that the whole end of the trailer, from floor to ceiling, was absolutely covered with them. I could not figure out what I had done to disturb them, but I grabbed a can of insecticide and proceeded to fumigate the area. I stepped out of the trailer to let the fumes die down, but in less than three seconds my lower legs were covered with hundreds more ants, and they all seemed to be biting. I stomped and jumped and skipped over to the top of a rock pile and, after clearing my legs and feet, used my flashlight to pan the area. There were *millions* of army ants swarming around, over, and through the trailer. They seemed only to have been slowed by the trailer walls, so I had been awakened when the exterior had already been completely surrounded. What a way to wake up.

Jacinto had awakened with my furious activity, and he was laughing at my problems with the ants. But after I cleared out he found his flashlight and began scanning. Then spraying. Then giving me a progress report every five seconds: "*¡Muchas hormigas!*" . . . "*¡Muchas hormigas!*" He did not abandon his bunk until the floor was covered and they were on their way up to get him. Then he joined me on the rock pile. We thought about trying to sleep in the truck, but it was inaccessible, so we stood waiting outside the ants' perimeter, monitoring their progress for about an hour before we felt it was safe to return. Then we mopped up the remaining ants and caught a short nap before a group from La Península came over and woke us up for a ride into town.

We were scheduled to go in that morning to get supplies and to drop Jacinto at the bus station, so we tiredly went about it. But we had not driven more than a hundred meters before I slammed on the brakes and leaped out the door, tearing my pants off and beating myself furiously from the waist down. I had not shaken out my pants before putting them on. Not only were my pants full of ants, but they had lain quietly until the signal was given to all bite me at once. I was amazed at this ant behavior. Six faces pressed up against the fogged glass of the Blazer looking astonished at the behavior of this really bizarre gringo leaping about on the lonely road with his pants around his ankles. Jacinto was laughing so hard he was practically crying, and the rest of the truckload joined him when I climbed back in and just said lamely, "Hormigas," before driving on.

A fair number of the birds we caught would bite for all they were worth, but it was generally only the bites of the occasional bat or the claws of the rare *Micrastur* forest-falcon that we had to be careful about. We did not catch them often. The bite that really surprised me was that of the Collared Aracari

Figure 20.4. Jacinto Hernández with a *sorda* (*Bothrops atrox*) that he killed on the La Península study site while checking mist nets, Sierra de Los Tuxtlas, Veracruz, October 22, 1983. Photo by K. Winker.

(*Pteroglossus torquatus*). Who would have guessed at the viciousness of these small toucans and at the amazing amount of pressure that they can bring to bear at the end of that long bill when they have their mandibles sunk into a wide-eyed biologist?

One animal of La Península that did *not* bite me was the fer-de-lance, or *sorda,* as it is known locally—*Bothrops atrox* to scientists. This very poisonous snake was universally feared by the residents of La Península. In the two years before the Wood Thrush project began, two members of the village had been killed by the bite of the *sorda*, and Mario Ramos had probably saved another person with the antivenin we carried in our packs. The *sorda* was not uncommon in the area; we ran across them occasionally going to and from the site and on net checks. We usually killed them when we found them to keep down the risk of being bitten on a subsequent encounter. This may not sound very conservation oriented, but it was prudent: we were working in a limited section of forest in a remote location, repeatedly going over the same trails. And with our sense of familiarity for these trails, we did not always pay a great deal of attention to where we stepped. Because we were many hours' drive from any medical attention besides our antivenin kits, a snakebite would have been a serious event; fortunately, nobody in our parties ever received one.

Jacinto killed a nice five-footer one day in October 1983, and it was the first chance I had had to try the meat. I had heard that people in the western United States enjoy rattlesnake, and after skinning this animal I was impressed by the quality of the fine, white meat. I kept a foot and a half of it for dinner—the first fresh meat we had had in more than three weeks. Only it wasn't to be "we."

When I asked him how much he wanted, Jacinto looked at me oddly and said none. That night, as I prepared the meat with salt, pepper, lemon juice, and garlic, Jacinto was looking at me very strangely. It sure smelled good. I don't know whether he thought I was pulling his leg or what, but as I sat down at the small table and picked up my fork he could contain himself no longer and finally made a very serious, questioning statement: "You're not going to die, right?"

Wow. I had had no idea why he'd been looking at me so strangely, but suddenly I realized that to him my snack was a deadly serious thing. He must have wondered whether I was nuts. As I tore into the feast to learn how tasty their bodies were, I explained to Jacinto how pit viper venom was produced and delivered in and by the head. He was delighted to find me still alive and well the next morning, and gleefully told anyone in the village who would listen the whole crazy story, showing them some of the cleaned bones for proof. I think they pretty much all thought we were crazy, anyway; this was just further proof. The next year I learned that to some in the village, we were not so much *biólogos* as *bió-locos*.

Micrastur ruficollis

The Barred Forest-Falcon (*Micrastur ruficollis*) is a small, rapacious-looking rain forest dweller. My first encounter with one was in a mist net, where it had become entangled while killing and attempting to eat two small birds that had been captured earlier—snacks delivered by biologists. The bird was unapologetic; it looked at me fiercely and sank its claws into my hands as I tried to free it from the net. I did not have a band that would fit it, so I carefully squared off the tips of the outer three rectrices with my knife against a tree trunk so that we would be able to recognize the bird as a recapture if we caught it again that season. Upon release, it flew off unperturbed. At the time, the nest and eggs of the species had yet to be described.

This species was a rather rare capture at the La Península study site; we caught only seven in several years of netting. Curious about their movements during the nonbreeding season, I put a radio transmitter on the next one captured (January 6, 1984), a male. I did not have a fresh transmitter at the field site, so I had to rush back to the trailer for one—half an hour each way, running down boulder-strewn trails and across the Coxcoapan River. Fortunately, I returned with all three of the currently functioning transmitters, for I wound up putting transmitters onto two Wood Thrushes as well. The two thrushes were floaters (nonterritorial individuals), and it required extra effort to keep track of them—including repeated trips (sans pants and boots) across the river. Because the *Micrastur* was so shy (I never could get a look at him), I decided to take it easy on him and let him get used to me for a few days, and so located him only once a day. This was a mistake, for the transmitter failed just a few days later; this was depressing. I wished I had pushed the bird and learned more, and I thought my chances of capturing another were poor. For good or ill, I was wrong.

That whole season was probably the wettest one I endured in Los Tuxtlas. One *norte* after another dumped cold rain almost continuously, making fieldwork extremely difficult. Also, I was alone during much of the season, and it was difficult even under the best of conditions to run mist nets and track transmitter-bearing birds. My journal captures some of the prevailing conditions. "29 December 1983: The 25th was such a miserable day that I officially moved Christmas up to the first day with decent weather. It was colder that day than I've ever felt it here, and on top of that it rained and rained all day." I spent the whole day shivering inside the trailer with the lamp and stove on for warmth, wearing my only dry clothes—underwear, socks, and a heavy wool shirt. I think I have felt more miserably cold only one other time, years later and also in Los Tuxtlas, but that time there were others around with whom to laugh about it.

My notes from this period bear little snippets of Tuxtlas wisdom: "If it rains for less than three days it's just a shower," and "15 minutes is one *hell* of a long time when you're standing on a ridge in the clouds, soaking wet, with a chill wind blowing and the rain a-falling." The last observation was made while tracking the next *Micrastur ruficollis*, which I was lucky enough to capture shortly after the transmitter on the first went dead, and which I was smart enough to track hard. I began trying to get a reading on him every two hours, but found that his movement rate was high enough that I could not get any other work done anyway, and so I began following him and taking readings every fifteen minutes. I quickly learned that I could not get closer than about fifty meters without causing him to move (learned from the first bird also), so I plotted his position through triangulation, moving about through the forest in oblique directions, measuring and mapping new reference points when off the main study site, which was frequently. The main site was gridded with location-specific flagging. Keeping abreast of his often rapid movements on topographically challenging, muddy, densely forested, and trackless mountain slopes in the pouring rain posed both mental and physical challenges. Our radio equipment was not up to the challenge, and my own abilities were pushed to the limit.

On January 20, while off the site and heading across some particularly rough terrain for a new fix on the bird, I slipped on the rim of a steep, muddy arroyo slope and tumbled and slid twenty or twenty-five feet. Both the antenna and the receiver were broken, and I knew I was lucky not to have broken something myself, for I was alone in the field and a long way from any of the usual trails on the study site. After trying to use the damaged equipment a little longer, I hobbled home to make repairs.

The journal says it all: "22 January 1984. I was pretty sore when I got up yesterday. I neglected to mention on the 20th that I have several *chocho* spines in me. One made its clever way into the cartilage and synovial fluid of my left little finger knuckle. Bending it is an act of stupidity, bravery, or masochism. Others are in my feet, and still others are in my right hand and head.

Despite being sore from the fall, I tried to locate the bird on its roosts before dawn. On the morning of the 23rd I arose at 4:00 a.m. and set out by flashlight for the study site, trotting down the familiar trail with my pack on my back. My notes are sketchy on the actual event, but I remember feeling as though someone had used a baseball bat to hit a home run off my head. One second I was jogging down a dark jungle trail in the rain, and the next moment I was weakly wriggling on my back on the muddy ground, still in my pack, with pieces of light falling gradually into place. The kaleidoscopic lights slowly became mostly dark, except for one part of my vision, which, upon my groaning and rolling over a little, became my flashlight, lying on the ground a little farther down the trail. When I finally felt able to get out of my pack, stagger to my feet, and pick up the flashlight, I rediscovered a *Cecropia* tree trunk that had recently blown across the trail to lie at exactly head height.

I did locate the bird's roost site that morning—and the next. But three days

Figure 20.5. Kevin Winker standing beside a felled tree in a corn field cleared for planting near La Península de Morenos, Sierra de Los Tuxtlas, Veracruz, March 1985. Photo by K. Winker.

later the entire upper front right part of my head still hurt terribly, with a steady pressure seeming to arise from inside my skull. I was sleeping fourteen hours a night and yet was still very tired. In retrospect, I suppose I had had a concussion, but at the time I just wished it would go away. On the 25th I hobbled up the hill to do battle again before dawn and found that the bird had used the same roost site as the night before and had been able to preen the transmitter away from its skin. We used eyelash adhesive to glue the transmitters onto the birds' backs, and this species proved too strong for this method of transmitter attachment. I was not nearly as depressed by the loss of this transmitter as I had been with the last. This bird had proven quite a trial.

The *Chocho*

Chocho is *Astrocaryum mexicanum*, a common understory palm in the undisturbed rain forests of Los Tuxtlas. This plant is remarkably vicious. Its trunk is encircled with densely bristling swordlike daggers 2–4 cm in length. These weapons are sharp and brittle, penetrating deeply and breaking off easily when bent by impaled flesh. The trunk's blades are the worst, but the leaf stems and fruits also bear spines—rounder, but just as brittle. The frequency of *chochos* in the rain forest understory in Los Tuxtlas rapidly trains one to adopt a hands-at-your-sides policy of walking and falling. The trunks are usually no more than about 5–6 cm in diameter without the spines, making them look peripherally like good saplings to grab when you are falling. It only takes a couple of *chocho* grabs before you automatically take the fall instead. I have both performed and witnessed some marvelous falls as a consequence. Bruises, bumps, and sorely twisted limbs are preferable to embedded *chocho* spines; the wounds always become infected. Even when you treat it with respect, however, the *chocho* will get you. Many times I have used the edge of a machete to steady my balance against a peripherally seen understory treeling as I walked a forest slope, only to curse as a lightly tapped *chocho* dropped its spine-laden fruits on my head.

The plant is not universally hated, however. The little rain forest squirrel *Sciurus deppei* regularly climbs the palms and feeds on the fruits, although how its paws avoid the infections of even the smallest prick of those spines mystifies me. Local people often harvest the flowers before the pods burst (yes, even the pods are densely spine-covered). How? Most of the harvesters I saw cut the whole tree down rather than use a tool to reach up and cut only the emerging blooms. This low-quality forest food is spineless, but it is rather bitter and bland, requiring cooking with some real food (like eggs) to be palatable, unless one is starving.

The Garbage Scow

During our remote fieldwork in Los Tuxtlas a vehicle was a critical piece of the operation, linking us to the outside world for supplies and occasional small airplane flights to look for missing Wood Thrush transmitters. The World Wildlife Fund/Texas A&I, Wood-Thrush-dedicated Chevy Blazer was that vehicle, but its performance and personality seemed to be cursed. I became a slave to the Blazer during my first season with the Wood Thrush project in the fall of 1983. At first, I was amazed at how deep a stream it could successfully cross. But its less respectable qualities, which accumulated rapidly, came to dominate my views. One day that season we promised to take some of the people from La Península into town. Apparently, however, our promise was also extended to several *pigs*. John Rappole and I were incredulous that anyone would have expected that a promise to haul people included pigs, but our Spanish was not good enough for us to be sure exactly what had been promised. The circus involved in getting several semi-wild pigs loaded into the vehicle was quite a spectacle, and I'll never forget Jacinto riding with his arm at the ready to fend off the very unhappy pigs riding behind him during the rough two-hour journey to town. As we rode, the pigs' digestive tracts continued to function perfectly, and the smell was terrible. To my nose, the vehicle never lost this smell, the antithesis of the new car smell, despite severe cleanings and plenty of new smells to overlay the old aromas during the next four years that I was associated with the vehicle.

We christened the Blazer the Garbage Scow during the winter of 1984–85, when each trip to town began by loading up our garbage to haul it out to the dump between Catemaco and San Andrés Tuxtla. We went to town only about once every two weeks; thus again it was an aromatic journey. These trips were generally made on days when it was too rainy to open mist nets, so the streams we had to cross to get out to the main road were generally pretty deep. We would just barely gurgle our stinking way out each time. It was always a pleasure to drop the garbage and drive fast on a real road with the windows rolled down.

During this season we had engine problems. One rainy morning in January we had to go into town, but the cursed vehicle would not start. I spent over an hour under the hood tinkering away until I finally located the problem. The carburetor had been reduced to the rudest of instruments by the tinkering of past mechanics—there was more stuff *un*hooked from it than there was hooked to it. I was finally able get it started by dumping relatively large quantities of gas directly down the beast's throat, a procedure that had to be repeated on subsequent trips that season. Once Steve Stucker was pouring gas down its throat while I was trying to start it, when it backfired and flames erupted from under the hood. Steve's alarmed "Whoop!" and rapid departure created a flaming spectacle as the remaining gasoline was spread burning in one direction while Steve ran in another. Unfortunately, this was not the only time the Blazer did just that.

On January 13, 1986, on a cold, wet night, John Rappole and I were heading back from San Andrés Tuxtla to El Bastonal in the Garbage Scow when we smelled a bad smell—worse than usual—and it seemed to be coming from us.

After a look in the side mirrors, John said something remarkably calm: "We're on fire."

In leaping out to check, I saw a merry blaze in the right rear wheel well. We had stopped on the side of the road leading to Catemaco from Highway 180, and there was a Pemex gas station nearby; I ran toward it for something to put out the fire, but before I got there a man came running toward me with a bucket of water. Meanwhile, John had grabbed a wet, muddy pair of pants he had been wearing earlier in the day, and by swinging them up behind the tire he had been able to put out the fire. When I returned, he was wrapping the pants up in there to keep things smothered. We had a lot of bad-smelling smoke and a quickly gathering crowd of people.

As we pulled out the jack and the lug wrench to remove the tire to see what was wrong, one helpful fellow took his flashlight and crawled in there far enough to get a good look at what might have caused the problem. He emerged with an expression of utter incredulity. Maintaining this face of amazed disbelief, he explained to the onlookers that the problem was that there was a pair of *pants* wrapped around the axle. A pair of *pants*! His facial expression and short speech said very eloquently that he had never been exposed to such absolute stupidity. Everyone knows that pants aren't supposed to be wrapped around axles—except two gringos, apparently. As emissaries from the north we failed that night, and the reputation of gringo intellectual capacity, perhaps never very high, took a steep dive in Catemaco.

By the time we had gotten the tire off and the axle had been cooled down with the water, the crowd had dispersed. With the tire briefly back on, we drove a short distance to a nearby motel to spend the night. Next morning we learned that the wheel bearing had gone out, causing the brakes to rub, causing the hub area to heat up and ignite the lubrication. We later discovered that the axle had also been irreparably damaged. This breakdown took literally weeks to fix because of mechanical mixups and the need for parts from the United States. In the meantime, our transportation became Mario Ramos's Datsun sedan, on loan from INIREB (Instituto Nacional de Investigaciones sobre Recursos Bioticos) until the Garbage Scow was fixed.

When parts from the north were required, it involved some interesting telephone conversations with people back in Texas—often including John's wife Bonnie. During these conversations we would stand there holding a part, trying to describe it effectively so that the proper piece could be purchased up there, driven to the border, and put on a bus to San Andrés Tuxtla. Sometimes, when the wrong part arrived a week or so later, we would learn that the conversation had not been effective. Perhaps it is not surprising that something occasionally got lost in translation along the communication chain of Mexican mechanic to gringo field biologist to helpful person in Texas to a parts store clerk in Kingsville. Amazingly, even complex repairs were usually accomplished within a week. This particular one proved more difficult parts-wise, but at least we had Mario's car as a substitute.

Besides its tendency to burst into flame, the Garbage Scow would also occasionally lose its brakes. This tended to happen on mountain roads. The first time it happened to me, I was heading back to Texas alone on January 31, 1984. I had detoured to drop some specimens and things off at INIREB in Xalapa and was on my way out of town, headed north. What I now remember as quite a hair-raising trip was only briefly recorded in my journal while I watched an ingenious mechanic in Tlapocoyan making repairs: "The funny noise in the front left wheel turned out to be the bearings—as I suspected. The brakes went out on the mountain road between here and Perote. One exciting ride."

My next bout with the Scow's brakes came almost three years later, when John Klicka arrived from the Playa Escondida at the Estación de Biología one morning in a foul mood. I had spent the night at the study site to keep a radio eye on transmitter-bearing Wood Thrushes, to see where they roosted and learn whether the relatively long distance movements made by nonterritorial birds occurred during the night. By doing so I had missed an interesting ride down the long slope to, and past, the station; it was on this slope that the brakes had given out for John.

I had to take the beast brake-free into San Andrés Tuxtla, a journey of more than passing excitement and one near accident. At the mechanic's, Escalera's, it was quickly determined that the front brakes had again failed due to lost bearings, but this time the entire hub had to be replaced. Not only that, but since the last bout with this problem, Mexico had gone through an economic crisis, and Mexican mechanics could not afford to stock parts for many American vehicles: we needed more parts from Texas. El Maestro's son Enrique dismantled the front brakes, stopped the brake fluid flow to them, then fixed the rear brakes so that they worked. As he did this, I remembered that they also had not been working when the brakes went out coming down from Xalapa three years before. As I drove out and tried them, I thought about how nice it was to have them back from the dead. They didn't last long.

A week later we drove up into the yard of the Hotel Playa Escondida with passengers, and when the time came to stop, all the stomping in the world had no effect. Nor did shutting off the engine. This motel is at the top of a cliff, and we were on a downhill slope with only a few hopelessly small trees and a large LP gas tank between us and the edge. We were not going very fast, but the vehicle had all the momentum needed for things to get ugly. Rather than go into or through the tank or into the restaurant, I turned the key back on and made a hard left, ninety degrees and dead-on into a big concrete pillar supporting the roof of a side building. The column just leaned a little, the front bumper was dented a bit, and everyone was very quiet. Old Pepe, the custodian and one of our passengers, had been alarmed about the possibility of our meeting that LP tank and seemed genuinely relieved that instead we had smashed into one of his buildings.

Of course this required another brake-free trip to Escalera's in San Andrés Tuxtla, and this time I wound up detouring into a pasture to avoid rear-ending someone. It seemed as if the Garbage Scow was taking revenge on us. John Klicka and I were glad we were soon returning to the north and leaving the vehicle behind for John Rappole and Dave Delehanty to continue with the Wood Thrush work. It was with no regrets that I bid farewell to the Garbage Scow—and I never saw it again. About a month later, with Dave Delehanty at the helm, the beast gave out completely and had to be towed hundreds of miles across the border and back to Kingsville. It was not yet destined to become scrap, however. Years later, the still-living Garbage Scow was driven to Belize to serve John Rappole, Courtney Conway, and Bill McShea on a study of migrants there. John rechristened the beast Louise in a vain effort to get it off to a new start in a new land; but with the Scow flattery had long ago proven useless. I heard that one day the cantankerous beast just burned up. I wish I'd been there to toss fuel on the flames.

Food of the Gods

When first meeting John Rappole at the La Península study site in February 1983 with John Gerwin and Dick Vogt, I had seen the little trailer—that of the army ant experience related earlier—on the Coxcoapan River at the Ejido de La Península. At the time, I had no idea that within months this same trailer would become my home. John and Mario had towed it there when setting up the Wood Thrush study site. On our way back from Mexico in February 1983, John Gerwin and I had stopped in to visit John Rappole at Texas A&I University in Kingsville (now Texas A&M–Kingsville). Back at the University of Minnesota, Mario Ramos was on temporary leave from INIREB, finishing up his dissertation, and he had told me that he and John were looking for good field assistants for that coming fall season. It sounded like fun to me, so in September I drove down from Minnesota to help John get things set up for the field season, and I become a part of the effort in October.

We roared down in the Blazer from Kingsville to La Península (via Xalapa to pick up Jacinto, as noted) in one long drive. One of my memories of that whirlwind drive involves going through Tampico when the Río Pánuco was in flood. The high bridge over the river was not yet completed, but there was a roundabout way to avoid the ferry, which could stop us for hours in a line to get aboard it. On that circuitous lowland route we drove through flooded barrios where the odor of human waste was like a fetid slap. I remember switching drivers on a crystal-clear dawn in the middle of a long and deserted piece of the coastal Highway 180. Mexico is a beautiful country. This was the first of a number of fast drives between Kingsville and La Península, but it is still the most memorable.

At the end of this long drive was the little trailer and the clear Coxcoapan. The cold, clear water felt so refreshing, first just splashed on the face, and later, after dark, for a good bath. Inside, the trailer was about six feet high, six feet wide, and thirteen long. For one person it was pretty good. For three it was fine. But for five, which is how many occupied it in early 1985, it was very cozy. More than twenty years later, I still know the inside of that trailer as though I moved out of it yesterday. Had we not been so geared toward fieldwork each day, eating and sleeping in such a small space might have become annoying. Being cooped up inside for more than a day by heavy rain did build up some pressures, usually forcing us out no matter what the weather. But it did feel like home.

Working long days in the field in the tropics means that at least some of that work will be done in the dark. We quickly learned to carry a raincoat and a flashlight every day. The darkness of Los Tuxtlas can swallow you up completely. With no urban lights and frequent total cloudiness, nights in Los Tuxtlas can be as black as black can be. Going out to the Great Outdoor Restroom on cloudy nights brought this darkness home to us. Without a flashlight you could not go far at all, and it was so dark that your sense of balance was quickly lost. Once a flashlight was turned off, your pupils would dilate to their maximum, and then the very soft light of phosphorescent fungi in the forest would appear. You could not do much by the light of these fungi, but the light they cast was at once eerie and reassuring.

Our field diet was often unique, as much from what we had readily available to cook as from our impatience and lack of time for elaborate cooking when we were hungry at the end of long field days. Tuna and refried beans with hot dog chunks mixed in was an early delicacy, but actual hot dogs were not common fare because bread went moldy too quickly to eat anything on a roll or bun. To make the chemically treated river water taste better, we would mix up some sort of fruit-flavored drink that José Luís Alcántara dubbed "ambrosia." Of course, with Nectar of the Gods we had to eat Food of the Gods, and so by default, anything we concocted that tasted good was considered just that. Tuna and refried beans with chiles was one Food of the Gods, particularly when eaten with the world-class tortillas that Rosa Mozo in La Península made for us every day.

Jacinto Hernández had a taste for hot food that I have rarely seen excelled. I like chiles, but Jacinto beat anyone I'd seen. He would first put a small pan over the gas flame with a little puddle of cooking oil in the bottom, then he would finely chop several *chile piquin* and some onions. When the oil was literally smoking, he would add the chopped chiles and onions and then stand over the intense steam that this generated and inhale deeply. Just being in the same

Figure 20.6. Hunter holding a fawn (*Mazama americana*) that his dog had killed, La Península study site, Sierra de Los Tuxtlas, Veracruz, 1984. Photo by K. Winker.

closed space with this did me in—my eyes watered and I could hardly breathe. After the first couple of times I asked him to tell me when he was about to work his magic so that I could leave the trailer until the air had cleared.

We usually did not have exquisite cuisine in Los Tuxtlas, although as Dave Delehanty said, hunger makes the best sauce. To spice our food we mostly used pickled jalapeños in cans, and we preferred to open the cans from the bottom so that we could eat the pickled carrot slices first. Probably the best of all, though, were canned chilpotles in an *adobo* sauce. The chilpotle is a true Food of the Gods. Some of the world's best were raised nearby in a drier area of Los Tuxtlas, and a Veracruz cannery made exquisite canned chilpotles in a rich, red, smoky sauce. Chilpotles are mature jalapeño chiles dried with the aid of a smoky fire—red because they are mature (unlike the popular, less mature commercial jalapeño, which is green). Their flavor is out of this world. I cannot imagine being without them, and I buy them dried by the kilo every time I go to Mexico. The name is of Native American origin, and in going from Nahuatl to Spanish and then to English, it has become chipotle, now becoming a favored ingredient in some cuisines of the United States.

Because going to town cost us a whole day in field time, we would go about once every two weeks when the weather made working difficult or impossible. And after two weeks our food stocks were usually getting pretty low. One evening the whole group ganged up on me to say that we needed to go into town the next day for food. I showed them that we had both crackers *and* canned sardines, and that we could therefore stave off a trip to town for at least one more day. I don't remember whether the requisite rain came to drive us to town the proper way, but I do remember that my decision was not popular. Others did not seem to enjoy crackers and sardines as much as I did.

An Expedition to Santa Marta

During the winter of 1984–85, my second field season with the Wood Thrush project and my third in Los Tuxtlas, John Rappole and Mario Ramos organized an endangered species survey into the Santa Marta wilderness. Steve Stucker and I had been down since mid-December 1984 working at the La Península site with Mara Neri Fajardo and José Luís Alcántara. John and Mario let Steve and me join their group; I was interested not only in the more remote areas of Los Tuxtlas but also in Wood Thrushes at higher elevations. The "Minnesota group" (Dwain Warner, Mario Ramos, and John Rappole) had hypothesized that the increase in lowland Wood Thrushes during *nortes* was a consequence of highland birds seeking refuge in the lowlands. It made sense: cloud cover would descend during *nortes*, and it got wetter even at slightly higher elevations. And highland species would occur in the lowlands during *nortes*, an even better indication that conditions were worse at higher elevations. Here was an opportunity to see whether this scenario was being played out on the other end.

There was a lot of scrambling to get everything and everyone ready for the trip, and in the rush there was some miscommunication about how much of a stock of rice and beans to buy. Unfortunately for all of us, the error was not apparent until much later. We squeezed our gear and all nine people into two vehicles (the Blazer and Mario's Datsun), and we drove from Catemaco to the "other side"—an uncomfortable ride of about four hours around the Tuxtlas to the drier side of the mountains. We stopped for the night at our destination,

Magallanes (settled in 1960), where the townspeople let us stay in the schoolhouse. I remember resoundingly bashing my head on the low doorframe and ringing the entire building like a big wooden bell. It can be hard being tall. On March 4 we packed our gear on our backs and on the backs of three horses we had hired. The horses could only go to Guadalupe Victoria; from there on it was up to human power. We repacked, loaded obscenely heavy packs on our backs, and headed out to cross a steep-walled valley. Four hours later we had topped out on the other side, exhausted, but thrilled with the increasingly exciting forest around us. We had crossed the river below on a strangler fig that had fallen across a rocky gorge through which the raging water plunged. When were contemplating that crossing, a pair of spider monkeys (*Ateles geoffroyi*) entertained us as they fed in the trees on the other side. And when we reached the top we were treated to the loud, double-tap "call" of the Guatemalan Ivory-billed Woodpecker (*Campephilus guatemalensis*) striking a dead tree.

We camped on this ridge for the night and the next morning went back to Guadalupe Victoria for the rest of our gear. We stopped at one point to watch spider monkeys and howler monkeys (*Alouatta palliata*) together. I was surprised to see the two species in the same tree and even more surprised to watch a spider monkey walk right by a howler monkey—they practically brushed fur—with absolutely no response from the howler. Neither seemed to mind the other's proximity. These animals were almost entirely absent from La Península (probably because they were at least occasionally hunted), and so were fascinating to us. Alejandro, whom we had hired in Guadalupe Victoria to guide and assist our efforts, told us that they used these *changos* for *camarone* bait in their freshwater prawn traps.

Rather than going back to Guadalupe Victoria with us, John Rappole and Eduardo Iñigo had scouted ahead for a base camp at least one kilometer into the *selva*. From the previous night's ridge camp this proved not too great a distance. But because it was getting late in the afternoon and many of the group were tired, only half of us elected to make a run for the new camp and get set up there before dark. It was a pleasant trip. We encountered several spider monkeys along the way, and at one point there was a pile of feathers beside the trail from a Great Curassow (*Crax rubra*) that a hunter had cleaned. We also heard for the first time the fantastic song of the Pheasant Cuckoo (*Dromococcyx phasianellus*). The ridgetop camp that John and Eduardo had chosen was a good jumping-off point for work in several directions. It lacked running water—the nearest was a seven-minute walk away—but the steepness of the terrain did not provide both flat places for tents and running water together. Once established, our camp took up all of the flat and flattish places on what was just a slight widening of a sharp and rocky ridge in the forest.

The next day, Steve Stucker and I went down into the next valley to find a site for setting up a net grid. This valley wall was incredibly steep, and it took us an hour to get down to the bottom. The terrain there was very rugged also. We plotted out some points and put up a small equipment tent so we would not have to haul all our gear up and down each day; it was impossible to haul a full load on this slope. It took us almost an hour to climb back up to base camp that evening. It took the rest of the next day to finish marking out a grid and to get eight net lanes cut and the nets set up. We found ourselves being watched by monkeys—an eerie feeling, being under observation. The site itself was a spectacular place. The river was wild and cold, and the forest was full of the giant trees that La Península and the other places we had been lacked. Unfortunately, however, it was more than a little rugged. Our sixteen net points, which were set on a 50 m grid, used up all available land with a slope of less than 45°. There were boulders scattered about that were the size of small houses and a water slide-fall about 40 m high. The visual impact of the site was quite overwhelming, making us feel small and insignificant as we crawled about on our ephemeral business.

By now we had learned of our error in stocking up on provisions for the trip. As I recall, the miscommunication in the scramble to get everything ready in Catemaco had resulted in two kilos each of rice and beans being purchased for everyone for two weeks—rather than some more reasonable amount. As a consequence, after arriving at our remote base camp and assembling a small cooking tent, we had been forced to cut rations down to a small breakfast and about two-thirds of an army cup of hot food at dinner time (the army cups being the metal ones that fit over the bottom half of a one-quart canteen). Having such low rations when doing so much physical work each day had everyone going more slowly and tiring more easily. Food became one of the main topics of discussion around the fire each night, and one night we all went around talking in ecstasy about what favorite dish we were thinking about.

On March 8 Steve and I moved down to our study site to avoid the two-hour round trip climb each day. The weather was not cooperative. We spent much of the day in pouring rain, and unfortunately I had brought all our radio transmitters down the day before and needed a fire to do the soldering required to hook them up and get them running. The transmitters required a light job of soldering to connect the battery before use, and I had been doing this with a red-hot nail held by a pair of pliers. I spent five straight hours working on getting a fire going, because I did not want to have to climb back up just to hook up transmitters. In retrospect, the climb would have been easier, but it kept on looking as if the fire was just about catch. To get dry wood I had to use my machete to cut deeply into the largest pieces of dead wood to get through the deeply soaked exterior and into the drier interior. Eventually the smoldering pile dried enough material to get a blaze going. After hooking up several radios, Steve and I cooked a hot dinner, enjoyed a cheery blaze, and tried to dry some socks before turning in, hoping for less rain the next day.

No luck. Everything was soaked. In fact, I had noticed this on previous climbs down and up: it was simply much wetter down in the valley. I am still not sure how that can happen, apparently based solely on elevation over such a comparatively short distance. But it soon became apparent that the two-hour round-trip climb might be worth it just to get a little drier each night. Each morning I opened the tent, picked up my pile of totally soaked clothing, wrung out each piece to reduce the moisture content gained in the night's rain, then put it on for another day. I remember sitting in a total downpour by a roaring river with a sewing awl, stitching the sole back onto one of my boots. Coupling such conditions with short rations was trying. March is usually drier here.

We got a peek at the sun on the 9th. Steve and I had the nets open and were catching birds, but we were down at the river with our clothes spread on rocks to dry as soon as the sun appeared. It was but a fleeting moment, though, serving only to accentuate the misery of the cold, wet conditions. After a particularly soaking cloudburst later that day, I wrote: "I guess that I can think of several times when I was that wet last year, but then I always had the dry trailer & food to return to. Here it's the wet tent and no food." In that wet tent one morning as it was raining too hard to net, Steve compiled three lists. His "Things to Buy" list probably still has value more than twenty years later. It would be difficult to get more insightful about equipment needs than from the bottom of a steep valley in rain forest in absolute pouring rain at the end of a long stint under such conditions. The second list was "Things to Do," of the type we all make. The third was "What to Eat on the Trip Home," and I can guarantee that there were eight more people in this part of the selva who were at least mentally compiling a similar list.

Our netting at that remote, difficult site was quite interesting. I remember seeing with astonishment the levels of fat deposition that occurred in sedentary species. It brought home to me the importance of feeding strategies in predictable versus unpredictable environments.

Steve and I left the camp below and retreated to the base camp on the night of March 11 when we ran out of food. We had milked our short rations as long as planned. Back up on the ridge that evening we found a roaring fire against which to dry wet feet after a *brimming cupful* of hot food for dinner and before retreating into a dry tent. This was the life!

During our absence John and Mario had set off on an aborted trip to the crater. The weather was so uncooperative that after one night out they had come back to base camp. Not being able to see anything and being cold, wet, and miserable could just as well be accomplished in base camp. The next day John had set off on his own to see whether he could get into the crater of Santa Marta from the first river we had crossed (both rivers were called Suchiapan). But John had not returned that night. When we arrived back up top we learned that Mario and Eduardo had set off downslope to find him—but then he returned from upslope. They never saw him until they too returned to the camp. John had gone upriver until it became impossible to proceed farther, then had begun scaling the north slope toward the ridge. Darkness had caught him in an awkward spot, and he had spent a long night shivering in his raincoat belted to a tree on a steep slope. Somewhere along the way John had slipped; he had been using the machete I had lent him as a staff, and his hand had slipped off its handle and down the blade. The wound to his thumb was substantial, and he had taped his hand closed to keep things stable. No doubt he bears the scar to this day. The machete itself was later lost on a particularly steep slope when a slip caused it to clatter down far below, where retrieval was not considered a good move.

One morning for breakfast I had the last tortilla, something nobody else wanted. It was carpeted with green mold, and even after beating it clean and spreading some peanut butter on it, puffs of mold spores went poofing out with each savory bite. We had had *chocho* flowers as a filler in some meals, but they were bitter, bland, and not as common as at La Península. And we had shot a squirrel (*Sciurus deppei*) and a couple of doves (*Leptotila plumbeiceps* and *Geotrygon carrikeri*—a Tuxtlas endemic) for additional nutriment, but to little gain. Real game was not sufficiently common, presumably because local hunters were able to get eight hundred pesos per kilo of meat from such succulent delicacies as *tepezcuintle* (*Agouti paca*), Great Curassow, and Crested Guan (*Penelope purpurascens*; we did not see a guan). In a region where laborers were paid five hundred pesos per day, this was a good wage for hunting.

Eventually John and Mario sent Alejandro on a trip to Guadalupe Victoria to pick up more beans and rice, and the product of this trip was a godsend to us starving idiots on the ridge. Relative to our previous diet we had so much food that Steve and I fairly raced up the valley wall each evening. With the additional calories, we were able to make it in an incredible twenty-two minutes (unburdened). Being in shape, reasonably nourished, and familiar with a steep and complex trail is a rare and wonderful thing. In the evenings we scouted holes for emerging beetles and tried to nab large, horned males as they emerged for a nocturnal rendezvous with females.

By March 14 the monkeys were becoming annoying. The howlers would howl at the onset of every rainfall, which seemed a legitimate rage against the elements. I too felt like howling each time I was in for a cold soaking. But the spider monkeys barked incessantly, which was highly irritating. John Howe counted three barks per second—a truly unpleasant rate of barking (to human sensibilities). If Steve and I had not been near a roaring river all day we might have become perturbed at their sound. As it was, though, it was only when they were quite close that we could hear them. They did have the extremely annoying habit, however, of dropping feces in our vicinity. I could not tell if it was on purpose, but a few sodden things dropping in your vicinity makes you move in a hurry so as not to learn whether they can improve their aim. Before long the whole study site smelled like a poorly kept zoo.

Our research efforts were not going at their usual pace, mostly because of the weather. And even though we were learning interesting things about a higher-elevation bird community, it was coming at a higher-than-usual cost. "I absolutely abhor clinging to a cliff while measuring a tree. Tripping and slipping over rocks is no treat either," I remarked in my field notes for March 15. Quantifying habitat characteristics by measuring distances to saplings and trees on bad terrain in lousy weather is sufficient reason to question the importance of research on avian ecology, or to question sanity itself. We called this "vegetating," and Steve and I were good at it. But one needs the proper frame of mind and better weather to enjoy it.

I saw a tayra (*Eira barbara*) one day at the edge of a large treefall gap and was impressed with this *viejo del monte*. I had not seen one before in Los Tuxtlas, nor would I again. One evening on the ridge everything became totally still as a roar could be heard approaching us. It sounded like a big wind approaching in the calm, but when it arrived it was an earthquake. Strange to be able to hear its approach. Another night we had a terrible windstorm. The trees thrashed mercilessly, and branches and whole trees could be heard cracking and falling during the night. I don't think I slept a wink, waiting for the next tearing gust to send a large branch or tree through the top of our tent or someone else's; but in the morning everyone was fine, despite the evidence of some big falls in and near our camp.

When the weather improved, we caught a Wood Thrush and put a transmitter on it, and I spent a lot of time over the subsequent days triangulating its position. This bird turned out to be a model of our hypothesis that highland birds rode out *nortes* in the lowlands: it was first caught when the weather cleared up, hung around while the weather was reasonably decent, then disappeared when the weather deteriorated again.

John and Mario succeeded in getting into the crater and found it topographically well isolated. It will be the last stronghold of the forested Tuxtlas. But they found no sign of tapir (*Tapirus bairdii*), jaguar (*Panthera onca*), or Harpy Eagle (*Harpia harpyja*). The local people told us about recent contacts with both tapir and jaguar, but we were not fortunate enough to find sign of either, and any remaining animals would have been very few.

We spent our last night on the ridge sitting around the fire talking in two languages over beans and chicken in foil packets, listening for more calls from Crested and Black-and-white owls (*Lophostrix cristata* and *Ciccaba nigrolineata*), species we had heard on previous nights. On March 20 we left the ridge in gloriously sunny weather. Once out of the forest we found kettle after kettle of Swainson's Hawks (*Buteo swainsonii*) migrating along the coastal thermals with some Broad-winged Hawks (*Buteo platypterus*) mixed in. At Guadalupe Victoria our friends and their horses were ready to help us out to Magallanes, and we made it back there by midafternoon. With everything all packed up anyway, it was a simple decision to load up the vehicles and drive back to Catemaco. Immediately after checking into the Hotel Berthangel, dirty as we were, we all walked down to one of the swanky lakefront restaurants and ordered up a *lot* of food.

El Bastonal

Shortly after returning to the United States from Los Tuxtlas in the spring of 1985, I was watching the news on television when I learned that something on the order of nineteen *federales* had been killed in a shootout during a raid on a small village near Minatitlán, which was a way of positioning anything happening in the eastern Tuxtlas. Los Tuxtlas had a bad reputation as a drug region, although we had never encountered anything suggesting a drug trade. We kept our noses out of other people's business and tried to have good relations with our neighbors. That winter (1985–86) we were going to make a stronger effort to follow floater (nonterritorial) Wood Thrushes, so we set up two sites: one back at La Península in some of the best lowland rain forest remaining in Los Tuxtlas and the other at a higher elevation near El Bastonal, a tiny community that sat high above the upper Coxcoapan River valley. I looked forward to working there, for Los Tuxtlas is known for its endemic forms of highland birds.

This was our most ambitious season. David Delehanty, Douglas Gomez,

Figure 20.7. El Bastonal crew: John Rappole, Jorge Vega, Doug Gomez, Rick Coleman, and Kevin Winker, Sierra de Los Tuxtlas, Veracruz, January 18, 1986. Photo by K. Winker.

Rick Coleman, and Samantha Baab came along and formed the backbone of our effort. With me and Mara Neri Fajardo, who was finishing her professional thesis at UNAM based on her field research at La Península, we had six people, and we set up half the group at La Península and the other half at El Bastonal. Jorge Vega and Sergio Barrios had done their professional theses at El Bastonal several years earlier, and Jorge had accompanied John Rappole to investigate the site before we committed to it. They found things as Jorge remembered them, with the site itself looking good and the pleasant neighbors of El Bastonal willing to let us use a cabin that had been given over to sheep and cattle. Once the manure had been scraped out and the floor washed, it was a quality place to live for the season. We had not expected a metal roof and a cement floor.

The study site at El Bastonal was far below in the valley. Before getting accustomed to the climb, and during the foolish phase of carrying too much gear back and forth, it was a forty-minute commute each way. We trimmed this to twenty-eight minutes each way once things were better established. The birds and the mountains here were wonderful.

But this year was the first when I seemed to spend way too much time keeping things running and too little time in the forest. With two field sites, six people, one vehicle, bad roads, and regular flights to find errant transmitter-bearing birds, I was being run ragged. Between flights I kept up with putting transmitters on birds that the field crews were capturing and also finding (or at least looking thoroughly for) the birds upon which those transmitters were being placed. Because we were focusing on floaters, we had a lot of disappearing transmitters, and I spent long days finding routes to remote peaks from which to "beam" remote valleys. The Yohualtajapan valley, which was over the next row of peaks, was one wild place. And the Sierra de Santa Marta is one rugged range—surely the reason there was still forest there.

Except for the army checkpoints set up at every road intersection and the enthusiastic vehicle and body-frisking searches conducted with comparatively high frequency during this season, things were fairly normal in Los Tuxtlas. At one point a military officer came to visit us to see what we were up to. He was satisfied that we were legitimate, and he was fascinated by the small radio transmitters I showed him and the idea that we glued these to small birds. Other than this heightened policing activity, there was no sign of the restlessness that had caused the heavy gunfight in which so many *federales* had been killed less than a year before. One day our landlord's brother stopped by to visit, and I asked him whether he had heard about this event. "Oh, yes. That was just over there," he said, pointing down the mountain. While I had realized the shootout had been in the eastern Tuxtlas, I had not guessed it would have been so close that someone would just wavingly point to it. That explained the military presence.

The weather up at El Bastonal was different from La Península. It was cooler and wetter, both because of the surrounding clouds (the forest at this elevation just qualifies as cloud forest in Los Tuxtlas) and because rain tended to fall with a higher frequency (though perhaps not with such volume). During a particularly cool period I remember someone commanding, "Close the door! You're letting the clouds in!" But by late February it began to get hot, and we would jump into the river to cool off during the day. There was a particularly nice small pool, a natural jacuzzi where the crystal clear water was heavily churned by a small waterfall. We had a good setup. We were productive and comfortable working in a comparatively remote area.

But I was getting tired of driving to La Península and back to El Bastonal to keep abreast of things, bringing in supplies and mail. The road up to El Bastonal was poor. Someone had begun to establish a mine for barite up past Bastonal; we could hear occasional dynamite blasts as people established the mine and camp, and they had dumped truckloads of fresh dirt along some of the lower stretches of the road, creating a mud circus. One day, rather than do that drive again, I decided to walk to La Península and back along the Coxcoapan. I had been in much of the valley from either end and had climbed most of the peaks along the rim, but it would be good to see the whole valley from the river itself.

I set out early after looking at the topo sheet to be sure I could make it there and back in one day. As usual, I carried too much, and to maximize rock hopping ability and minimize foot chafing, I wore leather boots instead of the usual rubber boots. This proved to be a mistake; half a day of rapid rock hopping can wear raw holes in the tops of one's feet in leather boots. Feeling tired already upon reaching the La Península study site, I did not spend much time with the group there before setting out again to return. On the way back I tried harder to stay on just one side of the river, which meant spending more time in the forest and less time on the riverbank; and that was how I got misplaced. Things seemed to be going fine, if slowly, when I had the feeling that I was not where I thought I was; the river was shrinking too fast. I kept going until I finally had to admit that I was on the wrong river. I knew where I was in general—on a substantial tributary, the mouth of which I had seen on the way down—but by the time I realized this, it was too late to turn back and correct my mistake. On my left were sizable peaks, so a correction back to the real river was not an option either, and it was getting late. I had a great spurt of speed when I realized this, but in my tired condition and with sore feet it did not last long.

The way grew steeper and steeper, and the river smaller and smaller. I began to wonder whether I would be spending the night in the forest. I did not have a jacket, but I did have a lighter, a knife, and a *bolillo*, one of the delicious French-bread-style rolls common in Mexican bakeries. With the increasing steepness, the now quite small river became difficult to follow, and eventually it was fruitless to continue trying. I knew there were cliffs in the area, though, and I was not sure which direction would be best in leaving the water. My notes give the helpful retrospective tip: "The place to leave is before the waterfalls become on the order of spectacular. They get pretty good." The problem was that you had to scale some steep ground to appreciate this. I remember flopping out on the lip of a precipice next to a waterfall near dark after a particularly hair-raising climb and feeling ready to stay there. I accidentally chose the right way to go, though, missing the impossible terrain and stumbling out into a clearing as darkness settled. Exhausted, I found my way back to the shack by starlight.

We pulled out of El Bastonal in the Garbage Scow on March 16, 1986, smoking big hand-rolled Mexican cigars and listening to Credence Clearwater Revival on the bird tape playback unit.

On the Trail of the Nonterritorial Wood Thrush

Micrastur ruficollis may have created an exciting diversion in radio tracking from time to time, but even they could not hold a candle to nonterritorial Wood Thrushes for interest level and unpredictability. Putting a transmitter on a nonterritorial bird was always an interesting proposition: where that individual would be in twenty-four hours' time was impossible to predict. Figuring out what was going on among this behavioral category of birds kept me and a number of other people occupied for two full seasons after I had completed data collection for my master's thesis. As pleasurable as those two seasons were, they remain for me lessons in what was ultimately marginally productive fieldwork, while at the same time providing some of my most poignant memories of Los Tuxtlas.

To determine the extent of the movements of nonterritorials, we netted and banded birds for a while before putting transmitters on those we suspected of being transient. After several years of working in this system we could often predict which birds would turn out to be wanderers, or floaters: an unbanded bird, usually carrying fat, that showed up during or just after a *norte*. In these seasons subsequent transmitter signals usually bore out our predictions. We kept transmitters on a couple of territorial birds as well just to make sure everything was working. On the ground each day we would run nets, and I would try to locate all the transmitters that had been set out, whether we were still receiving them or not. The nets were being run by our capable volunteers, in these seasons Dave Delehanty, Samantha Baab, Mara Neri Fajardo, Rick Coleman, Doug Gomez, and John Klicka. Once every week or two I would go into town and go flying with Moices Estrada to find the lost signals.

The day that might have ended it all was February 22, 1986. That was the year that we ran both La Península and El Bastonal. As usual, we had arisen before dawn at El Bastonal, and I took the Blazer into town for a flight. Moices liked to let the clouds burn off before going up, but the waiting game was fickle; we often finally made it up when their afternoon reformation was well under way. On this day Moices said we needed gas, so we headed for the small airport at Minatitlán. I was falling asleep, but he soon tapped me on the leg and pointed to the fuel gauge. Empty. What fun. I feel bad when my car tank gets near empty, but an *airplane*? Moices was very nervous, and as the airport kept failing to come into view he grew even more nervous. He spent some time on the radio talking with them, but that did not calm him at all. I pretended cool, trying to calm him, but I was getting nervous too. He handed me the manual and asked me to look up the quantity of the fuel reserve. The book didn't even mention a reserve. This really made him fret. I wondered how far below Empty the gauge could go, and I looked at the terrain below, taking no comfort in the fact that there could be no very successful emergency landing in this rough volcanic country. I read the emergency procedures for crash landing but found no comfort there, either. Moices was sweating profusely. There was nothing to do but try to act icily calm in hopes of keeping him together. We make mistakes when we're nervous.

We made it, of course. The errant airport eventually appeared, and we made a direct approach. At the last second the fellow in the tower yelled at us over the radio that the slight breeze had changed and to make our approach from the other end. Running on fumes, we were in no mood for this, but Moices, swearing profusely, swung around and landed successfully from the other end of the runway. As we waited for the tank to be filled, Moices smoked cigarettes with very shaky hands.

Back in the air we found Los Tuxtlas pretty well socked in by this time. I pushed for getting in as closely as possible to the Coxcoapan valley, but we could not go in. I was able to search for lost transmitters, but we were unable to pinpoint any locations on the ground due to the heavy cloud cover. This is not an area to fly in without visibility. The mountains and valleys are steep, and the turbulence can often be amazing. Moices knows the mountains well, however, and he was game to try things that were perhaps not too smart. After having survived almost running out of gas, I wondered if we were now going to be smeared against a mountainside. When you see valley walls above you while going into a cloud bank, and then have to circle repeatedly to gain enough altitude to get back out—all in dense cloud—you wonder whether you would even have time to see the forest reach out to grab you. I kept expecting to see trees in some close shaves, though I never did. And the turbulence was incredible. It was a stimulating ride. When we eventually returned to the airstrip at Lerdo, Moices was a wreck. I had been concentrating hard enough on trying to find signals that I had not realized how stressful the latter part of the trip had been for him. He was surprised I had not been more nervous during the day's flight. But once we had fuel again I had been concentrating on trying to get signals and determining where we were.

I have never written any papers on the results of those two seasons. We used up a lot of transmitters and followed a lot of birds for short periods over rough country. Moices and I flew the length and breadth of Los Tuxtlas hunting for the signals of the birds that had disappeared. Exactly what occurs among nonterritorial Wood Thrushes remains unclear. We gained a decent understanding of their movements within Los Tuxtlas. But too many transmitters simply disappeared after just a couple of days, never to be heard from again. The rate was unprecedented in relation to our previous studies, which had included a much larger proportion of territorial individuals. We found reception of some birds to be excellent, even at times from 8,000–9,000 feet, an altitude from which our receiver could cover a lot of ground. And yet when we covered that ground, finding one of the lost birds was rare. I began to suspect that some birds might be making much larger-scale movements than we had thought—as far, perhaps, as to the mountains of the Sierra Madre Oriental approximately ninety miles away, where the nearest equivalent habitat was available. But carrying on a search of that scope was beyond our capacity, so we continued to monitor nonterritorial movements in the vicinity of our study area; we never had a bird move between the Sierra San Martín and the Sierra Santa Marta.

Los Tuxtlas Retrospective

For more than twenty years now, when I mention to people that I do fieldwork in Mexico, I have heard sarcastic remarks like, "Oh, it must be rough!" Mexico is a desirable vacation destination, but people who have not done fieldwork in Los Tuxtlas have no idea how difficult and un-vacationlike it is. As much as I have enjoyed the years spent there, remote work in Los Tuxtlas exacts a steep price. In pursuit of the birds of Los Tuxtlas I have been beaten, bashed, rolled, pierced, bruised, and cut, usually while soaking wet. I have learned that everything grows mold, and that the true luxuries in life are simple: hot water, dry toilet paper, and cold beer. In retrospect it may all have been summed up one night by a boy at La Península. It was dark, pouring rain, and the river was high. It had been another long day, and it was good to get back to the trailer. But just down the road a short distance on the bank of the river we found a child about ten years old squatting on the ground under the belly of his horse, crying because he was unable to cross over and get home. The coastal slope of the Sierra de Santa Marta is a punishing place to keep on keeping on.

In the 1990s we moved back over to the San Martín portion of Los Tuxtlas, continuing the long-term work begun by the Minnesota group in the early 1970s. We were back again in the early 2000s, too, continuing to add data from a fourth decade to this now remarkable data set. My good friends and mentors Dwain Warner and Mario Ramos were not able to join us in the field, but they were as excited as we were to see what birds were hitting the nets and how things had changed. Dwain died in late 2005, still very engaged in what we were learning in Los Tuxtlas (see Winker 2006). Mario died unexpectedly in September 2006 (see Rappole 2007). Just a few days beforehand, he had been sending his comments on our most recent Los Tuxtlas manuscript and helping to plan for our next field effort there.

Afterword

How This Book Came to Be

I usually dislike a longwinded preface, wanting to tear directly into the meat of a book. But often I also find that by the time I'm finished reading it, I want to know more about a book's origins—something a brief introduction does not usually provide. For those like me, read on.

I first went to Mexico with my parents in 1965, driving down the west coast from California on a camping trip. We celebrated my third birthday with a *piñata* and created some of my earliest detailed memories. My next trip to Mexico occurred in the winter of 1982–83, and my twentieth birthday was spent very differently than my third had been. I was in Veracruz doing fieldwork with Dwain Warner, who himself had first been to Mexico in 1941 with George Miksch Sutton and Olin Sewall Pettingill. In retrospect, I was in the process of being "raised from a pup," as Dwain would put it.

Bibliophilia

Dwain used to threaten people at the University of Minnesota with whom he did not agree that he would stay on and "terrorize you until I'm seventy"—at that time the mandatory age of retirement. He did just that, remaining a dynamo of enthusiasm and activity until his death in 2005 at age eighty-eight. Dwain retired in the fall of 1986. I was headed to Veracruz to continue work with Mario Ramos and John Rappole on Wood Thrushes (*Hylocichla mustelina*) in the Sierra de Los Tuxtlas, and as a consequence I almost missed his retirement party. (Fortunately I did not miss it and was finally able to meet Bob Dickerman there). At the time, my student office was in the ornithology preparation lab on the third floor of the Bell Museum of Natural History in Minneapolis, connected to Dwain's somewhat cluttered office. Before I left that season for Veracruz, Dwain mentioned that by the time I returned, he would have cleaned up some forty years' accumulation of stuff and moved out. I made the request that if there was anything he contemplated throwing away,

Figure 21.1. Dwain Warner feigns biting back at a cantankerous, flightless White Pelican (*Pelecanus erythrorhynchos*), Sontecomapan, Sierra de Los Tuxtlas, Veracruz, January 1983. Photo by K. Winker.

he instead put it into my small office, which was just through his door (which, by the way, was always open).

When I returned in early January after two months, I was unable to enter my office because Dwain had piled so much stuff into it—he had simply stacked it all on the floor. I was ecstatic in going through it. The items accumulated by someone studying ornithology for forty years is an amazing collection of memorabilia and, importantly for me, literature. Dwain had left much of his personal library. This included publications such as a long run of *The Auk* and a complete set of Ridgway and Friedmann's *The Birds of North and Middle America* (Ridgway and Friedmann 1901–50). This was immensely kind of him. I pointed out that he could sell some of these things for a good price; for example the Ridgway and Friedmann volumes could not be found for less than $250 at that time. His answer was that much of it had been given to him as a graduate student and that he was just carrying on the tradition. He pointed out that as an example, the Ridgway and Friedmann volumes from 1901 through 1919 had been given to him before he left Cornell by Albert R. Brand. And so, it turned out, had a well-used copy of the Fourth Edition of the American Ornithologists' Union's *Check-list of North American Birds* (AOU 1931). On the flyleaf of this volume Brand had compared his life list in the checklist area (404 species as of May 1938) against the life list of Arthur A. Allen (703 species at that time).

There were many other little treasures in Dwain's piles. Much of what he left me immediately formed the core of my working office library. More than twenty years later, I still find that I use this literature regularly. In fact, my longstanding passion for books subsequently became very focused, for I realized that the excellent library just across the hall from my office in the Bell Museum (unfortunately closed and disbanded in about 1992) would not always be available. I began to keep a close eye on the ornithology sections of the used book stores in Minneapolis and Saint Paul and also to peruse book dealer catalogues. One happy surprise came when I worked in the field at the Welder Wildlife Foundation in Sinton, Texas, in the fall of 1988. Welder has an excellent library, particularly strong in ornithology. During the hot south Texas afternoons (when it was better for the birds to leave the nets closed) and late into the evenings I enjoyed myself by going through as much of the excellent collection as I could, not looking for anything in particular but going systematically through the shelves and reading anything that caught my eye. Spending months working with birds during the daylight hours and in the library at other times is a very pleasant way to pass the time.

The core of the Welder holdings came from the personal libraries of Clarence Cottam, the foundation's first director, and his friends Theodore Palmer and Alexander Wetmore, both of whom willed their libraries to Welder when they died. Wetmore was a first-class bibliophile. Not only was he an excellent collector, but he was also a dedicated curator of his books, and he had obviously had a long working relationship with an excellent binder. The quality of Wetmore's personal library was unmatched in my experience. Institutional libraries sometimes have more complete holdings, but they do not care for the volumes with the fastidiousness evident in Wetmore's collection. Of course, institutions have to bind for utility and heavy use, and therefore cannot revel in the binder's art, as Wetmore clearly had.

When the Wetmore volumes began arriving at Welder there was some overlap in the holdings, and to keep duplicates down to preserve space they sold the less desirable duplicate volumes at good prices to Welder students. Fortunately, few students of ornithology had been through before my visit, and I was able to purchase some useful duplicates. Years later, when I wound up at the Smithsonian Institution, I wrote to Alex's widow, the late Beatrice Wetmore, to learn where he had shopped for used books and where he had had them bound. Mrs. Wetmore was very helpful, telling me that he had purchased most of his books through used book catalogues, and she directed me to Storrs Olson regarding the current address of the binder. Storrs gave me the address of the Mount Pleasant Bookbinders in Augusta, West Virginia. Richard and Mari Smith, who had done the admirable binding Wetmore had obviously liked so much, had retired, but their daughters Madie Alkire and Laura McBride carry on the family business, producing hand-bound works of beautiful quality and variety in a workshop in a forest in the mountains of West Virginia. When I paid a visit there in August 1996, Richard Smith told me his sorting of bindery records had shown that Wetmore had had more than seven thousand volumes bound there over the years.

To some this may seem a digression from tales of exploration in Middle America, but it's not. The literature of the field represents the tracks of previous explorers, and one is most effective in one's efforts to learn what is new when one knows where these predecessors have been. (The explorer Richard Burton had the odd habit of visiting the graves of his predecessors; knowing where these graves were located suggests a superb grasp of available information.) This history is fascinating in its own right, but it is also an integral part of our field. Sadly, today's ready access to so much information—indeed, a bombardment of new data to process at an ever-increasing pace—makes it easy to overlook the history. Who has time for it? But when studying biological diversity and its distribution there is no better way to begin than to read the works of our predecessors. Most are out of print, and few libraries can be considered replete in the genre. And although electronic access is expanding, historical works have been slow to be added to online databases.

It was in part a fascination for this historic literature that led me to realize many tracks had yet to be recorded, and not just the scientific aspects, either. There is a strong oral history in field biology, rife with excitement, humor, and keen views of human nature. Unfortunately, that oral history is all too short-lived. I have always enjoyed a good story, and since beginning fieldwork in Mexico as an undergraduate with Dwain Warner, I have had the pleasure of hearing stories from many who have conducted biological explorations in distant places. One day I decided to begin a correspondence campaign to encourage explorers of the ornithology of northern Middle America to write of some of their experiences. This book is the result.

Authors Not Represented

When I began this correspondence campaign my goals were more selfish: I wanted to see a decent history written of recent ornithological exploration in Veracruz and neighboring Mexican states. I had heard a lot of stories that to my knowledge were not recorded. Many of these tales were both enlightening and entertaining. As the effort progressed, however, I realized that the limited number of people involved were unlikely to write at great length of their experiences (if they could be persuaded at all). I also began to realize that this harvest of unrecorded history could productively go farther afield, capturing a broader selection of geography and personalities.

As I write this afterword, at least eighteen of the people whom I initially approached have passed away. Fortunately for those of us left behind, several sent material for the book. Miguel Álvarez del Toro, Lula Coffey, Charles Sibley, Walter Thurber, and Walter Dalquest completed excellent chapters. Allan Phillips was just beginning to thaw a little to the idea and had sent a couple of memories. Robert McCabe had died before I actually wrote to him. His wife Marie penned a short note in response: "Dear Mr. Winker, Sorry, you're too late. My husband died May 29. I believe he would have enjoyed such a project, since the Chihuahua expedition [with A. Starker Leopold] was his first great field experience. He relished every detail and had great stories. They should have been recorded. Good luck on this project. Sincerely, Marie McCabe."

Roger Tory Peterson might have had something interesting to relate about the northern Neotropics and the work he and Edward Chalif did to produce what became the standard field guide of northern Middle America for more than twenty years (Peterson and Chalif 1973). A brief note not long before he died indicated that he could not write a chapter. Every time I visited the Field Museum I hoped to meet Emmet R. Blake, but it was not to be. His never-written chapter would have made fascinating reading. Charles Sibley, an excellent correspondent through email, passed away shortly after writing that he was ready to send a chapter, which his wife Fran kindly sent later. During the long course of putting the book together, others have passed away. John Emlen was kind enough to allow me to use excerpts from his autobiography, which he was in the process of finishing when I first wrote to him.

One of my goals in encouraging authors to write of their experiences was to get something recorded of people who went before us and could no longer contribute. Surprisingly, there seems to be little oral history left in the profession of some giants of Neotropical ornithology. It seems that stories of people such as W. W. Brown, Alexander Wetmore, Chester C. Lamb, George Lowery, Robert Newman, and Allan R. Phillips will have to be developed from historical materials. A book on these individuals similar to the volumes of ornithological biographies by Barbara and Richard Mearns (Mearns and Mearns 1992, 1998) would be a wonderful work indeed.

Some of the more than seventy people approached were unable to write chapters, usually because of other commitments that left no time. One of these responses I enjoyed immensely. Fred Loetscher, whose 1941 Ph.D. thesis on the *Ornithology of the Mexican State of Veracruz* (Loetscher 1941) remains the definitive work on the birds of that state, wrote that while he did not have time to write of his experiences in Mexico, "I can't recall a single experience I had there which would interest anyone; I never had an encounter with a bandit or with a rabid coatimundi; never once was questioned, let alone detained, by the *policia* when toting a (usually concealed) gun; nor did I ever let pimps lead me to their double-breasted mattress-thrashers—what could be duller reading?"

Looking to the Future

Although most of the material in this book is retrospective, the authors' enthusiasm for writing of their experiences shows that, like me, they found their explorations in field biology to be of lasting importance and value. In this respect, these experiences provided long-lasting motivation, both personally and professionally. And it is heartening to learn that books they had read by earlier explorers stimulated some of the authors to begin their own explorations. Times do change. For example, two of the authors represented here have shot Harpy Eagles. But adventures can still be had today on the frontiers of field biology, and while these experiences will differ from those of the past in many ways, we can look forward to future generations of field biologists continuing to pursue the boundaries of personal and scientific knowledge—and, I hope, sharing some of their experiences and insights with the rest of us.

Literature Cited

Acuña, R. 1984. *Relaciones geográficas del siglo XVI: Antequera.* México City: Universidad Nacional Autónoma de México, Instituto de Investigaciones Antropológicas.
Ahlquist, J. 1999. Charles G. Sibley: A commentary on 30 years of collaboration. *Auk* 116: 856–60.
Álvarez del Toro, M. 1971, 1980. *Las Aves de Chiapas.* Tuxtla Gutiérrez, Chiapas: Gobierno del Estado de Chiapas and Universidad Autónoma de Chiapas.
American Ornithologists' Union (AOU). 1931. *Check-list of North American Birds, 4th ed.* Baltimore: AOU.
———. 1957. *Check-list of North American Birds, 5th ed.* Baltimore: AOU.
Andrle, R. F. 1964. *A Biogeographical Investigation of the Sierra de Tuxtla in Veracruz, Mexico.* Ph.D. diss., Louisiana State University, Baton Rouge.
———. 1967a. The Horned Guan in México and Guatemala. *Condor* 69: 93–109.
———. 1967b. Birds of the Sierra de Tuxtla in Veracruz, Mexico. *Wilson Bulletin* 79: 163–87.
Andrle, R. F., and J. R. Carroll. 1988. *Atlas of Breeding Birds in New York State.* Ithaca, N.Y.: Cornell University Press.
Baker, R. H. 1951. The avifauna of Micronesia, its origin, evolution, and distribution. *University of Kansas Publications, Museum of Natural History* 3: 1–359.
Bates, J. M. 1992a. Frugivory on *Bursera microphylla* (Burseraceae) by wintering Gray Vireos (*Vireo vicinior*, Vireonidae) in the coastal deserts of Sonora, Mexico. *Southwestern Naturalist* 37: 252–58.
———. 1992b. Winter territorial behavior of Gray Vireos. *Wilson Bulletin* 104: 425–433.
Binford, L. C. 1989. A distributional survey of the birds of the Mexican state of Oaxaca. *Ornithological Monographs* 43: 1–418.
Blake, E. R. 1953. *Birds of Mexico: A Guide for Field Identification.* Chicago: University of Chicago Press.
Blom, F., and O. La Farge. 1926–27. *Tribes and Temples: A Record of the Tulane University Expedition to Middle America.* 2 vols. New Orleans: Tulane University.
Coffey, B. B., Jr. 1943. Post-juvenile migration of herons. *Bird Banding* 14: 34–39.
Coffey, B. B., Jr., and L. C. Coffey. 1984. *Bird Songs and Calls from Southeast Peru.* Madre de Dios, Peru: Tambopata Nature Reserve.
———. 1989. *Songs of Mexican Birds.* Gainesville, Fla.: ARA Records.

Corbin, K. W., and A. H. Brush. 1999. In memoriam: Charles Gald Sibley, 1917–1998. *Auk* 116: 806–14.

Courtenay, W. R., Jr., and C. H. Robins. 1997. C. Richard Robins: Yesterday and today. *Bulletin of Marine Science* 60: 629–42.

Cuarón, A. D. 1997. Miguel Álvarez del Toro: First and last of a kind. *Conservation Biology* 11: 566–68.

Deevey, E. S., Jr. 1949. Biogeography of the Pleistocene. *Bulletin of the Geological Society of America* 60: 1315–416.

Dickerman, R. W. 1961. A new subspecies of the Pinnated Bittern. *Wilson Bulletin* 73: 333–35.

———. 1974. Review of Red-winged Blackbirds (*Agelaius phoeniceus*) of eastern, west-central, and southern Mexico and Central America. *American Museum Novitates* 2538: 1–18.

Dickerman, R. W., ed. 1997. *The Era of Allan R. Phillips: A Festschrift*. Albuquerque, N.M.: Horizon Communications.

Dickey, D. R., and A. J. Van Rossem. 1938. *The Birds of El Salvador*. Publications of the Field Museum of Natural History, Zoological Series 23: 1–609.

Dirzo, R., and M. C. Garcia. 1992. Rates of deforestation in Los Tuxtlas, a Neotropical area of southeast Mexico. *Conservation Biology* 6: 84–90.

Dressler, R. L. 1962. Tropical orchids near the Texas border. *Missouri Botanical Garden Bulletin* 50: 15–19.

Dunn, E. R., and J. T. Emlen, Jr. 1932. Reptiles and amphibians from Honduras. *Proceedings of the National Academy of Sciences of Philadelphia* 84: 21–32.

Dunning, J. S. 1970. *Portraits of Tropical Birds*. Wynnewood, Pa.: Livingston Publishing.

Eaton, S. W. 1992. Wild Turkey (*Meleagris gallopavo*). *The Birds of North America* 22: 1–28.

———. 1995. Northern Waterthrush (*Seiurus noveboracensis*). *The Birds of North America* 182: 1–20.

Eaton, S. W., and E. F. Schrot. 1987. A flora of the vascular plants of Cattaraugus County, New York. *Bulletin of the Buffalo Society of Natural Sciences* 31: 1–235.

Edwards, E. P. 1955. *Finding Birds in Mexico*. Amherst, Va.: E. P. Edwards.

———. 1972. *A Field Guide to the Birds of Mexico*. Sweet Briar, Va.: Ernest P. Edwards.

———. 1998. *A Field Guide to the Birds of Mexico and Adjacent Areas*, 3rd edition. Austin: University of Texas Press.

Edwards, E. P., and P. S. Martin. 1955. Further notes on birds of the Lake Pátzcuaro region, Mexico. *Auk* 72: 174–78.

Emlen, J. T., Jr. 1950. Techniques for observing birds under natural conditions. *Annals of the New York Academy of Sciences* 51: 1103–12.

———. 1979. Land bird densities on Baja California islands. *Auk* 96: 152–67.

———. 1996. *Adventure Is Where You Find it: Recollections of a Twentieth Century American Naturalist*. Madison, Wis.: J. T. Emlen, Jr.

Flannery, K. V. 1982. *Maya Subsistence: Studies in Memory of Dennis E. Puleston.* New York: Academic Press.
Fogleman, J. C. 1990. William B. Heed, a biography. Pp. 1–10 in *Ecological and Evolutionary Genetics of* Drosophila, ed. J. S. F. Barker et al. New York: Plenum Press.
Friedlaender, I. 1923. Über das Vulkangebiet von San Martin Tuxtla in Mexiko. *Zeitschrift für Vulkanologie* 7: 162–87, plates 17–34.
Goldman, E. A. 1951. *Biological Investigations in Mexico.* Smithsonian Miscellaneous Collections 115: i–xiii, 1–476.
Greenberg, J. B. 1989. *Blood Ties: Life and Violence in Rural Mexico.* Tucson: University of Arizona Press.
Grinnell, H. W. 1940. Joseph Grinnell: 1877–1939. *Condor* 42: 3–34.
Haemig, P. D. 1977. A nest of the Mexican Red Warbler. *Condor* 79: 390–91.
———. 1978. Aztec Emperor Auitzotl and the Great-tailed Grackle. *Biotropica* 10: 11–17.
———. 1999. Predation risk alters interactions among species: Competition and facilitation between ants and nesting birds in a boreal forest. *Ecology Letters* 2: 178–84.
Haemig, P. D., J. Hernandez, J. Waldenström, J. Bonnedahl, and B. Olsen. 2008. Barn swallows (*Hirundo rustica*) test negative for Salmonella. *Vector-borne and Zoonotic Diseases* 8: 451–54.
Harrell, B. E. 1951. *The Birds of Rancho del Cielo: An Ecological Investigation in the Oak–Sweet Gum Forests of Tamaulipas, Mexico.* M.A. thesis, University of Minnesota, Minneapolis.
Hernandez X., E., H. Crum, W. B. Fox, and A. J. Sharp. 1951. A unique vegetational area in Tamaulipas. *Bulletin of the Torrey Botanical Club* 78: 458–63.
Horner, N. V., and F. B. Stangl, Jr. 2001. Obituary: Walter Woelber Dalquest: 1917–2000. *Journal of Mammalogy* 82: 604–12.
Howell, S. N. G., and S. Webb. 1995. *A Guide to the Birds of Mexico and Northern Central America.* New York: Oxford University Press.
Jackson, J. A. 1994. In memoriam: Ben B. Coffey, Jr., 1904–1993. *Auk* 111: 991–93.
Jehl, J. 1974. The near-shore avifauna of the Middle American west coast. *Auk* 91: 681–99.
Jobling, J. A. 1991. *A Dictionary of Scientific Bird Names.* Oxford: Oxford University Press.
Kerber, E. 1882. Eine alta mexicanischen Ruinenstaate bei San Andres Tuxtla. *Verhandl. Berliner Gesell. fur Anthropol., Ethnol., und Urgeschichte* 14: 488–89.
Koopman, K. P., and P. S. Martin 1959. Mammals from cave deposits in the Gómez Farías region of southern Tamaulipas, Mexico. *Journal of Mammalogy* 40: 1–12.
Lanyon, W. E., S. T. Emlen, and G. H. Orians. 2000. In memoriam: John Thompson Emlen, Jr., 1908–1997. *Auk* 117: 222–27.
Linsdale, J. 1942. In Memoriam: Joseph Grinnell. *Auk* 59: 269–85.
Loetscher, F. W., Jr. 1941. *Ornithology of the Mexican State of Veracruz, with an Annotated List of the Birds.* Ph.D. diss., Cornell University, Ithaca, N.Y.

Lowery, G. H., Jr., and W. W. Dalquest. 1951. Birds from the State of Veracruz, Mexico. *University of Kansas Publications, Museum of Natural History* 3: 531–649.

Marshall, J. T. 1943. Additional information concerning the birds of El Salvador. *Condor* 45: 21–33.

———. 1957. Birds of pine-oak woodland in southern Arizona and adjacent Mexico. *Pacific Coast Avifauna* 22: 1–125.

———. 1977. A synopsis of Asian species of *Mus* (Rodentia, Muridae). *Bulletin of the American Museum of Natural History* 158: 175–220.

———. 1988. Birds lost from a giant sequoia forest during fifty years. *Condor* 90: 359–72.

Martin, P. S. 1951. Black Robin in Tamaulipas, Mexico. *Wilson Bulletin* 63: 340.

———. 1956. *A Biogeography of Reptiles and Amphibians in the Gómez Farías region, Tamaulipas, Mexico*. Miscellaneous Publications of the Museum of Zoology, University of Michigan, no. 101, Ann Arbor.

Martin, P. S., and B. E. Harrell. 1957. The Pleistocene history of temperate biotas in Mexico and eastern United States. *Ecology* 38: 468–80.

Martin, P. S., C. R. Robins, and W. B. Heed. 1953. Birds and biogeography of the Sierra de Tamaulipas, an isolated pine-oak habitat. *Wilson Bulletin* 66: 38–57.

Mearns, B., and R. Mearns. *Audubon to Xántus*. London: Academic Press.

———. 1998. *The Bird Collectors*. San Diego, Calif.: Academic Press.

Morley, S. G. 1946. *The Ancient Maya*. Stanford, Calif.: Stanford University Press.

Navarro S., A. G., and J. E. Morales-Pérez. 1999. In memoriam: Miguel Álvarez del Toro, 1917–1996. *Auk* 116: 226–27.

Newton, I. 2008. *The Migration Ecology of Birds*. London: Academic Press.

Nice, M. M. 1937. *Studies in the Life History of the Song Sparrow*. Vol. 1. Transactions of the Linnean Society 4: 1–247.

Paynter, R. A., Jr. 1955. *The Ornithogeography of the Yucatán Peninsula*. Peabody Museum of Natural History, Yale University Bulletin 9: 1–347.

Peters, J. A. 1948. The northern limit of the range of *Laemanctus serratus*. *Natural History Miscellanea*, Chicago Academy of Sciences, no. 27: 1–3.

Peterson, A. T., A. G. Navarro-Sigüenza, B. E. Hernández-Baños, G. Escalona-Segura, F. Rebón-Gallardo, E. Rodríguez-Ayala, E. M. Figueroa-Esquivel, and L. Cabrera-Garcia. 2003. The Chimalapas region, Oaxaca, Mexico: A high-priority region for bird conservation in Mesoamerica. *Bird Conservation International* 13: 227–54.

Peterson, R. T., and E. L. Chalif. 1973. *A Field Guide to Mexican Birds*. Boston: Houghton Mifflin.

Phillips, A. R. 1969. An ornithological comedy of errors: *Catharus occidentalis* and *C. frantzii*. *Auk* 86: 605–23.

———. 1975. The migrations of Allen's and other hummingbirds. *Condor* 77: 196–205.

Phillips, A. R., R. W. Dickerman, A. M. Rea, and J. D. Webster. 1986. *The Known Birds of North and Middle America, Part 1*. Denver.: Allan R. Phillips.

Phillips, A. R., D. D. Gibson, K. C. Parkes, M. A. Ramos, and A. M. Rea. 1991. *The Known Birds of North and Middle America, Part 2*. Denver: Allan R. Phillips.

Pietz, P. 2000. David Freeland Parmelee (1924-98). *Ibis* 142: 182.

Ramos, M. A. 1989. Eco-evolutionary aspects of bird movements in the northern Neotropical region. Pp. 250-93 in *Proceedings of the XIX International Ornithological Congress*, Ottawa, Ontario, 1986.

Ramos, M. A., and J. H. Rappole. 1994. Relative homing abilities of migrants and residents in tropical rainforest of southern Veracruz, Mexico. *Bird Conservation International* 4: 175-80.

Ramos, M. A., and D. W. Warner. 1980. Analysis of North American subspecies of migrant birds wintering in Los Tuxtlas, southern Veracruz, Mexico. Pp. 173-80 in *Migrant Birds in the Neotropics: Ecology, Behavior, Distribution and Conservation*, ed. A. Keast and E. S. Morton. Washington, D.C.: Smithsonian Institution.

Rappole, J. H. 1995. *The Ecology of Migrant Birds: A Neotropical Perspective*. Washington, D.C.: Smithsonian Institution.

———. 2007. In memoriam: Mario Alberto Ramos Olmos, 1949-2006. *Auk* 124: 6-8.

Rappole, J. H., and E. S. Morton. 1985. Effects of habitat alteration on a tropical forest community. *Ornithological Monographs* 6: 1013-21.

Rappole, J. H., and D. W. Warner. 1980. Ecological aspects of migrant bird behavior in Veracruz, Mexico. Pp. 353-93 in *Migrant Birds in the Neotropics: Ecology, Behavior, Distribution and Conservation*, ed. A. Keast and E. S. Morton. Washington, D.C.: Smithsonian Institution.

Rappole, J. H., M. A. Ramos, and K. Winker. 1989. Wintering Wood Thrush movements and mortality in southern Veracruz. *Auk* 106: 402-10.

Remsen, J. V., Jr. 1995. The importance of continued collecting of bird specimens to ornithology and bird conservation. *Bird Conservation International* 5: 177-212.

Ridgway, R., and H. Friedmann. 1901-50. *The Birds of North and Middle America, Parts I-XI*. U.S. National Museum Bulletin 50. Washington, D.C.: U.S. Government Printing Office.

Robins, C. R., and W. B. Heed. 1951. Bird notes from La Joya de Salas, Tamaulipas. *Wilson Bulletin* 63: 263-70.

Robins, C. R., P. S. Martin, and W. B. Heed. 1951. Frigate-bird, oyster catcher, upland plover, and various terns on the coast of Tamaulipas, México. *Wilson Bulletin* 63: 338.

Rodríguez-Yañez, C. A., R. M. Villalón, and A. G. Navarro S. 1994. *Bibliografía de las aves de México (1825-1992)*. Publicaciones Especial Museo Zoologica (Facultad Ciencias, Universidad Nacional Autónoma de México) 8: 1-146.

Russell, S., and G. Monson. 1998. *The Birds of Sonora*. Tucson: University of Arizona Press.

Sanderson, I. 1941. *Living Treasure*. New York: Viking Press.

Scherer, W. F., R. W. Dickerman, E. W. Cupp, and J. V. Ordonez. 1985. Ecologic observations of Venezuelan encephalitis virus in vertebrates and isolations of Nepuyo and Patois viruses from sentinel hamsters at Pacific and Atlantic habitats in Guatemala, 1968–1980. *American Journal of Tropical Medicine and Hygiene* 34: 790–98.

Sharp, A. J., E. Hernandez X., H. Crum, and W. B. Fox. 1950. Nota floristica de una asociación importante del suroeste de Tamaulipas, México. *Sociedad Botanica de México* 11: 1–4.

Sibley, C. G. 1950. Species formation in the red-eyed towhees of Mexico. *University of California Publications in Zoology* 50: 109–194.

———. 1954. Hybridization in the red-eyed towhees of Mexico. *Evolution* 8: 252–90.

Sibley, C. G., and J. E. Ahlquist. 1990. *Phylogeny and Classification of Birds: A Study in Molecular Evolution.* New Haven, Conn.: Yale University Press.

Sibley, C. G., and J. Davis. 1946. Real del Arriba, Mexico, as a Deppe locality. *Condor* 48: 279.

Sibley, C. G., and B. L. Monroe, Jr. 1990. *Distribution and Taxonomy of Birds of the World.* New Haven, Conn.: Yale University Press.

Sibley, C. G., and F. C. Sibley. 1964. Hybridization in the red-eyed towhees of Mexico: The populations of the southeastern plateau region. *Auk* 81: 479–504.

Sibley, C. G., and D. A. West. 1958. Hybridization in the red-eyed towhees of Mexico: The eastern plateau populations. *Condor* 60: 85–104.

Simonian, L. 1995. *Defending the Land of the Jaguar: A History of Conservation in Mexico.* Austin: University of Texas Press.

Smithe, F. B. 1966. *The Birds of Tikal.* New York: Natural History Press.

Soriano, E., R. Dirzo, and R. Vogt, eds. 1997. *Historia Natural de Los Tuxtlas.* México City: Universidad Nacional Autónoma de México.

Stephens, J. L. 1841. *Incidents of Travel in Central America, Chiapas, and Yucatan.* 2 vols. New York: Harper and Brothers.

Stone, W. 1931. Three new birds from Honduras. *Proceedings of the Academy of Natural Sciences of Philadelphia* 83: 1–3.

Sutton, G. M. 1972. *At a Bend in a Mexican River.* New York: Paul Eriksson.

Thurber, W. A. 1978. *Cien Aves de El Salvador.* San Salvador, El Salvador: Ministerio de Educación.

———. 1980. Hurricane Fifi and the 1974 autumn migration in El Salvador. *Condor* 82: 212–18.

———. 1981. Aerial "play" of Black Vultures. *Wilson Bulletin* 93: 97.

Thurber, W. A., and A. Villeda C. 1976. Band returns in El Salvador, 1973–74 and 1974–75 seasons. *Bird-Banding* 47: 277–78.

———. 1980. Wintering site fidelity of migrant passerines in El Salvador, Central America. *North American Bird Bander* 5: 131–35.

Warner, D. W. 1947. *The Ornithology of New Caledonia and the Loyalty Islands.* Ph.D. diss., Cornell University, Ithaca, N.Y.

———. 1959. The song, nest, eggs, and young of *Dendrortyx macroura*. *Wilson Bulletin* 71: 307–12.

Warner, D. W., and J. R. Beer. 1957. Birds and mammals of the Mesa de San Diego, Puebla, Mexico. *Acta Zoologica Mexicana* 2: 1–21.

Warner, D. W., and B. E. Harrell. 1957. The systematics and biology of the Singing Quail, *Dactylortyx thoracicus*. *Wilson Bulletin* 69: 123–54.

Warner, D. W., and R. M. Mengel. 1951. Notes on birds of the Veracruz coastal plain. *Wilson Bulletin* 63: 288–95.

Webster, F., and M. S. Webster. 2002. *The Road to El Cielo*. Austin: University of Texas Press.

Western, D., and R. M. Wright, eds. 1994. *Natural Connections: Perspectives in Community-Based Conservation*. Washington, D.C.: Island Press.

Wetmore, A. 1943. The birds of southern Veracruz, Mexico. *Proceedings of the U.S. National Museum, Natural History* 93: 215–340.

Winker, K. 1995. Autumn stopover on the Isthmus of Tehuantepec by woodland Nearctic-Neotropic migrants. *Auk* 112: 690–700.

———. 1996. The crumbling infrastructure of biodiversity: The avian example. *Conservation Biology* 10: 703–7.

———. 1999. In memoriam: David F. Parmelee, 1924–1998. *Auk* 116: 816–17.

———. 2004. Natural history museums in a post-biodiversity era. *BioScience* 54: 455–59.

———. 2005. Bird collections: Development and use of a scientific resource. *Auk* 122: 966–71.

———. 2006. In Memoriam: Dwain W. Warner, 1917–2005. *Auk* 123: 911–12.

Winker, K., J. H. Rappole, and M. A. Ramos. 1990a. Population dynamics of the Wood Thrush (*Hylocichla mustelina*) on its wintering grounds in southern Veracruz, Mexico. *Condor* 92: 444–60.

Winker, K., J. H. Rappole, and M. A. Ramos. 1990b. Within-forest preferences of Wood Thrushes wintering in the rainforest of southern Veracruz. *Wilson Bulletin* 102: 715–20.

Winker, K., R. J. Oehlenschlager, M. A. Ramos, R. M. Zink, J. H. Rappole, and D. W. Warner. 1992. Avian distribution and abundance records for the Sierra de Los Tuxtlas, Veracruz. *Wilson Bulletin* 104: 699–718.

Winker, K., J. H. Rappole, and M. A. Ramos. 1995. The use of movement data as an assay of habitat quality. *Oecologia* 101: 211–16.

Winker, K., P. Escalante, J. H. Rappole, M. A. Ramos, R. J. Oehlenschlager, and D. W. Warner. 1997. Periodic migration and lowland forest refugia in a "sedentary" neotropical bird, Wetmore's Bush-Tanager. *Conservation Biology* 11: 692–97.

Winker, K., S. A. Weiss, J. L. Trejo, and P. Escalante. 1999. Notes on the avifauna of Tabasco. *Wilson Bulletin* 111: 229–35.

Winker, K., J. H. Rappole, and R. W. Dickerman. 2006. In Memoriam: Dwain W. Warner, 1917–2005. *Loon* 77: 191–94.

Index

Page numbers in italics refer to illustrations.

Abronia ochoterenai, 12
Academy of Natural Sciences of Philadelphia, 144, 148
Acapulco, 278
Acayucan, 33, 36
Accipiter, 305 (*striatus*), 326
Ack, Vicente, 247
Actias luna, 64
Afropavo congensis, 143
Agouti, 31, 119
Agouti paca, 31, 361
Agriocharis ocellata, 78, 92, 100, 104, 120
Agua Zarco, 218
Ahlquist, Jon, 276
Aimophila botterii, 129; *carpalis*, 51
Alamos, 272
Albuquerque, 83
Alcántara, José Luís, 355, 357
Alcorn, Ray, 87, 274, 294–295
Alexander, Annie, 268–69
Alkire, Madie, 374
Allen, Arthur A., 121–22, 142, 197, 207, 373
Alouatta palliata, 22, 29, 32, 48, 68, 87, 117–18, 358, 362
Alta California, 152
Altamira, 226
Álvarez del Toro, Miguel, 1, 36, 38–39, 100, 375
Amadon, Dean 44, 215
Amapala, 144–45
Amaya, Héctor, 321
Amazilia tzacatl, 33, 248
Amazona, 81; *autumnalis*, 81, 135; *farinosa*, 81; *ochrocephala*, 81; *viridigenalis*, 81, 130, 152, 210
American Museum of Natural History, 44, 83, 92, 118, 142–43, 181, 215, 275, 286, 332
American Ornithologists' Union (AOU), 276
American Philosophical Society, 291

American Rosario Silver Mine Company, 145
Amigo de Los Pájaros, El, 318, 320–21
Ammodramus maritimus, 277
Amphispiza bilineata, 56, 126
Anas discors, 79
Andrews, Ron, 38–39
Andrle, Robert F., 19, *20*, *39-40*
Ann Arbor, Mich., 209, 223–25, 229, 275
Anolis, 251, 256
Antbird: Ocellated, 118; Spotted, 117
Anthus rubescens, 168
Antigua Morelos, 58, 60, 286, 327
Ant, 24, 96, 110, 117, 147–48, 188, 213, 342–44
Antvireo, Plain, 118
Antwren, Dot-winged, 118
Aphelocoma ultramarina, 218
Aphriza virgata, 53
Aptenodytes forsteri, 276
Aracari, Collared, 171, 344
Ara macao, 81, 244, 246, 248, 321; *militaris*, 96, 206, 223
Aramides axillaris, 287; *cajanea*, 79
Aratinga astec, 81, 172; *holochlora*, 81, 130
Arbutus xalapensis, 218
Archilochus colubris, 306
Ardea herodias, 91
Arenaria melanocephala, 53
Armadillo, 25–27, 227
Arremon brunneinucha, 28, 97
Arremonops rufivirgatus, 94
Asclepias pellucida, 110; *tuberosa*, 112
Astrocaryum mexicanum, 349
Ateles geoffroyi, 32, 87–88, 195, 214, 358, 362
Atitlán, 46, 106-7
Audubon Society Camp, 115–16
Aulacorhynchus prasinus, 7, 22, 39, 253
Autlan, 67

Automeris io, 64
Avellana, La, 90–91
Axtell, Harold, 25, 30
Aythya affinis, 103
Aztec, 166, 179

Baab, Samantha, 364, 367
Baboquivari, 52
Baeolophus inornatus, 275
Bahía San Carlos, 271
Bahía Sontecomapan, 22, 24, 34–35
Bahía Visciano, 155
Baja California, 152, 155, 257
Baja Peninsula, 57, 150, 152–56
Baker, Rollin, 84, 86, 332
Balzapote, 264, 266
Bambito, 115–16
Bananaquit, 248
Barbachano family, 102
Barranca del Muerte, 98
Barro Colorado Island, 104, 108, 117–19
Basileuterus, 98; *belli*, 32, 39, 97–98; *rufifrons*, 98, 128
Basiliscus, 32
Bat, 30, 88, 120, 175, 185–86, 189, 213, 236, 288, 309; false vampire, 30, 88; vampire, 120, 175, 186, 189, 213
Bates, John, 49, *50*
Baton Rouge, 225, 233
Bauer, Edgar, 46
Baxin, Andrés, 24, 30
Bear, black, 138, 213, 218
Bee, 110, 116, 246, 248, 343
Beebe, William, 188, 197
Beer, Jim, 329
Beetle, 264, 342, 362
Begonia, 184, 192, 215–16
Belize, 104, 107, 238–49, 260, 354
Bell Museum of Natural History, 160, 167, 169, 182, 371, 373
Benito Juárez, Chimalapas, 254, 256, 258
Benson, Seth, 268–71, 279–82
Berkeley, 194–95, 206, 268–69, 272–74, 278–81, 283, 285, 287, 290–91
Bernoullia flammea, 29
Birds, seen or obtained: Biology Station and Playa Escondida, Los Tuxtlas, 172–74; Canal Zone, 89; Chichén Itzá, 103–4; Ciudad Victoria, 93–94; Costa Rica, 112–13; El Triunfo, 39; Escarsega, 101–2; Laguna de San Juan, El Salvador, 91; Lake Catemaco, 31, 33; Lake Pátzcuaro, 199, 206; Linares, 127–28; Madden Forest, 119–20; Martínez de la Torre, 169; Matamoros to Ciudad Mante, 160–61; Mérida, 102–3; Mesa de Llera, 128–32; Palenque, 101; Puerto Lobos, 54–57; Puerto Peñasco, 49; Rancho del Cielo, 221, 236–37; Reynosa to Linares, 125–26; Río San Gregoria, 106; Río Frio, near Mexico City, 99, 167, 178; San Fernando to the Río Corona, 160; San Salvador, 91; Sierra Espinazo del Diablo, 253; Tamazunchale, 94; Tres Cumbres, near Mexico City, 97; Xicotepec, 163
Bittern: Least, 91, 124; Pinnated, 87, 91
Blackbird, Red-winged, 89–91
Blake, Emmet R. 375
Blalock, Leland, 215
Blesse, Frank, 189, 216
Blom, Frans, 21
Blom, Gertrude Duby, 105
Bluebird, Western, 99
Boca Chalchijapa, 82
Bonker, Dee, 119
Bonpland, Aimé, 219
Boobie, Brown, 150, 273
Boquete, 114
Botaurus pinnatus, 87, 91
Bothrops, 16; *atrox*, 24, 203, 345; *goldmani*, 4
Bowers, James Basil, 285
Bowers, Rick, 50
Braulio Carrillo National Park, 45
Breckenridge, Walter J., 87
British Honduras, 238, 245. *See also* Belize
Brittlebush, 52, 54
Brodkorb, Pierce, 96
Bromelia, 201, 228
Brooks, Major Allan and Mrs., 270
Buffalo Museum of Science, 19
Bufo, 110, 203
Bunting, Painted, 249
Burgos, Felix, 214, 222
Burma, 238
Bursera, 54, 56, 201, 211
Burton, Richard, 374
Buteo fluviaticus, fossil, 276; *magnirostris*, 152, 169, 300; *platypterus*, 302–03, 363; *swainsonii*, 56, 302–3, 363

Butterfly, 8, 25, 27–28, 67, 116, 118, 151, 297, 302, 342; monarch, 302
Butz, Leonard, 114–16
Byers, Bill, 216
Byrd, Richard E., 276

Caborca, 51–53
Cabo San Lucas, 155
Cacaguatique, 303
Cactus, 52, 54, 98, 126–27, 129, 206, 219, 233, 271, 280–81, 294
Cairina moschata, 79, 152, 195
Calabasas, Paso or Rancho, 133, 202
California Academy of Sciences, 71
Calocitta, 102, 272
Caluromys derbianus, 32
Cambridge, Mass., 275
Camoa, 271
Campeche, 101–2, 104–5
Campephilus guatemalensis, 358; *imperialis*, 208
Campylopterus curvipennis, 80; *excellens*, 29; *hemileucurus*, 29
Campylorhynchus zonatus, 33, 106, 169, 172
Canal Zone, 89, 117, 120. *See also* Panama
Cancun, 103
Canis latrans, 57
Cantarranas, 146–47
Caprimulgus vociferus, 64, 100; *maculicaudus* 64, 100; *ridgwayi*, 127
Caracara cheriway, 160, 201
Caracara: Crested, 160, 201; Red-throated, 77
Cardellina rubrifrons, 100, 105
Carillon, U.S.S., 144
Carleton College, 327
Carnegiea gigantea, 54–55, 198
Casa de Piedras, 214
Casa Na Bolom, 105
Castillo, Leopoldo 28
Catemaco, 21–22, 25, 29, 31, 33, 100, 139, 171–72, 260, 263, 351–52, 357, 359, 363
Cathartes aura, 95, 130, 160, 302, 326
Catharus, 166; *dryas*, 39; *frantzii*, 166, 312–13; *guttatus*, 307; *mexicanus*, 28, 188, 232, 237; *occidentalis*, 166; *ustulatus*, 115
Catherpes mexicanus, 163
Catherwood, Frederick, 47
Cayetano, F. B. (Dondon), 240–41, 245
Central American Railway, 144
Cercidium, 54

Cereus, 52
Cerro Baúl, 254; Campanario, 24; El Fraile, 294; García, 292–93; Gordo, 293; Grande, 293; Prieto, 54, 56; de la Muerte, 112; Punta, 114–15; San Felipe, 284, 288; Tecolote, 291; Tequila, 292–93; Tuxtla, 20; Verde, 302, 305–7, 309, 313–15, 318, 323, 325; Viejo, 286–88, 293
Chachalaca, 17, 43; Plain, 61, 104, 127–28, 161, 227, 245
Chaetura vauxi, 209, 221
Chalchicomula, 283–84, 289
Chalchijapa, 74–75, 78, 82, 250–51
Chalif, Edward, 375
Chamaedorea, 212
Chamal, 203, 215, 220
Chamula, 100, 106
Changuitiro, 294
Chapala, Lake 286, 292
Chapin, James P., 143, 275
Chapman, Frank M., 143, 275
Chapultepec, 96
Chiapas, 1, 15, 18, 25, 27, 36–41, 44, 66, 100, 102, 105–6, 112, 114, 250–52, 258, 288
Chicago, 49, 232, 275
Chichén Itzá, 103–5, 179
Chichicastenango, 107
Chigger, 37, 46, 204, 228–29
Chihuahua, 130, 206, 219, 375
Childs, Henry E., 285, 295
Chilpancingo, 60, 277, 284
Chimalapas, 250–51, 254, 256–59
Chimo, 330
Chinanteco, 257
Chiriquí, 114, 116–17
Chlidonias niger, 118
Chloroceryle aenea, 80, 114; *amazona*, 80; *americana*, 80, 128, 305
Chlorophonia occipitalis, 174
Cholula, 167–68, 177–78
Chrotopterus, 30, 88
Ciccaba virgata, 28, 58, 77, 128, 217, 267; *nigrolineata*, 323, 363
Cinclus mexicanus, 170
Ciudad Hidalgo, 288
Ciudad Juárez, 88
Ciudad Mante, 141, 151, 161, 203, 230, 329
Ciudad México. *See* Mexico City
Ciudad Oaxaca. *See* Oaxaca

Ciudad Victoria, 58, 60, 93–94, 126, 128, 132–33, 151, 159, 161, 183, 189, 190, 201, 215, 226–27, 234–35, 329
Civil Service Commission, 196
Claravis mondetoura, 9
Clausen, Robert T., 215, 218
Cnidoscolus, 213
Coahuila, 83–85, 209, 257
Coatimundi, 119, 376
Coatzacoalcos, 74–75, 77–82, 85–86, 139, 333
Coccothraustes abeillei, 97, 209, 237
Coccyzus americanus, 64, 129; *minor*, 130
Cochlearius cochlearius, 79–80, 91
Cocula, Jalisco, 291
Coereba flaveola, 248
Coffey, Ben and Lula, 59, 65, 69, 58–70, 375
Cofre de Perote, 214, 283, 295
Colaptes rubiginosus, 24, 236
Coleman, Rick, 364, 367
Colima, 329
Colinus, 102, 329
Colonia Rodolfo Figueroa, 254
Columbina inca, 94, 96, 125, 184, 308; *passerina*, 94, 113; *talpacoti*, 248
Coma, Roberto, 323
Comitán, 65, 106
Concepción, Panama, 114, 117
Conepatus, 271
Coragyps atratus, 74, 95, 97, 120, 130, 171, 200, 315
Córdoba, 19, 177
Cormorant, Brandt's, 274; Neotropic, 21, 33, 134
Cornell Laboratory of Ornithology, 298, 310–12, 326
Cornell Library of Natural Sounds, 313–15
Cornell University, 92, 121–23, 130, 133, 142, 148, 163, 197–99, 207–8, 215–16, 218, 223, 225, 286, 315, 327, 372
Cornell University Medical College, 83
Corpus Christi, 93, 124, 199
Cortland State Teachers College, 320
Corvus brachyrhynchos, 315; *imparatus*, 130, 160
Costa Rica, 41, 44–45, 108–9, 111, 113–14, 117, 260, 262
Cottam, Clarence, 92, 332–33, 373
Cougar. *See* Mountain lion
Cowbird, Giant, 108
Coyame, 29, 263, 341
Cozumel Island, 104

Crax rubra, 16, 28, 31, 78, 213, 236, 244, 246, 248, 358, 361
Creosote, 52, 209, 219, 279
Crique Sarco, 240, 243, 245–46, 249
Crossbill, Red, 232
Crotalus horridus, 203; *lepidus*, 218. *See also* rattlesnake
Crow: American, 315; Tamaulipas, 130, 160
Crum, Howard, 215
Crypturellus boucardi, 28, 78; *cinnamomeus*, 78, 130–31, 152, 236
Ctenosaura, 203
Cuckoo: Mangrove, 130; Pheasant, 255, 358; Squirrel, 172, 221, 309, 326, 358; Yellow-billed, 64, 129
Cuetzalapan, 31
Cupressus, 218
Curassow, Great, 16, 28, 31, 78, 213, 236, 244, 246, 248, 358, 361
Cuyutlán, 286
Cyanerpes cyaneus, 28
Cyanocorax affinis, 114; *morio*, 102, 104–5, 111, 127, 169, 227; *stelleri*, 49, 95, 97, 167; *yncas*, 131, 169, 218; *yucatanicus*, 103
Cyclarhis gujanensis, 237, 305

Dactylortyx thoracicus, 181, 211, 327
Dalquest, Walter W., 71, *72*, 375
Danaus plexippus, 302
Darnell, Rezneat, 215
Dary, Mario, 324–326
Dasyprocta, 31, 119
Dasypus novemcinctus, 25, 227
Datura suaveolens, 217
Davis, George, 275–76; Irby, 61, 64, 151, 215, 225, 234, 277
Davis, John, 195, 274, 282–83, 285, 288–90
Davis, W. B., 332
Daytona Beach, Fla., 276–77
DeBell, Jean T., 215
Deer, 16, 138, 214, 245, 271, 280, 288, 295; red brocket, 17, 29, 31, 214, 264, 356; white-tailed, 151
Deevey, Ed, 233
Delaware Museum of Natural History, 234
Del Cielo, Rancho, 131, 181–82, 184–85, 187, 190–93, 210–11, 214–17, 219–24, 227–31, 233–37
Delehanty, David, 354, 356, 363, 367
Delgadillo, Margarito, 268–70, *272*, 279, *280*

Dendroica coronata 103–4; *occidentalis*, 95; *palmarum*, 103; *petechia*, 89, 92, *townsendi*, 95, 168, 306
Dendrortyx barbatus 331; *leucophrys*, 14, 314
Denver Museum of Natural History, 99
Desert Laboratory, 197–98, 200
Desmodus, 30. See also bat, vampire
DeSola, Carlos, 299, 321–22
Díaz Ordaz, 254–55, 258
Dickerman, Robert W., 31, 83, *84*, *90*, 96, 198, 331–32, 371
Dickey Collection, 194
Didelphis virginiana, 64
Diemictylis, 231
Dilger, Bill, 197–98, 207, 223
Dille, Fred, 279
Dioon edule, 215
Dipodomys, 49, 270
Dipper, American, 170
Ditmars, Raymond, 232
Don Rodrigo, 1, 5–6, 18
Don Salomón, 254–55
Doña María, 255–56
Doria, Sr., *139*–40
Dos Amates, 32, 263
Dove: Inca, 94, 96, 125, 184, 308; White-tipped, 131, 236; White-winged, 126, 130
Downs, Allan, 329, 334
Downs, Anita, 329, 334
Downs, Lila, 334
Dressler, Robert, 215
Dromococcyx phasianellus, 255, 358
Dryocopus lineatus, 305–6; *pileatus*, 277
Duby, Gertrude, 105
Duck, Muscovy, 79, 152, 195
Duke University, 118
Dunn, E. R., 144
Dunning, John, 316
Durango, 208, 218
Dysithamnus mentalis, 118

Eagle, Harpy, 17, 75–76, 195, 244–45, 251, 363, 376
Eaton, Betty, 92, 95–96, 98, 102, 106–*7*, 108–9, 112, 117
Eaton, Elon Howard, 122
Eaton, Stephen W., 92, 121–*22*, 136, 139, 141
Eckelberry, Don, 322
Edwards, Ernest P. (Buck), 92, 94, 121, *122*, *139*, 190, 197–98, 215, 225, 236, 286

Edwards, Mabel, 92
Eira barbara, 22, 147, 204, 362
El Amigo, 320, 321
El Bastonal, 32, 351, 363–67
El Bayo, 86, 88
El Carrizal, 255
El Catorce, 253, 254
El Cielo, 215–16, 234–36. See also del Cielo, Rancho
El Cielo Biosphere Reserve, 234
El Clarinero, 318
Electron carinatum, 74
El Faro, 295
El Fraile, 294
El Jícaro, 254
El Limón, 141, 186, 202–3, 285
El Paval, 1, 2
El Refugio Suchitlán, 330
El Salto, 60, 137, 206, 223
El Salvador, 96, 108–10, 194–96, 297–304, 306–7, 310–14, 317, 319, 322, 324–26
El Salvador Museum of Natural History, 299, 307
El Tesoro, 1, 13
El Triunfo, 1, 4–5, 13–18, 25, 27, 38–41
Eleutherodactylus hidalgoensis, 221
Emanuel, Victor, 40
Emlen, John T., 142, 375
Encelia, 52, 54
Engelhard, Lucy, 298, 310, 314
Engelhardtia, 26
Enrique Beltrán, 234
Ensenada del Perro, 279–81
Enterolobium, 201
Erethizon dorsatum, 281–82
Ergaticus ruber, 97, 99, 178
Escarsega, 101–2, 105
Eschrichtius robustus, 155
Espino, Alfredo 321
Estación de Biología Tropical Los Tuxtlas, 171, 206, 333, 340, 353
Estero Tastiota, 273–74
Estrada, Moices, 367–68
Eumomota superciliosa, 319, 321
Euphonia: Elegant, 116; Scrub, 33, 136–37; Yellow-throated, 136–37
Euphonia affinis, 136–37; *elegantissima*, 116; *hirundinacea*, 136–37
Euthlypis lachrymosa, 131

Falco deiroleucus, 47; *femoralis*, 272, 285; *rufigularis*, 47, 135, 236; *sparverius*, 55, 94
Falcons: Aplomado, 272, 285; Bat, 47, 135, 236
Fall, Bruce, 333
Farfan B., Santos, 91
Felis, 29, 42; *onca*, 247; *yagouaroundi*, 175
Fer-de-lance, 24–26, 203, 345. See also *Bothrops atrox*
Fiallos, Luis, 325
Ficus, 201
Field Museum, 49, 232, 375
Figueroa, José Mariano Moziño Suárez de, 20
Finca El Imposible, 300; Prusia, 38; Waldemar, 42–43
Flores, César Domínguez, 18
Flores, José Salvador, 323
Flores, Rafa, 260
Florida, 276–77
Florida Keys, 277
Florida State University, 114–15
Forbes, Dyfrig McHattie, 73, 77
Forest-Falcon, Barred, 22, 28, 39, 344, 346–49
Fort Guásima, 271
Fortuna Nacional, 86
Foster, Robin, 118, 120
Fouquieria, 52
Fox, gray, 101
Fox, William, 216
Frankson, Alec, 240
Fregata magnificens, 53, 120, 175, 279
Frigatebird, Magnificent, 53, 120, 175, 279
Frontera, 88
Fuertes, Louis Agassiz, 198, 207

Gallinule, Purple, 123–24
García, Raúl and Julieta, 263
Gatún, Lake, 118–19
Gaylord, Mr., 144–45
Gealey, Bill, 194–95
Geer, Nate, 195
Gehrlich, Paul, 214, 217, 222
General Bravo, 126, 200
Geothlypis flavovelata, 87; *nelsoni*, 98; *poliocephala*, 102, 104–5
Gerwin, John, 335–36, 354
Gila monster, 270–71
Gilbert, Albert, 38, 42
Glaucidium brasilianum, 77, 292–93
Glaucomys volans, 214

Glendora, 269, 279
Gnatcatcher, Tropical, 116
Golden Gate Park, 71
Goldman, E. A., 271, 329, 334
Gomez, Douglas, 363–64, 367
Gómez Farías, 187, 189, 190, 201–3, 209, 213–216, 221–22, 224–25, 228, 230–36
Gómez Pérez, Agustin, 286
Gómez Pompa, Arturo, 262
Grackle: Boat-tailed, 106; Great-tailed, 93–94, 108, 168, 179, 318
Grassquit, Blue-black, 311–12
Grebe, Atitlán, 46
Greenway, James, Jr., 44
Gregorio, Castulo and Chico, 74–75, 76, 81–82
Grenada, 110
Grijalva River, 86
Grinnell, Hilda Wood, 196, 274; Joseph, 268, 274, 277
Ground-Dove: Common, 94, 113; Maroon-chested, 9; Ruddy, 248
Grosbeak, Hooded, 97, 209, 237
Guadalajara, 149–50, 285–87, 291–96
Guadalupe Victoria, 1, 358, 361, 363
Guan: Crested, 28, 31, 72, 78, 213, 234, 236, 243–44, 361; Highland, 38, 45, 251, 255; Horned, 4–5, 8–12, 18, 25, 38–39, 41–43, 45–47, 100
Guanajuato, 86, 287
Guatemala, 19, 33, 38, 41–48, 65, 89–92, 100, 103–4, 106–9, 112, 117, 144–45, 201–2, 240–41, 288, 297, 319, 324–26, 358
Guatemala City, 41, 43–44, 47–48, 91, 104, 107–8, 144–45
Guatemala National Museum, 326
Guaymas, 152, 156, 271, 273
Guazuma, 201
Guerrero, 277
Guirocoba, 272–73
Gulf of California, 49–50, 53, 152, 273, 279
Gulf of Fonseca, 145
Gulf of Mexico, 19–24, 26, 28–31, 34, 37, 102–3, 120, 123, 158, 164, 172, 202, 233, 306, 333

Hacienda Acuña, 231
Hacienda de la Concepción, 96
Hacienda El Imposible, 324
Hacienda Los Pinos, 301, 308–9, 311, 313, 324
Hacienda Montecristo, 309, 312
Haemig, Paul, 158–59, 178–79, 262

Hagar, Connie, 333
Halffter, Gonzalo, 234
Hall, E. Raymond, 71, 73, 83, 196, 294, 331–32
Hardwicke family, 126, 128
Harlingen, Texas, 189, 215, 225
Harpia harpyja, 17, 75–76, 195, 244–45, 251, 363, 376
Harrell, Byron E., 37, 158, 181, 185, 189, 215–16, 220, 223, 228, 233–34, 236–37, 327–29
Harrison, Frank, 181–*82*, 184–86, *187*–90, 192–*93*, *211*–18, 221–23, 226, 228, 231, 234, 236
Harvard University, 216, 263, 275
Hastings Natural History Reservation, 268
Haverford College, 144
Hawk: Broad-winged, 302–3, 363; Roadside, 152, 169, 300; Swainson's, 56, 302–3, 363; White, 27, 74–75, 102, 171, 172, 263
Hawk-Eagle, 195; Black, 27, 251
Hawk Mountain, 302
Hayden, J., 117
Hayward, Bruce J., 90, 216
Hecht, Max, 208
Heck, Joyce, 181–*82*, *191*, 216
Heckenlaible, Joyce, 216
Heed, William B., 216, 223, 225–26, 233
Heliornis fulica, 79
Heloderma suspectum, 270–71
Henicorhina leucophrys, 170, 313; *leucosticta*, 22, 174
Hermit, Stripe-throated, 80–81
Hermosillo, 50, 152, 271, 273, 278–79, 281
Hernández, Efraím, 216, 234
Hernandez, Jacinto, 336, *345*
Hernández, Patrocinio, 13
Hernández Corzo, Rodolfo, 35
Heron: Boat-billed, 79–80, 91; Great Blue, 91
Hespenheider, Henry, 119
Hewitt, Oliver, *122*
Hidalgo, Carlos, 322
Hildebrand, Milton, 195
Hobart College, 121–22
Hoffmeister, Don, 196
Honeycreeper, Red-legged, 28
Howe, John, 362
Hoyt, J. Southgate, *122*
Huasteca, 133, 202, 204, 210
Hudson, W. H., 212
Huitzilac, 97–98
Huixtla, 13

Hulbert, Lloyd, 122
Hull University, 298
Humboldt, Alexander Von, 219
Hummingbird, 7, 11, 25, 29, 32–33, 39, 54–55, 80–81, 95, 98, 166, 173–74, 178, 213, 236, 248, 253, 304, 306, 309, 320, 324, 333; Ruby-throated, 306
Hunter, John, 216, 234–35
Hurd, Roger, 199, 204–6, 209–*11*, 215, 220, 224, 228, 286
Huxley, Aldous, 107
Hylocichla mustelina, 101, 172, 174, 176, 180, 335, 341, 347, 350, 353, 357, 362–63, 367, 369, 371
Hylomanes momotula, 74
Hylophylax naevioides, 117

Ibarra, Jorge, 44–45, 326
Ibycter americanus, 77
Icterus graduacauda, 127; *gularis*, 133
Illg, Paul, 196
Indiana University, 297
Instituto de Biología, UNAM, 296, 333, 340; de Historia Natural, 1, 38; de Turismo, El Salvador, 299, 318, 323
Instituto Nacional de Investigaciones sobre Recursos Bioticos (INIREB), 352, 354
Irapuato, 287, 296
Isthmus of Tehuantepec, 36, 71–72, 76, 78, 82, 88, 100, 137, 206, 256–58, 288–89
Ithaca, 83, 121, 123, 197, 221, 223, 225
Ixobrychus exilis, 91, 124
Ixtlán, 284, 294–95
Iztaccihuatl, 97, 99 168, 284

Jacksonville, 120, 277
Jacques, F. Lee, 332
Jaguar, 15–16, 35, 42, 78, 101, 106, 117, 138, 213, 236, 246–48, 253, 363
Jalapa, 278, 328, 336, 352–54
Jalisco, 67, 291–293, 329
James, Pauline, 216
Japan, 121, 319
Jaumave, 219
Jay: Black-chested, 114; Brown 102, 104–5, 111, 127, 169, 227; Green, 131, 169, 218; Mexican, 218; Steller's, 49, 95, 97, 167; Yucatan, 103
Jesús Carranza, 74, 76
Jicacal, 264, 267
Jimba, 75

Jitotol, 105
Jocotal, 91, 324
Johns Hopkins University, 120, 148
Johnson, Karl, 89
Johnston, Marshall, 216

Kagu, 197, 236
Kahle, Herman, 38
Kansas, 71, 73, 83–84, 216, 233, 250, 294–95, 331
Kansas University Natural History Museum, 79, 250, 295. *See also* University of Kansas
Kekchi, 238, 240–42, 245–46, 249
Kellogg, Peter Paul, 122–23, 197
Kentucky, 121–23
Kessel, Brina, 198
Kestrel, American, 55, 93
Key West, Fla., 277
Kincaid, Edgar, 216
Kingfisher: Amazon, 80; American Pygmy, 80, 114; Green, 80, 113, 128, 134, 163, 305; Ringed, 32, 80, 134
Kingston, Ken, 317
Kingsville, 124, 336, 352, 354
Kinkajou, 22, 101
Kiskadee, Great, 94, 127, 161, 169, 210, 248
Klicka, John T., 340, 353–54, 367
Koopman, Karl, 234
Korea, 292

La Avellana, 90–91
La Azteca, 203, 210
La Azteca, Ejido, 203, 210
LaBastille, Anne, 46
La Cocina, 22, 24, 30
Lacondon, 106
La Cumbre, 288
Laemanctus, 203, 225
Lago Atitlán, 46; Catemaco, 21–22, 25, 29, 31, 33; Petén Itzá, 48, 91; Sabaneta, 288
La Gringa, 252, 258
Laguna de San Juan, 91; Jocotal, 91, 324; Tisatal, 26
La Joya, 190, 206, 214, 216–20, 228, 230–31
Lake Atitlán, 106–7; Chapala, 286, 292; Nicaragua, 110–11; Okeechobee, 277; Olomega, 194–95; Pátzcuaro, 123, 198–99, 206, 208, 223, 285–86, 295
Lake Itasca Biological Station, 189, 331, 333
Lamb, Chester C., 287, 296, 375

Lancetillas Experiment Station, 148
La Paz, 152–55, 293
La Peninsula de Morenos, Ejido, 336, 338, 341–44, 347, 349–50, 354–59, 361, 363, 364–67, 369
Laredo, Texas, 58, 60, 283, 285, 290, 296
Larrea, 52, 209, 219, 279
Las Joyas, 294
Las Norias, 292
La Union, 145
La Venta, 101
Lawrence, Kans., 75, 83
Lea, Robert B., *122*, 126, 132–33, 197
LeFebvre, Eugene, 181, 216
Leopold, A. Starker, 26, 94–95, 100–101, 225, 375
Leptotila verreauxi, 131, 236
Lerdo, 368
Lerma, 105
Linares, 126–28, 135, 141, 225, 290
Lind, John, 25, 31
Linsdale, Jean M., 268
Lippmann, Manfredo, 41–42
Liquidambar, 22, 100, 168, 184, 188, 190, 212, 257
Loetscher, Fred, 375–76
Lof, Larry, 235–36
Loftin, Horace, 114
López Mateos, Ejido, 215
Lophostrix cristata, 363
Loreto, 152, 155–56
Los Angeles, 149, 152, 154, 192, 269
Los Esesmiles, 301
Los Tuxtlas, 20–21, 31, 34–35, 138, 158–59, 162, 166, 171, 177–78, 180, 260–63, 267, 327–29, 332–33, 335–36, 338–39, 342–43, 345, 347, 349–50, 355–57, 361–65, 367–72
Louisiana, 19, 25, 27, 49, 51, 58, 71, 73, 123, 225, 233
Louisiana State University, 19, 25, 27, 49, 51, 58, 71, 73, 225–26, 233, 286
Louisiana State University Museum of Zoology, 27, 73, 225
Loveridge, Arthur, 21
Lovo, Hilda, 304
Lowe, Chuck, 83
Lowery, George, 58, 71, 73, 75, 92, 225, 233, 286, 375
Loxia curvirostra, 232
Lutra longicaudis, 86
Lycopodium, 112

Macaw: Military, 96, 206, 223; Scarlet, 81, 244, 246, 248, 321
MacDougall, Thomas, 38, 256
Maciewicz, John, 216
MacNeish, Richard, 216
Macuspana, 86, 88
Madden Forest (Canal Zone), 119–20
Magallanes, 358, 363
Magnolia, 218
Mahogany, 240, 242
Malaria, 33, 204, 210, 213, 215, 228, 241
Mammoth, 216
Manakin, Red-capped, 117, 119, 173
Mangroves, 22, 53, 103–4, 169–70, 232, 271, 287
Mapastepec, 1, 18, 41
Marien, Danny, 208
Marshall, Joe, 194–95, 301
Martin: Gray-breasted, 102; Purple, 104
Martin, Marian, 216
Martin, Paul, 181, 189, 197, *211*, 286
Martín del Campo, Rafael, 296
Marx, Hyman, 232
Mason, Olive and Nancy, 100
Massachusetts, 275
Matamoros, 93, 125, 151, 160, 182–83, 189–90, 226
Matehuala, 273
Matías Romero, 250, 254
Maya, 98, 238, 240, 245
Mayr, Ernst, 275
Mazama americana, 17, 29, 31, 214, 264, 356
Mazamitla, 293
Mazatlán, 149–50, 152–55
Mazza, Gerardo, 75, 77
McAllen, 121, 125, 199
McBride, Laura, 374
McCabe, Robert, 375
McCamey, Ginny, 58
McCarty family, 272–73
McShea, Bill, 354
Megaceryle torquata, 32, 80, 134
Melanerpes aurifrons, 125, 174, 314; *formicivorus*, 163, 232, 236
Meleagris gallopavo, 92–93, 96, 248
Memphis, Tenn., 60, 69
Mengel, Robert, 128, 332
Mérida, 102, 104–5
Merritt Island, 276
Mesa Central, 163
Mesa de Chipinque, 285
Mesa de Llera, 94, 128–29, 132, 135, 140
Mesquite, 52, 93, 95, 129, 230, 287
Mexico City, 59, 82, 85–86, 88–89, 91, 93, 96–97, 99, 137, 139, 153, 163–64, 166–67, 173, 176–77, 179, 182, 200, 206, 218–19, 234–35, 255, 271, 277, 279, 283–86, 288–91, 294–96, 331–33
Mice, 49, 210, 213, 268, 270
Michigan, 181, 203, 215, 216, 221, 224–25, 268, 275
Michigan State University, 215
Michoacán, 198, 205–6, 218, 223, 286, 288, 293–94
Micrastur ruficollis, 22, 28, 39, 344, 346–49
Micrathene whitneyi, 55
Microrhopias quixensis, 118
Micrurus, 211–12
Middle American Research Unit (Canal Zone), 89
Midwestern State University, 71
Miguel Álvarez del Toro Museum, 100
Mil Cumbres, 286
Miller, Alden, 194–95, 276, 290
Miller, Robert C., 71
Miller, Ted, 216
Miller, Waldron DeWitt, 143
Millerton, Pa., 199
Mimus polyglottos, 55–56, 64, 236
Minatitlán, 64, 363, 367
Minneapolis, 159, 168, 177, 229, 327, 371, 373
Minnesota, 83, 158–60, 177–79, 181–82, 189–90, 215–16, 228–29, 260, 327, 329, 331–35, 354, 357, 369, 371
Mississippi, 64, 277
Mississippi River, 199
Missouri Farms, 238–39
Mistletoe, 54, 137
Mitla, 284
Mockingbird, Northern, 55–56, 64, 236
Momotus momota, 22, 73–74, 131, 137, 173, 204, 217, 236, 337
Monkey, 17, 118–19, 206, 209, 214, 235, 359, 362; howler, 22, 29, 32, 48, 68, 87, 117–18, 358, 362; spider, 32, 87–88, 195, 214, 358, 362
Montagna, William, *122*
Montecristo, 307, 309, 312
Montemorelos, 201
Montepío, 23, 29–30, 34
Monterrey, 60, 125–27, 164, 200, 209, 216, 285

Monzón, Raúl, 320, 322
Moore, Robert T., 287
Morbeck, Mary Ellen, 236
Morelia, 59, 285-87
Morelos, 58, 60, 103-4, 114, 286, 295, 327
Morgan, Henry, 110
Morpho butterfly, 27, 28, 118, 151, 342
Morton, Eugene, 119-20
Mosiman, James E., 216
Mosquito, 1, 2, 13, 72, 87, 88, 90-91, 124, 129, 134, 185-86, 213, 231, 276, 277, 279, 288, 299-300, 305, 309, 343
Motmot: Blue-crowned, 22, 73-74, 131, 137, 173, 204, 217, 236, 337; Keel-billed, 74; Tody, 74; Turquoise-browed, 319, 321
Mountain lion, 31, 138, 147, 189
Moynihan, Martin, 119
Mozo, Rosa, 355
Murchison, Clint, 231-32
Murphy, Robert Cushman, 143
Museo de Ciencias Naturales, 318
Museo Nacional de Costa Rica, 112
Museo Nacional de Historia Natural, Guatemala, 44; México, 295
Museum of Comparative Zoology, 275; of Southwestern Biology, 83
Mustela frenata, 169-70
Myadestes melanops, 112; *occidentalis*, 39, 127, 170, 188, 199, 211, 237, 313; *unicolor*, 22, 174, 253, 312-13
Myanmar. *See* Burma
Myioborus miniatus, 39, 97-99, 101, 114, 116, 178; *pictus*, 101; *torquatus*, 116
Myrica, 218
Myrtillocactus, 219

Nabhan, Gary, 234
Nahua, 168, 357
National Museum of Canada, 216
National Science Foundation, 233
National University of El Salvador, 299, 318, 323
Nava S., Juan, 91
Nayarit, 179, 292, 295
Nelson, E. W., 271, 329, 334
Neotoma, 219, 270, 272
Neri Fajardo, Mara, 357, 364, 367
Nevada, 274
New Caledonia, 197
New Jersey, 92, 143, 276
Newman, Marcella, 58, 233

Newman, Robert, 92, 286, 375
New Mexico, 83, 87, 218, 268
New York, 19, 38, 83, 92, 100, 120-23, 142-43, 197, 200, 260, 275, 320, 325
New York Botanical Society, 38
New York State Museum, 122
New York Zoological Society, 197
Nicaragua, 109-11, 255, 306
Night-Heron, Yellow-crowned, 104, 169
Nightingale-Thrush: Black-headed, 28, 188, 229, 232, 237; Ruddy-capped, 166, 312-13; Spotted, 39
Nightjar: Buff-collared, 127; Spot-tailed, 64, 67, 100
Noctilio, 88
Nogales, 52, 152, 268, 270, 279, 281
Norman, Okla., 182
North Carolina, 216, 276
North Dakota, 79
Northfield, Minn., 331
Norton, Elwin, 100-101
Nosillero, 1
Notiochelidon pileata, 108
Novillero River, 2
Nuevo León, 126, 164, 285, 290
Nuevo Morelos, 286, 327
Nyctibius jamaicensis, 77
Nycticorax violaceus, 104, 169
Nyctidromus albicollis, 33, 67, 77-78, 127
Nyctiphrynus mcleodii, 67-68

Oaks, 95, 97-100, 106, 108, 146, 151, 163, 167-68, 178, 184, 188, 190, 199-200, 202, 206, 208, 212, 218, 220-21, 223, 228, 230-32, 256-57, 284, 286, 288, 292-94
Oaxaca, 19, 36, 88, 102, 137, 179, 217, 250-52, 254, 256-58, 284-85, 288-89
Obregón, 273
Ocotal Chico, 25, 31
Ocotillo, 52, 54, 156
ODECA. *See* Organazión de Estados Centro-Americanos
Odocoileus virginianus, 151, 214
Odontophorus guttatus, 28, 331
Oehlenschlager, Richard J., 160, 164, 169-70, 172-77, 179, 262, 333
Ohio State University, 216
Oklahoma, 182, 216, 224-25
Olmec, 20, 158
Olneya, 54

Olomega, 194–95
Olson, Eugene A. ("Olie"), 291–93, 295
Olson, Storrs, 374
Omilteme, 284
Onchocerca, 47
Oppenheimer, John and Lisa, 118–19
Opuntia, 54, 129, 206
Oreophasis derbianus, 4–5, 8–12, 18, 25, 38–39, 41–43, 45–47, 100
Organazión de Estados Centro-Americanos (ODECA), 298, 325
Organ Pipe Cactus National Monument, 49
Oriole: Altamira, 133; Audubon's, 127
Orizaba, 19, 168, 283, 289–90, 295
Orlando, 277
Ortalis vetula, 61, 104, 127–28, 161, 227, 245
Orthoptera, 144
Osorio family, 205, 219; Antonio, 217; Cayetano 219–20; Demetrio, *211*
Osprey, 55, 57
Ostrich, 143
Otoxha, British Honduras, 240, 249
Otter, river, 86
Ovis canadensis, 52
Owen-Lewis, Don, 238–39
Owl, 64, 73, 77, 101, 112, 146, 213–14, 217, 230, 264, 267, 322, 330; Black-and-white, 323; Crested, 363; Elf, 55; Fulvous, 45; Mottled, 28, 58, 77, 128, 217, 221, 236, 267; Spectacled, 77, 267; Striped, 77
Oyster, 271

Paca, 31, 361
Pachuca, 96, 283–84, 289, 332
Pachycereus pringlei, 52, 54–55, 57
Padre Island, 93
Palenque, 47, 68, 101, 105
Palmer, Theodore, 373
Palms, 7, 28, 104, 168, 201, 212, 311, 349–50
Panama, 89, 92–93, 104, 108–9, 111, 114–17, 120, 197, 297–98, 303
Pan-American Health Organization, 89
Pandion haliaetus, 55, 57
Pano Ayuctle, Rancho, 132–34, 137–41, 202, 205, 209, 215–17, 228
Panthera onca, 15–16, 35, 42, 78, 101, 106, 117, 138, 213, 236, 246–48, 253, 363
Parakeet: Aztec, 81; Green, 81, 130
Paricutín, 137, 206
Parkes, Ken, 92, 96, 208, 236

Parmelee, David, 167
Parque Cerro Verde, 314, 323
Parque Cuscutlán, 317
Parrot, 58, 68, 81, 129, 133–34, 146, 169, 171–73, 200–1, 321; Maroon-fronted, 218, 228; Mealy, 81; Red-crowned, 81, 130, 134–35, 152, 210; Red-lored, 81, 135; White-crowned, 81, 95, 236, 274; Yellow-crowned, 81
Parula pitiayumi, 127, 135–36, 230
Parula, Tropical, 127, 135–36, 230
Passerculus sandwichensis, 55
Passerina ciris, 249
Patagioenas fasciata, 127; *flavirostris*, 152, 210, 227; *nigrirostris*, 79, 253; *speciosa*, 28, 79
Pauraque, Common, 33, 67, 77–78, 127
Peafowl, Congo, 143
Peccary, 31, 75, 118, 147, 151, 253, 264
Pelecanus erythrorhynchos, 57, 372; *occidentalis*, 49, 53, 107, 173, 273–74, 279
Pelican: Brown, 49, 53, 107, 173, 273–74, 279; White, 57, 372
Pelican Island, 279
Pemex City, 86
Penelope purpurascens, 28, 31, 72, 78, 213, 234, 236, 243–44, 361
Penelopina nigra, 38, 45, 251, 255
Penguin, Emperor, 276
Penn State University, 216, 223
Peppershrike, Rufous-browed, 237, 305
Pérez Gómez, Agustín, 286
Perognathus, 49, 268
Perote, 168, 353
Peru, 68, 262
Petén, 47–48, 91
Peters, James L., 275
Peterson, A. Townsend, 250
Peterson, Roger Tory, 204, 375
Petra, 211
Pettingill, Olin Sewall, 133, 197, 201, 327, 371
Peucedramis taeniatus, 97, 99–100
Phaenostictus mcleannani, 118
Phaeothlypis fulvicauda, 116, 119–20
Phaethornis striigularis, 80–81
Phalacrocorax, 53; *brasilianus*, 21, 33, 134; *penicillatus*, 274
Phalaenoptilus nuttallii, 57
Pharomachrus mocinno, 5, 8, 12, 36, 38, 42, 80, 251, 253, 255, 319, 325
Philadelphia, 144–45, 148
Philippines, 282

Phillips, Allan, 31, 67, *90*, 96, 122, 163–66, 176–78, 329, 331, 333, 375
Phoenix, 83, 333
Phoradendron, 54
Piaya cayana, 172, 221, 309, 326, 358
Pie de La Cuesta, 278
Pigeon: Band-tailed, 127; Red-billed, 152, 210, 227; Scaled, 28, 79; Short-billed, 79, 253
Pijijiapan, 66–67
Pines, 2, 4, 22, 37, 95, 97–100, 106, 108, 110, 127, 145–46, 163, 167–68, 178, 199, 202, 206, 208, 218, 221, 223, 228, 230, 232, 254, 256–57, 277, 283, 286, 288, 292–94
Pinus, 168, 218. *See also* pines
Pionus senilis, 81, 95, 236, 274
Pipilo, 219; *fuscus*, 282–85 *maculatus*, 282–87, 290, 294–95; *ocai*, 283–88, 290, 292–95
Pipit, American, 168
Pitangus sulphuratus, 94, 127, 161, 169, 210, 248
Pitelka, Frank, 282
Pituophis, 105
Platalea ajaja, 243
Playa Escondida, 171–76, 263, 266–67, 328, 342, 353
Pliocercus, 211
Poblado Catorce, 252
Poblado Once, 252
Podilymbus gigas, 46
Podocarpus, 218
Polioptila plumbea, 116
Poorwill: Common, 57; Eared, 67–68
Popocatepetl, 137, 168, 284
Popoluca, 25
Poppy, Jim, 216
Porphyrio martinica, 123–24
Port Newark, 117, 120
Pospichal, Steve, 329
Potoo, Northern, 77
Potos flavus, 22, 101
Potrero Viejo, 73
Powell, George, 260
Prawn, 202
Priori, Andrea, 298, 310, 314
Procyon lotor, 64, 104
Progne chalybea, 102; *subis*, 104
Prosopis, 52, 93, 95, 129, 230, 287
Protonotaria citrea, 103, 330
Pseudoeurycea scandens, 221
Pseudoscops clamator, 77
Pteroglossus torquatus, 171, 344–45

Pueblo Nuevo, 36
Pueblo Nuevo Solistahaucan, 100
Puente Talismán, 44
Puerto Barrios, 107, 144
Puerto Castillo, 144
Puerto Juárez, 103
Puerto Kino, 279, 281
Puerto Lobos, 50–55
Puerto Morelos, 103–4, 295
Puerto Peñasco, 49–50
Puerto Vallarta, 330
Puleston, Dennis, 178–79
Pulsatrix perspicillata, 77, 267
Puma concolor, 31, 138, 147, 189
Punta Gorda, 240–42, 245, 249
Punta Villa Rica, 169
Putla, 329
Pygmy-Owl, Ferruginous, 77, 292–93
Pygochelidon cyanoleuca, 112

Quail, 329, 331–32; Singing, 181, 187, 211, 236, 327
Quercus, 168, 184. *See also* oaks
Querétaro, 296
Quesada, Alvaro, 42–*43*
Quetzal, Resplendant, 5, 8, 12, 36, 38, 42, 80, 251, 253, 255, 319, 325
Quetzaltenango, 46, 106
Quintana Roo, 103–4
Quiscalus major, 106; *mexicanus*, 93–94, 108, 168, 179, 318

Rabbit, 20, 64, 198
Raccoon, 64, 104
Rader, Elsie, 196
Rail, King, 124
Rallus elegans, 124
Ramírez, Carlos, 35
Ramos, Mario, 333, 335–37, 346, 352, 354, 357, 361, 363, 369–70, 371
Ramphastos sulfuratus, 26, 28, 118, 172, 251
Ramphocelus passerinii, 113
Rappole, John, 159–60, 170, 261, 333, 335–36, 338–40, 350–51, 354, 357–58, 364, 371
Rash, Santiago, 246
Rat, 14, 169–70, 213, 219, 270–71; kangaroo, 49, 270–71
Rattlesnake, 189, 203, 218, 232, 271, 280–81, 346
Rattus, 169
Ray, Milton S., 284

Redstart: American, 98, 101; Collared, 116; Painted, 101; Slate-throated, 39, 97–99, 101, 114, 116, 178
Reed, Howard, 231–32
Rehn, A. G., 143–44, 148
Reilly, Ed, 197
Reserva Ecológica Campesinal, 258
Reynosa, 125–26, 190, 199, 204
Rhynchopsitta terrisi, 218, 228
Rhynochetos jubatus, 197, 236
Rice University, 233
Richardson, William B., 268
Ridgely, Robert, 89
Ridgway, Robert, 163
Rinconada, Rancho, 126, 133–34, 201
Río: Bravo, 151; Camacho, 128; Chalchijapa, 74–75, 78, 250; Chiriquí Viejo, 114, 116; Coatzacoalcos, 74, 77–78, 80–81; Col, 29; Corona, 58, 160; Corte, 258; Coxcoapan, 24, 335–36, 338–341, 347, 354–55, 363, 366, 368; Frio, 99, 167, 178, 202; General, 113; Grande, 125–26, 131, 151, 160, 183, 200, 220, 227, 244–46; Grijalva, 86; Guayalejo, 132–33, 203; Lacantun, 100; Máquina, 29; Mayo, 271; Moctezuma, 94; Papaloapan, 171; Sabinas, 94, 131–34, 136–38, 183–84, 192, 201–4, 206, 209–10, 215–16, 220, 222, 225–27, 234, 329; Samalá, 46; San Gregoria, 106; Solosuchil, 72, 74–75; Soto, 227; Suchiapan, 361; Tuxpan, 162; Usumacinta, 86, 106; Uxpanapa, 252, 257; Yaqui, 50; Yohualtajapan, 365
Riparia riparia, 110–11
Robin, American, 99
Robins, C. Richard, 216, 223, 225–26, 233–34, 236
Robles, Ben, 340
Ross, Gary, 25, 27
Rowley, J. Stuart, 255
Royal Agricultural College, 238
Rozas, Eduardo Turrent, 35
Russell, Steve, 50–51, 236
Ruth, Babe, 275–76

Sabaneta, 288
Sabinas, 83–84
Sabrewing: Long-tailed, 29, 32; Violet, 29, 172, 174, 253; Wedge-tailed, 80
Saguaro, 54–55, 198
St. Bonaventure College/University, 92, 122

St. Vincent Island, 41
Salamander, 170, 211–12, 218, 221, 228
Salvador Flores, José, 323
San Andrés Tuxtla, 19–20, 22, 30, 33, 35, 75, 171, 176, 329
San Antonio Agua Caliente, 91
San Blas, 287, 292
San Cristóbal de Las Casas, 105, 288
Sanderson, Ivan, 48
San Francisco, 71, 152, 196, 252, 254, 284, 291
San Isidro La Gringa, 252, 258
San José, 44, 112
San Jose State College, 291
San Lorenzo, 145
San Luis Potosí, 58, 60, 94, 96, 161, 166, 206, 223, 226, 233, 250, 273, 279, 285–86
San Miguel, 110
San Miguel Chimalapa, 250, 257
San Pablo, 214, 217, 222
San Salvador, 91, 144–45, 299, 307, 320–21, 325
Santa María Chimalapa, 250, 257
Santa Rosalia, 155–56
Santa Teresa, 243–44, 247
Santiago Atitlán, 46, 106
Santiago Tuxtla, 20
Sarabia, 251
Sarcoramphus papa, 74–75, 195, 226
Sasabe, 52
Sayula, 285
Scaup, Lesser, 103
Sceloporus, 203
Schaldach, William, 34, 67, 216, 251
Schmidt, Karl Patterson, 232
Schwartz, Paul, 307
Sciurus aureogaster, 28; *deppei*, 350, 361
Sedum, 208, 218
Sefuentes Baron, Jesús, 86
Seiurus motacilla, 101, 122; *noveboracensis*, 101, 307
Seravia, Carlos, 216
Seri, 50, 53, 55
Serrano, J. Francisco, 299
Serrano, Juliano, 289–90
Setophaga ruticilla, 98, 101
Shanks, Royal, 216
Sharp, Jack, 214, 234
Shaw, David, 58
Shorebirds, 49, 53, 169, 232, 303
Shropshire, 238
Sialia mexicana, 99

Sibley, Charles G., 206–8, 223, 268, *272*, *278*, *280–81*, 375
Sierra: Colorado, 95; de Cuyutlán, 286; de Los Tuxtlas, 138, 158, 162, 178, 261, 328, 335–36, 338, 342, 345, 349, 356, 364, 371–72. *See also* Los Tuxtlas; de Santa Marta, 357, 361, 365, 369. *See also* Volcán Santa Marta; Espinazo del Diablo, 251–53, 259; Madre de Chiapas, 25, 27, 38–41, 250; Madre Occidental, 152, 208, 218, 272, 287, 292–93; Madre Oriental, 95, 126, 133, 161, 182, 184, 200–2, 218–19, 226, 230, 234, 369
Simuliidae, 47
Sinton, 92–93, 373
Skunk, 195, 271–72
Skutch, Alexander, 113, 148–49
Smith, H. H., 284; Neal, 118; Mari and Richard, 374
Smithsonian Institution, 260, 276, 373
Smithsonian Tropical Research Institute, 117
Snail, 104, 253
Snake, 4, 14, 24–25, 74, 103, 105, 114, 189, 203, 210–12, 218–19, 226, 228, 232, 262, 271, 280–81, 309, 345–46
Solanum, 54
Solitaire: Black-faced, 112; Brown-backed, 39, 127, 170, 188, 199, 211, 237, 313; Slate-colored, 22, 174, 253, 312–13
Sonora, 49–52, 54, 57, 90, 152, 156, 200, 268–70, 272, 278–81
Sontecomapan, 22, 24–25, 33–35, 263, 372
Sosa, Humberto, 234
Soto la Marina, 218, 224, 226–27, 231
South Africa, 323
South America, 49, 51, 111, 201, 269
Spain, 20, 257, 269, 319
Sparrow, 50, 129, 204, 237, 305; Black-throated, 56, 126; Botteri's, 129; Rufous-collared, 106; Rufous-winged, 51; Savannah, 55; Seaside, 277; White-crowned, 56
Spence, Robert, III, 83
Spilotes, 74, 226
Spinetail, Rufous-breasted, 148, 167
Spizaetus, 195; *tyrannus*, 27, 251
Spoonbill, Roseate, 243
Squirrel, 28, 187, 198, 214, 250, 350, 361
Stelgidopteryx serripennis, 94, 304
Stevenson, David, 101; Henry, 116, 122
Stewart, Dave, 260

Stirton, R. A., 194–95
Stone, Witmer, 143
Storer, Robert W., 276–77
Storms, Everts, 48, 133–34, 137–38, 183, 201–2, 211, 214–16, 234
Streptoprocne zonaris, 60
Stresemann, Erwin, 284
Strix fulvescens, 45
Struthio camelus, 143
Stucker, Steve, 335, 351, 357, 359–62
Sula leucogaster, 150, 273
Sungrebe, 79
Surfbirds, 53
Sutton, George Miksch, 58, 126, 133, 182, 197–98, *211*, 216, 231, 235–37, 327–28, 371
Swainson, William, 283
Swallow: Bank, 110–11; Barn 110–11, 117, 120; Black-capped, 108; Blue-and-white, 112; Northern Rough-winged, 94, 304
Swarthmore College, 144
Sweet Briar College, 121–22
Sweetgum, 22, 100, 168, 184, 188, 190, 212, 257
Swift, 209, 304; Vaux's, 221, 236; White-collared, 60
Symphonia, 120
Synallaxis erythrothorax, 148, 170

Tabasco, 19, 83–84, 86–88, 101, 225–26
Tabebuia, 118, 211
Tamaulipas, 93, 96, 126, 130, 133, 139, 141, 151, 159–61, 166, 177, 181–82, 187, 191, 193, 197, 199–204, 206, 209, 212, 214, 217, 223–26, 228–37, 328
Tamazunchale, 94, 137, 206, 279
Tampico, 202, 226, 230, 232, 329, 354
Tanager: Azure-rumped, 18; Passerini's or Scarlet-rumped, 113
Tangara cabanisi, 18
Tapachula, 41, 44
Tapalapan, 21, 25–27
Tapanatepec, 288–89
Tapir, 31, 75; Baird's, 16, 30, 119, 289, 363
Tapirus bairdii, 16, 30, 119, 289, 363
Tashian, Richard, 138
Tattler, Wandering, 53
Taxodium, 160, 201
Taxus, 218
Tayassu, 31, 75, 118, 147, 151, 253, 264
Tayra, 22, 147, 204, 362

Teapa, 87–88, 105
Tegoma, Epigmenio, 25–27
Tegucigalpa, 145–47
Tehuantepec, 36, 136, 256–57, 288. *See also* Isthmus of Tehuantepec
Telea, 64
Temascaltepec, 285
Temash River, 240
Tennessee, 64, 69, 214, 216
Teotihuacán, 98, 177, 285
Tepatitlán, 293
Tern: Black, 118; Common 303
Ternstroemia, 218
Texas, 58, 71, 92, 121, 123–27, 131, 135, 150, 159–60, 177, 183, 189, 193, 199–200, 216, 218, 220, 225–26, 233–35, 260, 277, 279, 283, 290, 303, 326, 332, 336–37, 350, 352–54, 373
Texas Southmost College, 193, 216, 234–35
Teziutlan, 168, 170
Thrush: Black, 223; Clay-colored, 33, 112, 131–32, 188, 229, 249, 311; Hermit, 307; Sooty, 113; Swainson's, 115; White-throated, 188; Wood, 101, 172, 174, 176, 180, 335, 341, 347, 350, 353, 357, 362–63, 367, 369, 371
Thryothorus maculipectus, 61, 172; *rufalbus*, 313
Thurber, Walter A., 297, 375
Tiburón Island, 156, 279–81
Tick, 37, 47, 130, 195, 204, 228, 285, 309, 330
Tiger-Heron, Bare-throated, 80, 201
Tigrisoma mexicanum, 80, 201
Tikal, 47, 104, 107
Tilia, 218
Tillandsia, 212
Tinamou, 8, 78, 81, 140, 146, 151, 181, 187, 228, 255; Great, 28, 78, 244, 253; Slaty-breasted, 28, 78; Thicket, 78, 130–31, 152, 236
Tinamus major, 28, 78, 244, 253
Titmouse, Oak, 275
Tlapocoyan, 353
Tlaxiaco, 329, 334
Toad, 20, 64, 110, 119
Toledo District, 238–39, 247
Torreón, 85, 209
Toucan, 81, 200, 226, 233, 235, 249, 345; Keel-billed, 26, 28, 118, 172, 251
Toucanet, Emerald, 7, 22, 39, 253
Towhee: Canyon, 282–85; Collared, 283–88, 290, 292–95; Spotted, 282–87, 290, 294–95
Tres Cumbres, 97–99

Tres Marias Islands, 149–50, 152
Tres Picos, 250–51
Tres Zapotes, 20, 27
Tringa incana, 53
Troglodytes musculus, 248; *solsitialis*, 114
Trogon, 7, 58, 60, 80, 146, 249; Citreoline, 80; Collared, 28, 80; Elegant, 127–28, 137, 151, 161, 232; Mountain, 105, 211, 221; Slaty-tailed, 80; Violaceus, 80
Trogon citreolus, 80; *collaris*, 28, 80; *elegans*, 127–28, 137, 151, 161, 232; *massena*, 80; *mexicanus*, 105, 211, 221; *violaceus*, 80
Tucker, John, 195; Robert, 58
Tucson, 49, 51–52, 153–54, 198, 200, 216, 270
Tulancingo, 289, 332
Turdus assimilis, 188; *grayi*, 33, 112, 131–32, 188, 229, 249, 311; *infuscatus*, 223; *migratorius*, 99; *nigrescens*, 113
Turkey: Ocellated, 78, 92, 100, 104, 120; Wild, 93, 96, 248
Turnstone, Black, 53
Turtle, 102, 150, 202, 227
Tuxpan, 161–62
Tuxtla Gutiérrez, 5, 7, 12, 18, 36, 40, 100, 105, 288
Tuxtla Mountains, 20–21, 23, 26–27, 30, 33–34, 36, 174, 260, 262. *See also* Los Tuxtlas

United Fruit Company, 144, 148
Universidad Autónoma de Tamaulipas, 234–35
Universidad Nacional Autónoma de México (UNAM), 96, 164–66, 171, 235, 262, 333, 340, 364
Universidad San Carlos, 324
University of: Arizona, 49–50, 83, 197–98, 200, 202, 216, 233, 270; California–Berkeley, 194, 206, 225, 268, 291; California–Berkeley Museum of Vertebrate Zoology, 194, 268, 273, 282; California–Berkeley Vertebrate Paleontology Museum, 194; Kansas, 71, 73, 83–84, 216, 233, 250, 294–95, 331; Kentucky, 121, 123; Michigan, 181, 203, 216, 221, 224–25, 268, 275; Michigan Museum of Zoology, 223–25, 275; Minnesota, 83, 158–60, 177–79, 181, 189, 215–16, 229, 260, 327, 331–35, 354, 371; New Mexico, 83, 87; Oklahoma, 182, 216, 224–25; Tennessee, 214, 216; Texas–Brownsville, 216; the Americas, 167–68, 177–79; Washington, 71; Wisconsin, 142. *See also* Universidad

Urera, 213
Urocyon cinereoargenteus, 101
Uropsila leucogastra, 131–32, 209
Ursus americanus, 138, 213, 218
U.S. National Museum of Natural History, 27, 262
Uxmal, 102
Uxpanapa, 250–52, 254, 256–57
Uzzell, Thomas, 216

Van Rossem, Adrian J., 194, 284, 301–3
Van Tyne, Josselyn, 224, 275
Vaquerano, René, 323
Vasquez, Jacky, 246
Vega, Jorge, 260, *364*
Velasco Suárez, Manuel, 18
Venezuela, 83, 90, 197, 212, 307
Veracruz, 19, 36–37, 56, 62, 64, 73, 75, 77, 79–82, 85, 100, 131, 138, 158, 162, 164, 166–67, 171, 176–79, 213–14, 219, 231–32, 251, 260–62, 278, 295, 326, 328, 335–36, 338, 342, 345, 349, 356, 364, 371–72, 374, 376
Vermivora peregrina, 306, 310; *ruficapilla*, 95, 307
Viejo, Rancho, 214, 222
Vietnam, 162, 333
Villa, Bernardo, 85, 166, 171–72, 175, 177, 333
Villahermosa, 86–87, 101, 104–5
Villa Juárez, 289
Villeda, Amanda, 297–301, 304–10, 312–14, 317–26
Vireo, Gray, 50, 56
Vireo vicinior, 50–51, 53–54, 56–57
Virginia, 55, 64, 92, 121–23, 151, 214, 260, 374
Vogt, Dick, 335–36, 354
Volatinia jacarina, 311–12
Volcán San Martín Tuxtla, 19–23, 25–26, 28–31, 341, 369; Santa María, 45–46; Santa Marta, 20, 24–25. *See also* Sierra de Santa Marta; Tacaná, 41; Tajumulco, 42–43
Vorhies, Charles, 270
Vulture: Black, 74, 95, 97, 120, 130, 171, 200, 315; King, 74–75, 195, 226; Turkey, 95, 97, 130, 160, 169, 302–3, 326

Wagner, Helmuth, 282, 284
Walker, Charles F., 216, 221
Wannamaker, John, *122*
Warbler: Buff-rumped, 116, 119–20; Canada, 118, 237; Fan-tailed, 131; Golden-browed, 32, 39, 97–98, 170; Hermit, 95; Nashville, 95, 307; Olive, 97, 99–100; Palm, 103; Prothonotary, 103, 330; Red, 97, 99, 178; Red-faced, 100, 105; Rufous-capped, 128; Tennessee, 306, 310; Townsend's, 95, 168, 170, 306; Yellow, 89; Yellow-rumped, 103–4
Warburton, Barbara, 235
Warner, Dwain, *ii*, *122*, 126, 128, 130, 133, 158–62, 164–78, 181, 185, 197, 229, 236, 260, 262, 265, 267, 327–*28*, 357, 369–*72*, 374
Wasp, 263, 342
Waterthrush: Louisiana, 101, 122; Northern, 101, 307
Weasel, 105, 169–70
Webster, Fred and Marie, 214, 220, 235–36
Welder Wildlife Foundation and Refuge, 92–93, 150, 332–33, 373
Wells, Tex, 329
West Indies, 41, 110, 142
Wetmore, Alexander, 21, 276, 373–75
Wetmore, Beatrice, 373
Whip-poor-will, 64, 100
Whittemore, Wendell, 67
Williams, George, 233
Williams, Raymond E., 291–92
Williamson, Mrs. Fred, 215
Wilmington, 234
Windnagle, Shirley, 225
Winker, Kevin, 236, 260, 335, *349*, *364*
Wolfe, John, 216
Wood-Partridge: Bearded, 331; Buffy-crowned, 14, 314
Woodpecker: Acorn, 163, 232, 236; Golden-fronted, 125, 174, 314; Golden-olive, 24, 236; Imperial, 208; Ivory-billed, 358; Lineated, 305–6; Pileated, 277
Wood-Quail, Spotted, 28, 331
Wood-Rail, Gray-necked, 79
Wood-Wren: Gray-breasted, 170, 313; White-breasted, 22, 174. *See also* Wren
World War II, 24, 121, 133, 142, 197, 199, 214, 220, 238, 277, 327, 332
Worth, Brooke, 144
Worthington, Willis W., 224
Wren: Band-backed, 33, 106, 169, 172; Banded, 132; Canyon, 98, 163; House, 94, 132, 248; Mountain, 114; Rufous-and-white, 313; Southern House, 248; Spot-breasted, 61,

172, 236; White-bellied, 131–32, 209. *See also* Wood-Wren
Wrenthrush, 113
Wright, Bert, 36, 45
Wyoming, 274

Xalapa, 278, 328, 336, 352–54
Xenops, Plain, 167, 173–74
Xenops minutus, 167, 173–74
Xenosaurus, 251, 256
Xicotencatl, 203, 216
Xicotepec, 163
Xilitla, 151, 226, 279

Yahualica, 293
Yaqui, 271
Yellowthroat: Altamira, 87; Gray-crowned, 102, 104–5; Hooded, 98

Young, Carol, 244
Yucatan, 103–4, 120
Yucatán Peninsula, 91, 96

Zacapu, 285, 294
Zamora, 294
Zapotal, 81–82
Zapotec, 284
Zapotlanejo, 293
Zeledonia coronata, 113
Zenaida asiatica, 126, 130
Zimmer, John T., 275
Zitácuaro, 286
Zonotrichia capensis, 106, 112–14; *leucophrys*, 56
ZOOMAT, 40
Zoque, 257
Zunil, 45–46

Kevin Winker is curator of birds and professor of biology and wildlife at the University of Alaska Museum, the Department of Biology and Wildlife, and the Institute of Arctic Biology at the University of Alaska Fairbanks.

www.ingramcontent.com/pod-product-compliance
Lightning Source LLC
Chambersburg PA
CBHW070817250426
43672CB00031B/2759